◉ REGENT'S   Park Campus

This book is due for return on or before the last date shown below.

D1356615

MODERN
JAPANESE
AESTHETICS

MODERN JAPANESE AESTHETICS

A READER

MICHELE MARRA

University of Hawai'i Press

Honolulu

Publication of this book has been assisted by a grant from
the Kajiyama Publications Fund for Japanese History,
Culture, and Literature at the University of Hawai'i at Mānoa.

99 00 01 02 03 04   5 4 3 2 1

Library of Congress Cataloging-in-Publication Data

Marra, Michele.
    Modern Japanese aesthetics : a reader / Michele Marra.
      p.   cm.
    Includes bibliographical references and index.
    ISBN 0–8248–2173–4 (cloth : alk. paper)
    1. Aesthetics, Japanese—19th century.   2. Aesethetics,
Japanese—20th century.   I. Title.
BH221.J3M36   1999
111'.85'0952—dc21   99–27949
                                          CIP

Designed by Ken Miyamoto
Printed by The Maple-Vail Book Manufacturing Group

To Professor Robert E. Morrell

and to Mrs. Sachiko Morrell

on the occasion of their retirement from

Washington University in St. Louis

CONTENTS

POETIC EXPRESSION

POSTMODERNISM AND AESTHETICS

ACKNOWLEDGMENTS

THE BASIC IDEA behind this book came from a combination of fortunate circumstances that brought me into contact with distinguished scholars of aesthetics from Japan and the West. As a fellow of the Japan Foundation in 1993, I was privileged to work in the Department of Aesthetics and Art History of the University of Osaka under the supervision of Professor Tsunemichi Kambayashi, the current president of the Japanese Association of Aesthetics. Professor Kambayashi was then organizing a major symposium on the future of philosophical thought to which he invited major twentieth-century philosophers, including Professor Gianni Vattimo of the University of Turin. It was ironic indeed that I, a graduate of the University of Turin, would meet my former dean of humanities for the first time in Japan and would be asked to be his interpreter. This encounter encouraged me to reread the insightful work of Professor Vattimo, who has been very vocal on the need to make the past relevant to the present in the humanities. As a scholar of medieval Japan, I grew considerably interested in the role played by aesthetic categories in the formation of contemporary discourses on premodern Japan. Urged by a desire to know more about the use of Western hermeneutics in the construction of images of Japan, I began to teach a series of undergraduate courses on Japanese aesthetics and hermeneutics at the University of California, Los Angeles. Unfortunately, I soon discovered the paucity of materials on these topics. What one needed on the Japanese side was a publication similar to Gianni Vattimo's brilliant anthology of texts on aesthetics, *Modern Aesthetics* (*Estetica Moderna*, 1977). Although the present work falls short of reaching the completeness of Vattimo's work, it is nevertheless a step in that direction. To Professors Kambayashi and Vattimo, therefore, go my deepest thanks for allowing me to envision this book. To the Japan Foundation I am particularly grateful for financing four months of research at the University of Osaka.

From 1993 to 1995 at UCLA I held several graduate seminars on Japanese aesthetics in which students worked on preliminary drafts of some of the texts presented in this book. Bruce Baird, Joseph Essertier, Ryuko Flores, Makiko Fujiwara, Gregory Golley, and Leslie Winston were among them. Christopher Bush of the Department of Comparative Literature took upon himself the task of reading the entire manuscript. Several colleagues from my home department were very supportive of this project, foremost among them Professor Herbert Plutschow, a truly learned, generous, and ideal colleague. Conversations with Haun Saussy, now of Stanford University, were inspirational in making me aware of the complexities of "the problem of a Chinese aesthetic," to use the title of his thought-provoking book. Fred Notehelfer, director of the UCLA Center for Japanese Studies, has made the UCLA experience truly enjoyable and rewarding by shaping the center into UCLA's most vital organization on Japan. Mihoko Miki and Toshie Marra of the Richard C. Rudolph East Asian Library shared with me, as always, their unique bibliographic expertise. The UCLA Council on Research Award was very generous in supporting this study.

The completion of this book's first draft was made possible by a lavish grant from the International Research Center for Japanese Studies (Kokusai Nihon Bungaku Kenkyū Sentā) where I spent a most rewarding year from 1996 to 1997. I deeply thank Professor Haga Tōru, emeritus, of the University of Tokyo for his kind invitation. At the Nichibunken I benefited from the expertise of Professors Suzuki Sadami (modern Japanese literature), Inaga Shigemi (Japanese and Western art), Mitsuta Kazunobu (premodern Japanese literature), Hayakawa Monta (Japanese art), Kasaya Kazuhiko (Japanese history), and Inoue Shōichi (Japanese architecture, design, and popular culture).

My interest in issues related to Japanese aesthetics and hermeneutics would not have evolved without the guidance of my teachers of Japanese literature. Without their pioneering efforts in making philosophy relevant to the field of Japanese literature, in fact, this book would not exist. It gives me infinite pleasure to acknowledge my indebtedness to them once again. They are Professors Robert E. Morrell (M.A. adviser), William R. LaFleur (Ph.D. adviser), and J. Thomas Rimer (whole life adviser). It is with deep regret that I think of all the mistakes they will find in this book despite such a strong didactic presence. Responsibility, of course, stays with the imperfect student.

Patricia Crosby, executive editor of the University of Hawai'i Press, is the embodiment of loyalty and determination in the field of publishing. I thank her deeply for all her hard work in defending and promoting my research. I also want to thank Masako Ikeda, managing editor, and Don Yoder, copy editor for the press, for their professional care.

INTRODUCTION

THE READER, I hope, will excuse the tautology that appears in the title of this book and is often repeated throughout: "modern aesthetics." Of course—it may be argued—aesthetics can only be modern, since it is part of modernity and did not exist as a field prior to the mid-eighteenth century. Moreover—it might be added—the field of aesthetics was born in Europe as a branch of philosophy, and, therefore, the application of the category of aesthetics to Japan is a clear act of hermeneutical hegemony.

I chose the expression "modern aesthetics" to show that aesthetics is indeed a product of modernity and that, therefore, whenever we talk of "Japanese taste," or of a "Japanese sense of beauty," thus making the particular into a universal, and apply the notion of aesthetics to premodern Japan, we are actually referring to a fairly modern construct called "aesthetics" whose wide popularity in Japan is directly related to its ability to produce images of what we call "Japan." Unless the notion of aesthetics is subjected to genealogical scrutiny, we will continue to use the word "aesthetics" in the ambiguous sense of something that always existed out there and was naturally visible to everybody—for example, the "aesthetics of feminine sensibility" of the Heian period, the "aesthetics of formlessness and impermanence" of the Kamakura and Muromachi periods, the "aesthetics of the floating world" of the Edo period—rather than as a modern mechanism that is responsible for a number of hermeneutical strategies directly related to the production of subject and state.[1]

As for the second objection—the charge of hermeneutical hegemony—this book presents the works of modern Japanese thinkers who either were trained in, or had a good knowledge of, Western philosophy and applied their knowledge of Western aesthetics—if I may be allowed another tau-

---

1. For several examples of this approach see the articles contained in Nancy G. Hume, ed., *Japanese Aesthetics and Culture* (Albany: SUNY Press, 1995).

1

tology—to the explanation/production of "Japan." The expression "Japanese aesthetics," therefore, refers to a process of philosophical negotiation between Japanese thinkers and Western hermeneutical practices in the creation and development of images of Japan. Inasmuch as we consider it the work done in Japan on the topic of the philosophy of arts, "Japanese aesthetics" does indeed exist as a field.

The aesthetic project would not have raised so much interest in Japan were it not for its political relevance—particularly at a time, such as the beginning of the Meiji period, when the burgeoning state was grappling with the problem of modernization. Nishi Amane (1829–1897), who introduced modern aesthetics to Japan (see Chapter 1), perceived the political implications of aesthetics. This we can see from the following statement, which he addressed to the Meiji emperor and to the most distinguished members of the Meiji government:

> It goes without saying, then, that art fosters the flourishing of civilization; it elevates the human world into a lofty realm. Naturally, the ministers and officials appointed to legislate laws and govern society must not neglect it. Although it is not the purpose of the fine arts to have a direct bearing on policies, they nevertheless are an indirect objective of political tactics. That is why you will not find any example in any country of a sovereign who has not paid attention to this topic. After all, the true purpose of aesthetics does not conflict with the comparable purposes of morality, law, and economics. If one is too partial in one direction, however, he will not be free from the abuse of making them reciprocally incompatible. Therefore, we should clearly distinguish what is of importance and find a proper balance between them. Here I end my theory of aesthetics. [Nishi Amane, *The Theory of Aesthetics (Bimyōgaku Setsu)*]

Nishi was quite successful in his endeavor. The Japanese Ministry of Education invited several foreign scholars to lecture on aesthetics at Tokyo Imperial University. From the United States came Ernest F. Fenollosa (1853–1908), who taught Western philosophy from 1882 to 1885, and George William Knox (1853–1912), who was entrusted with an independent course on aesthetics from 1885 to 1887. Appointments were also made to the German Ludwig Busse (1862–1907) from 1887 to 1892 and to the Russian Raphael von Koeber (1848–1923) from 1893 to 1914. In 1899 Professor Ōtsuka Yasuji (1868–1931) became the first tenured Japanese professor of aesthetics at Tokyo Imperial University, followed in 1910 by Fukada Yasukazu (1878–1927) at Kyoto University. The state must have had its reasons for finding the field worthy of such attention. As Nishi pointed out in his lecture, the political relevance of aesthetics to the well-being of the state was too great to be ignored. The major role played by aesthetics in the formation of judgments could not be underestimated at a time when politicians were searching for new ways of eliciting agreement within and between communities. How could any agreement be reached without first devising a mechanism that would allow one to ground the immanence of subjectivity in some kind of transcendent objectivity? How could a multiplicity of subjects find any consensus unless an abstract "common sense" was theorized and grounded in some sort of convincing objectivity?

Once the consolatory truths of Platonic "Ideas," Plotinian emanations from the "One," and the "God" of Catholic hermeneutics had lost credibility after the close scrutiny of the Enlightenment, a new bond was required to keep members of communities together. A secularized version of the divine could be found in the cult of "Beauty," whose inscrutability, rooted in the depth and mystery of one's innermost feelings, was as profound as the path leading to God. The way to beauty brought philosophers back to the study of its origin, that is, man's affects, sensations, perceptions (Gk. *"aisthesis,"* from which the word "aesthetics" is derived). The role played by Immanuel Kant (1724–1804) in the issue of taste was utterly central to the interest that Meiji politicians showed for the notion of the intersubjective validity of the category of taste as a common response to beauty. Kant had searched for answers to the paradox of the antinomy of taste: How do we reconcile the alleged universality of aesthetic judgment with the particularity of the subject pronouncing that judgment? How do we keep the idea of a possible universality of taste based on a notion of common sense without the principle of this common sense negating the subjectivity conceived of in a nonmetaphysical way?

If we accept the formula "to each his own taste," then we destroy the claim to universality without which the aesthetic field would collapse—and, with it, the possibility of communal cohesion. Kant solved the problem by positing two kinds of judgment: determinant judgment, or the judgment of cognition, and reflective judgment, or the judgment of taste. Reflective = aesthetic judgment proceeds from the particular to the universal. The general (or universal) is not given prior to the activity of reflection, but only through it and after it. If we were to stop at this point, however, we would never be able to agree. Therefore, Kant argued that this judgment presupposes an indeterminate horizon of expectation or principle to reflection—meaning that the real will let itself be classified in conformity to logic. This activity of reflection is at the origin of what Kant calls aesthetic satisfaction. Such a satisfaction is felt when the reflective subject observes an agreement between the real and his requirement (agreement between what is and what ought to be): a reconciliation of sensibility and intelligence. The beautiful is a partial reconciliation of sensibility and concepts. The judgment of taste is not based on determinate concepts or rules. It is thus impossible to argue about it as if it were a judgment of scientific knowledge. At the same time it is not confined to a pure empirical subjectivity of feeling, since it rests on the presence of an object that, if it is beautiful, will awaken an idea necessary to reason and, as such, common to humanity. It is thanks to this indeterminate idea that it becomes possible to argue about taste. But while scientific debates are regulated by disputation, in which the subjective particularity is erased within an imperious rationality, aesthetics is ruled by discussion, in which the same particularity, while remaining particular, aims to expand to the point of claiming universality, without demonstration, without the mediation of a concept. Taste becomes an autonomous human delight allegedly deprived of interest and purpose. Here we have Kant's famous four moments of the judgment of taste:

> 1. First moment: "*Taste* is the faculty of an object or a method of representing it by an *entirely disinterested* satisfaction or dissatisfaction. The object of such satisfaction is called *beautiful.*"
> 2. Second moment: "The *beautiful* is that which pleases universally without requiring a concept."
> 3. Third moment: "*Beauty* is the form of the *purposiveness* of an object, so far as this is perceived in it *without any representation of a purpose.*"
> 4. Fourth moment: "The *beautiful* is that which without any concept is cognized as the object of a *necessary* satisfaction."[2]

This necessary satisfaction is what explains the possibility of an intersubjective aesthetic common sense. The construction of a community based on the universal communicability of sensation, and ruled by notions of taste, had tremendous political consequences with regard to the burgeoning modern states, which the aesthetic program provided with internalized aesthetic imperatives. From the disinterested contemplation of beauty, a social bonding could be derived in which the unity, totality, and harmony of the work of art translated into the unity, totality, and harmony of an "ideal" society. The satisfaction of aesthetic contemplation, or the pleasure of a finality without an end, a purposiveness without a purpose, turned into principles of "spontaneous" consensus, so that beauty became the internalization of a moral imperative—a sort of pleasant repression. Once in the hands of the ideologues of the emerging states, Kant's "purposiveness without a purpose" easily translated into the practice of a "purposiveness without expressing its purpose."[3]

---

2. Immanuel Kant, *Critique of Judgment* (New York: Hafner, 1951), pp. 37–81.

3. The expression comes from Gregory Jusdanis, *Belated Modernity and Aesthetic Culture: Inventing National Literature* (Minneapolis: University of Minnesota Press, 1991).

Theoretical developments in the field of aesthetics kept treading over the path of reconciliation between the present world and the world of transcendence through the mediation of the "beautiful"—"the wide realm of the beautiful" that, according to G. W. F. Hegel (1770–1831), is the province of the fine arts.[4] Belief in the potential of art to bridge final actuality and the infinite freedom of reason—metaphysical universality and the determinateness of real particularity—made the work of art an epiphany of the Absolute Spirit in front of a newly constituted assembly of believers (the art critics and the appreciators of art) who filled with aesthetics the void left by theology. Hegel's *Introductory Lectures on Aesthetics* is eloquent on this point:

> This is an attribute which art shares with religion and philosophy, only in this peculiar mode, that it represents even the highest ideas *in sensuous forms,* thereby bringing them nearer to the character of natural phenomena, to the senses, and to feeling. The world, into whose depth *thought* penetrates, is a supra-sensuous world, which is thus, to begin with, erected as a *beyond* over against immediate consciousness and present situation; the power which thus rescues itself from the *here,* that consists in the actuality and finiteness of sense, is the freedom of thought in cognition. But the mind is able to heal this schism which its advance creates; it generates out of itself the works of fine art as the first middle term of reconciliation between pure thought and what is external, sensuous, and transitory, between nature with its finite actuality and the infinite freedom of the reason that comprehends. . . . The philosophic conception of the beautiful, to indicate its true nature at least by anticipation, must contain, reconciled within it, the two extremes which have been mentioned, by combining metaphysical universality with the determinateness of real particularity. Only thus is it apprehended in its truth, in its real and explicit nature. It is then fertile out of its own resources, in contrast to the barrenness of one-sided reflection. For it has in accordance with its own conception to develop into a totality of attributes, while the conception itself as well as its detailed exposition contains the necessity of its particulars, as also of their progress and transition one into another. On the other hand, again, these particulars, to which the transition is made, carry in themselves the universality and essentiality of the conception as the particulars of which they appear.[5]

Aestheticians entrusted aesthetic categories with the reduction of the chaos engendered by particularity to the order of universality. The issue of the antinomy of taste remained at the center of debates on aesthetics, in-

---

4. G. W. F. Hegel, *Introductory Lectures on Aesthetics,* trans. Bernard Bosanquet (London: Penguin, 1993), p. 3.

5. Ibid., pp. 9–10 and 25–26.

forming basic techniques of aesthetic practices such as the reduction of historical "difference" to some sort of categorical specificity. In an effort to explain the diversity of particularity with a commonly understood language of objectivity, history was presented in specific moments of ideality and representativeness. Ages and cultures began to be described according to alleged major characteristics—whether major authors, styles, or works of the literary canon—or according to general aesthetic categories in which the richness of historical diversity was reduced to aesthetic principles of alleged ideality. Such a method actually came to the field of aesthetics from physics. We might think of Newton, for example, who reduced the multiplicity of celestial phenomena to a single principle: universal gravitation. In an analogous manner,[6] aesthetics searches for universal rules behind human feelings, in the human responses to the world where these feelings are best exteriorized and expressed in an observable way, what we today call the work of art. We see the same reduction at work in the title of Charles Batteux's *Les Beaux-Arts Réduit à un Même Principe* (The Fine Arts Reduced to a Single Principle, 1746)—that is, beauty. We see it too in the title of Nishi Amane's *New Theory of the One Hundred and One* (*Hyakuichi Shinron*, 1874), which refers to the notion of harmony that finds "unity" *(ichi)* among the "diverse" *(hyaku).*[7]

The answers provided by the field of aesthetics to the problem of the antinomy of taste have proved extremely influential to the formation of cultural images of Japan since Nishi's introduction of the field up to the present time. When we consider the impact that Western philosophy has had on Japanese scholars since the late nineteenth century—and the impact that Japanese scholarship still has to this day on the ways in which Westerners represent Japan to themselves—attention to the work of Japanese aestheticians clarifies the complex web of paradoxes in which all scholars of Japan, East and West, are inevitably trapped when talking about their subject matter. The realization that moments of cultural specificities are

---

6. The concept of analogy plays a fundamental role in aesthetics, since the field was set up by Alexander Gottlieb Baumgarten (1714–1762) in his *Aesthetica* (1750) as a "science of sensible knowledge" *(scientia cognitionis sensitivae)* that invested the sensible world with the perfection of logic. Moved by the need to justify the existence of a "science" of the senses independently from physical sciences, however, Baumgarten described aesthetics as "an inferior form of knowledge" *(ratio inferior)* grounded in what he called "the analogue of reason" *(analogon rationis)*. Baumgarten's *Aesthetica* begins as follows: "Aesthetics (theory of the liberal arts, doctrine of inferior knowledge, art of beautiful thinking, art of the analogue of reason) is the science of sensible knowledge." See Alexander Gottlieb Baumgarten, *Estetica* (Milan: Vita e Pensiero, 1993), p. 17.

7. On the analogy of aesthetics and science see Luc Ferry, *Homo Aestheticus: The Invention of Taste in the Democratic Age* (Chicago: University of Chicago Press, 1993), p. 41.

often couched in the language of Western realities is one of the major concerns of present-day aestheticians.[8] Such a realization, however, cannot be achieved unless we analyze the hermeneutics of major Japanese aestheticians of the past (and a few modern responses to them)—thinkers whose heroic intellectual experiments are exemplified in the selections gathered in this book.

The reader will notice several common patterns in the writings that follow. All the authors are moved by an impulse to define Japan to themselves in an attempt at clarifying their own subjectivities to themselves. Such an awakening to the pressing issue of the subject follows the forceful intervention of the West in producing questions that otherwise might have been left without formulation or might have been formulated differently. As a result, all the authors engage, at different levels of consciousness, in dialogues with Western thinkers and Western hermeneutical practices that I have tried to clarify either in the prefaces to the translations or in the footnotes. Moreover, each author is to some degree responsible for explaining the mechanism of hermeneutical practices that scholars in other fields— as, for example, the history of Japanese literature or the history of Japanese art—tend to take for granted and apply to their work without realizing that their images of Japan speak a foreign (most of the time German) idiom.

The first section of the book ("The Subject of Aesthetics") focuses on responses given by Japanese aestheticians to the introduction in Japan of the Western vocabulary of aesthetics. New words such as "aesthetics," "subjectivity," "objectivity," "sensitivity," and "imagination" had to be created in order to accommodate foreign concepts to the discussion of local artistic productions. Nishi Amane was undoubtedly the champion in the adaptation of an essentially Neo-Confucian idiom to the idiosyncrasies of the German technical language of philosophy (Chapter 1).

Okakura Kakuzō (1862–1913) used the same German vocabulary to reverse Hegel's philosophy and replace Germany with Japan in the journey of the Absolute Spirit toward self-transparency (Chapter 3). By subverting Hegel's Eurocentrism and attacking his notion of dialectics, Okakura located in the nondualism of Indian Buddhism the universality of the East, which

---

8. Private conversations with contemporary aestheticians—Amagasaki Akira of Gakushūin Women's University, Hamashita Masahiro of Kobe Women's University, Iwaki Ken'ichi of the University of Kyoto, Kambayashi Tsunemichi of Osaka University, and Sasaki Ken'ichi of the University of Tokyo—have clarified to me the struggle faced by scholars in presenting images of Japan that are somehow free from metalinguistic paradoxes. Due to the experimental nature of their writing, I think their work deserves a separate book and therefore decided not to include them in the present anthology.

transcended the Western version of universality and was, in Okakura's opinion, much less violent since it did not depend on the cannibalistic method of a synthesis feeding on a thesis and an antithesis. Okakura played a leading role in setting up the practice of aesthetic hermeneutics with regard to Japan that, independently from the attacks of later detractors, shaped notions of dichotomy (East/West) and strong local subjectivity (the specificity of the land) that to this day remain common coinage in studies of Japan. Okakura can be considered the founding father of the "myth of Asian spiritualism," which came as a result of his negotiations with the philosophy of idealism and the mediation of a Westerner, Ernest Fenollosa (1853–1908), an active lecturer in Japan in the late 1870s and early 1880s. Paradoxically, the lecture selected for this anthology deconstructs Okakura's own myth of Asian spiritualism by arguing against the emptiness of discourses on uniqueness and struggling to find answers to the thorny search for the subject.

Responses to the vocabulary of idealism, and to newly imported notions such as "idea" and "spirit," were mixed. Tsubouchi Shōyō's (1858–1935) fierce attack on Fenollosa (Chapter 2) indicates the uneasiness that a major practitioner of the art of writing felt with the abstract language of aesthetics—a language that, in Tsubouchi's opinion, was not conducive to the actual production of the work of art. His skepticism about the significance that the Western project of metaphysics could have for his land contrasts with the position taken by a professional aesthetician, Ōnishi Hajime (1864–1900), who followed Okakura's lead in analyzing Japan in light of the notion of spiritual peace (Chapter 4). Ōnishi's hermeneutics are truly remarkable as they bring to the reader's attention the difficulty of constructing images of a land based on a theory that was actually contradicted by practice. Since Okakura had envisioned Japan as a receptacle of Asian spiritualism, Japanese scholars felt that every facet of their society should live up to those standards. Whenever they did not, the aesthetician would remind his contemporaries that they were not fulfilling the reality required by the myth. Ōnishi embodied the moral voice of the land, telling his audience that reality should match the ideality of "what ought to be" and reproduce in visible terms the ideality of the work of art. If the evidence spoke against theory, then the land should be mobilized to create new evidence that would eventually match the stereotype. In the essay selected for this book Ōnishi engages Christian hermeneutics in an attempt to strengthen the myth of Asian spiritualism and find a method that would increase spiritual depth in local forms of artistic expression.

Appeals to live aesthetically reached their peak at the beginning of the century in the work of Takayama Chogyū (1871–1902), who engaged Friedrich Nietzsche's (1844–1900) philosophy of the "overman" (*Über-*

mensch) in the production of a strong Japanese subjectivity (Chapter 5). Takayama's wide knowledge of aesthetics is well exemplified in his "Observations on Aesthetic Pleasure," translated here, in which the author enters into a dialogue with major Western voices, past and modern, from Kant to Schiller (1759–1805), from Julius Heinrich von Kirchman (1802–1884) to Alexander Bain (1818–1903), from Herbert Spencer (1820–1903) to Grant Allen (1848–1899), from Eduard von Hartmann (1842–1906) to Jean-Marie Guyau (1854–1888), from Henry R. Marshall (1852–1927) to George Santayana (1863–1952).

The second part of the book ("Aesthetic Categories") addresses the thorny issue of the reduction of particularity to the unified structure of "universals" *(aware* and *yojō)* that are at the center of all debates on Japan's literary arts. Originally belonging to the vocabulary of premodern Japanese poetics, *aware* and *yojō* (in combination with *yūgen)* were transformed into aesthetic discourses in the modern period when they came to be used to indicate the "spirit" of, respectively, the Heian (794–1191) and Kamakura (1192–1333) periods. No one has paid more attention to the notion of *aware* than Ōnishi Yoshinori (1888–1959), who taught aesthetics at the University of Tokyo from 1922 until his retirement in 1949 (Chapter 6). To his lifelong research on Japanese "aesthetic categories" *(biteki hanchū)* he brought his vast knowledge of Western phenomenology. Genuinely interested in the philosophical implications of the notion of *aware,* Ōnishi provided a theoretical basis for a dialogue with thinkers such as Okazaki Yoshie (1892–1982) and Watsuji Tetsurō (1889–1960), as well as with literary historians such as Hisamatsu Sen'ichi (1894–1976), who employed categories theorized by Ōnishi in his examination of premodern Japanese literature. We may think of Hisamatsu's concern with explaining the specificity of each literary age in terms of the degree of, for example, "humor" *(kokkei),* "sublimity" *(sōbi),* or "elegance" *(yūbi)* found in the writings of that age.

The category of *yojō* (surplus of meaning) is taken up by the philosopher Kusanagi Masao (b. 1900), whose apologia of incompleteness clarifies to the reader the major arguments that were proposed to explain the "essence" of Japanese art in terms of its alleged lack of final form (Chapter 7). Kusanagi was an active participant in the creation and sustenance of what in hindsight could be called "the myth of formlessness," which he discussed by engaging the philosophy of Karl Jaspers (1883–1969) in his explanation of the "overtones" of the medieval notion of *yojō.* Kusanagi relied on Jaspers' existentialism, accepting the idea that art works as a "cipher of transcendence" and makes the invisibility of transcendence visible. Since the infinity of transcendence can only be caught in glimpses—the argument goes—incompleteness is the only chance we have to get in touch with the infinite. As the essay translated in this book demonstrates, Kusanagi's net of references is breathtaking. In addition to investigating the genealogy of the concept prior to its translation into an aesthetic category—an investigation that takes him through the works of medieval Japanese poets and theorists such as Minamoto no Tsunenobu (1016–1097), Fujiwara no Shunzei (1114–1204), Saigyō (1118–1190), Kamo no Chōmei (1153–1216), Fujiwara Teika (1162–1259), Nijō Yoshimoto (1320–1388), Shōtetsu (1381–1459), and Shinkei (1406–1475), as well as Chinese and Japanese painters such as Kuo Hsi (b. 1020), Tosa Mitsuoki (1617–1691), Nakabayashi Chikutō (1776–1853), Nakayama Kōyō (1717–1780), and Kuwayama Gyokushū (1737–1812)—Kusanagi interrogates the work of major art historians of the West, such as Joseph Gantner (1896–1988), Dagobert Frey (1883–1962), and Herbert von Einem (1905–1983).

The third section of the book ("Poetic Expression") contains examples from two major Japanese philosophers on the issue of the local poetic voice and the difficulty of articulating it through a philosophical vocabulary informed by Western metaphysical thought. Nishitani Keiji (1900–1990) mobilizes the vocabulary of Tertullian (b. ca. 150), Nāgārjuna (ca. 150–ca. 250), Yün-men Wen-yen (864–949), Ch'eng Ming-tao (1032–1085), Dōgen (1200–1253), Johannes Eckard (?1260–1327), Niccolò da Cusa (1400–1464), Gottfried Wilhelm Leibniz (1646–1716), and, albeit unacknowledgedly, Martin Heidegger (1889–1976) to make sense of the rhetorical specificity of the Japanese language (Chapter 8). Nishitani searches for such specificity by locating the poetry of Saigyō, Myōe Shōnin (1173–1232), and Bashō (1644–1694) in what Nishida Kitarō (1870–1945) called the "place" (basho) of "absolute negation-qua-affirmation"—a space where the logic of grammar (bunpō) makes room for a poetics of grams (aya), which resists the articulation of the world in terms of logical continuities between subjects and objects. The eclecticism of Nishitani's thinking elicits thought-provoking readings of his native literary tradition in which poetic imagination is grounded in a "field of nothingness" (mu no basho), thus anticipating postmodernist concerns with the arbitrariness of selection of a prioris as starting points in the process of interpretation.

The notion of expression is discussed in the essay by Imamichi Tomonobu (b. 1922), professor of aesthetics at the University of Tokyo from 1968 until his retirement in 1983 (Chapter 9). Reinforcing the orthodox view of an alleged East/West dichotomy, he argues that whereas in Europe "expression" is part of the modern vocabulary devised as a replacement of what was previously called "representation" (in the sense of mimesis), the reverse order applies to Japan. Following the myth of formlessness championed by Kusanagi Masao, Imamichi sees in the incompleteness of native artistic products a sign that the Japanese artist used to privilege the "imitation of his own conscience" (expression or "drawing the innerside") over the imitation of the external world—a pattern that Imamichi extends to the arts of Asia in general. The argument is buttressed by an analysis of Western and Eastern epistemologies built upon different notions of truth. The debt that Imamichi owes to Western philosophy is apparent from the very name of his system: "calonology," a contemporary revival of the Greek notions of beauty *(kalon),* existence *(on),* reason *(nous),* and science *(logos),* the four major ingredients of Western metaphysics. The metaphysical undertones of Imamichi's philosophy are particularly pronounced in his notion of art, which he associates with depth and profundity—a means to counterbalance, with its verticality, the horizontal structure of ordinary life (time extension) and make the appreciator ascend to absolute heights. Imamichi appears to be unconcerned with the consequences that the reproduction of a "strong" interpretative model entails: the conservation and regeneration of violence generated by clashes between strong subjectivities—the Western subjectivity, anchored in representation and mimesis as a result of the alleged Western dichotomy between subject and object, and the Eastern subjectivity, rooted in expression, that resists the division of spirit and matter, body and soul, immanence and transcendence.

The impasse that a thought grounded in "strong" notions of truth has created in philosophical discussions constitutes a major concern for thinkers active in the debate on postmodernism—a topic addressed in the final section of the book ("Postmodernism and Aesthetics"). The philosopher Sakabe Megumi (b. 1936) of Tokyo University has been very vocal on the need to reduce the weight of subjectivities in an age that seems to be committed more than any other period in history to the reduction of conflict on a global scale (Chapter 10). Sakabe's project is the closest example in Japan to what the Italian philosopher Gianni Vattimo (b. 1936) has called "weak thought"—a move from a strong to a weaker sense of Being that attempts to reduce the heaviness of metaphysical thought.[9] In the first essay presented here, Sakabe introduces the Japanese version of a soft or weak subject, whose surface *(omote)* is caught in a structure of what Sakabe

---

9. The term "weak thought" *(pensiero debole),* currently indicating Gianni Vattimo's philosophy and school, first appeared in a book that gathers several articles discussing resistance to the "strong" images informed by metaphysics: Gianni Vattimo and Pier Aldo Rovatti, eds., *Il Pensiero Debole* (Milan: Feltrinelli, 1983). See also Vattimo's *The End of Modernity: Nihilism and Hermeneutics in Post-Modern Culture* (Cambridge: Polity Press, 1988) and *The Adventure of Difference: Philosophy After Nietzsche and Heidegger* (Cambridge: Polity Press, 1993). For a discussion of "weak thought" in the light of Japanese epistemology see my article, "Yowaki Shii: Kaishakugaku no Mirai wo Minagara (Weak Thought: A Look at the Future of Hermeneutics)," *Nichibunken Forum* 95 (1997):1–39.

calls "reciprocity" *(sōgosei)* and "reversibility" *(kagyakusei)*. The subject is displaced in a web of reflections in which it is reduced to "something that is seen by others, that sees itself, and that sees itself as another." Sakabe resurrects an argument that is originally rooted in local hermeneutics—the theory of detached view *(riken no ken)* advanced by the medieval playwright Zeami (1364–1443)—while, at the same time, reworking it in the light of the phenomenology of the French philosopher Maurice Merleau-Ponty (1908–1961). In the second essay, Sakabe's findings are applied to his analysis of the notion of "imitation."

The book ends with an essay by Japan's foremost literary critic, Karatani Kōjin (b. 1941), who has written extensively on the process of domestication and taming that Western hermeneutics tends to impose on non-Western texts: silencing the Other by making it another image of the same (Chapter 11). Karatani's research on the political implications of aesthetic practices has redirected the attention of scholars of Japan all over the world on the need to reexamine the process of discourse formation before blindly accepting orthodox interpretations of realities that actually resist the epistemological apparatus through which these realities are interpreted. Karatani has perceptively pointed out that since the encounter with the West in the second half of the nineteenth century, Japan has been made into the Museum of Asia by Westerners who thought to "overcome" the problems of modernity through their "discovery" of an alien reality made exotic.[10]

Karatani considers the construction of Japan as an aesthetic object an act of compensation on the part of a worshiper of art who participates in the guilt of silencing the Other while at the same time enshrining it in the hall of beauty. He builds his critique by analyzing how Kant's project of aesthetic disinterest actually affects political interests. He starts by outlining the fact that one of Kant's major philosophical achievements was the organization of knowledge along the lines of logic (true and false), ethics (good and bad), and aesthetics (beautiful and ugly). The ultimate point, however, remained the formulation of judgments (right and wrong). The argument, then, proceeds as follows. Unlike "premodern" times, ruled by religious beliefs, in which the three spheres were interdependent—so that beauty could not be false and bad, truth could not be bad and ugly, and goodness could not be false or ugly—modernity grounded its distinction in the notion that each sphere enjoyed independence from the other. This was made possible by the belief in the inherent value of each type of knowledge (the Kantian "purposiveness without a purpose"), which resulted from the crisis faced by the very

---

10. Karatani has made this argument in the article "Bijutsukan to Shite no Nihon: Okakura Tenshin to Fenorosa," *Hihyō Kūkan* 2(1) (1994).

notion of belief: a single authority in charge of the process of legitimation. Markets on their way to development needed different justificatory devices for actions that could be profitable (true) but ethically questionable (bad) and aesthetically unacceptable (ugly). Truth had to be found in what used to be considered false (evil and ugliness), so that beauty could also be spotted in what was perceived as morally reprehensible and logically absurd. This logic provided the European "discoverers" of the world with a powerful argument for accepting (and revering) on an aesthetic level what was rejected (and despised) as barbarous and uncivil on all other grounds. Since judgment in the modern world was the result of a putting into brackets concerns that belonged to a different sphere of knowledge, the judgment of taste required that ethical/logical notions such as goodness and truth be scrapped from the process of judging. Karatani notes that unless the brackets are removed once the aesthetic judgment has taken place, we fall into the trap of self-deception by thinking that we have finally established a relation of equality with the Other, whose aesthetic existence we acknowledge and admire. Karatani warns his readers not to ignore the basic mechanism of aesthetics, which operates by setting up separating screens and producing aesthetic appreciation out of a guilt the observer is bound to feel, should he judge the same situation from an ethical point of view.[11]

The aesthetic construction of Japan, for example, frees the observer from the guilt of contributing to the loss of a world for which the process of modernity—aesthetics included—is responsible as a result of colonial and imperialistic policies of expansion. This is not just the case with a French and American audience that fell in love with Japanese prints *(ukiyo-e)* at a time when Western powers were showing off their military muscle in the Far East, threatening to destroy a world by forcing it to adopt a Western lifestyle and a Western management of knowledge.[12] It also applies to local guilt—as in the case of Okakura Kakuzō, who realized that he had to assume a detached and scientific attitude in his aesthetic appreciation of the Guze Kannon statue in Nara during a survey of "artistic products" in his land.[13] It is also the guilt of the Japanese colonialist who praises the

---

11. Karatani develops this argument in the article "Bigaku no Kōyō: *Orientarizumu* Igo," *Hihyō Kūkan* 2(14) (1997).

12. On an analogous issue see the powerful essay by Renato Rosaldo, "Imperialist Nostalgia," in his *Culture and Truth: The Remaking of Social Analysis* (Boston: Beacon Press, 1989), pp. 68–87.

13. Okakura's attitude contrasts with the reverent behavior of the monks of the Hōryūji temple who fear that exposure of the statue might invite the revenge of the gods in the form of thunder or other natural calamity. For the different attitudes taken by the monks, by Okakura, and by Fenollosa during fieldwork at the temple see Stefan Tanaka, "Imaging History: Inscribing Belief in the Nation," *Journal of Asian Studies* 53(1) (February 1994):24–44.

popular arts of Korea as "mighty beauty" *(idai na bi)* at a time when the Japanese army was reproducing on Korean soil the Western logic of expansion and repression.[14] The displacement of reality into the aesthetic realm exonerates the worshiper of art from feelings of self-blame to which rational thoughts would inevitably expose him, while providing pleasure in the possibility of aesthetic evasion.

Together with Tsubouchi Shōyō, Karatani is undoubtedly the most critical voice in this anthology. His warnings, combined with a chorus of analogous statements coming from the field of cultural studies,[15] cannot be neglected in the present age in which social and political issues are often displaced in the realm of fashion. It seems appropriate, therefore, to bring this book to a conclusion with a deconstructive act in the very "spirit"—if a return to Hegel is allowed—of the postmodern age.

---

14. This is the case of Yanagi Muneyoshi (1889–1961), whose defense of Korean independence during the Japanese colonial days did not spare him from the sharp criticism of Korean intellectuals on the ground of his complicity with the aesthetic project. See Karatani, "Bigaku no Kōyō," pp. 52–54.

15. See, for example, Terry Eagleton's fierce critique of aesthetics in *The Ideology of the Aesthetic* (Oxford: Blackwell, 1990).

THE SUBJECT OF AESTHETICS

ONE

The Introduction of Aesthetics
Nishi Amane

THE INTRODUCTION to Japan of the field of aesthetics in the 1870s entailed a subtle and complex reorganization of local epistemological systems. At the same time, Japanese intellectuals were challenged with the creation of a technical vocabulary that was sensitive to the newly imported ideas. Alien concepts, such as the Western distinction between mechanical and liberal arts, had to be assimilated during what Yamamoto Masao has called "the enlightenment period" of Japanese aesthetics.[1] A major challenge came when the purposiveness and practicality of craftsmanship *(gijutsu)* had to be differentiated from the ideality of artistic creation *(geijutsu)*. The basic difficulty—to find Japanese counterparts to the meanings that the Greek expression *"techne"* had come to assume in the West during the centuries—was further compounded by the idealistic argument that justified grouping under the same category different activities such as architecture, sculpture, painting, music, and poetry: the argument that each particular "fine art" *(bijutsu)* partook of an alleged universal element.[2]

It was not simply a linguistic problem. Behind the vocabulary of aesthetics stood a thick layer of Western philosophy that extended from Pla-

---

1. The contemporary aesthetician Yamamoto Masao distinguishes three moments in the history of Japanese aesthetics. The first is the period of enlightenment (1868–1878), which is characterized by the translation and adaptation of Western works on aesthetics on the part of Nishi Amane (1829–1897), Nakae Chōmin (1847–1901), and Kikuchi Dairoku (1855–1917). This is also the time when the American scholar Ernest Francisco Fenollosa (1853–1908) was touring Japan and delivering lectures on aesthetics and the arts. The second moment is the period of criticism (1878–1888) as represented by Tsubouchi Shōyō (1859–1935), Futabatei Shimei (1864–1909), Toyama Masakazu (1848–1900), Ōnishi Hajime (1864–1900), Mori Ōgai (1862–1922), and Takayama Chogyū (1871–1902). The third is the period of reflection (1888–1910), which coincides with the institutionalization of aesthetics in Japanese academia. In 1899 Ōtsuka Yasuji (1868–1931) was asked to fill the first permanent chair of aesthetics at Tokyo Imperial University, followed in 1910 by Fukada Yasukazu (1878–1927) at Kyoto University. See Yamamoto Masao, *Tōzai Geijutsu Seishin no Dentō to Kōryū* (Tokyo: Risōsha, 1965), pp. 15–115.
2. See Chapter 3, note 16.

to's notion of Idea to the Hegelian system of Absolute Spirit. The importation of aesthetics required Japanese scholars to explain and justify the new "science" in the light of Western epistemology. In the last three decades of the nineteenth century, Japan was faced with the introduction, study, and digestion—or indigestion—of more than two thousand years of Western thought.

In addition to the problem of mastering in a brief period of time the secrets of the political other, Japanese intellectuals were also faced with the delicate task of linking their traditional thought to the newly imported philosophical systems. In the field of aesthetics, the major challenge was to explain a basic paradox: how to make sense of fields of knowledge such as literature, for example, that for centuries had been justified by Neo-Confucian scholars in terms of ethical principles—"to promote good and chastise evil" *(kanzen chōaku)*—according to the Kantian notion of "purposiveness without a purpose." How could the dependence (either religious or political) to which art had been submitted in Japan, on practical grounds, be transformed to a moment of autonomy and freedom?[3]

Nishi Amane (1829–1897) faced this challenge when, back from a few years of study at the University of Leiden in Holland, he translated "aesthetics" as "the science of good and beauty" *(zenbigaku).*[4] The basic premise behind Nishi's choice was a belief in a strong relationship between the ethical and aesthetic moments—with the obvious implications that only the person versed in the fine arts is good and that only an ethically good person understands beauty.[5] Nishi could count on solid sources from both the Eastern and Western traditions: a combination of the Confucian "theory of good, beauty, capability, and refinement" *(shan mei liang ueng)* and the Greek "theory of goodness and beauty" *(kalosk' agathos).*[6]

---

3. Although, as Thomas Havens has argued, "it is doubtful that Nishi ever read Kant at all" (Thomas R. H. Havens, *Nishi Amane and Modern Japanese Thought* [Princeton: Princeton University Press, 1970], p. 55), we know from a letter that he sent in 1863 to Johann Joseph Hoffman (1805–1878), a professor of Japanese studies at Leiden University, about Nishi's interest in studying Kant's philosophy. In the letter we read: "In addition to what I previously mentioned, I would like to study the field of philosophy. I would like to learn from Descartes, Locke, Hegel, and Kant since what they expound is different from the religious thoughts allowed in my country." There is no doubt that Nishi was exposed to German philosophy during his studies at Leiden under Professor C. W. Opzoomer (1812–1892), the most distinguished scholar of philosophy in Holland at the time, beginning in April 1863. See Ōkubo Toshiaki, ed., *Nishi Amane Zenshū,* 2 (Tokyo: Munetaka Shobō, 1960), pp. 701–702.

4. Nishi Amane used the translation *"zenbigaku"* in a work on politics and ethics entitled *New Theory of the One Hundred and One (Hyakuichi Shinron,* 1874), in which he analyzed the notion of harmony that finds "unity *(ichi)* among the diverse *(hyaku)."* See Havens, *Nishi Amane and Modern Japanese Thought,* p. 118.

5. Nishi Amane, *Hyakuichi Shinron,* in Ōkubo, *Nishi Amane Zenshū,* 1, p. 251 [hereafter *HS*].

6. Kaneda Tamio, *Nihon Kindai Bigaku Josetsu* (Tokyo: Hōritsu Bunkasha, 1990), p. 12; Yamamoto, *Tōzai Geijutsu Seishin no Dentō to Kōryū,* p. 24.

The strong Confucian background of Nishi's education is evident when we think of the beginning of his *New Theory of the One Hundred and One (Hyakuichi Shinron)* in which he explains the word "learning" *(oshie)* as a process of cultivation that is strictly related to the regulation of the family, the order of the state, and the peace of the world. The message came primarily from *The Great Learning (Ta Hsüe)* in which we read: "The extension of knowledge lay in the investigation of things. For only when things are investigated is knowledge extended; only when knowledge is extended are thoughts sincere; only when thoughts are sincere are minds rectified; only when minds are rectified are our persons cultivated; only when our persons are cultivated are our families regulated; only when families are regulated are states well governed; and only when states are well governed is there peace in the world."[7]

The acceptability in Japan of the new field of aesthetics depended on its potential for inclusion in the network of knowledge leading to the *Bildung* of the Meiji citizen. Nishi understood aesthetics as an answer to the conflicts that had resulted from the encounter between the Confucian ethical system and the legalistic system imported from the West. In an effort to live up to the standards of "enlightened" nations by adopting their cultural and political systems, Japan was favoring the replacement of ritual with laws in the political administration of the country. The embracing of the other, however, meant a relaxing of the Confucian rules of morality. The easy availability of the written rule exonerated humankind from the painstaking search for moral improvement—or learning, whose basic structure had, in the Confucian world, been provided by the unwritten laws of ritual.

Nishi argued that whereas laws helped humanity to achieve a deep sense of justice *(sei)*, only learning elevated people to the supreme goal of the ethical good *(zen)*. While laws regulated the realm of human reason *(chi)*, learning had the power to regulate the freer, but more dangerous, sphere of the will *(i)*. Aesthetics was related to the good inasmuch as ethical good showed itself as form in beauty *(bi)*, appearing in actual things as skill *(nō)* and in matter as taste *(kō)*. In Nishi's thought, aesthetics had the potential to replace ritual, whose effectiveness was challenged by the strengthening of the law. Aesthetics could express the ethical world of the good in the form of beauty through the skill of a producer and the taste of a consumer *(zenbi nōkō)*.[8]

---

7. William Theodore de Bary, Wing-tsit Chan, and Burton Watson, eds., *Sources of Chinese Tradition,* vol. 1 (New York: Columbia University Press, 1960), p. 114; *HS,* pp. 236–237.

8. *HS,* p. 265.

If, on the one hand, aesthetics could be seen as a moment of resistance against the power of the Western notion of the law, it could on the other hand also help resist the temptation to alienate humanity from the natural world along the lines of the Western natural sciences that were conquering nature by analyzing and classifying it. This explains Nishi's efforts to locate aesthetics within the sphere of the human sciences—and, more specifically, "psychology" *(shinri)*—opposing it to that other science which regulates nature rather than appreciating it, namely "physics" *(butsuri)*. Although Nishi was a fervent "enlightener" inasmuch as he spent most of his life writing on the benefits that Western science could bring to the Japanese government, he nonetheless saw in aesthetics the possibility of bringing a degree of moderation to the epistemological conflicts that were challenging his country during the Meiji period. The value of aesthetics, he argued, could be maximized when it was applied to the explanation of human behavior and human socialization.

Aesthetics could be used as a safety valve while importing natural sciences that were less concerned with human beings, their lives, and their values. Yet aesthetics should not be used to explain the physical world. Here lies a major difference between Nishi and Confucian thought. Nishi resisted the thought of collapsing "psychology" and "physics" according to the Confucian notion of analogical patterns between nature (the way of heaven) and the present human reality (the way of man). The naïveté of explaining natural phenomena according to the pattern of heaven, Nishi argued, was after all the main cause behind the fanciful interpretation by Shinto scholars of the failed Mongol invasion of Japan in the thirteenth century: divine rather than physical winds *(kamikaze)*.[9]

We cannot neglect the importance that Joseph Haven's (1816–1874) *Mental Philosophy* (1857) had on Nishi's notion of aesthetics. Nishi, in fact, translated this work, shortening the title to *Psychology (Shinrigaku,* 1870–1871). In his book Haven distinguishes what he calls "mental philosophy" from philosophy proper, inasmuch as the latter "seeks to discover, and scientifically to state, the general laws both of matter and mind," while the former targets a narrower field of inquiry that is restricted to the human mind. To quote Haven: "Mental philosophy has for its object to ascertain the facts and laws of mental operation."[10] In the introduction, Haven distinguishes what he calls "the two great departments of human knowledge," physics and metaphysics, to which he wants to add psychology.

9. *HS,* pp. 279–280.
10. Joseph Haven, *Mental Philosophy: Including the Intellect, Sensibilities, and Will* (Boston: Gould & Lincoln, 1857), p. 15.

Joseph Haven tackled the problem of aesthetics—or, as he called it, "the science of the beautiful"—in the section on intuitive power. The difficulty of finding a common denominator for the highly abstract category of the beautiful forced Haven to approach the matter historically by listing different definitions given to the subject in the past. Beauty, then, is portrayed in a multiplicity of ways: as the producer of feelings and sensations of the mind rather than as an objective reality; as the result of "associations of idea and feeling with the object contemplated"; as the sign or expression awakening emotions in the viewer or listener; or, for those who take beauty to be an objective category, as novelty, as unity in variety, as order and proportion, as "spiritual life in its immediate sensible manifestations."[11]

The quarrel between theories supporting the objective nature of the beautiful—the real presence of beauty in the object itself—and those that construct beauty as the result of the mental process of the imagination leads Haven to uphold a position in between: beauty as a relational encounter of mind and its object of contemplation.[12] But he did not deny the objective presence of beauty in the external object that is perceived differently by different subjects and whose difference is dictated by social class, education, and personal sensibility.[13]

In Nishi's translation of Haven's book we find the expression "the science of good and beauty" *(zenbigaku)* used for the first time. Nishi must have felt the inadequacy of this word, however, since he decided to change it to "the discipline of good taste" *(kashuron)* in a series of lectures he gave in his private academy.[14] This new definition of aesthetics was based on the pragmatism of experience in the process of aesthetic appreciation, a strain of thought that was rooted in the positivism of Auguste Comte (1798–1857) and the utilitarianism of John Stuart Mill (1806–1873). This was a kind of aesthetic psychologism that led to "the aesthetics from below" *(die Ästhetik von unten)* of Gustav Theodor Fechner's (1834–1887) *Elementary*

11. Ibid., pp. 263–266.

12. "As the spark from the smitten steel is not strictly to be regarded as itself a property of the steel, nor yet of the flint, but as a relative phenomenon arising from the collision of the two, so beauty, it may be said, dwells not absolutely in the object per se, nor yet in the intelligent subject, but is a phenomenon resulting from the relation of the two." Ibid., p. 271.

13. "The perception and enjoyment of the beauty are subjective, relative, dependent; the beauty itself not so." Ibid., p. 274.

14. Nishi published these lectures as *Encyclopedia (Hyakugaku Renkan,* 1870), a work in which he organized Western knowledge into the "common sciences" (history, geography, literature, and mathematics) and two "particular sciences"—the "intellectual sciences" (theology, philosophy, politics, political economy, and statistics) and the "physical sciences" (physics, astronomy, chemistry, and natural history). See Havens, *Nishi Amane and Modern Japanese Thought,* pp. 93–94; Douglas Howland, "Nishi Amane's Efforts to Translate Western Knowledge: Sound, Written Character, and Meaning," *Semiotica* 83(3/4) (1991):292.

Course in Aesthetics (Vorschule der Ästhetik, 1876), as opposed to the ideality of the Hegelian system—"the aesthetics from above" *(die Ästhetik von oben).*[15]

At this point in time Nishi adopted the "modern" strain of aesthetics of the age of science, when around 1870 the idealistic and metaphysical schools were being severely challenged in Europe. A general mistrust for the grand systems of Kant, Schelling, and Hegel was inducing philosophers to concentrate on the contingency of facts before gradually rising to the formulation of a generalized aesthetic system. This empirical approach to aesthetics led scholars to borrow from the fields of physiology, biology, psychiatry, sociology, and ethnology in the formulation of theories of experimental aesthetics.[16]

The concept of aesthetics takes center stage in a series of lectures that Nishi gave in 1877 in the presence of Emperor Meiji, later published as *The Theory of Aesthetics (Bimyōgaku Setsu).*[17] Nishi's decision to modify further the Japanese translation of the word "aesthetics" into "the science of the beautiful and mysterious" *(bimyōgaku)* might have been dictated by his attempt to single out aesthetics as an independent field of study worthy of the attention of specialists. We should be careful, however, not to overemphasize Nishi's belief in the autonomous status of art. He never became free of the Confucian belief in the ethical implications of the artistic object. In this work, Nishi considers "aesthetics" a third "elemental form" *(genso)* that, together with ethics and law, constitutes the pattern of human civilization *(jinbun).* While ethics is the science that codifies the human sense of morality *(dōtoku no sei)* which leads people to distinguish good from evil, and while the law is the result of a feeling of justice *(seigi no kankaku)* set up for the protection of the individual as a "natural" need to promote good and punish evil, aesthetics finds its justification as a science that explains the human need to distinguish beauty from ugliness. It is also the science that deals with the fuzzy realm of perception and feelings, which for centuries had been the target of Confucian contempt on the ground that passions disrupted the moral order and the perfection of the "principle of nature" *(ri).*

With respect to Neo-Confucianism, therefore, Nishi's work was definitively a step ahead in daring to address the topic of the human psyche—always a challenge for political philosophers. At the same time, however,

---

15. Gustav Theodor Fechner, *Vorschule der Ästhetik* (Leipzig: Breitkopf & Härtel, 1925), pp. 1–7. See also Yamamoto, *Tōzai Geijutsu Seishin no Dentō to Kōryū,* p. 28.

16. Katharine Everett Gilbert and Helmut Kuhn, *A History of Esthetics* (Bloomington: Indiana University Press, 1954), pp. 524–549.

17. The text appears in Aoki Shigeru and Sakai Tadayasu, eds., *Bijutsu, NKST* 17 (Tokyo: Iwanami Shoten, 1989), pp. 3–14 [hereafter *BS*].

Nishi presented aesthetics as a way to codify and control the last bastion of human freedom by connecting it with ethics and law in a triad that was required to operate simultaneously. On this Nishi maintained a position that was well in tune with the aspirations of the ideologues of the Meiji state: Beauty is found in the sage whose behavior is virtuous, and the writer's brush is said to be right when his heart is honest.[18]

Nishi's major concern in this series of lectures was to make the abstractness of the field of aesthetics acceptable to government officials in the hope that they might sponsor the new science at the level of academia. The problem had already been solved in Europe when the alleged autonomy of the aesthetic field, as expounded by Kant and the emerging intellectual bourgeoisie, was transformed into a "scientific" discipline competing for power at the time of state formations. The crisis of metaphysical aesthetics during the second half of the nineteenth century allowed Nishi to stress at the end of his lectures the role that art can play as "an indirect objective of political tactics" (seiryakujō kansetsu no mokuteki),[19] without any fear of being untruthful to the Western development of the field. This softening of the Kantian position on the independence of the arts was also salvaging the traditional view of Confucian pragmatics.

The basic paradox of the social utility of an autonomous sphere of knowledge surfaced again when Nishi was obliged to justify the distinctiveness and the purpose of aesthetics. The answer came to Nishi from the theory of nonappropriation of Théodore Jouffroy (1796–1842). According to Jouffroy, art cannot be appropriated for practical ends. Nishi's source was again Joseph Haven, who explained the theory in the following terms:

> That only is useful which can be *appropriated,* and turned to account. But the beautiful, in its very nature, cannot be appropriated or possessed. You may appropriate the picture, the statue, the mountain, the waterfall, but not their beauty. These do not belong to you, and never can. They are the property of every beholder. Hence, as Jouffroy has well observed, the possession of a beautiful object never fully satisfies. The beauty is ideal, and cannot be possessed. It is an ethereal spirit that floats away as a silver cloud, ever near, yet ever beyond your grasp. It is a bow, spanning the blue arch, many-colored, wonderful; yonder, just yonder, is its base, where the rosy light seems to hover over the wood, and touch gently the earth; but you cannot, by any flight or speed of travel, come up with it. It is here, there, everywhere, except where you are. It is given you to behold, not to possess it.[20]

---

18. *BS*, pp. 4–5.
19. *BS*, p. 14.
20. Haven, *Mental Philosophy*, p. 278.

Nishi showed his originality by applying this theory to Japanese linguistics and concentrating on the Japanese process of adjectivation. He distinguished between adjectives expressing "ethical feelings" and those voicing "aesthetic feelings." In the former he included words such as "good" (*yoshi*), "evil" (*ashi*), "cute" (*kawayushi*), "hateful" (*nikushi*), "happy" (*ureshi*), "pleasurable" (*tanoshi*), and "joyful" (*yorokobashi*). Nishi argued that in expressing joy, anger, sadness, pleasure, love, hatred, and desire, these adjectives are immediately related to the speaker's or listener's possible advantages and disadvantages, merits and demerits, profits and losses. He felt that these adjectives were complicit with personal interests. On the other hand, "aesthetic adjectives" such as "interesting" (*omoshiroshi*) and "funny" (*okashi*) convey what Nishi called "innocent feelings" (*tsumi no naki sayō*)—feelings that are unrelated to the action of the will and do not lead to the formulation of any moral judgment. Pure interest does not engender any anxiety of possession, for it is located outside the boundaries of property rights (*shoyūken*) and causality (*in'yu*).[21]

The delicate balance between aesthetics and ethics—on which Nishi felt that the destiny of the philosophy of art depended—was masterfully articulated by Joseph Haven in a manner that must have pleased Nishi:

> [The beautiful] differs from the true in that the true is not, like the beautiful, expressed under sensible forms, but is isolated, pure, abstract, not addressed to the senses, but to reason. It differs from the good, in that the good always proposes an end to be accomplished, and involves the idea of obligation, while the beautiful, on the contrary, proposes no end to be accomplished, acknowledges no obligation or necessity, but is purely free and spontaneous. Yet, though differing in these aspects, the good, the true, and the beautiful are at basis essentially the same, even as old Plato taught, differing rather in their mode of expression, and the relations which they sustain to us, than in essence.[22]

Nishi's psychologization of aesthetics presented the experience of beauty as an encounter between the imagination (*sōzōryoku*)—a faculty inherent in the self that exists within human sensibility or internal feeling (*kanju*)—and the beauty inherent in the external object (*mono*). The theory was a rehearsal of Haven's mental philosophy that stressed the subjectivity of perception and the objectivity of beauty.

As for the achievement of artistic beauty, Nishi was again indebted to the work of Haven when he introduced what he called "the major elemental form" (*ichidai genso*) of the aesthetic field: "the pattern of difference and

---

21. *BS*, pp. 12–13.
22. Haven, *Mental Philosophy*, p. 281.

sameness" *(idō seibun).* Nishi explained it as the artist's need to avoid the weariness of repetition by bringing variety into the unity of his work. Although an excessive number of variations destabilizes a work of art and confuses the observer, an obsession with sameness inevitably engenders boredom.[23] Known as "the theory of unity in variety"—a totalizing view of the artistic object whose parts must be related to the whole—the basic idea had been made popular by Victor Cousin (1792–1867). Nishi took it from Haven's *Mental Philosophy,* in which we read:

> The intellect demands a general unity, as, e.g., in a piece of music, a painting, or a play, and is not satisfied unless it can perceive such unity. The parts must be not only connected but related, and that relation must be obvious. At the same time the sensibility demands variety, as, e.g., of the tone and time in the music, of color and shade in the painting, of expression in both. The same note of a music instrument continuously produced, or the same color unvaried in the painting, would be intolerable. The due combination of these two principles, unity and variety, say these writers, constitutes what we call beauty in an object.[24]

What Nishi left out was the important objection that Haven had already moved against this Hegelian theory twenty years prior to Nishi's work:

> Not every thing is beautiful which presents both unity and variety. Some things, on the other hand, are beautiful which lack this combination. Some colors are beautiful, taken by themselves, and the same is true of certain forms, which, nevertheless, lack the element of variety. . . . A bright red pebble, or a bit of stained glass, appears to a child very beautiful. It is the color that is the object of his admiration. We have simple unity but no variety there. On the other hand, in a beautiful sunset we have the greatest variety, but not unity, other than simply a numerical unity.[25]

Perhaps it would be unreasonable to ask of Nishi a state-of-the-art presentation of the aesthetic field at the end of the nineteenth century. His unmatched contribution lies in devising a language that would be sensitive to alien epistemologies and making it understandable to a reader who was mainly trained in the language of the Confucian classics. Nishi coined 787 original terms that cannot be found in dictionaries prior to 1874. Among them, 447 words were the result of newly devised Sino-Japanese compounds; 340 words were drawn from the Chinese and Japanese classics.[26] Many of these words are common currency in contemporary language: "phi-

23. *BS,* p. 9.
24. Haven, *Mental Philosophy,* pp. 278–279.
25. Ibid., p. 279.
26. Morioka Kenji, ed., *Kindaigo no Seiritsu: Goi Hen* (Tokyo: Meiji Shoin, 1990), pp. 138–161.

losophy" *(tetsugaku),* "subjectivity" *(shukan),* "objectivity" *(kyakkan),* "reality" *(jitsuzai),* "phenomenon" *(genshō),* "chemistry" *(kagaku),* "history" *(rek-ishi),* "consciousness" *(ishiki),* "thought" *(shisō),* "idea" *(kannen),* "impression" *(inshō),* and many more.

It is curious to notice, however, that the word devised to indicate the very field that Nishi introduced to Japan for the first time, "modern aesthetics" *(bimyōgaku),* is no longer in use in the field. Nowadays in Japan aesthetics is known simply as "the science of beauty" *(bigaku),* an expression first used by the journalist and political scientist Nakae Chōmin (1847–1901) in his translation of Eugène Véron's (1825–1889) *L'Esthétique* (1878): *The Aesthetics of Mr. V. (Ishi Bigaku,* 1883–1884).[27]

The Theory of Aesthetics
by Nishi Amane

1

THERE IS A BRANCH of philosophy called "aesthetics" that is related to the fine arts and thoroughly investigates its underlying principles.[28] It goes without saying that human nature is originally endowed with the nature of morality and with a mechanism that allows people to discern good from evil, right from wrong. Additionally, another branch of this nature is endowed with a feeling of justice that provides an avenue for protecting oneself and governing others. These two elements, morality and justice, are elemental forms essential to the formation of human society. Nothing surpasses them despite the myriad theories developed by the sages in ancient times. Confucianism calls them "humanity," Buddhism calls them "compassion," Christianity calls them "love." Although the name differs, arguments about the good and evil of human nature are simply to promote good and chastise evil.

Moreover, with regard to the sense of justice, all over the world, in both the ancient and modern countries, there exists the so-called elemental form of

---

27. Nakae Chōmin's translation appears in *Meiji Bunka Zensho,* add. 1 (Tokyo: Nihon Hyōronsha, 1970).

28. The original text of this essay, *Bimyōgaku Setsu,* appears in Aoki Shigeru and Sakai Tadayasu, eds., *Bijutsu, NKST* 17 (Tokyo: Iwanami Shoten, 1989), pp. 3–14.

the law. It started in China with the five punishments of Kao Yao[29] and in the Western world with the Greeks Solon[30] and Lycurgus.[31] So long as societies exist at all, everything is grounded in the law. Therefore, a discussion of the sources of these two elemental forms, accompanied by an exhaustive exploration, is the substance of philosophy. Even though there are infinite differences in people's life, nothing exceeds the boundaries of morality and justice. Therefore, nothing is independent from the working of these two principles, neither the regulation of the life of the common people nor, on a larger scale, the governance of the country; not even the emerging from one's own arena into the international sphere.

Although everything pertaining to human life is likely to be subsumed in these two elements, still one elemental form remains: namely, that of aesthetics. Besides the two elemental forms of morality, which distinguishes between good and evil, and law, which determines what is just and what is unjust, human nature is endowed with a third element that discusses beauty and ugliness. By the time human beings had barely moved away from the stage of savagery, a long time ago, this element had already become conspicuous in society and was having a powerful effect on it. The legend goes that Nüwa[32] heard the phoenix bird's song and made a free-reed mouth organ; using the zither, Emperor Shun[33] created the southern airs; and when K'uei[34] broke off stones and

---

29. Kao Yao was minister of crime under Emperor Shun. The five punishments in question include tattooing; the cutting of the nose, feet, and reproductive organs; and capital punishment. The Confucian *Analects* (12:22) refer to Kao Yao as follows: "When Shun had all that is under Heaven, choosing from among the multitude he raised up Kao Yao, and straightway Wickedness disappeared." See Arthur Waley, trans., *The Analects of Confucius* (New York: Vintage Books, 1938), p. 169. The *Book of Documents* further adds: "The Emperor said, 'Kao Yao, the barbarous tribes disturb our bright great land. There are also robbers, murderers, insurgents, and traitors. It is yours, as the minister of Crime, to employ the five punishments for the treatment of offenses, for the infliction of which there are three appointed places; and the five banishments, with their several places of detention, for which three localities are assigned. Perform your duties with intelligence, and you will secure a sincere submission.'" See James Legge, *The Chinese Classics,* vol. 3, pt. 1 (London: Oxford University Press, 1939), pp. 44–45.

30. Solon (early sixth century B.C.) was an Athenian statesman and lawmaker who resisted the establishment of Pisistratus as tyrant of Athens ca. 561.

31. Lycurgus (ca. 390–324 B.C.), Athenian statesman and orator, was well known for his efficient administration and his rigorous prosecution of crime.

32. A goddess in Chinese mythology. See the *Book of Rites* (12:25): "Ils avait le tambour à pieds des Hia, le tambour fixé sur un poteau selon l'usage des In, le tambour suspendu des Tcheou, le carillon de Chouei, les tablettes de pierre de Chou assemblées de manière à donner les différents sons de la gamme, l'orgue à bouche de Niu koua avec ses languettes." See Séraphin Couvreur, *Mémoires sur les Bienséances et les Cérémonies,* vol. 1 (Paris: Cathasia, 1950), pp. 738–739.

33. A culture hero of China, Emperor Shun was considered one of the three model emperors together with Yao and Yü. The *Book of Rites* (17:1) states: "Anciennement Chouen inventa le luth à cinq cordes, et s'en servi pour exécuter le chant *Nân fôung* (le Vent de Midi)." See Couvreur, *Mémoires sur les Bienséances et les Cérémonies,* vol. 2, p. 67.

34. Director of music under Emperor Shun. The *Book of Documents* (1:5.24) states: "The emperor said, 'K'wei, I appoint you to be director of music, and to teach our sons, so that the straightforward may yet be mild, the gentle may yet be dignified, the strong not tyrannical, and the impetuous not arrogant. Poetry is

struck them like chimes, one hundred animals were enchanted into dancing. Likewise, even in this country, in the ancient age of the gods there were *kagura* dances.[35] Moreover, it is said that the thirty-one-syllable poem originated with Susanoo no Mikoto.[36]

As soon as the course of human society was established, we instantly witness the germination of this elemental form. But far from being related solely to music, the object of aesthetic discussion applies to a much broader field. Presently included in Western art are painting, sculpture, engraving, and architecture. Yet it is appropriate to say that the principle of aesthetics applies also to poetry, prose, and music, as well as to Chinese calligraphy. Dance and drama should also be included in the list. All of these arts are the reverse side of practical sciences, and yet they are not at odds with practical sciences. Even practical sciences, when they truly flourish, no doubt imply the radiation of the aesthetic doctrine.

When we attempt to discuss what a division of the major philosophical categories means, we see that morality designates the study of good and evil; law encompasses justice and injustice; aesthetics designates the realm of beauty and ugliness. Once we understand this parallelism, we can argue that a good person is naturally moved to justice and his external appearance cannot be deprived of beauty. Likewise, an evil person is naturally unjust and his appearance ugly. Therefore, we can conclude that, even though the aesthetic doctrine is mainly discussed with regard to the fine arts, it is certainly not limited to them but also applies directly to everyday human society.

Consequently, the person who should be called a gentleman, regardless of his innate beauty or ugliness, has a complexion and appearance endowed with

---

the expression of earnest thought; singing is the prolonged utterance of that expression. The notes accompany that utterance, and they are harmonized themselves by the pitch pipes. In this way the eight different kinds of instruments can all be adjusted so that one shall not take from or interfere with another, and spirits and men will thereby be brought into harmony.' K'wei said, 'Oh! I smite the stone; I smite the stone. The various animals lead on one another to dance.'" See Legge, *The Chinese Classics*, vol. 3, pt. 1, pp. 48–49.

35. Nishi refers to the fact that the sacred dances of Shinto rituals allegedly originated from the mad dance of Ama no Uzume, which the deity performed in an attempt to persuade the Sun Goddess Amaterasu to leave the cave where she had secluded herself. The *Kojiki* reads: "Ame no Tachikara no Kami stood concealed beside the door, while Ame no Uzume no Mikoto bound up her sleeves with a cord of heavenly *hi-kage* vine, tied around her head a head-band of the heavenly *ma-saki* vine, bound together bundles of *sasa* leaves to hold in her hands, and overturning a bucket before the heavenly rock-cave door, stamped resoundingly upon it. Then she became divinely possessed, exposed her breasts, and pushed her skirt-band down to her genitals." See Donald L. Philippi, trans., *Kojiki* (Tokyo: University of Tokyo Press, 1968), p. 84.

36. The poem in question *(waka)* appears again in the *Kojiki* at the time of Susanoo's exile to the human world. "Arriving at Suga, he said: 'Coming here, my heart is refreshed.' In that place he built his palace and dwelt there. Therefore that place is still called Suga. When this great deity first built the palace of Suga, clouds rose from that place. He made a song, which said: The many-fenced palace of Izumo / Of the many clouds rising— / To dwell there with my spouse / Do I build a many-fenced palace: / Ah, that many-fenced palace!" See Philippi, *Kojiki*, p. 91.

both a warm, gentle nature that deserves to be loved and a solemn, austere aspect that musters respect. Even though a petty person may possess great beauty, his vulgarity will come out of its own accord, marking the man's foolish demeanor, so that you will easily spot the man's violent nature. That is, whether one is a gentleman or a petty person, what he carries inside will eventually reveal itself to the outside world. He cannot conceal his true heart, nor can he avoid "what ten eyes behold, what ten hands point to."[37] If this is the case with a petty person, you can imagine the demeanor of a thoroughly virtuous man: his virtue will glow from his visage and emanate from his stature. Chu Kuang-t'ing praised Ch'eng Min-tao,[38] saying that to be with him was like sitting in a spring breeze for a month: future generations will continue to think about Ch'eng's moral reputation.

Moreover, although they are certainly reflected in appearance and dignified manners, these characteristics also show in the performance of deeds and will remain as models for future generations. Confucius commented that Shao court music was both beautiful and good, while the Wu martial dance was beautiful but not yet good.[39] This means that the performative aspect of raising arms and legs and violently stepping on the ground spontaneously reveals itself when singing and dancing, and nothing can be done to hide it. How much more so when composing Chinese poetry, reciting a Japanese poem, or making a calligraphic sample! The inside of the creator surfaces between the lines and emerges in the stroke of the brush, with no possibility for deception. Liu Kung-ch'uan[40] said: "When the heart is rectified, one's brush will be so too." In short, the elemental form of aesthetics that emanates into society forms with the other element of morality the longitude and latitude through which human civilization is structured—something that cannot be taken lightly.

So far I have discussed how the elements of aesthetics, morality, and law form an enlightened society through their relation to each other. Yet we still need to ask where the principle of aesthetics lies and to what degree its influ-

---

37. That is: the criticism of others from whom injustice and evil cannot be hidden. Here Nishi quotes from *The Great Learning (Ta Hsüe):* "The disciple Tsang said, 'What ten eyes behold, what ten hands point to, is to be regarded with reverence!'" See James Legge, *The Chinese Classics,* vol. 1: *Confucian Analects, The Great Learning, The Doctrine of the Mean* (Hong Kong: Hong Kong University Press, 1970), p. 367.

38. Chu Kuang-t'ing (1037–1094) entered the Neo-Confucian school of the Ch'eng brothers, Ch'eng Hao (also known as Ch'eng Min-tao, 1032–1085) and Ch'eng I (also called Ch'eng I-ch'uan, 1033–1107).

39. Shao was the name of the music made by Emperor Shun; Wu was the music of King Wu. According to James Legge, the first was "perfect in melody and sentiment" while the latter was "also perfect in melody, but breathing the martial air, indicative of its author." Arthur Waley argues that the first dance "mimed the peaceful accession of the legendary Emperor Shun" while the latter "mimed the accession by conquest of the Emperor Wu, who overthrew the Yin." Nishi is referring to the Confucian *Analects* (3:25): "The Master said of the Shao that it was perfectly beautiful and also perfectly good. He said of the Wu that it was perfectly beautiful but not perfectly good." See Legge, *The Chinese Classics,* p. 164. Waley's comments appear in Waley, *Analects of Confucius,* p. 101.

40. Famous calligrapher of the Tang period who lived between 778 and 865.

ence on society results in benefit and harm. This I will save for the following discussion.

2

We have seen in the previous section that, although the elemental principles of aesthetics, morality, and law are reciprocally interrelated and at the same time individually distinguished, they are not at cross purposes. They structure human civilization through their being inextricably linked to each other. Therefore, here we must discuss what kind of elemental forms aesthetics is made of.

The form of aesthetics is divided into two parts: one is inherent to the object; the other belongs to the subject. The form inherent to the object is its beauty as it fits our taste; the element belonging to the subject is our imagination. According to the logic of aesthetics, first of all there must be an external object whose beauty is appreciated through the auspices of the subject's imagination. Even with a celebrated hanging scroll, for example, if we lack natural sensitivity then we see nothing but ink and paint smeared on a silk fabric or rice paper. On the other hand, once we possess sensitivity, we sense refinement even in one mere ink painting, and we perceive elegance in one word of a verse.

As for the beauty belonging to the external object, even birds and beasts are likely to perceive it to a slight degree. Yet it seems that they are not endowed with any inner imagination whatsoever. It goes without saying that among birds, beasts, insects, fish, and life of that kind, those of substantial size not only possess by nature the outer element of aesthetics but also have in their nature the elemental form of the law, as well as a bit of morality. Among the hundred species of animals, for example, they all know how to protect themselves; should someone step onto their rights, they become enraged and fiercely attack and bite the intruder. This attitude stems from the animals sharing with human beings the same elemental form of the law, which is at the root of the right to self-protection. This explains why fierce animals such as tigers and wolves make it their habit always to avoid humans. But if humans approach their den, the animals will attack and bite them without fail. This is why a tiger feeding her young should be feared.

Another example is a dog going from street to street with his tail hanging down, begging for pity. But if a dog from outside goes so far as to enter the gate of another dog's master, the home dog will become enraged and growl and bare his teeth. This is how property rights come about in humans. Even birds and other animals possess a small bit of the elemental form of the law. To understand this, we sometimes find clues in examples like the ones mentioned here.

The elemental form of morality is often seen in situations that extend from the love between male and female to the raising of children: the space of unbound love. As everyone knows, it is like the pheasant saving its chicks first when its home is burning or the crane protecting the young from the cold under its warm wings. To return to our example of dogs, they love their master not only in order to be fed but also because they have a developed sense of duty: think of the Swiss Saint Bernard, which rescues humans in the snow. We can also think of animals such as oxen and horses, which often show their dutiful nature. There used to be a farmer who would feed an ox at dawn every day, pack supplies on its back, and send it off near and far. Only on rainy days would the ox rest. One day the ox did not eat. It was as if the ox thought, "If I eat this food, I'll have to carry this load." The farmer, reading the ox's mind, sprinkled water from the roof of the barn. As the water dripped from the eaves of the barn, the ox thought, "It's raining today, so even if I eat I won't have to carry anything." So he began to eat. Finally though, the farmer packed a load on the ox and put him on the road. This story shows that the ox knew that in order to eat, he had to work. It is as if the ox understood that it was his duty to work if he wanted to eat.

The elemental form of morality somehow seems to exist even in birds and beasts, and so too does the form of law. It appears that only the element of aesthetics is absent. And yet we can discover that even animals possess the faculty to perceive external elegance. Colorful birds like peacocks take pride in their beauty, and, it is said, if a person dressed in filthy, old rags comes close to its nest, the peacock will become indignant. Birds attract each other through the beauty of their plumage or the charm of their song. It is believed that they can differentiate between beauty and ugliness and can also appreciate beauty and disdain ugliness. The fact that dogs and cats cover their feces themselves is an indication of how highly developed the outer element of aesthetics is in them.

Yet when it comes to human beings, the inner element of aesthetics is developed from infancy. Not only do we see that a child in the early stages of language acquisition already has the ability to distinguish beauty and ugliness, purity and contamination; we are also witnesses to the fact that the imagination is already formed in childhood. When a butterfly sees a famous painting of a peony, for example, rarely will it light on it and try to draw nectar, mistaking it for the real thing. Similarly, when a kitten sees a fine painting of a sparrow or a mouse, rarely will it want to catch it. Although the proverb goes that animals can be deceived by pictures, it is probably not true.

But when a child who already understands language sees a picture of Chung Kui[41] or a devil, though it may not be a great painting, he will certainly be seized with terror and will scream and cry hysterically. After a while, when the child grows and starts to play with brush and ink, he will inevitably draw a

---

41. Chinese deity who protects humans from demons spreading illness. The name Chung Kui belonged to a scholar recluse who, according to Chinese legend, cured the sick emperor Hsuing-tsung by driving away his devils in a dream. The frightening appearance of Chung Kui comes from the fact that he was represented with large eyes, a bearded chin, high boots, and a head covered with a black scholar's hat.

picture. He will draw a cross with a round shape at the top like a dumpling and call it a person. Even if he draws skillfully, it will still look like a wood-carved doll. This demonstrates that his imagination has developed sufficiently to where he sees that a person is like a cross with arms extending on both sides, a lower portion with legs, and an upper portion with a round head like a dumpling. He is not at all concerned with what the real thing looks like. This presents evidence that as a person matures, even a little, his imagination will develop.

Human language consists mainly of the ability to abstract, which for the most part springs from the imagination. For example, the expressions "purity" and "impurity" are both figures extracted from our ability to think abstractly. Should we try to grasp the meaning of purity and impurity in actuality, we realize that there is no substance behind these two concepts. Even if one tries to dissect the body of Confucius, one cannot find the site of benevolence. And if one were to dissect the body of robber Chih,[42] there would be no site of injustice or immorality. If one perceives Hsi-shih[43] as a bag of blood, then she becomes the symbol of utmost filth; if one believes a sardine head is a deity, then one expects fortune and misfortune to come from it. The imagination that looms over us, one step higher than abstraction, has a limitless impact on morality and aesthetics. Accordingly, it is thought that the millet Po-yi grew was pure, while the millet robber Chih grew was dirty. This is all the work of imagination.

Ultimately, then, we must ask: Where in art do we find the external and internal elemental forms? I will reserve this topic for some other day.

3

Last time we discussed the distinction between the outer and inner elements that make up the elemental form of aesthetics. Now we will turn our attention to the outer element. Similarly to the natural sciences, aesthetics' external element comes into human consciousness through the five sensory organs: the ears, eyes, nose, mouth, and skin. Therefore, the outside object takes on color and form through the eye, sounds through the ears, aromas through the nose, taste through the mouth, and texture and gloss through

---

42. "Robber Chih, with a band of nine thousand followers, rampaged back and forth across the empire, assaulting and terrorizing the feudal lords, tunneling into houses, prying open doors, herding off men's horses and cattle, seizing their wives and daughters. Greedy for gain, he forgot his kin, gave not a look to father or mother, elder or younger brother, and performed no sacrifices to his ancestors. Whenever he approached a city, if it was that of a great state, the inhabitants manned their walls; if that of a small state, they fled into their strongholds. The ten thousand people all lived in a dread of him." See Burton Watson, trans. *The Complete Works of Chuang Tzu* (New York: Columbia University Press, 1968), p. 323.

43. A Chinese legendary beauty who was offered by King Kou Chien of Yueh as a gift to King Fu Chai of Wu so that the latter would be blinded by the woman's beauty and lose control of his kingdom.

the sense of touch. Among the five organs, however, the ears and eyes are superior. Although the five organs share the same principle inasmuch as they all depend on the characteristics of the external thing, the pleasure derived through the three remaining senses depends exclusively on each specific organ. The pleasure emerging from the eyes and ears can be shared by everyone at the same time. With the pleasure of drinking and eating, it is only the person who indulges who can savor it. On the other hand, with regard to music, the person who does not play an instrument is precisely the one who enjoys it. This is why hearing and sight occupy a privileged position among the five senses.

The elemental form of aesthetics, together with the five senses, is endowed with a major elemental form that we will call the differential style. The pattern of the entire universe arises from the fact that there is sameness in difference and difference in sameness. If we incline toward difference, even in the slightest degree, we will reach the spiteful and loathsome limit of irregularity. If, on the other hand, we lean toward sameness, although we may follow the rules, a sense of weariness will grow to the point where it will be hard to stand. Therefore, the elegance of patterns arises from the sameness in difference and difference in sameness. The more detailed this pattern, the greater its ingenuity.

This is the outer element of aesthetics, and every object has evidence of this: think, for example, in the natural world of leaves, flower petals, or the feathers of birds. Everyone should know that the flatfish has a strange form. Now, roads that are flat are considered to be the best. But if one continues on a straight, even road for seventy miles, one will inevitably become tired. And in poetry, especially that which is monotonous, having the same beginning and the same conclusion is the most detested. But if there is the so-called occurrence of endless changes—despite the same repetitious thirty-one-syllable pattern, the same meter, and the following of the same compositional rules—the poem is much loved so long as there appear unexpected changes and each idea is different. This is the desired difference in sameness.

Having said this, however, if one composes poems and songs without following rules at all, merely expressing whatever comes to mind, surely what results is not a form of poetry. If a road is very dangerous, winding to the right, turning to the left, climbing a precipice, then it must not be called a road. This shows the necessity of sameness in difference: proportion and balance cannot be lacking.

If we take the five senses as an example, we will see that listening to the same tone at the same intervals is unbearable. Music can first be heard when there is pitch; tempo; the seven notes, *do, re, mi, fa, sol, la, si,* as well as the Chinese notes, *kung, shang, chüe, chih, yü, pien-yü, pien-kung;* the combinations of two and three of these notes that produce harmonies; and melody, in which notes jump unexpectedly from the lowest to the highest. Think of a concert in which you hear the diverse sounds that are peculiar to each instrument: bells and chimes, string instruments, gourd and earth instruments, drums and wood instruments. Although you hear diversity, a final sameness of harmonious tunes and notes is achieved. Differences are valued in sameness.

So too, when looking at the seven colors of red, orange, yellow, green, blue, indigo, and purple, and the opposites of black and white, colors close in hue do not please the eye as much as contrasts do. Therefore, red complements green (a mixture of yellow and blue), yellow complements purple (a mixture of indigo and red), and indigo complements orange (a mixture of yellow and red). So when we put black and white on opposite ends of a spectrum, with yellow, orange, green, blue, purple, and indigo streaming out in order from the white side, the opposites of black and white match well; orange and indigo, and green and purple, do not match as well. But because white, yellow, orange, green, and blue are similar in hue to blue, purple, indigo, and black, they do not match at all. Yet among them all, red complements almost all the other colors. Purple and indigo are other examples of two colors not matching because they reside next to each other. Therefore, if one seeks harmony among colors, the difference between any two colors must be a stark contrast. This is why sameness is necessary among differences.

When considering the human voice, "*a*" is produced as a middle sound; "*u*" and "*o*" are produced back in the throat; "*e*" and "*i*" are pronounced in the front of the mouth. Therefore, when pronouncing these sounds from back in the throat to the front of the mouth, the vowels should be in the order "*u, o, a, e, i.*" But it is inconvenient to pronounce them accordingly, because sounds of the same type stand side by side. Therefore, it sounds refreshing to pronounce the vowels alternately in the order of "*a, i, u, e, o*" starting with the middle sound, "*a,*" then moving to the very front of the mouth to produce the sound "*i,*" returning to the back of the throat to produce the sound "*u,*" reaching back to "*e,*" which is a sound produced between the middle and front of the mouth, and ending at "*o,*" which is a sound produced in between the back of the throat and the middle of the mouth. This is a further example of the necessity of difference in sameness.

Although there is not yet scientific research on whether this principle also applies to the other three senses of smell, taste, and touch, I have no doubt as to its applicability. With regard to taste, it is obvious that rich food complements simpler or spicy hot food. Therefore, broiled eel and carp should be seasoned with Japanese pepper; sea bream soup also requires pepper. After a satisfying meal, plain pickled radish is just what is needed. This is proof that rich and plain tastes complement each other. Therefore, people who eat mainly Western meals with a lot of meat prefer bitter beer or sour wine, while those who eat plain Japanese food are fond of rich, mellow sake. Once again we see that rich and simple tastes complement each other. This does not go beyond the principle of seeking difference in sameness and sameness in difference.

We still need much more explanation to see whether this principle also applies to the fine arts, such as drawing, sculpture, music, and poetry. Here I have only discussed the principle of aesthetics—specifically, how external objects let people sense beauty.

4

As I discussed in the previous section, aesthetics values difference in sameness and sameness in difference, which means that this theory avoids the continuous repetition of the same pattern. Therefore, to keep repeating the same subject matter in this lecture violates the theory of aesthetics and creates feelings of boredom in the listeners. Yet there is still more to discuss, so I must continue until I have exhausted this topic. With all this in mind, I will make this section the final one.

What is called the inner element of aesthetics is human feeling. The imagination, which helps to formulate this feeling, is what makes human beings such that they cannot stop being moved. According to the findings of contemporary linguistics, generally the words that describe people's character and feelings are those which follow the so-called *shiku*-conjugation: for example, "good" *(yoshi),* "evil" *(ashi),* "cute" *(kawayushi),* "hateful" *(nikushi),* "happy" *(ureshi),* "pleasurable" *(tanoshi),* "joyful" *(yorokobashi),* and so on. Yet even though these words belong to one category, upon further analysis one finds a distinction between those that describe feelings of morality and those that indicate aesthetic feelings. Namely, the adjectives "good," "evil," "cute," "hateful," and so on all express feelings of morality. There is a voluminous number of words belonging to this category, probably because human action does not extend over and beyond the sphere of morality. Yet there are only two adjectives following the *shiku*-conjugation that denote aesthetic feelings: "interesting" *(omoshiroshi)* and "funny" *(okashi).* These two emotions arise as a result of the matching of the outer element with the principle of aesthetics.

What, then, makes these two adjectives indicate aesthetic feelings? Unlike the seven passions of joy, anger, sadness, pleasure, love, evil, and greed, "interesting" and "funny" do not occur in correlation with one's personal interests. Feelings of joy, for example, arise in human beings when they obtain what they want and what benefits them. And feelings of anger arise when they sense something that they hate, abhor, and might harm them. This is all part of the ordinary course of nature. But in regard to feeling that something is interesting or funny, personal interest is not a consideration. Simply the sight of a particular thing is interesting or funny. Only when a person goes so far as to wanting to possess this interesting thing does he start positing the aim of judging good and bad, thus making his feelings the work of the will. It goes the same way for the feeling of amusement. When you simply think that something is funny, there should not arise any sense of moral judgment. But once it falls into the will's hands and a person goes so far as to laugh at people or ridicule them, that immediately indicates the purposiveness of moral judgment.

Therefore, these two feelings are an operation of pure aesthetics, an innocent pursuit that does not fall prey to the will in the slightest measure, completely unrelated to the sphere of human morality. In contrast, the moral feelings of joy, anger, love, evil, and so on are somehow related to the consequences stemming from them, so that they put in motion a chain of causality. If I find delight in a person, for example, then that person will love me too. If I become angry with a person, then that person will come to hate me. Yet if I think something is interesting or funny, of course it has no bearing on others. When I look at a landscape painting and find it interesting, for example, or see a child at play and think it funny, these situations have absolutely no relation to my personal interests whatsoever.

Moreover, being different from moral feelings, these two emotions are located outside the boundary of property rights. If one finds a child delightful, then the parent will be happy. If one encounters a slave and becomes angry with him, then the master too will become angry. But if one looks at somebody's garden or collection of calligraphy and paintings and regards them as interesting, the owner is not distressed by fear that the observer might want them. And when someone finds the garden and the house funny, there is no harm done. Therefore, because aesthetic feelings do not impose themselves on the will at all, they are outside the sphere of right and wrong.

Nevertheless, there is no mistaking that the feeling that something is interesting or funny is still a feeling. This is evidenced by the fact that these feelings are expressed facially like other feelings. When one is sad, for example, one cries; when one is angry, one's eyes flash with rage. If one finds something interesting, it too will appear on the countenance to some degree. If one feels that something is funny, it will immediately give an impulse to the lungs, erupting in a spontaneous burst of laughter.

As we have seen, these two feelings arise from the outer element. In whatever one finds interesting, there is difference in sameness and sameness in difference; variation in regulation and regulation in variation; irregularity in order and order in irregularity. Nothing escapes this principle.

Although there are various theories by ancient philosophers regarding the origins of humor, we do not have one standard theory. Among those theories that should be considered is the aforementioned concept of variation in regulation. Feelings of humor seem to arise when unexpected changes occur in things that follow rules consistently and maintain internal order. One example would be when an extremely serious person dressed decorously, proceeding in a stately and dignified manner, suddenly loses his footing and trips and falls. Another would be when ten or more people of the same height and appearance line up and pass by, and among them one conspicuously tall man stands out. One more instance would be if during a refined and logical conversation, one suddenly makes a vulgar and gratuitous statement. Feelings of humor are evoked when something unexpected springs up from what you think will continue in a customary fashion. Nothing is funny when it is anticipated or it is repetitious. Laughter is psychologically an essential and lofty feeling that is limited to the human species. Birds and beasts lack this capacity, their nature being particularly earnest and straightforward in all matters. They do not know the pleasure of laughing, joking, or frolicking.

The preceding has been a discussion of the inner element of aesthetics. To expand both inner and outer principles and apply them to human civilization—calligraphy and paintings, engravings, architecture, music and dance, poetry and prose, utensils and toys—would require an inordinate amount of time, since each of them has its own subtle, logical rules.

It goes without saying, then, that art fosters the flourishing of civilization; it elevates the human world into a lofty realm. Naturally, the ministers and officials appointed to legislate laws and govern society must not neglect it. Although it is not the purpose of the fine arts to have a direct bearing on policies, they nevertheless are an indirect objective of political tactics. This is why you will not find any example in any country of a sovereign who has not paid attention to this topic. After all, the true purpose of aesthetics does not conflict with the comparable purposes of morality, law, and economics. But if one is too partial in one direction, he will not be free from the abuse of making them reciprocally incompatible. Therefore, we should clearly distinguish what is of importance and find a proper balance between them. Here I end my theory of aesthetics.

TWO

A Voice of Resistance
Tsubouchi Shōyō

THE CRITIQUE that Tsubouchi Shōyō (1858–1935) moved against Western aesthetics was directly related to two major events that shook the Japanese intelligentsia during the last two decades of the nineteenth century: the arrival in Japan of Ernest Francisco Fenollosa (1853–1908) and Nakae Chōmin's translation of E. Véron's *L'Esthétique.*

Fenollosa reached Japan in 1878 as a lecturer of philosophy at Tokyo Imperial University where he played a major role in introducing Hegelian thought.[1] He presented the major issues of his philosophy of art in a speech that he gave to the members of the Dragon Pond Society (Ryūchikai) in May 1882.[2] The text was later published in Japanese as *Bijutsu Shinsetsu* (The True Conception of the Fine Arts, November 1882) by Ōmori Ichū (1844–1908), who based his translation on notes taken during the lecture. Fenollosa's talk was a summary of several lectures he had given in Tokyo to artists and scholars since April of the previous year.[3]

In his speech Fenollosa argued for the autonomous status of the arts which, rather than fulfilling a practical purpose, had to be appreciated for their ornamental value *(sōshoku).* This argument contributed to clarifying the difference between arts *(bijutsu)* and crafts *(kōgei),* whose independent and practical aspects were rarely kept separate in Japan. Fenollosa stressed the idea that the main function of art was to please the heart and elevate the spirit. But art was not simply play—a notion that would still privilege

---

1. "Although the full details of Fenollosa's activities in Japan are difficult to determine, his influence on early Meiji connoisseurship and art appreciation was a decisive one. His lectures—often adaptations of Hegelian theory—threw new light on the nature and importance of Japanese art, and opened Japanese eyes to the necessity of reexamining and revaluing their heritage. Fenollosa, carried away by his enthusiasm, even went so far as to argue the superiority of Japanese painting over Western oil painting." See Uyeno Naoteru, ed., *Japanese Arts and Crafts in the Meiji Era* (Tokyo: Pan-Pacific Press, 1958), p. 18.

2. The Ryūchikai, founded in 1879 by Japanese artists in traditional styles, was headed by Sano Tsunetami and Kawase Hideharu. It was renamed the Japanese Art Society (Nihon Bijutsu Kyōkai) in 1887.

3. The original text in English has not yet been found. The Japanese translation by Ōmori appears in Aoki Shigeru and Sakai Tadayasu, eds., *Bijutsu, NKST* 13 (Tokyo: Iwanami Shoten, 1989), pp. 35–65.

the idea of practical utility in life. It was not a plaything provided with the purpose of bringing joy to the user. The goodness of art was not located in its ability to produce *jouissance*. Rather, it produced *jouissance* because of its independent goodness. Fenollosa strongly restated this point in a later series of lectures on the theory of literature that he gave at Tokyo's Higher Normal School on 25 January 1898.[4] In these lectures Fenollosa introduced the heavy language of metaphysics in an attempt to explain the world in terms of authenticity and inauthenticity, interiority and exteriority, universality and particularity, being and not-being. Following the dialectic of negative theology, Fenollosa proposed four negative propositions in his definition of literature.

First: Literature is not its utility, and yet it partakes of some sort of inherent value.[5] This statement echoes the third moment of Kant's analytic of the beautiful, according to which "beauty is the form of the purposiveness of an object, so far as this is perceived without any representation of a purpose."[6]

Second: Literature is not constituted by pleasure, and yet there is something called "literary pleasure."[7] Here Fenollosa follows the Kantian notion

---

4. See "Preliminary Lectures on the Theory of Literature—Higher Normal School—Tokyo—Jan. 25th '98," in Akiko Murakata, ed., *The Ernest F. Fenollosa Papers: The Houghton Library, Harvard University,* vol. 3: *Literature* (Tokyo: Museum Press, 1987), pp. 115–162 [hereafter PLTL].

5. "I shall first maintain that the essential thing in literature is not its utility. If, by utility, we mean the furthering of ordinary human interests, then some writings which have it and some writing which do not have it are equally literature. . . . In literature, however, the peculiar value cannot lie in some outside end for which the book is valuable. Literary value is no adventitious or temporary value, but something inherent directly in the very body of the words. It does not follow, however, merely because literature is not defined by use, that it has no use. Even beyond the ordinary use which, as we have seen, it *may* have, there often lies a separate and higher use of a very special kind. All value must be useful in some way, even literary value. Even a poem may uplift the human soul. Literary value broadens man's mind, softens his heart, stimulates his patriotism, or claims his reverence. Man is a finer being because of it. But there is a most important difference between this special kind of utility, and ordinary, personal, material utility. It is this. The excellence of the latter utility consists solely in its use; but the use of the former utility consists in its excellence. . . . Such utility is a new and higher sort which may be named *literary utility,* and which, far from helping to define literature, needs the help of literature for its own definition." See PLTL, pp. 118–119.

6. Immanuel Kant, *Critique of Judgment* (New York: Hafner, 1951), p. 73 [hereafter *CJ*].

7. "Literary excellence is not defined or constituted by pleasure. . . . But, because literature is in no way defined by pleasure, it does not follow that it is incapable of imparting pleasure. There is no doubt that to read a splendid poem or a fine martial speech thrills us with an inward excitement which, for want of a better word, we call pleasure. But, though language lacks the word, we must nonetheless recognize that this meaning of pleasure is something quite new and special. The thrill is an accompaniment of the reading, but not its purpose, and not the admirable quality in the piece we are reading. It is the subjective correlative in use of an excellence in the literature, but it would never exist in us if that excellence did not exist first. The literature is not good because it gives pleasure, it gives pleasure only because it is good. Here lies the difference between ordinary pleasure, and this higher kind of special pleasure. In the former the pleasure is primary, and the excellence of things, their utility, is derivative; in the latter, the pleasure is derivative, and the excellence of the thing is primary. In short, we have no resource but to name it 'literary pleasure'; and, thus, this pleasure, so far from defining literature, needs literature to establish its own definition." See PLTL, pp. 122–123.

that beauty cannot be bound by any kind of interest or purpose, thus tracing a line between a "pure satisfaction" and a satisfaction that implies the presence of an object or action. The gratification of mere pleasure (the pleasant) does not match up to the disinterested and free satisfaction of the beautiful since, as Kant argued in the first moment of his analytic, "taste is the faculty of judging an object or a method of representing it by an entirely disinterested satisfaction or dissatisfaction. The object of such satisfaction is called beautiful."[8]

Third: Literature is not a means for producing information, and yet it conveys some sort of "literary information" or "literary education."[9] Here Fenollosa distinguishes the discursiveness of the arts from mere transmission of knowledge, searching for a justification in the second moment of Kant's analytic—the ability of the beautiful to provide a universal satisfaction independently of the presence of concepts, or, to use Kant's words, "the beautiful is that which pleases universally without [requiring] a concept."[10]

Fourth: Literature does not stimulate moral growth, and yet there is an integrity to literature that justifies the usage of the special name "literary ethics."[11] Again, Kant's first moment is invoked, which resulted from the

---

8. *CJ*, p. 45.

9. "My third negative proposition concerning Literature is one that still more decidedly contradicts popular, and much of critical, opinion. It is that the essence of Literature cannot lie in the fact of imparting information. . . . Now, of course, I do not deny that all literature, even poetry, does and must impart a certain quantity of information. What I deny is that it is this fact which constitutes it literature. . . . But, as we saw before in the cases of use and pleasure, it does not follow that, though not so defined, literature does not, in fact, contribute to general information and to mental growth. But it does follow, that beside the ordinary ways of doing this, it has its own higher, more special, and characteristic way. . . . If literature should introduce an entirely new significance and efficiency into these as wholes, it would merit the specific name of 'literary information,' or 'literary education'; and, in that case, so far from defining the function of literature, it would have to incorporate that function in its own definition." See PLTL, pp. 122–123.

10. *CJ*, p. 54.

11. "My fourth proposition under this head is that the essence of Literature cannot consist in its tendency to stimulate moral growth. . . . But it does not follow that Literature may not, after all, stimulate moral growth, and that in a quite peculiar way. Like use, and pleasure, and information it may be an accompaniment, rather than a test. . . . Literature groups thoughts and facts together in a peculiar way, a way which gives them an added value without increasing their substance, analogous to the arrangement of a heap of bricks in a wall. Beside a special literary mental growth involved in such a grouping, it is quite possible that Literary grouping may also exhibit qualities which tend to stimulate the moral character of men. After all 'integrity' means 'wholeness'; and the power of firm resistance in a grand literary idea to all disintegrating suggestions—personal, emotional, or logical—is a typical analogue of that round self-mastery of our actions which we denominate character. It is probable that this is what Confucius had in mind when he identified moral with literary excellence. It is this which belongs to the higher end of man's growth; and is something so special, so supplementary to ordinary textbooks on Ethics, that we ought to give it a special name: 'Literary Ethics,' or 'Literary Integrity.' It follows that the independent definition of literature logically precedes and enters into its own." See PLTL, pp. 123–124.

following preamble: "Whatever by means of reason pleases through the mere concept is *good*. That which pleases only as a means we call *good for something* (the useful), but that which pleases for itself is *good in itself*. In both there is always involved the concept of a purpose, and consequently the relation of reason to the (at least possible) volition, and thus a satisfaction in the *presence* of an object or an action, i.e., some kind of interest."[12]

This negative theology in which the unnameable can only be represented by negative attributes introduces the majesty of a transcendent Being (God/literature) which is then grasped in "four positive propositions": (1) The being of literature is inherent to itself and is self-subsistent;[13] (2) it is purely individual, independent from an external authority and, therefore, it is unique;[14] (3) it is wholeness in which every part of the whole is determined by the combination of all—a spirit revealed by a literary genius;[15] and (4) it is made of the harmony of its parts.[16] To sum it all up in Fenollosa's words: "In four negative propositions I showed that Literary excellence does not lie in any external relations; material, personal, abstract, universal, or moral. In four positive propositions I have now shown that Literary excellence does lie in an individual harmonious wholeness of internal relations."[17]

---

12. *CJ*, p. 41.

13. "The value of a work of literature is one that is inherent in its very being, or substance. . . . Utility, we saw, is not inherent. It is the outsideness of an end. Pleasure, we saw, though a measure of utility, lies in our own personality, not in the Literature." See PLTL, p. 127.

14. "My second proposition is, now, that such inherent literary value must be purely individual. . . . Books which have value in themselves differ infinitely from one another, and must do so. Each has its own peculiar treatment of subject, its own peculiar expression of feeling, its own peculiar choice and combination of words. . . . Granting that each great piece has value in itself, that it is its own end, then it is a jewel, an inestimable treasure which can never be produced again, something as precious as if it had dropped to us from heaven. And the History of Literature is nothing but the single rosary of such individual jewels, strung together in their unique order." See PLTL, pp. 128–129.

15. "My third proposition, perhaps the most important of all, is that the peculiar value of a piece of Literature consists in its *wholeness*. . . . In a fine work of literature every part is most carefully calculated, and the order of the parts is most carefully calculated. Not one thought more or less must come in, not one word or figure of speech changed. The whole combination is absolutely determined, individualized. By what? By itself, by its own unity. Then the unity must be present to the consciousness of the author, to guide him in the very selection and grouping of his parts. He must see the whole and the parts together, as one individual. . . . The wonderful fact is that just that concrete idea, that literary individuality, can exist only just in that perfect combination of the parts. Each defines the other, because each *is* the other. How can the author think of such a unique whole, out of the infinite possibilities of the world? There is no rule to follow. It must come upon him as a revelation. . . . Only the rare author has the exceptional gift or clear sight, and when he shows you what he sees, it strikes you like a revelation. Such clearness does not come from without, but from within. It is not utility, pleasure, or information that produces it. It is individual, then it is self-produced." See PLTL, pp. 133–134.

16. "My fourth proposition is that every case of Literary value consists in the harmony of its parts. . . . Out of all infinity, only in that combination does the individual subsist. The individual lives in the bosom of its harmonies." See PLTL, p. 134 and p. 137.

17. PLTL, p. 150.

Tsubouchi Shōyō, who in his *Essence of the Novel (Shōsetsu Shinzui,* 1885) saluted Fenollosa as "the learned Doctor from the United States" *(Beikoku no monoshiri),* pushed Fenollosa's four negative propositions even further by stressing the absolute self-sufficiency and independence of the arts from all possible purposes, including the alleged aim of pleasing the heart and elevating the spirit as Fenollosa had argued.[18] Another important notion that plays a major role in Tsubouchi's aesthetic discussions is the concept of the "idea" *(myōsō)* that, according to Fenollosa's *True Conception of the Fine Arts,* brings the work of art to life and provides a standard for the distinction between good and bad art. German idealism had created all sorts of variations on the notion that the idea was made concrete in a work of art by the power of the artist's imagination. Fenollosa's emphasis on ideas led him to the famous apologia of traditional Japanese arts, whose rejection of imitational representation facilitated the achievement on the part of Japanese arts of the fulfillment of ideal beauty. In his *Aesthetics* Hegel had provided the classic definition of the idea of the beauty of art:

> The Idea as the beauty of art is not the Idea as such, in the way that metaphysical logic has to apprehend it as the Absolute, but the Idea as shaped forward into reality and as having advanced to immediate unit and correspondence with this reality. For the *Idea as such* is indeed the absolute truth itself, but the truth only in its not yet objectified universality, while the Idea as the *beauty of art* is the Idea with the nearer qualification of being both essentially individual reality and also an individual configuration of reality destined essentially to embody and reveal the Idea. Accordingly there is here expressed the demand that the Idea and its configuration as a concrete reality shall be made completely adequate to one another. Taken thus, the Idea as reality, shaped in accordance with the Concept of the Idea, is the *Ideal.*[19]

Fenollosa's discussion of the Hegelian notions of "ideas" and "ideals" created considerable confusion among Japanese scholars. Toyama Masakazu (1848–1900), for example, in his *Nihon Kaiga no Mirai* (The Future of

---

18. This might have come as a reaction of Tsubouchi's Confucian upbringing, which originally made him interpret the value of literature according to its ability to "promote good and punish evil." According to Okazaki Yoshie (1892–1982): "The reason that Shōyō came to write *Shōsetsu Shinzui* is that from his youth he had the intention of clarifying literary theory; the immediate reason, however, is that while at Tokyo University, during a final examination in an English literature course, he was asked by the professor, who was an Englishman, to write a character analysis of Queen Gertrude in *Hamlet,* but because he wrote primarily a moral critique, he received a low grade. He profited by this experience, and under the guidance of Takada Hanpō he began to read criticism of Western novels. Such reading resulted in his later introducing a new style into the Meiji novel." See Okazaki Yoshie, *Japanese Literature in the Meiji Era* (Tokyo: Ōbunsha, 1955), pp. 74–75.

19. G. W. F. Hegel, "Philosophy of Fine Art," in Stephen David Ross, ed., *Art and Its Significance: An Anthology of Aesthetic Theory* (Albany: SUNY Press, 1994), p. 147.

Japanese Painting, 1890) misunderstood Fenollosa's promotion of "ideas" as an appeal to Japanese artists to portray thoughts and, therefore, to concentrate their efforts on the depiction of existential and social problems.[20] For Shōyō, the grasping of an idea meant giving a faithful representation of things "as they are." Shōyō's resistance to what he perceived as the abstractness of idealism is clear in the series of essays known as *Bi to wa Nani zo ya* (What Is Beauty?, 1886). This text shows how indebted he was to Nakae Chōmin's translation of Véron, which became the basis of Shōyō's strong criticism of idealistic philosophy.

It was through the auspices of the Japanese Ministry of Education that Nakae Chōmin was able to publish his translation-adaptation of Véron's *L'Esthétique,* the first volume of which appeared in 1883, the second in 1884. With Nishi Amane, Chōmin introduced to Japan the positivism of Auguste Comte and the utilitarianism of John Stuart Mill, giving a materialistic turn to the Japanese reception of Western philosophy. Véron provided Chōmin with powerful arguments against the metaphysical ground of idealism—particularly in the appendix to *L'Esthétique,* in which Plato becomes the target of Véron's criticism. In his summary of Plato's theory of ideas, Véron distinguishes three essential principles that led Plato to formulate three basic hypotheses. First, human intelligence is inert; its main function is the passive mirroring of the ideal essences of things, which are located in a different space from our actual world. Second, reason allows us to penetrate the intelligibles, which are otherwise impenetrable to the physical eye. Third, we are privy to the world of ideas on account of our former divine status, making us fallen gods with the ability to retain a recollection of heaven.

This summary is followed by a criticism of the purely imaginary nature of these hypotheses that, by reducing the ideal of beauty to a play of mirrors, deprive human intelligence of the skills to conceive and create such an ideal.[21] If art is a human reproduction of the ideal world that is located between heaven and earth, reason plays a major part in the ascent toward the perfection of God. Imagination and its freedom are cut off from the

---

20. Toyama's text appears in Aoki and Sakai, *Bijutsu,* pp. 144–152.

21. "We must confess that a system that starts with two propositions such as these has great need of further demonstration. But demonstration is only conspicuous by its absence. From a scientific standpoint, we should be justified in considering it to be without foundation from this fact alone: were it not that the unreflecting adhesion of pretended philosophers—men who prefer imagination to truth, and judge scientific theories by their own prejudices and fancies—has given it an authority to which it has no internal claim." See Eugène Véron, *Aesthetics,* transl. W. H. Armstrong (London: Chapman & Hall, 1879), p. 395 [hereafter WHA]. The original text appears in Eugène Véron, *L'Esthétique* (Paris: C. Reinwald, 1878), pp. 465–466 [hereafter EV].

artistic process, however, inasmuch as they, like the senses and passions, are heavy with a material body that hinders the soul's rising into ideal perfection. The exclusion of matter from Plato's system and its reliance on a metaphysical ground make it far from compatible with the age of positivistic reason.[22] Véron's attack on Plato's idealism is severe:

> But then, we may say to him—By what right do you assert that your conception of the ideal is the correct one? How can you possibly give an accurate account of all the qualities of this invisible thing, which, according to your own confession, bears shapes so various? How can it be at once so vague and so precise, so obscure and uncertain to the rest of the world, and so clear to you alone? Have you received the power and peculiar privilege to enter the abstract world of celestial metaphysics, from which everyone else is excluded?[23]

Conformity to tradition, Véron argues, is the main reason for the success of Plato's ideas, rather than any demonstrable truth whose applicability to art can be proved.[24] The exemption of the ideal from the laws regulating existence—time, space, and movement—impugns Plato's argument that the artistic object must be modeled after the perfection of the ideal. Art finds its expression through a material form and through what Véron calls "a natural manifestation of vitality," the passions, that are alien to a world of ideal beauty, whose major target is instead the suppression of all passions.[25] By introducing Véron's views on aesthetics, Chōmin was taking a clear stand on the issue of idealism and its alleged irrelevance to the Japanese process of modernization. Idealism had found in Véron a formidable opponent:

---

22. "The shapes and lines are, then, the result of experimental observation, of sensation—of such material conditions, in fact, as can never be reconciled with platonic *ideas*. These ideas represent nothing from a scientific point of view, but a conception having the double disability of being at once hypothetical and self-contradictory." See WHA, p. 403; EV, p. 468.

23. WHA, p. 403; EV, p. 469.

24. "We may be justly astonished that it has not struck those metaphysicians who are the chief supporters of the artistic theory of Plato—a support founded, as we may well believe, upon its conformity with the fundamental characteristics of their own metaphysical creeds, rather than upon any truth in its application to art." See WHA, p. 405; EV, p. 472.

25. "Even if he did not confess these things, they would follow necessarily from his theory of the ideal. What is the special character of the ideal? Exemption from all laws of time, space, or movement. Immutability and immobility constitute the larger part of its perfection. The art that takes the manifestation of the ideal for its aim, should do its utmost to eliminate from its representations whatever it does not find in its model. The Aesthetics of Plato were in complete accord with the moral theories of antiquity, which had, for their principal aim, the suppression of all passions; that is, of the emotions that are the expression and natural manifestation of vitality. The consummation of this doctrine is found: in art, in the serene immobility of the gods of Phidias; in morals, in the *ataraxy* of the Stoics; in religion, in the asceticism of an Indian Fakir." See WHA, pp. 405–406; EV, pp. 472–473.

We may now leave the subject. An artistic theory that rests entirely upon unproved hypotheses, and that logically results in the negation of all expression, life, and progress; that separates man from his work, and reduces him to the condition of a mere copyist; that, at the same time and by a strange contradiction, would elevate the productions of a being thus degraded over those of God himself—is refuted by its mere recital, and so spares us the examination of the details of less important objections.[26]

Véron is uncomfortable with the very notion of beauty that he agrees, in the chapter on the definition of aesthetics, to be the object of "the science of the beautiful." He feels that the notion is too abstract to be analyzed, and too close to the ideas of the absolute and the divine, which are separated from the human realm.[27] Art, in Véron's opinion, is simply the product of human creation, the result of a genial act that mediates between the imperfection of an object and the perfection of its representation, the product of talent.[28] This explains Véron's modification of the traditional definition of aesthetics—"the science of beauty"—by adding a component that would stress active human intervention in the aesthetic process, thus identifying it as "the science of beauty in art" or "the science whose object is the study and elucidation of the manifestation of artistic genius."[29]

Véron's positivistic aesthetic system was a frontal attack on the idealism of Hegel (1770–1831) and Victor Cousin (1792–1867),[30] or, to use Véron's

---

26. WHA, p. 406; EV, p. 473.

27. "The science of the beautiful be it, but then, what is beauty? This abstract term has an air of Platonic entity which, like everything touched by metaphysical philosophy, refuses to submit to analysis. From ancient days down to our own, almost all the aesthetic doctrines founded upon the 'beauty' theory have considered it as something abstract, divine, with an absolute and distinct reality quite apart from man. The small number of metaphysicians who have held a different view has exercised a very restricted influence over art, to which we need not refer here." See WHA, p. 96; EV, p. 114.

28. "Beauty in art is a purely human creation. Imitation may be its means, as in sculpture and painting; or, on the other hand, it may have nothing to do with it, as in poetry and music. This beauty is of so peculiar a nature that it may exist even in ugliness itself; inasmuch as the exact reproduction of an ugly model may be a beautiful work of art, by the ensemble of qualities which the composition of it may prove are possessed by its author. The very theory of imitation is but the incomplete and superficial statement of the ideas which we are here advocating. What is it that we admire in imitation? The resemblance? We have that much better in the object itself. But how is it that the similitude of an ugly object can be beautiful? It is obvious that between the object and its counterfeit some new element intervenes. This element is the personality, or, at least, the skill of the artist. This latter, indeed, is what they admire who will have it that beauty consists in imitation. What these applaud, in fact, is the talent of the artist. If we look below the surface and analyze their admiration we shall find that it is so; whether they mean it or not, what they praise in a work is the worker." See WHA, pp. 107–108; EV, pp. 127–128.

29. WHA, p. 109; EV, p. 129.

30. "Cousin, author of an essay *On the True, the Beautiful, the Good,* assures his fellow countrymen, who are always naturally distrustful of German philosophical abstruseness, that his spiritualism is a reasonable and moderate one, which keeps clear of any kind of 'chimeric and dangerous mysticism.' Cousin and his fol-

words, "a reaction against ontology so chimerical."[31] Although *L'Esthétique* did not have the same repercussion as Hippolyte Taine's (1828–1893) *Philosophy of Art* (1865) or Jean-Marie Guyau's (1854–1888) *Art from the Sociological Point of View* (1889), it enjoyed a long period of fame in France, where reprints continued into the twentieth century, as well in the English-speaking world, as attested by the English translation of 1879.

Nakae Chōmin's translation of Véron's work was fundamental in setting in motion the famous debate between Shōyō and Mori Ōgai (1862–1922) who bitterly attacked each other in the pages of the journals *Waseda Literature (Waseda Bungaku)* and *Shigarami Zōshi* in the years 1891 and 1892. Ōgai attacked Tsubouchi's rejection of idealism by advocating the idealistic philosophy of Karl Robert Eduard von Hartmann (1842–1906). This series of polemics focused, on the one hand, on Shōyō's belief in the value of literature as a site for "reporting facts" *(kijitsu)* and, on the other, on Ōgai's advocacy of the need for "a discussion of ideas" *(danri).*[32]

As Karatani Kōjin has pointed out,[33] Shōyō's resistance to idealism was predicated on his disavowal of the Western notion of perspectival construction that privileged the verticality of profundity and depth over the horizontality of juxtaposition. The grounding of idealism in transcendental meaning and in a vanishing point—the point of ultimate depth— fostered a belief in the existence of a concrete ideal or essence allegedly hidden beneath the surface of the literary work. The assemblage of these ideals in the process of historical reconstruction allows the "idealist" historian to recapture the "spirit of the age." Shōyō contested the recoverability of meaning, seen "as transparent reduction to any kind of ideals," arguing that the literary text was filled with "submerged ideals" that were open to multiple interpretations. Karatani's evaluation of Shōyō's rejection of idealism as precursor of Western postmodern, antimetaphysical thought also explains why Ōgai is usually seen as the winner of the "submerged ideals" debate—given that Ōgai was espousing a Western view

---

lowers hardly fall behind their positivistic antagonists. Their ideas on the metaphysics of beauty exhibit no marked originality. Cousin, combining his somewhat vague Platonism with ideas derived from French eighteenth century moralists, emphasizes the ethical implications of his concept of beauty, and in doing so he verges on looseness in his use of terms. In a formula that reminds us of Shaftesbury he defines the purpose of art as the 'expression of moral beauty with the help of physical beauty.'" See Gilbert and Kuhn, *History of Esthetics,* p. 474.

31. WHA, p. v; EV, p. v.

32. For a summary of the debate see Okazaki, *Japanese Literature in the Meiji Era,* pp. 617–621, and Richard John Bowring, *Mori Ōgai and the Modernization of Japanese Culture* (Cambridge: Cambridge University Press, 1979), pp. 73–79.

33. Karatani Kōjin, *Origins of Modern Japanese Literature* (Durham: Duke University Press, 1983), pp. 145–154.

of depth and interiority that we have come to associate with the modern confessional novel.[34]

Shōyō's indebtedness to Chōmin's translation of Véron's work is undeniable. He came to know *L'Esthétique* during August 1885 and was initially so impressed as to praise it, in an article that appeared the following year in *Chūō Gakujutsu Zasshi,* as "the words of a true critic, the voice of a true aesthetician."[35] Although, as we can see from the following translation, he eventually grew quite critical of Véron's work, we cannot overlook the impact that *L'Esthétique* had on Shōyō's defense of the realist novel. It should be enough to recall the following passage that Véron dedicated to the novel:

> A new school has now sprung into existence which has already produced a large number of remarkable works, with most various titles: *Mme. Bovary, Manette Salomon, Germinie Lacerteux, René Mauperin, Les Rougon-Macquart, l'Assommoir, Fromont jeune et Risler aîné, le Nabab,* and others. The principal members are MM. Flaubert, De Goncourt, Zola, Alphonse Daudet, Hector Malot. This school, which unquestionably takes its origin from Balzac, founds all its art on supreme accuracy of observation. Such naturalism implies a condition of mind always open to impressions of a realistic nature; and which follows them through every change of form or of surrounding. Man, the real man, is the object of its study. Not that ideal of which it knows nothing, but man as he is moulded by society, with all his individual manifestations, be they good or evil.[36]

It would be a mistake to take literally the statement that Ōgai made in *Gessōjo* (1896) alleging that Chōmin's translation of the aesthetics of Véron—"a man who belonged to the Unlearned school rather than to the Metaphysical school"—"had no impact whatsoever on the literary arts of our country."[37] Ōgai's personal leanings toward the German idealistic school, which he introduced to Japan,[38] were not unrelated to his harsh assessment of a rival aesthetic theory. Even so, Véron's aesthetic system was in a sense guilty of introducing a kind of literature which was critical of

34. "Western writers have only achieved this perspective after entering a period when the West has been decentered vis-à-vis the rest of the world. It was, in fact, for this reason that Shōyō appeared to have been overpowered by Ōgai at the time that the debates took place (to some extent this impression persists today), even though Shōyō's views now seem quite fresh to us. Shōyō lacked a perspective of 'vertical depth.'" See Karatani, *Origins of Modern Japanese Literature,* p. 148.

35. Quoted in Shimamoto Haruo, "*Ishi Bigaku* to Nakae Atsusuke," in *Meiji Bunka Zenshū,* add. 1 (Tokyo: Nihon Hyōronsha, 1970), p. 124.

36. WHA, pp. 357–358; EV, pp. 412–413.

37. Mori Rintarō, *Ōgai Zenshū,* vol. 23 (Tokyo: Iwanami Shoten, 1973), p. 299.

38. Ōgai presented a translation-cum-adaptation of Eduard von Hartmann's *Ästhetik* (1890) in his *Shinbi Ron* (Theory of Aesthetics, 1892–1893) and *Shinbi Kōryō* (Outline of Aesthetics, 1899).

that very bourgeois society which Meiji Japan was struggling to build from the ashes of a feudal past. *L'Esthétique* was ahead of the process of Japanese modernization and could hardly foster in Japan the same critical awareness it had engendered in the West. Moreover, Shōyō's numerous misreadings of the text did not help the cause of the French philosophy of social engagement which, in Japan, was soon to be crushed under the pressure of German thought.

What Is Beauty?
by Tsubouchi Shōyō

THE QUESTION "what is beauty" was raised two thousand years ago, during the height of Greek civilization, by those inquisitive animals called humans.[39] Great thinkers like Socrates, Plato, and Aristotle explored and researched this issue but failed to obtain a clear answer. Since that time, for more than two thousand years, innumerable scholars and specialists of Britain, France, Germany, and Russia have ceaselessly investigated theories of truth, but the question of "beauty," along with other major philosophical issues, has never been clearly answered. It seems that even philosophers have managed only to offer a few speculative hypotheses to satisfy their nagging curiosity. Because "beauty" is often associated with ornamentation, unless one is in the field of philosophy one tends to think of the truth of beauty as a useless luxury—less urgent and essential than other, more practical truths. One usually considers vague interpretations of beauty sufficient, not fully pursuing them to the end, and leaving the notion of beauty as something very general.

But when we step back and think it over, even "beauty" is one of the truths of the universe and its value should not be considered less than other truths. If human beings are obliged to investigate the truth thoroughly, how can they avoid investigating the truth of beauty? If moral and political truths are essential objects of investigation, how can we avoid studying the theory of beau-

---

39. The original text of this essay appears in Aoki Shigeru and Sakai Tadayasu, eds., *Bijutsu, NKST* 17 (Tokyo: Iwanami Shoten, 1989), pp. 15–34.

ty? Human beings seek the truth as "truth," and that is all. In other words, we love truth for the fact that it *is* truth; we do not love it because it has some utilitarian merit. Therefore, we should not ask what sort of truth it is, because among truths, all are equal.

If a human being who has spiritual ability intends to seek the truth, he should not categorize each truth as he wishes, nor should he privilege one truth over another. One should consider all kinds of truth, just as the merciful Avalokitesvara seeks to save all sentient beings with her virtue which she exercises freely and generously: she rectifies an evil person; she assists a virtuous person, without ever hating the first and loving the other; she employs all possible methods in order to realize her desire to save them. Unfortunately, however, even today we have not attained the truth of beauty and are still in the midst of a thick fog. Even artists whose skill and talent depend on the logic of beauty must feel as if they are looking for something in the darkness of night without light. We must admit that this is indeed a regrettable situation.

When we look at art circles in our country, it is clear that our culture has developed significantly. We now live in an age when, for instance, music, painting, literary arts such as poems and prose, and performing arts such as dancing and theater are all in the process of improvement and rapidly progressing. Yet, oddly, people who are confident enough to call themselves artists do not show any intention of offering an opinion as to what art is, but rather embrace erroneous theories, looking proud and self-complacent. For instance, some people have respectfully adopted the empty theory of a certain figure,[40] pretending vaguely to comprehend that the purpose of art is to please one's eyes and heart and to refine oneself. Alas, what can we do about this? The theory of aesthetics is to determine the fundamentals of art as well as its purpose. But if the discussion remains as vague as the one I have mentioned and answers nothing accurately, how can artists define art's purpose? How can they possibly define the purpose and the standards of art?

Furthermore, they might often misunderstand its valuable essence and, in turn, hinder its development, eventually leading young artists to bizarre mistakes. The effects could be immeasurable. Perhaps the main cause of this abuse is that the field of aesthetics is not progressing. This is because the big question "what is beauty?" has not yet been answered correctly. If this situation existed during ordinary times, this lack of discussion could be dismissed as simply a fault without worrying about it too much. Yet now is a time when the cultural movement has finally started to mature and is ready to progress. In this phase, we should not rejoice at such illness. One must say something, if one desires cultural development for the empire.

Originally I was not a specialist of aesthetics and have not devoted myself

---

40. Tsubouchi refers to the American scholar Ernest Fenollosa (1853–1908), a contemporary of Shōyō and champion of the "rediscovery" of Japanese art.

entirely to aesthetics. Therefore, I might be criticized as a reckless blind man unafraid of snakes when I dare to tackle this important issue and give a lecture on the truth of beauty. When I think of it, I feel a little uneasy. Yet I have a deep karmic relationship with the literary arts since I spent some years in literary circles. I revere that lovable thing called the arts as much as life itself or as a god; it is undoubtedly my good friend who must be loved and adored. Thus it is against the rules of friendship to betray my friend just because I am afraid of being criticized slightly or receiving caustic remarks. It is all the more so when my fellow brother, the Misty House in Spring,[41] keeps company with artists and, furthermore, pretends to be a person from the world of art and engaged in writing about art. It would be against my true intention if I did not say what I know even if my theory might not be accurate, and even if my proposal might be erroneous nonsense. Worse, I would be criticized as disloyal to the country and insensitive toward art.

Therefore, from today on I will be brave and withstand the accusation of being forward. With my limited knowledge I will remove arbitrary misconceptions and determine the true essence of the great truth of "beauty" by discussing the reasons why art should be valued and letting people know why aesthetics should be revered, thereby contributing to speeding up the process of cultural development.

When I think about it deeply, beauty in the realm of art is different from beauty in its ordinary sense; it is different from the beauty you find in just any object. Should I be wrong on this, then we would not be able to consider fine artists the great master of all ages and would have no choice but to chase them out of the world of arts and letters. The representation of ugliness, filth, and wretchedness, scenes that defy beauty in its ordinary sense, is dissimilar from the aim of the fine arts striving after true beauty—indeed a complete transgression of art's purpose. Does not the French aesthetician Véron[42] say:

> "From the beginning, the beauty of art and the beauty of nature have always been completely different, and we should not mix the two. The beauty of nature constitutes perfection, purity, sensuality, the complete opposite of ugly and wretched forms. Artistic beauty is a kind of special beauty; its essence is not located in the beauty of its outer appearance," but has a different source? [summary][43]

---

41. Harunoya Oboro is another name for Tsubouchi Shōyō.

42. Eugéne Vèron (1825–1889) was a French scholar and political commentator.

43. Quotation marks indicate Tsubouchi's use of the Japanese translation of Véron's *L'Esthétique* [hereafter EV] by Nakae Chōmin: *Ishi Bigaku* [hereafter NC]. For Nakae's translation I consulted *Meiji Bunka Zenshū*, add. 1 (Tokyo: Nihon Hyōronsha, 1970), p. 124. Actually Véron was arguing along slightly different lines: justifying the presence of the ugly in the work of art as an act of mimesis that elevates the ugliness of reality to the heights of aesthetic representation. Moreover, Véron was also presenting the Platonic notion that reality is closer to the ideal form than art, thus elevating natural beauty above artistic beauty. Tsubouchi misreads the text as an apologia for the special status of artistic beauty. Nakae's translation is

He also says:

"If we look from the perspective of beauty and gracefulness at Gros' painting of Eylau (the place where Napoleon the first fought and defeated the Russian army), the verses that Dante (an Italian poet) composed to sing Hell, and things like the histories written by Tacitus (a Roman historian), there is nothing to recommend them," since these are all extreme representations of ugliness, filth, and cruelty. [summary][44]

He also says:

"As a rule, among poets as well as painters, from every nation, of all times, there are many who narrate or depict unfaithful acts toward both ruler and parent, and the extremes of ugliness. For the most part, these kinds of evil actually make us grimace and repulse us when we encounter them first hand. We try only to remain undefiled. However, if one expresses this ugliness in a poem or a painting with great talent, then suddenly all the critics in the world admire it as something skillful and superb. Why is this?" [summary][45]

Scholars of all times have struggled to answer this question, often expanding the territory of "beauty" and trying to explain its meaning by adding the two ingredients of sublimity and novelty. There are also others who examine beauty in detail, as if they were chemists analyzing the elements of an object. If I were to give them a name, I would call them the dissectionist school of aesthetics. The group is made up of Addison, Hogarth, Burke, and Ruskin.[46]

---

partly to be blamed for Tsubouchi's questionable hermeneutics. The original says: "We are thus compelled to refuse acquiescence in any theory that describes beauty as the result of perfection. The examples we have given imply also a duplication of the question at issue and prove that an essential distinction exists between the beauty of nature and that of art. The former alone has to do with ideal perfection, while the latter arises from a purely human and accidental circumstance, imitation." See WHA, p. 99; for the original see EV, p. 117.

44. The original text argues that even the most brutal situation is material for great art. "Art, in truth, addresses all the feelings without exception; hope or fear, joy or grief, love or hatred. It interprets every emotion that agitates the human heart, and never troubles itself with its relation to visible or ideal perfection. It even expresses what is ugly and horrible, without ceasing to be art and worthy of admiration. The battle field of Eylau, the hideous and awful tortures of the damned, the crimes and ignominies of those ferocious beasts who under the name of Caesars struck so great horror into Roman civilization—have not these afforded to Gros, to Dante, to Tacitus, opportunities for magnificent works whose models would hardly be found in the world of the intellectualists [that is, ideas]? What beauty is to be found in a battle field strewed with dead and dying? What in a vision of Ugolino devouring the head of his enemy, or of Tiberius at Capri?" See WHA, pp. 97–98; EV, p. 116; NC, p. 123.

45. The original says: "What beauty lurks in the more or less odious and shameful vices of that great multitude of wretches which peoples the literature of all times and countries? Where is it to be found in such men as Nero, such women as Agrippina, in Madame Bovary or La Marneffe? Whence comes it that the description of baseness and degradations, themselves horrible to us, can produce in works of art, so different a feeling?" See WHA, p. 98; EV, p. 117; NC, pp. 123–124.

46. Joseph Addison (1672–1719) was a British critic and essayist. William Hogarth (1697–1764) was a British artist and aesthetician. Edmund Burke (1729–1797) was a British politician and aesthetician. John Ruskin (1819–1900) was a British art critic and social philosopher.

Originally, however, beauty is formless; you will not find it in the real object. In other words, it is something expressed in the form of art. Furthermore, to give some other examples, it is more or less the same as the sweetness of sugar or the sourness of pickled plums. Although one can, using chemical methods, determine the components of sugar's sweetness and a plum's sourness, and explain in detail why they are sweet and why they are sour, unless you touch these things to your tongue and taste them, you will only have a very vague idea about sweetness and sourness and will never acquire true knowledge. It is the same with "beauty." While you can very closely determine the original elements of beauty through philosophical dissection, still your knowledge of beauty will be vague and will never be of any use to the practice of fine arts. On the contrary, it will cause enthusiastic artists to lament the fact that this dissection is extremely vague and groundless. When I think of it, beauty does not reside in individual parts but solely in a synthesis of those parts. One must perceive it with one's feelings and not by means of intellectual dissection.

The Kiyomoto school of puppet theater is chic *(iki),* and the art of Danjūrō is cool *(shibushi).*[47] When we say "chic" and when we say "cool" both are, in the realm of art, "beauty." But when we ask a "dissectionist" the principle behind these phenomena, he will surely explain them by means of logic. He will rationalize matters by arguing that Kiyomoto chanting is like this, the rate of its tempo is like that, the fluctuations of pitch are like this, and because it is rapid it is beautiful, and because the chanting is low in this manner it is beautiful. . . . They might say Danjūrō keeps silent, and that's why it is beautiful; because he does not intensify his gaze, it is beautiful. Alas, how are these judgments useful to the field of the fine arts? To be silent—does this always constitute art's beauty? Fast rhythm—will it always make for beauty in the realm of art? By no means is this so. There must be one reason why beauty is beauty.

Beauty is not in the least something that appears without rules, its elements existing in an unsystematic manner, having one component in one place and showing another element in another place; it is not as inconsistent as this. Even if each element is different, as explained above, in the ever-changing world of art (where you can tell from the combined result whether something constitutes beauty or not) you might interpret in detail what the components are, but this does not mean, from the enthusiast point of view of us aestheticians, that you have discovered the essence of beauty. I think the true essence of beauty cannot be understood if you do not rely upon emotions. Human beings are naturally moved to create art, and they make efforts to understand it as an expression of the human heart. But without realizing this principle, stupidly enough, they force their analyses on art, dissecting it with their intellect, a useless endeavor that fractures the meaning of art. Since ancient times the dili-

---

47. Kiyomoto is the name of a school of *jōruri* active during the Edo period and known for its complex style as well as its sensuous music and lyrics. Ichikawa Danjūrō IX (1838–1903) was one of the creators of historical documentary theater.

gence of the dissectionists has been very impressive, but when you see how erroneous their methods are, you cannot but deplore their achievements.

Thus it is completely impossible, by means of dissection, to capture the
truth of beauty. This is why serious philosophers do not discuss the true entity of "beauty" as a whole using abstract language. Specifically they try to find
the cause of "beauty" not in the appearance of the object itself but somewhere
else. We might call this school the "synthesis school." Their main argument
was started by the Greek Plato. Since then hundreds of theories have added
confusion—theories that either saw in Plato their revered forefather, or added
and twisted Plato's meaning, or proposed a new method opposing the main
theory. Even today, the debate seems endless and we have no idea which theory is correct. Because there is no standard, they continue to discuss hundreds
of empty theories that, generally speaking, are based only on speculation. I will
discuss each theory at a later time. [*Gakugei Zasshi* 2, 20 September 1886]

I explained in the previous section that the meaning of beauty cannot be shown
through dissection. I would now like to discuss this subject further and explain why every aesthetic theory in the world is improper. Although we may
say that all over the world aesthetic theories are plentiful, I believe that there
are no more than three, four, or five fundamental types. We should discuss
them in order, starting with the most prominent one.

First I would like to draw your attention to the so-called theory of imitationism. The followers of this school say: "The reason why art pleases the eye
and heart is because it imitates with skill the external form of actual objects,
entirely approaching their truth." Therefore, according to these theorists, so-
called artistic beauty does not go beyond the word "imitation." Many aestheticians past and present, East and West, endorse this theory. For example,
to name some of the celebrated and great philosophers known in this country,
Aristotle, Bacon and, more recently, Spencer all follow this theory. Spencer,
however, proposed, vaguely, that one should imitate the spontaneity of nature
rather than forcing oneself to make a servile copy of the object. Thus, I think,
his main theory is a bit different from that of the pure imitationists.

In fact, for our generation, in our country, imitationism is practiced through
photorealistic drama performances at the Shintomi[48] and Chitose[49] theaters.
Where can we find artistic beauty in the shakuhachi of Danjūrō or the ladder
climbing of Baikō, who suffer the abuses of imitationism? Recently, even Toyama[50] has vehemently criticized this trend. Even in the field of painting, imi-

---

48. The Shintomiza was a kabuki theater that took its name from the district in Tokyo where it was located.

49. The Chitoseza was renamed the Meiji Theater (Meijiza) in 1893.

50. Toyama Masakazu (1848–1900) was a cultural reformer very active during the Meiji period. His
criticism of actors behaving like fools on stage appears in his *Personal Views on the Reform of Theater* (*Engeki
Kairyō Ron Shikō*, 1896).

tationism has begun to flourish, and the graceful paintings that are indigenous to the East have been mercilessly displaced by Western painting. Their lifeline has become as thin as a thread. A certain figure,[51] lamenting this situation and suddenly poking his nose into it, has offered an opposing theory saying that the essence of art is not anything like what the imitationists claim. With his superior and flowing eloquence, he praised the Tosa and Kanō schools of painting and pointed out the singularity of the Shijō and Maruyama schools.

Those who originally had absolutely no idea of what aesthetics was, whose coarse mind could be called a tabula rasa deprived of all knowledge, were quite astonished and impressed listening to those novel ideas. Since then they have revered this person as if he were a god and have started rejecting imitationism. But because their intellect was insufficient to comprehend fully the theory this person was spreading, they fruitlessly ended up with a superficial understanding and insisted on wrong explanations. Although it is right to pose as a pedagogue, saying that "the purpose of art is to please the heart and eyes and to refine the human character," if one simply copies paintings that were created by the ancients and makes no effort to create something new, this proves that one has not completely broken away from imitationism—a true laughing matter indeed! The main theory of this person lies mainly in the representation of "ideas," not in *copying* the ancients. After giving his definition of art, however, he went astray and strangely played the role of "educator," unintentionally leading his disciples into a fog. Since I have elsewhere discussed, some time ago, the appropriateness of this theory (see my *Essence of the Novel*),[52] I do not intend to touch upon it here in detail. I believe it is not right to discuss such matters under the heading of imitationism.

As for the appropriateness of imitationism, I can only offer a negative opinion. The term "to imitate" is generally taken to mean "to copy." It is only possible to copy things that are in front of our eyes, things that have already been formed, or that are in the process of being formed. Otherwise there is no need for imitation. How can we copy things that do not appear in this world, or things that have no form or sounds, like the thin fur of animals in autumn? So-called professional impersonators are extremely skillful at imitating the voice of others. But when asked to imitate a particular timbre of voice that has no original, even the most accomplished performer falls silent, defeated. Of course, if there is no original it is hard to come up with a copy!

When we consider works of art, however, there are many cases that have moved peoples of the world by representing in paintings or in poems things that cannot exist and cannot generally be seen in reality. I do not know how

---

51. Tsubouchi refers to Ernest Fenollosa, who since April 1891 was lecturing actively in Tokyo on the need for a revival of native art. Fenollosa had taught Tsubouchi Shōyō at Tokyo University, failing him in the examination on Western politics.

52. *Shōsetsu Shinzui*—the essay on novels that Tsubouchi published in 1885–1886, in which he criticizes Fenollosa's *True Conception of the Fine Arts (Bijutsu Shinsetsu,* 1882).

aestheticians of the imitationist school would explain that. The French Véron has made the following remarks:

> Italy's fresco painted by Michael Angelo in the Sistine Chapel, which depicts the way the Creator created the earth, portrays a scene of creation which human beings have never witnessed, a scene which, therefore, has no original model. However, Michael Angelo managed to depict it. Although in his head there was no model from which to copy, I am sure that he represented things that deeply moved him, allowing his emotions and thoughts to flow. The skillfulness of design and the beauty of the colors are quite impressive. What makes this picture so outstanding? Some people say that Michael Angelo used the Bible as a model, reproducing its content in the painting. But how could this be true? In the scriptures, it simply says, "And God said, 'Let there be light!'" How could this serve as a sufficient model for this painting? Etc. etc. . . . [53]

Véron's statement is good; there is nothing in it to be criticized. There are famous paintings both old and new, as well as masterpieces of literature, that are not based on models. But if I offer a simple refutation against those minds that are caught up in imitationism and cannot easily get free from it, then I would be no more than a ghost whose inability to find enlightenment hinders his future destiny. Therefore I will briefly attack this problem anew in order to awaken those who have gone astray.

If we look at the essence of beauty from the point of view of imitationism, representations of ugliness and wretchedness should not be rejected. If these depictions accurately reflect reality, then should they not be considered as aesthetically beautiful? Why is it that decaying corpses are ignored? Why are pornographic paintings disliked? It does not make sense. If I take my criticism to these extremes, then imitationists would interrupt me to say that the important point of art is not to imitate things as they are but to imitate the spirit of things. This is why they do not necessarily imitate an object clinging to its outer appearance.

This, again, is a strange argument. As I stated previously, the word "to imitate" by definition requires an original model. One can talk about imitating formless spirits, but it is impossible actually to do it. Furthermore, what do they mean by "spirit"? We must examine the definition of this word. It is pos-

---

53. The original appears in part 2 ("What we admire in a work of art is the genius of the artist") of chapter 6 ("Definition of Aesthetics") of Véron's *L'Esthétique:* "To give other examples—what is it that strikes us in the fresco of the Sistine chapel, where Michael Angelo has represented the separation of light from darkness? Evidently imitation has nothing to do with it. No man, Michael Angelo no more than any other, saw the creation of light. The imagination of the artist had absolutely free scope. The arrangement of his work was completely subordinate to the power which he could put into the interpretation of his idea of a spectacle, whose elements were only to be found within himself. The Bible, even, could be no guide to him, so far as imitation is concerned. Jehovah said: 'Let there be light, and there was light.' How is the energy of these creative words to be represented in painting?" See WHA, p. 103; EV, pp. 122–123; NC, p. 128.

sible to imitate a sad voice or a happy face in paintings, poems, and music, but I have never heard of imitating a sad spirit (maybe as a rabbit's horn in the dark!). How could one imitate formless things? I should like to hear the answer.

If beauty is based on imitation, then why do we not employ photography, which is bound to evolve increasingly, and abandon the indirect methods of painting? As the reader might know very well, these days the technology of photography has progressed a great deal. Not only can they take full-sized pictures, but they can faithfully reproduce the colors of clothes and background scenery. In the debate that takes photography as the true image of representation, not even the most skillful painting can beat photographic techniques.

Furthermore, regarding writing, stenography is the technique of copying words as they are. When secretly transcribing children's conversations and women's gossip, every word and each phrase can be so accurately recorded that it is as if we were actually having a discussion with them. At a speech, for example, why do we not describe in detail the speaker's demeanor and the modulation of his voice, even the applauding "yeahs" and "nays" of the audience? The atmosphere of the day of the speech should also be faithfully reproduced on paper. Is this not the way a photographic report should be? Judging it at a glance, is this not perfect literature? But true connoisseurs reject photographically realistic sentences as mere "stenography." Instead they find pleasure in fictional literature produced by the imagination of the Sanba school.[54] I think this is because artistic beauty does not reside in the notions of "imitation" or "photography," but lies somewhere else.

Night has come. The distant temple bell has fallen silent. Even insects, who stir up feelings in the garden covered with grasses, have tired and ceased their chirping. Even the autumn breeze that blows over the ancient pond blows uselessly, as the leaves have been stripped from the trees, and spares only a little wind for the towel hanging near the shutters, bringing tidings from far away. At three in the morning there is no human sound, as if everyone were dead. Isn't that a frog jumping "plop" into the water that makes a sound from the direction of the pond? Etc. etc. . . . Such awkwardly prolific descriptions, even if they depict exactly what you hear in the middle of the night, contain nothing very interesting. Instead the sharp image, "The ancient pond / A frog jumps in / The sound of water" captures the essence of the situation, and one cannot help feeling a sense of admiration, as these seventeen syllables implicitly contain a mysterious beauty and the exquisite taste of silence.

Based on this discussion, it should be understood that imitation is not equal to "beauty." Although there are many other things I would like to say, it seems to me that a certain figure has already attacked these errors. Therefore I will

---

54. Shikitei Sanba (1776–1822) was a major writer of the late Edo period.

stop here, reserving for some other time my critique of other aesthetic theories. [*Gakugei Zasshi* 4, 20 October 1886]

I should turn again to the aesthetic theories of the Frenchman Véron. First I will outline his conclusions and then examine them. In his *Aesthetics* Véron argues as follows:

> To consider beauty a kind of mysterious activity, and to find its essence in God, is the fallacy of academicians that surely should not even be considered. (In this section Véron refutes Cuvillier-Fleury's[55] discussion of Plato's theory of "ideals." I have a different opinion about this theory and will discuss it in a later section.) I believe that trying to find beauty in imitation is not baseless, but it fails to capture the truth of beauty. If one believes that the beauty of ordinary things and the beauty of art are the same, when representations of ugliness and wretchedness are extremely close to their models, how could we call such depictions beautiful? I think that when representations of ugliness impress the connoisseur of art, and he calls it "beautiful," there must be something between the artwork and the object it represents. I believe this thing is nothing but the talent, emotion, and skill of the *artist*. Therefore, when we see the artwork and call it pleasant and beautiful, it is not that we are calling the artwork beautiful, nor are we calling the object beautiful, but, unconsciously, we recognize beauty in the talent of the artist. Even if one dissects and examines the principles explaining the nature of the world, putting all his energies into this effort, he will find that what a connoisseur calls beautiful or extraordinary does not exist anywhere but in the beauty and excellence of the artist's talent. I say, therefore, that the beauty of art does not reside in form or style, but in the talent of the artist.[56]

Furthermore, Véron quotes from Bürger[57] and says:

> The thesis of Bürger is acceptable to me. Therefore, I would like to bolster my theory with his ideas. Bürger says that when the artwork moves people, it is because the artist puts himself in the artwork in place of the actual object. How else could art impress people? I think when art has the power to move people, this is because even an artist with ordinary talent creates an artwork confronting the original model with an emotion quite different from ordinary people, and

---

55. Alfred Auguste Cuvillier-Fleury (1802–1887) was a French man of letters.

56. The original text says: "The very theory of imitation is but the incomplete and superficial statement of the ideas which we are here advocating. What is it that we admire in imitation? The resemblance? We have that much better in the object itself. But how is it that the similitude of an ugly object can be beautiful? It is obvious that between the object and its counterfeit some new element intervenes. This element is the personality, or, at least, the skill of the artist. This latter, indeed, is what they admire who will have it that beauty consists in imitation. What these applaud, in fact, is the talent of the artist. If we look below the surface and analyze their admiration we shall find that it is so; whether they mean it or not, what they praise in a work is the worker." See WHA, pp. 107–108; EV, pp. 127–128; NC, pp. 133–134.

57. Thoré-Bürger, or Théophile Thoré (1807–1869), was a French art critic.

sees it with different eyes than ordinary people, and, therefore, it must be that his talent emerges within the artwork. Therefore, when we see an extraordinary painting and call it beautiful, we are not admiring the painting itself, but are admiring the painter's talent.[58]

In summary, beauty in Véron's theory is not a beauty that has form, but a beauty that exists in the artist's talent, which is formless; it is an extraordinary talent that we cannot discuss in an inclusive and satisfactory manner. I think talent is different from one person to another, changing constantly, and so we cannot say that such-and-such a talent is indeed the main element of art. Isn't Véron's confidence in giving—without ever showing any hesitation—such a vague definition of art suspicious? Alas, it is hard to tell theory from practice. Theory talks about the truth of art and defines its rules. It is impossible to deny the relationship between the theory of economics and the practice of economics, or the theory of political science and political engagement. When one lectures about theory, it should become the guideline for artistic implementation. Theoreticians should pay attention to this point and should particularly guard against being concerned with empty talk.

Véron, however—I do not know what he thought—constantly criticizes Plato's ideals as something vague and baseless. Véron himself fell into the trap of empty theory, offering very pointless definitions, acting as if he had found the truth of beauty—a truly suspicious endeavor. I do not know but, should his ideas be valid, then what sort of standards should future artists employ and what artistic purpose should they pursue? I wonder whether such a formless thing as "extraordinary talent," which is extremely varied, could become a standard. I think that Véron, in his self-absorption, unconsciously misunderstood the true calling of the aesthetician and took the stand of a dilettante, providing interpretations accordingly. Perhaps, as a dilettante, he can say that the most important quality of art is the talent of the artist, but the "beauty of art" in general is never anything like this.

The group of experts known as the "critics of the second row"[59] concentrate on the skill of Danshū[60] and Baikō without ever being concerned with their outer appearance. On the other hand, ordinary spectators like us pay no attention to the actors' ability and content ourselves with being inexplicably

---

58. The original text says: "This was the opinion of Bürger, who, in his *Salon* of 1863, says: 'In works which interest us the authors in a way substitute themselves for nature. However common or vulgar the latter may be, they have some rare and peculiar way of looking at it. It is Chardin himself whom we admire in his representation of a glass of water. We admire the genius of Rembrandt in the profound and individual character which he imparted to every head that posed before him. Thus did they seem to him, and this explains everything simple or fantastic in his expression and execution.'" See WHA, p. 108; EV, p. 128; NC, p. 134.

59. This name indicates a group of influential critics who used to sit in the second row at the center of the theater.

60. This is another name for the actor Ichikawa Danjūrō.

moved by the simple surface appearance of the performance. The same thing goes when one looks at paintings. Those who admire a painting do not think of the artist, but there is something that impresses them naturally. When one is moved either by uniqueness or sublimity—or from crying, or in anger— how could one even think, from the midst of passions, of the technique and skill of the artist? It is due solely to the unilateral guidance of the emotions that, when you look at a painting, you perceive beauty, and when you read great literature, you admire its greatness.

Although I believe there is some help from the intellect, I think we should consider this as secondary. When one acknowledges the skill of the artist and admires his talent and powers, is he not solely following the operation of the intellect? Because the average person is not a connoisseur and is without the full abilities of appreciation, it is not possible for him to employ the intellectual function. Thus Véron's theory should be regarded as the opinion of a connoisseur, rather than the argument of an aesthetician who plans the progress of the art world by obligingly interpreting the principle of "beauty" and defining standards for future artists. His indifferent theory satisfies himself alone and helps no one else. It is not something that artists of the world revere or observe as truth. But if this is the opinion of a connoisseur, is it a rational argument? Aestheticians will surely counter that for some theoreticians, once they explain the truth and explain why it is the truth, they consider their job done. Their duty, they think, is not to set future standards. There is a point to this perspective. Rather than ignoring it and sticking my head in the sand, I will address this point directly.

Véron's theory of aesthetics seems to aim at being a meticulous doctrine safe from criticism. Unfortunately, when it comes to the vital definition of beauty, he gives an illogical interpretation and uses extremely vague language. Therefore, when you read his definition, there is nothing to hang your hat on. This is the most prominent weakness of his theory. Why am I so insulting? Mainly because I cannot help being skeptical at seeing the explanation of the meaning of the word "beauty" simply reduced to the expression "talent." Alas, does this "talent" reside only in artists? Is it something that never appears in objects produced by technicians or craftsmen? Certainly not! How could it be so?

Consider the extremely detailed mechanism of a pocket watch or the amazing efficiency of a locomotive. Even the most absentminded person would be impressed by these things and admire the talent of their creator. Practical, patented products spring from their creators' intellects and extraordinary minds, and whenever we use these things we cannot help being impressed by the results of their ability. But from ancient times to the present, I have never heard people, refer to these products as "artistic." Why is this so? Véron would surely say that "aesthetic talent" is different from "practical talent." If this is the case, Véron used rather ordinary terms to indicate this special talent, and in a way that was unfitting for a real theoretician. I must say that it is a truly imperfect definition.

In the scholastic field, there is nothing more important than a definition. If a definition is incomplete, the reeds accumulated over years will become a pile of ashes in a moment. Therefore in the study of economics, as well as in the study of law, scholars insist upon correct definitions. Definitions are the foundation and ground of a discussion; vague and unclear definitions must be avoided most scrupulously because they lead to misunderstandings. But Véron's definition epitomizes extreme vagueness. Should you present it to the world, you would be attacked from all sides and be required to defend yourself on all counts. This is because the vague word "talent" varies in meaning. If the definition is such a troublesome one, it is better not to have it at all, as it is completely useless. Therefore, I declare here: "The theory that explains beauty as the artist's talent not only violates the truth in most instances, but even in the most specific and exceptional cases (such as in the case of the connoisseur) it is too vague to be considered the foundation of aesthetics."

This declaration kills two birds with one stone. I would like to advance this discussion further, by addressing the most elegant artistic debates that have occurred since the most ancient times, and reach some conclusions. Although I promised that I would move to a different topic, I feel there are still some areas of Véron's aesthetic theory that I touched upon the other day but did not sufficiently examine. Therefore, I will make up for my previous omissions and add a few words on this topic. This is, of course, because I am afraid that it would be a great sin to offer an incorrect judgment of Véron's brilliance.

A supporter of Véron might say defensively: "You vehemently criticized Véron's definition of beauty in the previous article and rejected 'talent' as the essence of art because it is difficult to distinguish it from practical technology. You said that 'talent' resides in various kinds of techniques that appear in many different things and proudly proclaimed that, if one considers 'talent' as beauty, what about practical talent? This is a rather peculiar critique. What Véron called 'talent' is the talent of the artist; it is not talent in the ordinary sense. If the word 'talent' is too vague, you could use the term 'artistic talent.' Then your lengthy discussion will collapse and turn out to be nothing more than useless babbling. How can you move such an objection and say such offensive things?" Thus might this person say poignantly.

I regret very much that I offered such an extreme opinion, but I am not yet convinced of the validity of Véron's definition. The reason is that when you say "artistic talent," what kind of talent are you talking about? Is it a talent for depicting beauty, or is it a talent for representing the author's intention? Or is it a talent for imitating exactly the actual object? Did Véron not declare vehemently that imitation is not beauty, and did he not reject the notion of beauty in ordinary things? Therefore, according to this definition, if we concentrate exclusively on the artist's talent, what is the point of asking about the object of representation? If that is the case, this "talent" becomes a very vague concept that eventually leads to no conclusion. In other words, how can we understand correctly what sort of talent it is unless we first know what this talent is representing? If we hypothesize that true "artistic talent" is the talent to depict such-and-such a thing, this such-and-such a thing ought to be beautiful—ought to be the essence of art. Because if there is no such-and-such a thing, even the most outstanding talent cannot represent it in art.

Véron's supporter would turn the spear against my rebuttal and say: "Véron aimed at providing a successful definition. If there is exquisite talent that moves a connoisseur in an extraordinary manner, that would be called 'artistic talent.'" I would answer by saying: "If one copies the object in a way that makes it extremely close to the actual thing, the viewer would be impressed with the talent of the artist. Would you call this true art? There are some who make a painting seeking beauty in form, paying attention only to the distribution of lines. Should this be called true art? Didn't Véron himself emphasize the necessity of the author's intention? How uneasy it must make him feel when the person who equates "beauty" with "talent" talks about the necessity of intentionality! It must be because the word "talent" does not completely cover the phenomenon of beauty. Therefore, I still insist upon the theory that I expressed earlier, and I reiterate that Véron's definition is unclear.

Now, I would like to discuss and criticize "idealism." There are two schools of idealism: one is Plato's idealism; the other is its modern version. I will summarize the major ideas of both schools to provide readers with some reference:

Plato says that between heaven and earth there exist two kinds of things, each within its own realm. One is present in everything in the universe, and it is understood by the five senses. This is the realm of forms. The other is the realm of formlessness, which only contains the essence of things. Things that have form are limited spatially. Also, they will disappear in time. On the other hand, formless things are not like this. Since they have no form, they do not know limitation in space, nor do they fear destruction. These are the "ideal things."

The ideal is the ultimate authority that lies behind everything, and it is a perfect essence. That is, things in the realm of forms become formed things by conforming to the formless essences. However, there is no one thing that contains all essences and that is free of all defects. This is because the essences of things reside only in the realm of formlessness and do not transmit their perfection to forms.

Insofar as they exist in the realm of formlessness, one cannot know the essences by means of the five senses. How, then, can we know them? Plato says that human beings have two faculties. One is called "sensation," through which we know the realm of forms. The other is an ability called "intellect," by means of which humans comprehend formless truth. If this is the case, to comprehend the ideals that I mentioned earlier, and to display them in scholarship and art, depends solely upon the intellect. How can the function of the intellect possess such a subtle power? Why do we human beings never tire of seeking pure beauty and pure truth? Moreover, upon which truth do I base the conclusion that there are ideals?[61]

At this point, Plato is completely at a loss, ultimately presenting the following fallacious theory:

Human beings were originally all gods. Therefore, when they were in the celestial world, human beings were also formless. They were nothing but the essence of humans. The celestial world is the realm of essences: there is nothing there that is not ideal and nothing that is not perfect. After the fall of man and the subsequent appearance of so-called human beings, however, these humans soon lost the ability to see the realm of ideals, becoming, eventually, like lowly animals, vainly roaming around, polluted, imperfect, and impermanent things. Since the intellect, the true nature of human beings, still exists in them, even in this impermanent, limited, polluted, and imperfect world of forms, humans can remember the lost happiness by discovering traces of the essences they had been accustomed to in their previous existence. And yet the level of human intellect differs from one person to another. So certain people will be attracted by things alone, not perceiving any trace of essence and remaining unable to achieve happiness. Others, on the other hand, are blessed with extreme intelligence and can accidentally realize the presence of minute essences that the intellect of ordinary people could never perceive. People call them geniuses. Brilliant theoreticians, writers, mathematicians, are all geniuses of this kind. Although ordinary people do possess a little bit of intellect and tend to love ideals, the majority of them cannot perceive the traces of essences that are obscured by the world of forms. Therefore, if an outstanding genius realizes a pure

---

61. The original text appears in the appendix to *L'Esthétique* titled "The Aesthetics of Plato." It says: "First hypothesis.—Above the actual world in which we live, another world exists which is peopled by the ideal essences of things. Individual objects, subject to the limits of time and space as we know them, are there replaced by their ideal or perfect types, such as they first emerged from the divine brain. Each of these types has been utilized in succession as the model for the infinite multitude of objects of the same category. There is the *ideal bed,* the *"lit en soi,"* absolutely perfect, after which individual beds are constructed by mortal joiners! There also is the *ideal tree,* whose perfection nature imitates with more or less success in the trees that we see growing around us! There, too, are absolute types of happiness, truth, beauty, which man strives after in his terrestrial life with a greater or less modicum of success.

"Second hypothesis.—How is man to penetrate into this world of *intelligibles,* which is impenetrable to the physical eye? This question is answered by a second hypothesis, no less ingenious than the first. By the side of and in addition to the senses which enable us to see and feel material objects, we have a special faculty, that we call reason, which acts as an intermediary between our tangible world and the other. Reason is the most godlike of the faculties. It is a kind of open window though which human sight is enabled to penetrate into the sphere of pure ideas. But not the less on that account is it a purely passive quality. It, too, is a mirror, superior, indeed, to the other by the nature of the images which it reflects, but able to do no more than reflect. Man, try as he will, can only repeat a lesson which he has learned. All the ideas that he has the power to express have their type and model in the world of *intelligibles.* He is nothing but a plagiarist. The greatest geniuses, in philosophy, in arts or in letters, are those to whom the divine essences of things have been most completely laid open, and who have most accurately reproduced such revelations." See WHA, pp. 393–394; EV, pp. 454–456; NC, pp. 393–394.

ideal, expresses it in art or literature, and shows it to other human beings, who will not feel its good and beauty? Etc. etc.[62]

The foregoing ideas are the main points of Plato's theory of ideals, which I have paraphrased in a way that the reader will understand. In some parts the original text has been expanded. Nevertheless, I firmly believe that the original meaning has been retained.

Véron also discusses the absurdities of Plato's theory of ideals, so I will not add more here. The main fault in Plato is that he employs the very vague notion of a celestial world to prove the existence of ideals without ever clarifying on which ground he bases his hypothesis.

I believe that modern idealism originates from Plato. Even Véron, in his aesthetics, extrapolates from the works of idealists. To summarize, they say:

When we talk about the origin of beauty, we see it as one of the many godly virtues—purely simple, without ever changing through the ages. Therefore, human beings never discuss the temporal framework in which they encounter beauty. They never ask what sort of race it belongs to. When we engage in literature and art, we should make beauty the ultimate goal and purpose. "Aesthetics" is the science that studies beauty.

They also say: Beauty is the original aspect of all things. Before the Creator started to make the world, he first contemplated the truth of beauty. Then he made all creatures, covering them with beauty. Once things take on form, however, their life is not perfect, and they always have some blemishes. Therefore,

---

62. The original text says: "Third hypothesis.—There is but one thing now to be accounted for—and that is, the strange attraction which all that belongs to the ideal world exercises over man. This is a formidable difficulty, because it is obvious that if the human intellect be purely passive, it must also be quite indifferent to the nature of objects and the ideas which they reflect. But every thing combines to prove that such indifference does not exist; that man is naturally drawn to whatever is great, generous, or beautiful.

"A third hypothesis is formed, then, to explain this moral phenomenon:

Man is a fallen god, who retains his recollection of Heaven!

"Before his descent into this vale of tears and misery—man, as Plato tells us, contemplated the essences of things and lived among the Gods. Before being subjected to the yoke of his senses and the dark prison of his body, he was a pure spirit; nothing interposed between the absolute types and himself; his intelligence was not prevented from entire comprehension of pure truth and supreme beauty. His happiness was complete.

"When he fell from heaven upon this earth, he brought with him some vague souvenir of his primitive dignity, sufficient to keep alive in his heart an inextinguishable regret for what he had lost, an incessant desire to enjoy once more the happiness that had been his. So, too, the sight of the imperfect and gross objects that he perceived on all sides recalled, from the depth of his memory, the more or less confused and obliterated images of the perfect types which he formerly beheld around him; and excited in him an ever more and more active desire to build up truthful reproductions [unities] from these scanty and incomplete materials. This is the theory of recollection founded upon that Indian doctrine of Metempsychosis, which is to be found, in various forms, at the root of most religions.

"We have now arrived at Plato's system of Aesthetics." See WHA, pp. 394–395; EV, pp. 456–457; NC, pp. 394–395.

if one wants to understand the real meaning of beauty, the last thing to do is to study the world of forms. Rather, one should focus on abstract matters seeking beauty's original aspect, going back to the time before the Creator actually gave form to the world. Then you will be blessed with a happy result.[63]

In other words, it seems that the idealists call something ideal when it is perfectly beautiful. Therefore, "ideal" means extreme, perfect, and essential beauty. Or it may not be wrong to interpret idealism as "standardism." Because it is the desire of idealists to let people know the standards of things that human beings should value.

In his aesthetics, Véron criticized the obscurities of this theory and questioned the availability of proofs that might explain the existence of such standards. He also politely asked how we can know ideal beauty in its abstract form. Rather than be redundant, I will leave you to Véron's rebuttal and reserve my own doubts for some other time. [*Gakugei Zasshi* 5–6, 20 December 1886]

---

63. Tsubouchi quotes again from the sixth chapter of *L'Esthétique*: "Plato, Winckelmann and the academic school of our own day consider abstract beauty to be one of the attributes of divine perfection; a thing absolute, one and indivisible, consequently unique and universal; unchanged and unchangeable, dominating all peoples and all art in all times.

"To apply their theory, beauty is the essential form of all creatures before they took actual bodily shape; it is, in fact, the prototype of creation such as it must have presented itself in the brain of the Divine Creator, before the degradation consequent on its material realization had taken place.

"So soon as the mind has been induced to form a conception of the beautiful divorced from any connection with material reality, the definition and determination of metaphysical beauty, which must be universal and unchangeable, becomes a mere matter of logical induction. The starting point or premises may be utterly absurd, but this has never troubled metaphysicians, as they succeeded in establishing their conclusion by regularly formed syllogism.

"Beauty, as understood by them, naturally became the unique and supreme aim of all the arts, the eternal model for every effort of man, and the goal of all his aspirations. Considered from this point of view, it calls itself the ideal, though it is nothing but a feeble reflection of truth, only existing in the world of the intellectualists and their abstract ideas." See WHA, pp. 96–97; EV, pp. 114–115; NC, p. 121.

THREE

Hegelian Reversal
Okakura Kakuzō

THE IMAGE OF Japan as a site of Eastern spirituality, to be distinguished from a materialistically oriented West, is very much indebted to the Japanese adaptation of Hegel's philosophy. The explanation of reality as the journey of spirit in time until its ultimate realization provided potent arguments to Hegelian thinkers such as Ernest Fenollosa, who reversed the trajectory of spiritual fulfillment toward the place from where the spirit had originated: namely the East.[1]

While introducing Hegel to Japan, Fenollosa was also suggesting a way of appropriating his philosophy for the creation of an Eastern subjectivity. He was actually indicating how to challenge the Western notion of dialectics, which was at the core of Hegel's explanation of the superiority of European civilization. The language of harmonious wholeness—reminiscent of Augustinian, Thomistic, and Hegelian hermeneutics—was paradoxically used by Fenollosa's Japanese audience to construct the identity of their nation whose spirit was perceived in its alleged harmony and universality. Japan, in a sense, was made into a work of art: a part of a system called "Asia," whose distinctive characteristics were made into images that the West had reserved for centuries to representations of its God. The language of Western metaphysics came to be used to reverse the Hegelian argument of the Teutonic fulfillment of the ideality of art in favor of an alleged myth of Asian spiritualism.

---

1. "Using the Hegelian model Fenollosa argued that at the core of Japanese art lay the universal spiritual ideals of Asia. These stood in stark contrast to the technical facility and materialism of the West. Fenollosa's simplistic thesis-antithesis logic counterposed Asia's (read Japan's) spirituality and idealism with the West's preoccupation with realism, materialism, and technical facility. By the 1890s he had advanced his argument to the point where he clearly saw a new synthesis emerging out of the global confrontation between East and West. Eastern spiritualism, which he identified with the traditional Japanese arts, would be combined with Western technical achievements to create a higher culture in both East and West." See F. G. Notehelfer, "On Idealism and Realism in the Thought of Okakura Tenshin," *Journal of Japanese Studies* 16(2) (1990):321–322.

Fenollosa mediated the process through which Okakura Kakuzō (1862–1913)—or Tenshin—appropriated Hegelianism in order to stress the eternal nature of what he called "the Eastern spirit," which was shared by all nations of Asia.[2] Okakura simply subverted Hegel's Eurocentrism and attacked the Hegelian notion of dialectics, locating in the nondualism (advaita) of Indian Buddhism the "universality" of the East. He took issue with the Western brand of universality that was propelled by the violence of dialectics: the struggle of historical processes. If the spirit could be explained in terms of its being contained spatially in its area of origin (the East)—his argument goes—then there was no reason to employ dialectics to trace the journey of the development of the spirit from ancient Egypt to Germany, as Hegel had suggested. The dialectical adventure that put Germany at the end of the spirit's journey—and identified the Teutonic spirit with the fulfillment on earth of the Absolute Spirit—could easily be replaced by a philosophy of "sameness" that would explain reality as something which was constantly present to itself without any need for spatial or temporal articulation.[3] Okakura conceived Japan as the lasting museum of the metaphysicalization of Asia. Or as he wrote in 1903 in his *Ideals of the East:* "The unique blessing of unbroken sovereignty, the proud self-reliance of an unconquered race, and the insular isolation which protected ancestral ideas and instincts at the cost of expansion made Japan the real repository of the trust of Asiatic thought and culture."[4]

---

2. "Yet Okakura could not be satisfied with the idea of 'oneness' as the destiny of an Asia that was disintegrating under the onslaught of colonialism. For Okakura, 'the East' or Asia is not simply that which was imagined and defined by the West, nor can it refer to a unity created by the common destiny of colonialization. Okakura sought historically for principles of unity internal to Asia. To this end he tried to overturn Hegel's philosophy of history and art, trying not only to subvert Hegel's Eurocentrism but to attack the concept of dialectics itself. The notion of contradiction is crucial to Hegelian thought as that which gives rise to struggle and advances history. Okakura counterposed to this the philosophy of Advaita (nondualism), which had its origins in Indian Buddhism. The Sanskrit term 'Advaita' signified the oneness of that which is manifold and contradictory. Okakura sought to transcend the universality of the West in a universality of the East." See Karatani Kōjin, *Origins of Modern Japanese Literature* (Durham: Duke University Press, 1993), p. 43.

3. "Asia is one. The Himalayas divide, only to accentuate, two mighty civilizations, the Chinese with its communism of Confucius, and the Indian with its individualism of the Vedas. But not even the snowy barriers can interrupt for one moment that broad expanse of love for the Ultimate and Universal, which is the common thought-inheritance of every Asiatic race, enabling them to produce all the great religions of the world, and distinguishing them from those maritime peoples of the Mediterranean and the Baltic, who love to dwell on the Particular, and to search out the means, not the end, of life." See Okakura Kakasu [*sic*], *The Ideals of the East with Special Reference to the Art of Japan* (London: John Murray, 1903), p. 1.

4. Okakura, *Ideals of the East,* p. 5. He continues: "It is in Japan alone that the historic wealth of Asiatic culture can be consecutively studied through its treasured specimens. The Imperial collection, the Shinto temples, and the opened dolmens reveal the subtle curves of Hâng workmanship. The temples of Nara are rich in representations of Tâng culture, and of that Indian art, then in its splendour, which so much in-

Grounding his argument in the Hegelian notion that "the Idea as the *beauty of art* is the Idea with the nearer qualification of being both essentially individual reality and also an individual configuration of reality destined essentially to embody and reveal the Idea," Okakura conceived the history of Japanese art and its repository—the museum—as the history of Asiatic ideals.[5] At the same time, he constructed Japanese art along the Spencerian lines of an evolving organism—as suggested by Fenollosa, a transcendent wholeness that reflects itself in all its particulars,[6] a resilient organic union that withstood changes throughout the ages.[7] The vocabulary used by Okakura to express the local "aesthetic energy" speaks the language of "tender simplicity," "romantic purity," "innate love of cleanness," "free creativeness," "a living spirit of Freedom," and a "heroic spirit."[8]

---

fluenced the creations of this classic period—natural heirlooms of a nation which has preserved the music, pronunciation, ceremony, and costumes, not to speak of the religious rites and philosophy, of so remarkable an age intact. . . . Thus Japan is a museum of Asiatic civilization; and yet more than a museum, because the singular genius of the race leads it to dwell on all phases of the ideals of the past, in that spirit of living Advaitism which welcomes the new without losing the old. The Shinto still adheres to his pre-Buddhistic rites of ancestor-worship; and the Buddhists themselves cling to each various school of religious development which has come in its natural order to enrich the soil." Ibid., pp. 6–8.

5. "The history of Japanese art becomes thus the history of Asiatic ideals—the beach where each successive wave of Eastern thought has left its sand-ripple as it beat against the national consciousness." See Okakura, *Ideals of the East,* pp. 8–9.

6. "For art, like the diamond net of Indra, reflects the whole chain in every link. It exists at no period in any final mould. It is always a growth, defying the dissecting knife of the chronologist. To discourse on a particular phase of its development means to deal with infinite causes and effects throughout its past and present. Art with us, as elsewhere, is the expression of the highest and noblest of our national culture, so that, in order to understand it, we must pass in review the various phases of Confucian philosophy; the different ideals which the Buddhist mind has from time to time revealed; those mighty political cycles which have one after another unfurled the banner of nationality; the reflection in patriotic thought of the lights of poetry and the shadows of heroic characters; and the echoes, alike of the wailing of a multitude, and of the mad-seeming merriment of the laughter of a race." Ibid., pp. 9–10.

7. "Apart from this, her unassailable original destiny, the geographical position of Japan would seem to have offered her the intellectual role of a Chinese province or an Indian colony. But the rock of our race-pride and organic union has stood firm throughout the ages, notwithstanding the mighty billows that surged upon it from the two great poles of Asiatic civilisation." Ibid., p. 19.

8. "The waters of the waving rice-fields, the variegated contour of the archipelago . . . of all these was born that tender simplicity, that romantic purity, which so tempers the soul of Japanese art. . . . That innate love of cleanness which, though sometimes detrimental to grandeur, gives its exquisite finish to our industrial and decorative art, is probably nowhere to be found in Continental work. . . . We can only say that the original spirit of our primitive art has never been allowed to die. . . . There has always been abundant energy for the acceptance and re-application of the influence received, however massive. It is the glory of Continental Asia that her touch upon Japan has made always for new life and inspiration: it is the most sacred honour of the race of Ama to hold itself invincible, not in some mere political sense alone, but still more and more profoundly, as a living spirit of Freedom, in life, and thought, and art. . . . And it is for Japan herself never to forget that it is by right of this same heroic spirit that she stands to-day face to face with new problems, for which she needs still deeper accessions of self-reverence." Ibid., pp. 16–21.

Okakura played a central role in articulating a philosophy of subjectivity that was paradoxically grounded from its very inception in Western epistemology in the attempt to overcome the cultural inferiority complex of the Asian nation. On the one hand, he opposed the program of Meiji "enlighteners," such as Fukuzawa Yukichi (1834–1901), according to whom Japan ought to separate itself from Asia if it wanted to avoid the colonialization suffered by other Asian nations. On the other, Okakura remained, perhaps unconsciously, loyal to Fukuzawa's program by adopting Western categories in his creation of an Asian subjectivity. To put it in the compelling words of Karatani Kōjin, "'the traditionalist faction' that propelled with passion the cause of the art school and the museum was the most vocal faction propounding modernism and westernization."[9] Foremost among such categories is the notion of the "East" (Tōyō), which constitutes the backbone of all Okakura's reflections on Japan and its genealogy. The genealogical process in which he locates Japanese art, explaining it as the result of influences from northern China (Confucianism), southern China (Laoism and Taoism), and India (Buddhism), carefully follows the Western master plan of a Greek and Latin origin of Western art.[10]

At times, Okakura's language draws from the rhetoric of Western liturgical writings—as in the case of his *Awakening of Japan,* where the "Restoration" of the Meiji period is followed by a "Reformation" and then a "Reincarnation" in which "Japan accepts the new without sacrificing the old" while "the heart of Old Japan still beats strongly" and "in art Japan stands alone against all the world."[11] When he was requested to lecture on the subject of Japanese art ("Nihon Bijutsu Shi"), Okakura followed the scheme provided by the Western model of modernization: he periodized the development of Japanese art with the time frames of ancient *(kodai),* medieval *(chūsei),* and modern *(kindai)* Japan. The source was William Swinton's (1833–1892) *Outlines of the World's History, Ancient, Mediaeval, and Modern, with Special Relation to the History of Civilization and the Progress of Mankind* (1874), which was very popular in Japan at the beginning of the Meiji period.[12]

9. Karatani Kōjin, "Bijutsukan to Shite no Nihon: Okakura Tenshin to Fenorosa," *Hihyō Kūkan* 2(1) (1994):60.

10. In the table of contents of Okakura's *Ideals of the East* (1903), "The Primitive Arts of Japan" is followed by "Confucianism—Northern China," "Laoism and Taoism—Southern China," and "Buddhism and Indian Art." See Okakura Kakuzō, *Collected English Writings,* vol. 1 (Tokyo: Heibonsha, 1984), p. 5.

11. These are quotations from the table of contents of *The Awakening of Japan.* See Okakura, *Collected English Writings,* vol. 1, p. 72.

12. Isoda Kōichi, "Okakura Tenshin: Sono Rekishiteki Ichi wo Megutte," *Nihon no Bigaku* 1(4) (Spring 1985):96–99.

Okakura lectured widely on the alleged differences "between Eastern and Western art."[13] He told his audience in Boston in 1911:

> Eastern art is not interested in beauty as such. The quest of art is not the beautiful but the interesting. In the whole range of Eastern criticism you will rarely find a painting praised because it is beautiful, but always because it is aesthetically interesting. The Japanese term for artistic, "Omoshiroi," is not an equivalent of the word "interesting," but is derived from a word which means "white-faced." Its origin is very peculiar. The story of the word is told in terms like this: The Sun-Goddess once became disgusted with the world. There were many things which vexed her, and she withdrew into a cavern, leaving the whole world in darkness. The gods assembled and tried to entice her out of her retreat. They danced and sang until the Sun-Goddess emerged, and as the first ray broke upon the darkness, the gods, who had seen nothing before, recognized that their faces were white. It is significant that a word recalling this legend of recognition should be used to signify artistic delight. For the pleasure we derive from art is in recognition, in re-discovery of what we have felt ourselves. We find our memories awakened by an artist, awakened on a higher plane and with a wider significance, and we rejoice. Thus everything and anything could be interesting and artistic in a master's hand. We have no ideal types of beauty, therefore no so-called golden section, no rules of proportion which define artistic excellence.[14]

Okakura and Fenollosa's appeal to recover the voice of the Eastern spirit in Japanese artistic production found its institutional victory in the reorganization of the Technological Art School (Kōbu Bijutsu Gakkō). The school was originally founded in 1876 within Tokyo's Engineering College (Kōgaku-ryō), when three Italian artists were invited as teachers: the architect Giovanni Vincenzo Cappelletti (d. 1887), the painter Antonio Fontanesi (1818–1882), and the sculptor Vincenzo Ragusa (1841–1928). The development of the first Japanese school of art as an annex to the building where Western natural science, engineering, and the drawing of military maps were taught clearly indicates the pragmatic role that the arts played in Japan in the 1870s. The study of Western techniques, such as the use of chiaroscuro and perspective in paintings, was meant to explain nature scientifically, in order to master it and conquer it in imitation of the West. What was known in the West as art found its justification in early Meiji Japan in its being fit to be employed as a tool for a faithful representation/reproduction of nature. This explains the good fortune that "naturalism" encountered when Western poetics were first introduced to Japan.

---

13. This is the subject, for example, of Okakura's lecture "Nature in East Asian Painting." See Okakura, *Collected English Writings,* vol. 2, p. 145.

14. Ibid., pp. 148–149.

In February 1889, however, under the pressure of revivalists such as Okakura, the school was restructured as an independent body of learning and renamed the Tokyo Art School (Tokyo Bijutsu Gakkō).[15] Fenollosa's lectures on the ideal nature of art *(bijutsu)*,[16] independent of the purposiveness of crafts *(gijutsu)*, had found in Okakura a strong supporter, eventually leading to the formation of a school that focused less on the naturalism of the artistic product than on the idealism of its conception. The result was a privileging of the abstractness of traditional Japanese paintings at the expense of realist oil paintings from Europe.[17]

The purpose of the new school conformed to Okakura's notion of "pure design" as the essence of Eastern art and supposedly unconcerned with the detailed representation of specific natural forms such as, for example, the human body. The essentialization of form in Asia depends, according to Okakura, on the Eastern tendency to draw from memory rather than from actual models.[18] To quote again from his lecture on nature in East Asian paintings:

> What an absurd creature is man, who talks of spiritual things and the universal, and yet twice or thrice a day puts food through a opening in his head, and is subject to every variety of physical limitations. Portraiture has never obtained such a prominent place in our art. Why should we perpetuate this evanescent thing, this cradle and nest of lust and mean desires. We have no desire to glorify the human body as the Greeks did, or to give special reverence to man as the image of God. The nude does not appeal to us at all. We have not, therefore, conceived an ideal type of human beauty. We have no Apollo Belvedere, we have no Venus of Melos. The outward man is not more important than other manifestations of outward nature—trees, rocks, wa-

---

15. "The School was established by Imperial Decree in October of 1888, and in December the site of the former Education Museum in Ueno Park was selected as its grounds. Students were screened, and in February of the following year classes began." See Uyeno Naoteru, ed., *Japanese Arts and Crafts in the Meiji Era* (Tokyo: Pan-Pacific Press, 1958), p. 30.

16. Although the word *"bijutsu"* was used as early as 1872 to translate "art" in the Japanese version of the rules for the exhibit of the Vienna Exposition of 1873 (in which we read that "in the West art indicates music, painting, sculpture, and poetry"), the word at the time still had a technical connotation. *"Bijutsu"* started to connote what is meant in the West by art only after Fenollosa explained the concept in his 1882 lecture to the members of the Ryūchikai, a lecture that is known today as "Bijutsu Shinsetsu" (An Explanation of Truth in Art). For the Japanese text of the classification of the objects exhibited at the Vienna Exposition see Aoki and Sakai, *Bijutsu,* pp. 403–405.

17. On this subject see Kambayashi Tsunemichi, "Okakura Tenshin Geijutsu Shisō," in Kambayashi Tsunemichi, ed., *Nihon no Bi no Katachi* (Kyoto: Sekai Shisō Sha, 1991), pp. 231–249.

18. "Another difference of practice in the East is also responsible for the way in which we approach nature. We do not draw from models, but from memory. The training of an artist is to memorize first from works of art themselves, and then from nature." See Okakura, "Nature in East Asiatic Painting," in *Collected English Writings,* vol. 2, p. 150.

ters. All outward nature is a mask. The trees which we see before us present the forces of nature struggling through them. It is not the branches and leaves merely which are important, but as in all nature, what is important is the joy of life coursing through these forms and striving for higher achievements. The Eastern artist tried to take from nature what was essential. He did not take in all details but chose what he thought the most important. His work was therefore an essay on nature instead of an imitation of nature.[19]

Already in 1879 an art society was formed, the Ryūchikai, which promoted a revival of the traditional heritage and the introduction of Japanese art to the West. Both Fenollosa and Okakura were frequent speakers at the society's meetings. And both were supporters of the idea that knowledge of the past should help develop a new style of Japanese painting that could be exported to the West. This is the main gist of a famous speech that Okakura gave to the members of another prominent art society: the Painting Appreciation Society (Kanga-kai).[20]

A Lecture to the Painting Appreciation Society
by Okakura Kakuzō

SINCE MR. FENOLLOSA has already given a very thorough speech on this subject,[21] the reason for me to deliver this lecture does not come from any partic-

19. Ibid., pp. 147–148.

20. "In 1884 another art group was formed under the name Painting Appreciation Society. Fenollosa was prominent in the founding of this new group, the principal purpose of which was to exhibit works of ancient art in private collections. Secondary functions of the group included lectures on art history and expert advice on the authenticity of paintings. . . . The Society was reorganized more efficiently the following year, with Kawase Hideji as President, Fenollosa as Director, and Okakura Kakuzō and Ariga Nagao— Fenollosa's students at Tokyo University—as assistants." See Uyeno, *Japanese Arts and Crafts in the Meiji Era,* pp. 17–18.

21. Okakura refers to a lecture delivered by Ernest Fenollosa in front of the same society, in which he described the relationship of Japanese and Western art with the metaphor of "the spring flowing from the same mountain spring and dividing in two."

ular opinion I might have.[22] As he mentioned, the art of the East and the art of the West seem to be two streams coming from the same wellspring. Since I want to elaborate this point a little further, I will be imposing on your attention a little while longer.

Now that people have finally started to pay attention to art, they have primarily deliberated over which to choose: the art of the East or the art of the West? This is actually exceedingly important in everyday life, in industry, and in trade. With relation to the construction of homes, for example, which way of building is superior or most fitting: the Eastern or the Western? Or we might think of the need to choose when it comes to interior design, the furnishings of a room, or clothing. People who are engaged in technology and trade will have to decide the direction of future business activities based on the answer to this question.

Because our group has been criticized as a radical Western school of art, as well as having been blamed as a stubborn Japanese school of art, I think it is of the utmost importance, now that I have examined the art of foreign countries on my recent trip,[23] that we establish the principles of the group. Therefore, I will attempt to argue about four kinds of propositions. There are roughly four positions on this topic:

1. Those who argue in favor of a pure Western art
2. Those who argue in favor of a pure Japanese art
3. Those who argue in favor of an equal status of Eastern and Western art—in other words, eclecticism
4. Those who argue in favor of a natural development of the arts

1

Today there is a struggle over customs and manners, institutions, food, and clothing, and in that struggle we are essentially lapping up the leftover drops of the West's drink. We talk of the West without ever discriminating between what is right or wrong, or suitable, and apply everything. We just hear the word "Orient" and immediately we imagine something vulgar. This attitude has now reached the realm of the arts and is starting to appear among the proponents of Western art. Their opinion is that all paintings except those of the West are deficient, and that any sculpture apart from Western sculpture is not worth the name. Now, there are a few questions I would like to address to these

---

22. Okakura Kakuzō (1862–1913) delivered this lecture on 6 November 1887, one month after the Japanese government had established the Tokyo School of Art (Tokyo Bijutsu Gakkō), known today as Tokyo Geijutsu Daigaku. The original text appears in Aoki Shigeru and Sakai Tadayasu, eds., *Bijutsu, NKST* 17 (Tokyo: Iwanami Shoten, 1989), pp. 85–91.

23. Okakura refers to his trip to Europe and the United States together with Fenollosa from October 1886 to October 1887 in order to get acquainted with matters of art education, the establishment of museums, and the preservation of art.

specialists. When today's fashionable scholars discuss the affairs of the world, they inevitably open their mouth with "in Europe it is like this, in America it is like that," and go on to cite examples from those countries. Even here, in a paper such as this, it is probably unusual that I do not insert the phrase "therefore, in the countries of Europe and America . . . "

In any case, where are these so-called people of Europe and America? The institutions and histories of each of the countries of Europe and America are different and their religion, customs, and manners are not uniform. There are cases where in one country something may be right while in another country it is wrong. If one just all-inclusively says "Europe" it sounds magnificent, but in fact there is no such thing as "Europe." West of the Ural Mountain range and east of the Atlantic Ocean lie the countries of Italy, Austria, France, Germany, and Great Britain, but so far no one has heard of a country called "Europe."

It is the same with art. It is easy to discuss "Western art" sweepingly. But if we start paying attention to detail, we need to go back to ancient Egypt and Assyria, think about the prosperity of ancient Greece, consider the imitative power of Rome, compare the downfall of the various countries during the Middle Ages, research the causes of the Italian Renaissance. Then, based on the characteristics of the many different countries of today, we would need to analyze and determine the similarities and differences, the superiorities and inferiorities, of their art. How can we consider the artistic process uniformly by reducing the entire phenomenon to the simple expression "Europe and America"?

Even looking at just the Venetian school's style of painting that rose up in the single city of Venice, Italy, if the works of such artists as Carlo Crivelli[24] or Basaiti[25] are compared with the works of Tintoretto,[26] you have the impression of looking at the works of completely different schools. The same applies to the minor works of the old Sukekiyo[27] and to the masterpieces of Isen[28] and Seisen,[29] although they all belonged to the same Kanō school. We could say the same for the other schools. Except that we, gentleman, having learned the Western style in Japan, usually seem to take that particular method as unique, thus rejecting all other schools of painting. When we call both the pictures of Chinese yams and the masterpieces by Hsia Kuei and Ma Yuan[30] "Chinese landscapes," it is the same as if we were discussing empresses Su-liu[31]

---

24. Carlo Crivelli (ca. 1430–ca. 1493).
25. Marco Basaiti (ca. 1470–after 1530).
26. Jacopo Robusti (1518–1594).
27. Unknown artist.
28. Kanō Naganobu (1775–1828).
29. Kanō Osanobu (1796–1846).
30. Both artists were active in the years 1190–1224.
31. Consort of Min Wang of Ch'i, Spring and Autumn period (772–481 B.C.).

and Wu-yen[32] together with empresses Yü-huan[33] and Fei-yen.[34] Italian art reached its pinnacle during the fifteenth century with its advanced design and refined methods—achievements that we should compare to the masterpieces of Tang and Sung China—the same time as our Kose and Takuma schools.[35]

These, however, are achievements of days long gone. The art of today has generally entered a period of decline. This is not my individual prejudice. The people of foreign countries themselves have all come to lament this. A Leonardo da Vinci, with his refinement and profundity, had the presence of a Li Kung-lin.[36] A Fra Angelico,[37] with his sublimity and elegance, was he not a reincarnation of Kasuga Motomitsu?[38] A Perugino,[39] with his purity, seems to capture the frame of Japanese apricot blossoms. A Botticelli,[40] with his warmth, is like spring clouds coming out of the mountaintop. With the excellence of a Raphael or the strength and vigor of a Michelangelo, it is like snaking through a land of dragons. They all arouse in us a precious sense of reverence.

But since people nowadays have idly become slaves to sketching, we are no more than the guardians of painting techniques. In recent years intellectuals from England and France have made great efforts to recover from the present decline, actually bringing some dignity to today's discussions on the arts. There are roughly two methods to elicit this recovery. One is to understand how masters in ancient times became true masters and, based on the principles of aesthetics, to plan an improvement of the field. The other is for the East, particularly Japan, to search for new artistic methods.

A famous artist by the name of Guillaume[41] who teaches at the School of Fine Arts in Paris, gave a remarkable lecture in the spring of this year. His main point was the following: "Since, until now, people who have talked about the arts have mainly focused on the artistic developments that occurred in European countries, the discussions have been tremendously prejudiced. In the future the debate on the arts will have to include the arts of the East. Western art has been discussed by focusing particularly on Greece. Eastern art will need to center on Japan."

---

32. Consort of Hsüan Wang of Ch'i, Spring and Autumn period.

33. Yang Yü-huan is the name of Yang Kuei-fei as a child. She was the favorite consort of Hsüan Tsung of the late Tang dynasty.

34. Chao Fei-yen was the consort of Hsiao-ch'eng Ti of the Former Han dynasty (33–7 B.C.). While the first two empresses were known for their particularly repulsive figure, the latter two were taken as symbols of feminine beauty.

35. These are schools of painters who belonged to a Buddhist temple and specialized in religious paintings.

36. Li kung-lin (1049–1106), Chinese calligrapher and painter.

37. Fra Angelico (ca. 1387–1455), Italian painter.

38. Fujiwara no Motomitsu (latter half of the eleventh century) was the originator of the Tosa school of painting.

39. Pietro di Cristofero Vanucci (ca. 1450–1523).

40. Sandro Botticelli (ca. 1444–1510).

41. Jean-Baptiste-Claude-Eugène Guillaume (1822–1905) taught at the École des Beaux-Arts.

If that is the case with scholars, the lay world too is going the same direction with museums in Berlin, London, and all the national art museums in America embarking upon the investment of remarkable amounts of capital in the acquisition of Japanese artifacts. We have reached a point where every art school in France, Germany, England, and Austria utilizes Japanese illustrated copybooks. When we think about this, we see that while the Japanese have been blindly clamoring for the arts of the West, over there in the West they do not know what to do with their artistic heritage and are turning to the East for an answer.

Someone who thinks of himself as an artist should pay attention to the present situation and avoid rushing to imitate the West. He should then go a step further and deny that the import of Western styles to Japan leads to a good result. Like other social phenomena, art is deeply rooted in history; it is not something that suddenly springs to life like the mythological plant.[42] The nature of art is born out of the characteristics of a race, the climate of the land, and the conditions of social institutions. It cannot be transplanted into a different era, nor can it be used in a different country, since it belongs exclusively to a specific time and people.

Even in Europe, Latin peoples developed an art that is different from that of Teutonic peoples. Regardless of their present close relationships in terms of communication and national boundaries, these cultures did not mingle; they did not even try to mingle. They built their countries and governed their families on the models of Greek and Roman civilizations. We organized our present culture on the basis of Indian and Chinese civilizations. When we look at history and judge from the perspective of the race, how there can be identity behind these civilizations?

If we truly want to produce "pure Western art" in Japan, unless we adopt Western customs in everything, from dying our beards and hair purple to making our eyes blue, we will be absolutely unable to acquire their spirit. This would be no different from discarding our national identity. The future civilizations of the whole world will not be dealing with worldly affairs in the same, equal way; they will strive to make this world perfect by preserving the characteristics of each country. It is like the crimson peach and the white plum that together make spring on earth.

When we wonder whether something from the West applies to our country or not, we should not rush at an indiscriminate and immediate implementation. To give an example from architecture, one might ask whether or not the construction of brick buildings fits the humidity and the heat of our region, and whether such structures would be feasible in a seismic area. Actually, this spring in northern Italy there was an earthquake that was a little larg-

---

42. Literally "like the *udumbara* plant"—referring to the plant of Indian mythology that blossoms once every three thousand years.

er than normal—in which buildings made of stone and brick were destroyed and no little damage was done to life and property. Immediately a delegate was dispatched by the Italian government with the task of investigating the situation and making a report. The man advised the government mainly about the danger of stone and brick constructions, insisted on the need to use wooden buildings in seismic areas, and placed a limit on the height of houses. In accordance with the report, the government proclaimed a series of regulations on building codes for those areas.

In Japan we should pay particular attention to this news. Should we again meet with great tremors of the magnitude of those that occurred during the Ansei era,[43] what sort of nightmares will our brick buildings be facing? People with some sense should think about all this. We should learn from this, since what I am saying is not limited to architecture but applies to other arts as well.

Now, taking this discussion a little bit further, let me test the suitability of so-called Western art for trade. In the future, arts and handicrafts will play the most important role in our country's foreign trade. Until the present day, the reason why Japan became known to the West was not because of the profundity of its science, nor because of the elaborateness of its machines, nor for its promptness in copying foreign customs and manners. Rather, it was on account of its natural ability to transcend the dust of worldly matters through the spirit of art. I have no doubt that Japan, without ever straying from its course, will reach the point where it successfully dictates the tastes of foreign markets, eventually climbing to the leading position in exports. But in order for art objects to become widespread in foreign markets, they must have the Japanese elegance. If instead these products are made according to Western forms, no one will take notice of them. The so-called painters in the Western style are not fit even to be considered for this purpose. Perhaps this is because over there they set up a distinction between pure art and applied arts, and the separation of artists from designers is especially strong. Since this is a very important matter, I should clarify it later to this assembly. For the preceding reasons, then, I cannot avoid the feeling that insistence on a purely Western style is extremely disadvantageous for Japan.

2

Now I must address and interrogate the proponents of a purely Japanese art. Although this group of people always uses the expression "Japanese uniqueness," I wonder where I can find such uniqueness. I do not know about the arts of ancient Japan. But when I think of the developments that art underwent

---

43. Between 1854 and 1860 there were thirteen sizable earthquakes in Japan, the largest of which devastated Edo and vicinity in 1855.

from the time it started to take shape up until now, there have been so many changes that it becomes impossible to establish a particular Japanese uniqueness. The art of the Tenpyō era[44] has its origin in Korea; the art of the Engi era[45] was influenced by the culture of the Tang dynasty. The prosperity of Higashiyama culture[46] is rooted in the Zen flavor of the Sung dynasty. The brilliance of Momoyama culture[47] is deeply related to the conquest of Korea and the trade with Holland. The Genroku[48] and Kyōhō[49] periods aped the style of Ming China, while the Tenmei[50] and Kansei[51] eras followed the elegance of the Manchu dynasty. Where do we find Japanese uniqueness?

Although the many art schools that have sprung up in Japan so far have loomed large in the East with their exquisite and extraordinary qualities, recently they have decayed and now lie in a pitiful state. There are some differences in the causes of this decadence, but for the most part they are similar to the reasons that have led the arts of the European nations into decline. To recover from this deterioration, a simple study of ancient art will only lead to a fall into imitation and will never open the doors to a genuine revival. The Japan of the future is not the Japan of the past. We should not look at today— such a strategic moment in the development of the world—with the same eyes that we used to watch over three hundred years of isolation from the world. If we are to cope with foreign demands in trade, we must understand how foreigners live and then adapt to the changing times. Therefore, those who simply preserve a "unique" art cannot survive in the present world.

3

These days some fairly astute people are insisting on the establishment of an "East-West art." This -ism without an -ism is grounded in the belief that people in today's society live at a transitional time in which the past has become meaningless and no definite goal has been set for the future. But as I have argued before, a combination of Eastern and Western art can only be imperfect, since, taken individually, each element is already useless: doubling them would only increase the damage. Proponents of this current, in art as well as other areas of society, are swayed back and forth, yesterday with the East, tomorrow the West, so that even at the economic level, losses are not indifferent. Should we be enduring this with a simple sigh?

---

44. Tenpyō era (729–766).
45. Engi era (901–922).
46. Second half of the fifteenth century.
47. Sixteenth century.
48. Genroku period (1688–1703).
49. Kyōhō period (1716–1735).
50. Tenmei era (1781–1788).
51. Kansei era (1789–1800).

I once paid a visit to a famous European painter, carrying with me the problem of art. At the end of our discussion he turned to me and said: "According to what I hear lately, everything in Japan is an imitation of English and German landscapes. Even in the field of religion, I hear that they have embraced the Christian faith. Well, now that I am face-to-face with a Japanese, I would like to recommend a type of faith: faith in self-confidence. Without such a faith, you will do no more than just imitate the outward look of others, and it will be hard to assume an absolutely outstanding national style."

This was a painful comment to hear, but what can we do about the truth of the Japanese hastiness to change? We must take a lesson from this.

4

Since the foregoing three arguments have ceased to have any force, we must turn to the fourth and last: the natural development of the arts. Natural development does not make any distinction between East and West. It is the ground for the true principle of art. If there is a logic, it follows it; if there is beauty, it investigates it. It is a development that goes along with the present situation and is based on traditional heritage. If there is a reason to consult an Italian master, go ahead and consult him. If you need to use the technique of oil painting, use it. But you also need to experiment and search for new techniques that are appropriate for the man of the future. This is a principle that members of the Painting Appreciation Society always take to heart and put into practice. Therefore, I cannot nurture any doubt about it.

To all of you—Japanese artists!—art is the common property of heaven and earth. How could there be any distinction between East and West? Sectarianism is the source of evil. If you open wide your heart and express the spirit that dwells in it, you will inevitably reach the depth of art. I truly believe it and harbor no doubts. The business of art is related on a high level to the honor of the empire, and it is associated on a lower level with the ups and downs of trade. Responsibility weighs heavily on you, gentlemen! This duty that all of you must fulfill will grow even heavier in the future. I beg you to cultivate this spirit as much as possible, and to look forward to its future full realization. I myself trust this, and do not doubt it. [*Dai Nihon Bijutsu Shinpō* 50, 31 December 1887]

FOUR

Idealism, Christianity, and Poetics
Ōnishi Hajime

ŌNISHI HAJIME (Sōzan) (1864–1900) graduated from the English Department of Dōshisha University in 1884. After pursuing graduate studies at Tokyo Imperial University, he taught logic, psychology, ethics, aesthetics, and Western philosophy at Waseda University from 1891 to 1898. In February 1898 he decided to leave for Germany where he studied at the University of Leipzig with the experimentalist aesthetician Wilhelm Wundt (1832–1920) and with Johannes Volkelt (1848–1930), the German developer of the notion of empathy *(Einfühlung)*. Forced to return to Japan for medical reasons after only two years, Ōnishi died on 2 November 1900 at the age of thirty-six. He left among his disciples such prominent aestheticians as Tsunashima Ryōsen (1873–1907) and Shimamura Hōgetsu (1871–1918).[1]

Tsunashima contributed to the image of his teacher as a leader in the philosophical world of the Meiji period by portraying him as a critical spirit who understood that the duty of philosophy during state formation was to provide a model of "teleological evolution" that would hasten the country's revival.[2] Tsunashima, therefore, called Ōnishi's program of purpose and progress a kind of "evolutionistic idealism"[3] that could not be viewed independently of Ōnishi's deep interest in Christian and Hegelian thought.

Ōnishi applied to Japanese poetry the same basic idea that Okakura Kakuzō had applied to Japanese painting: in order to be competitive with his Western colleagues, the Japanese poet must find a new form of expression that frees poetic tradition from its current stagnation. Ōnishi came to

---

1. See Kaneda Tamio, *Nihon Kindai Bigaku Josetsu* (Kyoto: Hōritsu Bunka Sha, 1990), pp. 38–41.

2. One of Ōnishi's most famous early essays was actually titled "Criticism" ("Hihyōron"). It appeared in the May 1888 issue of the journal *Kokumin no Tomo.*

3. Quoted in Hijikata Teiichi, "Bigakusha to Shite no Ōnishi Hajime: Waga Kuni Romanshugi Tetsugaku to Shinrigaku Bigaku no Seiritsu no Mondai ni Yoseru," in Hijikata Teiichi, ed., *Meiji Geijutsu, Bungaku Ronshū,* MBZ 79 (Tokyo: Chikuma Shobō, 1975), pp. 385–386.

this conclusion in the essay "Waka ni Shūkyō Nashi" (There Is no Religion in *Waka,* 1887) by comparing Japanese traditional poetry *(waka)* with Indian, Chinese, and European poetry. He found the local poetic production poor in religious overtones—mainly because of the formal constraints to which the thirty-one-syllable poem was subjected. He therefore advocated a freer poetic form as well as the need to embrace a religious system that would facilitate poets' spiritual expression. Since, in Ōnishi's opinion, Shinto and Buddhism had failed to do so, he believed that the resurgence of Christianity in Japan might well provide poets with a deeper sense of interiority. The essay, originally published in *Rikugo Zasshi,* a journal of Christian inspiration, is part of a series of articles written by Ōnishi between 1887 and 1889 on the relationship between religion and art.[4]

Ōnishi's definition of art redirected toward the inner spirituality of the poet what Toyama Masakazu had reserved for the exteriority of the artist— namely, the materialistic representation of social phenomena. Since Ōnishi was well read in aesthetic thought, he could not entrust the autonomy of artistic expression with the purposiveness of social commentaries. In the essay "Bijutsu to Shūkyō" (Art and Religion), which he published in *Rikugo Zasshi* in April 1888, Ōnishi made clear that his emphasis on the importance of religion in the achievement of a mature poetic expression did not mean that poetry was in the service of religion or any other ideological construct. Although the arts and religious systems might develop in history independently of each other, and although truth, good, and beauty are regulated by independent value systems, Ōnishi argued that the philosophical, ethical, and aesthetic moments are somehow united in the perfection of human nature. The contradictions of the three moments are resolved in the unified body of idealism and Christianity, as we can see from the following statement: "The philosopher, the poet, and the prophet are three brothers who have made the universe their house. Although their features differ from one another, they all penetrate the secrets of the same universe. We should call good, beauty, and truth the Trinity of the ideal world."[5] The contradiction between art and morality exists only within the framework of a finite, impure world in which art has not yet fulfilled its task of living in harmony with the "good" of the ethical world, thus reaching the heights of an "ideal world." According to Ōnishi, beauty in art must appeal to the ethical and religious feelings of the appreciator, as well as to his sense of taste.

In addition to Christianity and idealism, Ōnishi also turned to the po-

---

4. The essay is translated later in the chapter.
5. *Ōnishi Hakase Zenshū,* vol. 7: *Ronbun Oyobi Kashū* (Tokyo: Keiseisha Shoten, 1904), p. 402.

etics of the Edo period to explain what he believed to be the universality of poetic content. In 1892, while writing his "Essay on Poetics" (Shika Ron), Ōnishi was also working on a study of the scholar Kagawa Kageki (1768–1843) that he published as "Kagawa Kageki Okina no Karon" (The Poetic Treatises of Master Kagawa Kageki). In the essay "A Different Opinion on New Learning" (Niimanabi Iken, 1811), Kageki had taken issue with a major scholar of the Edo period, Kamo no Mabuchi (1697–1769). Kageki's polemical treatise followed an acrimonious criticism that two major disciples of Mabuchi, Katō Chikage (1735–1808) and Murata Harumi (1746–1811), had leveled against several poems by Kageki. The resulting controversy was named after Chikage and Harumi's coauthored essay, "The Nature of the Brush" (Fude no Saga, 1802), in which Kageki was attacked for his excessive use of popular expressions (zoku) in a medium such as waka, which, according to an orthodox view, was supposed to set standards of refinement (ga).[6]

According to Kageki, the rhythm (shirabe) of poetry was the direct voice of human "sincerity" (magokoro),[7] the rhythmic expression of a cosmic totality (ametsuchi no shirabe), the sound of a wind blowing in the sky, a form that took different shapes according to the objects encountered in its path. The rhythm of the truth of cosmic/human expression came into being naturally (onozukara) without the help of consciousness (kokoro) or culture (takumeru ga gotoku, kazareru ga gotoku). As Kageki had argued in his Summary of Poetics (Kagaku Teiyō), poetry must preserve in its expression the freedom of the cosmic rhythm (jinen no shirabe) so as to incorporate in its language the form of what comes into being spontaneously (jinen no sugata). The mediation between cosmic and individual rhythm takes place at the level of the human body (shinjin) whose immersion in the reality of nature (san'ya kaihin ni toji) leads to the verbal articulation of the immediacy of experience.[8]

Ōnishi praised Kageki's attempts at freeing poetry from the restrictions of form and making it a medium suitable to the expression of daily and popular emotions.[9] His reevaluation of Kageki did not, however, blind him to the weaknesses of Kageki's thought, which, obviously, could not take ad-

---

6. For an overview of the "Fude no Saga" controversy see Roger K. Thomas, "'High' Versus 'Low': The Fude no Saga Controversy and Bakumatsu Poetics," Monumenta Nipponica 49(4) (Winter 1994):455–469.

7. In another major poetic treatise, A Summary of Poetics (Kagaku Teiyō), Kageki argued that successful poetry erased all gaps between "cosmic rhythm" (ametsuchi no shirabe) and the "individual rhythm of expression" (kan). See Nakamura Yukihiko, ed., Kinsei Bungaku Ronshū, NKBT 94 (Tokyo: Iwanami Shoten, 1966), p. 146.

8. Ibid., p. 151 and p. 155.

9. Ōnishi Hakase Zenshū, vol. 7, p. 500.

vantage of the knowledge derived from Western aesthetics. Ōnishi was now fully aware that it was no longer possible to follow Kageki's strategy and thus collapse into the poetic act the diverse moments of the self-engendering process of nature, its perception in human experience, and its articulation in poetic expression. "Sincerity" *(magokoro)* and "rhythm" *(shirabe),* content and form, could hardly be explained as the vague workings of nature. Simply put, Kageki was lacking the concept of "art." Ōnishi was taking issue with the fact that Kageki had not paid enough attention to the specific components of poetry: matter *(busshitsu),* rules of composition *(hōsoku),* and form *(shisō).* [10]

In an article published in the December 1888 issue of *Jogaku Zasshi,* Ōnishi pointed out that so long as foreigners considered as Japanese art the so-called Japanese crafts of ceramics, lacquerwork, fans, screens, and textiles, the Japanese had no reason to feel proud of their artistic heritage. It was not enough that foreigners regarded Japan as "an artistic country," since such a statement was not supported by any theoretical proof or explanation. The major problem, according to Ōnishi, was Japan's lack of a truly aesthetic education "based on the principles of the philosophy of art," one that would allow the creation of a new, original art of which to be proud. [11]

Between 1895 and 1897, Ōnishi wrote a series of articles on aesthetics that were clearly geared toward a philosophical analysis of the field. In "The Heart of External Beauty and Physical Sensation" (Kanbishin to Nikukan), published in the August 1895 issue of *Rikugo Zasshi,* he introduced the sensualist school of aesthetics. [12] A month later he published "On Aesthetic Senses" (Shinbiteki Kankan wo Ronzu), an article in which he analyzed the reasons behind the privileging of hearing and sight in the perception of beauty, commenting upon theories advanced by earlier aestheticians such as Schiller, Hegel, Hartmann, Spencer, Allen, and Guyau. [13] Moreover, in "An Outline of Modern Aesthetic Thought" (Kinsei Bigaku Shisō Ippan), published in *Waseda Literature (Waseda Bungaku)* in 1897, he traced the major differences between Hegel's idealistic approach to aesthetics and the experimental psychological approach. [14]

Ōnishi paved the way to the professional study of aesthetics in Japanese academia by training and sponsoring those who would become the major

10. Ibid., pp. 528–534. See also Yamamoto Masao, *Tōzai Geijutsu Seishin no Dentō to Kōryū* (Tokyo: Risōsha, 1965), pp. 65–66.

11. The essay, titled "Is the Japanese Endowed with an Artistic Sense?" (Nihonjin wa Bijutsushin ni Tomeru Kana), appears in *Ōnishi Hakase Zenshū,* vol. 7, pp. 414–427.

12. *Ōnishi Hakase Zenshū,* vol. 6: *Shichō Hyōron* (Tokyo: Keiseisha Shoten, 1905), pp. 324–333.

13. *Ōnishi Hakase Zenshū,* vol. 7, pp. 324–344.

14. Ibid., pp. 344–370.

players in the field. Although the subject of "aesthetics" *(shinbigaku)* had been included in the curriculum of Tokyo Imperial University since 1881, the first lectures on aesthetics were delivered by Fenollosa in 1882 as part of his course on Western philosophy. Courses on aesthetics were offered by Toyama Masakazu, as well, who was appointed professor in 1877, the same year that Tokyo University was founded. But considering the fact that Toyama was also in charge of courses in English, philosophy, psychology, and, after 1893, sociology, we may surmise that aesthetics was not the subject of Toyama's undivided attention. The only proof of Toyama's lectures on aesthetics is the title of the textbook he used in his courses: Herbert Spencer's *Philosophy of Style.*[15]

The course on aesthetics finally became independent in 1886, when it was entrusted to Professor George William Knox (1853–1912), the successor of Fenollosa after the latter's retirement in that year. From 1887 to 1892 the appointment went to Ludwig Busse (1862–1907) and from 1893 to 1914 to the Russian Raphael von Koeber (1848–1923). In 1900, Tokyo Imperial University made the first tenured appointment in aesthetics by giving the chair to Ōtsuka Yasuji (1868–1931), who had previously lectured on the aesthetics of Eduard von Hartmann at Waseda University upon the recommendation of Ōnishi Hajime. Ōtsuka remained in his post until he retired in 1929.

There Is No Religion in *Waka*
by Ōnishi Hajime

LISTENING TO THE SOUND of the waves breaking against the bottom of the Whitby monastery which stood at the top of the cliff, while looking in the distance at the horizon on the German sea, that famous Caedmon[16] composed the

---

15. Kaneda, *Nihon Kindai Bigaku Josetsu,* p. 33.

16. Caedmon (fl. 670), English poet, entered the monastery of Streaneshalch between 658 and 680. Although he was originally thought to be the author of long scriptural poems, such as *Genesis, Exodus, Daniel,* and *Christ and Satan,* modern scholarship only attributes to him the composition of the short "Hymn of Creation" cited by Bede.

most ancient English poems, singing the origin of heaven and earth, and celebrating the history of the Jewish people.[17] Since then, a common thread has clearly run through English poetry up to the elegant and delicate poetry of Wordsworth[18] and Tennyson[19] of modern times: religious thought.

The *Short History of English Literature* says: "How could English literature decline? It certainly revived in poetry, and the first poems of this revival were inevitably related to religion." This is something on which everyone even only slightly acquainted with English literature will agree. Now, when I compare our native poetic production with English poetry, I must reach the unpleasant conclusion that in *waka* there is no religion. Starting from the ancient poems that appear in the *Record of Ancient Matters*[20] and in the *Chronicles of Japan*,[21] down to the most beloved poetry of the present time by the school of Kagawa Kageki,[22] how much religious thought can we see in those poems? Of course in the ancient poetry prior to the *Ten Thousand Leaves*,[23] there is no poem that does not celebrate a deity. Among the eight collections of imperial poetry,[24] as well, there is none that has no Shinto hymns.[25] But do these hymns sufficiently cultivate a religious sentiment?

Let's take a look, for example, at the section of Shinto hymns from the *New Collection of Ancient and Modern Times*.[26] Let us begin with the very first poem, which, no matter what, one cannot overlook:

Shirurame ya   Do you realize it?
Kyō no ne no hi no   The lovable young pine tree
Himekomatsu   That you pulled on this day of the rat

---

17. The original text of this essay, "Waka ni Shūkyō Nashi," appears in Ōnishi Hajime, *Ōnishi Hakase Zenshū*, vol. 7, pp. 403–414. *Waka* is the Japanese thirty-one-syllable poem.

18. William Wordsworth (1770–1850) is the author of the *Lyric Ballads* (1798), a landmark in the history of English romanticism.

19. Alfred Tennyson (1809–1892), English poet.

20. *Kojiki* (712).

21. *Nihongi* (720).

22. Kagawa Kageki (1768–1843) argued that poetry should reflect the true feeling of the poet, rather than being concerned with rhetorical rules.

23. *Man'yōshū* (756).

24. *Hachidaishū* includes the *Collection of Ancient and Modern Times* (*Kokinshū*, 905), the *Later Collection* (*Gosenshū*, 951), the *Collection of Gleanings* (*Shūishū*, ca. 986), the *Later Collection of Gleanings* (*Goshūishū*, 1086), the *Collection of Golden Leaves* (*Kin'yōshū*, 1124–1127), the *Collection of Verbal Flowers* (*Shikashū*, 1151–1154), the *Collection of a Thousand Years* (*Senzaishū*, 1188), and the *New Collection of Ancient and Modern Times* (*Shinkokinshū*, 1206). For basic information on *waka* I have relied on Robert H. Brower and Earl Miner, *Japanese Court Poetry* (Stanford: Stanford University Press, 1961).

25. In fact the practice of including an entire section on Shinto hymns (*jingika*) in imperial collections started from the *Goshūishū*. These poems include oracles and poems composed on the occasion of Shinto festivals at Shinto shrines.

26. The compilation of the *Shinkokinshū* was ordered in 1201 by ex-Emperor Go-Toba; it was compiled by Fujiwara Teika, Fujiwara Ariie, Fujiwara Ietaka, the priest Jakuren, Minamoto Michitomo, and Asukai Masatsune.

| Oimu sue made | Will prosper, growing |
| Sakayubeshi to wa | Until the end of its long days.[27] |

Although I try hard to bear in mind the element of religious feeling in interpreting the meaning of this poem, no matter how I proceed in my analysis I am unable to find the slightest presence of religious thought in it. Generally speaking, it is the same with the Shinto hymns of the *Later Collection of Gleanings*[28] and the *Collection of a Thousand Years.*[29] Moreover, it is not that there are no poems dealing with matters related to the deities beside the Shinto hymns. These poems, however, are not any different from the hymns. In fact, among them there are poems that truly hurt my feelings, such as the following from the *Collection of Ancient and Modern Times:*[30]

Tamuke ni wa	Instead of the usual offerings
Tsuzuri no sode mo	I should make cloth strips
Kirubeki ni	Cutting the sleeves of this priest's garb:
Momiji ni akeru	Perhaps the god will return them,
Kami ya kaesamu	He who has got tired of beautiful maple leaves.[31]

Each time I read this poem I cannot help feeling how ridiculously childish is the poet's thought vis-à-vis god. Poems like this do not express a truly religious feeling. They only relate the imagination of an interesting, amusing poet.

In the *Later Collection*[32] there is a poem preceded by this note: "A woman came to hate a man and—I wonder what she might have thought—she composed the following poem:"

Chihayaburu	We are not
Kami ni mo aranu	Almighty gods,
Waga naka no	And yet our relationship
Kumoi haruka ni	Grows increasingly far,
Nari mo yuku kana	Far in the sky.[33]

---

27. *Shinkokinshū* 19:1852. See Kubota Jun, ed., *Shinkokin Waka Shū, Ge,* SNKS 30 (Tokyo: Shinchōsha, 1979), p. 283. The poem refers to the ancient Japanese custom of pulling young pine trees and picking up young herbs on the new year's first day of the rat. A note says that this poem came in a dream to the priest of the Hiyoshi shrine on the day that he went to the hill behind the shrine to pull a young pine tree. With this poem the god of Hiyoshi offers his protection to the shrine and its priest.

28. The *Goshūishū* was ordered in 1075 by Emperor Shirakawa; it was compiled by Fujiwara Michitoshi.

29. The *Senzaishū* was ordered in 1183 by ex-Emperor Go-Shirakawa; it was compiled by Fujiwara Shunzei.

30. The *Kokinshū* was ordered by Emperor Daigo and completed ca. 905; it was compiled by Ki no Tsurayuki, Ki no Tomonori, Ōshikōchi no Mitsune, and Mibu no Tadamine.

31. *Kokinshū* 9:421. The poem is attributed to Sosei Hōshi. See Okumura Tsuneya, ed., *Kokin Waka Shū,* SNKS 19 (Tokyo: Shinchōsha, 1978), p. 163.

32. The *Gosenshū* was ordered in 951 by Emperor Murakami; it was compiled by the so-called Five Poets of the Pear Jar Room: Ōnakatomi Yoshinobu, Kiyowara Motosuke, Minamoto Shitagō, Ki no Tokibumi, and Sakanoe Mochiki.

33. *Gosenshū* 14:1025. See Kubota Jun and Kawamura Teruo, eds., *Gappon Hachidaishū* (Tokyo: Miyai Shoten, 1986), p. 101.

Waka usually present not only the god of thunder, to which this poem refers,[34] but all deities, no matter which, as useless. To cite an extreme example, there are songs saying that if the prayer for love that I hang on the fence of a Shinto shrine fails to achieve the result I hope for, then god's existence is useless. How can poems like these inspire pious feelings?

Someone might argue that our ancestors worshiped a million deities and there is no reason at all to be skeptical about the childishness of thoughts about god in *waka*—certainly a reasonable argument. Yet our traditional, national thought concerning the deities is not simply vulgar and childish. You can also find very noble examples. As we can see from the following passage, for instance, we might say that what contains religious thought steps out into the faraway field of Buddhism.

We read in the *Jeweled Comb Basket:*[35] "High above, the ranks are high. It knows every country and province. It forces people to obedience and it is respected by everybody in the world. Everyone there lives in affluence and happiness. On a lower level, they eat without ever starving. They have warm clothes. They live in peace. Here you have the blessing of your lord, the blessing of the ancestors, the blessing of father and mother. When you investigate the origin of all things, starting from those mentioned above, you will find there is nothing that exists in the world which is not the spirit of the gods. However, people of this world do not go to the trouble of revering the gods. It has become customary not to keep the gods in one's heart, to forget them, never thinking of the benevolence of lord and ancestors. Everybody forgets about the spirit of the gods. They do not pay any attention to the gods—not a very wise thing to do! People do not realize it; they do not think about it. They consider the deities an alien entity. How blasphemous to see that if the prayer they only occasionally address to the god is not realized, they begin hating the deity. When we are in god's debt from the time we are born until the time we die, how can we begrudge a deity for a trifle that does not suit our wishes? How can we think that because our prayer has gone unanswered, it is useless to revere the gods?"

We also read in a variant version of the *Jeweled Comb Box:*[36] "There are many people who think that we are wasting too much money on useless religious rites, but this is a mistake. Without the blessings and the protection of the gods, nothing good would happen in this world. The more we are in distress

---

34. There is a pun in the poem according to the double meaning of *"naru"*: to become and to reverberate. The thunder is literally "the reverberating god" (*narukami*).

35. Motoori Norinaga (1730–1801) wrote *Tamakatsuma* from 1794 until his death. The original text appears in Yoshikawa Kōjirō, Satake Akihiro, and Hino Tatsuo, eds., *Motoori Norinaga,* NST 40 (Tokyo: Iwanami Shoten, 1978), p. 480.

36. Motoori Norinaga wrote the *Hihon Tamakushige* (Secret Jeweled Comb Box) in 1787. The original text appears in Ōkubo Tadashi, ed., *Motoori Norinaga Zenshū,* vol. 8 (Tokyo: Chikuma Shobō, 1972), pp. 368–369.

and hardships, the more deeply we must worship the gods. Also wrong is the thought that to perform as elegant actors during these religious rites, to drink rice wine and have a good time, are useless endeavors. You should not only worship the deity with offerings. The god also rejoices at the thought that people are eating and drinking, entertaining themselves, and having a good time."

Although these are the words of a rare and farsighted man, Motoori Norinaga, he was not the only one to harbor such thoughts in his mind. At least that much thought existed at the time. But when I think of poetry, I do not see even that much. Therefore, I can safely assert that in our country ancient Shintoism did not have the power to breathe religious life into *waka*.

As for the influence exerted by Buddhism on *waka*, we can say that it is extremely extensive. Yet we can easily exhaust this great influence in one word and summarize it in a single thought: to realize the wretchedness of this life, to abhor it, and to escape from it. We still encounter this thought, which came down from the poetry of the Man'yō period,[37] in the poetry of modern times, to the point of being nauseated. I only wish we were about to abhor and escape from this thought!

We can say that poetry such as that appearing in the eighteenth roll of the *Collection of Ancient and Modern Times* overflows with the kind of Buddhist thought mentioned above. Although there are several masterpieces in this roll that I often love to recite, I will concentrate on an analogous poem from a later collection. I will take the first poem opening the section on "Buddhist Poems" of the *Collection of a Thousand Years*:

Koko ni kie	This body of mine
Kashiko ni musubu	Spins in this floating world
Mizu no awa no	Where bubbles
Ukiyo ni meguru	Are forming here,
Mi ni koso arikere	Disappearing there.[38]

Although there are many Buddhist poems in the *Later Collection of Gleanings* and in the *New Collection of Ancient and Modern Times,* if you read the foregoing poem you can guess all the rest. If this is the case, I wonder how much this solitary thought that Buddhism injected into *waka* nurtured a religious sentiment in our nation. I seriously doubt that we can call it religious thought. I am truly skeptical that the Buddhist *waka* has the power to make its reader a devout believer in the Buddha and make him find delight in nirvana. How does such thought as Buddhist pessimism foster the vitality of our nation? On the contrary, I wonder whether this thought does not make our nation stagnant. How much lofty and subtle thought can we find in a genre that became the amusement of monks during their leisurely hours? Very little, I am afraid. Therefore, I assert that Buddhism does not pour any effective religious thought in *waka*.

---

37. The period covered by the poems that appear in *Ten Thousand Leaves:* approximately 347–759.
38. *Senzaishū* 19:1202. See Kubota Jun, ed., *Senzai Waka Shū* (Tokyo: Iwanami Shoten, 1986), p. 280.

When we compare Indian poetry to *waka,* we ought to see a big difference between them. We should be able to recognize, too, that the statement contending there is no religion in *waka* is not exaggerated. The following poems are folk songs of the Tamil people who live in the south of India:

1

My God is not a chiselled stone,
Or lime, so bright and white:
Nor is he cleaned with tamarind,
Like images of bronze.

2

I cannot worship such as these,
But loudly make my boast
That in my heart I place the feet,
The golden feet of God.

3

If he be mine what can I need?
My God is everywhere.
Within, beyond man's highest word,
My God existeth still.

4

In sacred books, in darkest night,
In deepest, bluest sky,
In those who know the truth, and in
The faithful few on earth;—

5

My God is found in all of these,
But can the Deity
Descend to images of stone
Or copper dark and red?[39]

Again, the following poem also belongs to the same genre:

God is the one great *all.* Can such as He,
Eternal Being, see our praise or prayer
In outward acts? If thou wouldst worship Him,
Lift up thy heart—in spirit serve thy God.

---

39. I used Charles Gover's original translation: "True Knowledge," in Charles E. Gover, *The Folk-Songs of Southern India* (Madras: South India Saiva Siddhanta, 1959; 1st ed., 1871), pp. 155–156.

Some bow themselves, lie prostrate on the earth,
In meditation spend their days. Some tell
Their beads in prayers, or mantras whisper oft,
Pay dues at sacred shrines. All this is nought.
External objects cannot help. They bring
Great grief to those who trust them. Life is thine
And endless bliss, if thou wilt look within . . . [40]

Clearly, all the poems mentioned here sing religious thought, which is quite common for the people of India. The neighboring northeastern nations could not attain the same degree of loftiness and religiosity. From this point of view, does *waka* compare favorably with Chinese poetry?

Not only is *waka* not religious, even from the perspective of philosophical thought, it is extremely poor. This is a point in which *waka* is definitely inferior to Chinese poetry. You will never see in *waka* the noble taste and lofty thought that you find, for example, in the following poem:

With time to spare, no matter what I do, my heart is calm, at ease.
Late I sleep in the morning: when I wake up, from the eastern window the sun
    I see already red.
Everything I observe with no worry; with everything I am satisfied.
With everybody else I share the pleasure of the seasons.
My concerns are outside the present world of forms.
I think I need to be like a cloud whose form is changed by the wind.
Do not indulge in riches, find pleasure in poverty.
If a man reaches that stage, you can call him a hero![41]

Moreover, the following poem is remarkably influenced by Buddhist doctrines and yet it is never dull:

Human life has no roots nor stem; it is dust blown on the street by the wind.
It spins, scattering under the wind; this body is no longer permanent.
Born on earth, we become brothers; it is only a relationship of bones and flesh.
If happiness comes, happiness you take; when wine is available, you gather the
    neighbors.
Fulfilling years do not pile forever; the same day knows no two mornings.
Catch the time, and yet strive after duties; time does not wait for people.[42]

---

40. The original translation appears with the title "The True God," ibid., pp. 151–152.

41. Titled "Impromptu on an Autumn Day," this poem was written by the philosopher Ch'eng Hao (1032–1085). See Imazeki Tenpō and Karashima Takeshi, eds., *Sōshi Sen, KT* 16 (Tokyo: Shūeisha, 1966), pp. 311–312.

42. Titled "A Miscellaneous Poem," this is the work of T'ao Ch'ien (365–427). See Hoshikawa Kyotaka, ed., *Koshigen, Ge, KT* 5 (Tokyo: Shūeisha, 1965), p. 102.

I personally think that the following poem from the *Collection of Ancient and Modern Times* is the most philosophical composition you can find in *waka*:

Yo no naka wa	What is contained in this world—
Yume ka utsutsu ka	Is it dream or reality?
Utsutsu to mo	I do not know whether it is
Yume to mo shirazu	Reality or dream,
Arite nakereba	Since I am and I am not.[43]

This poem reminds me of what the Greek philosopher Heraclitus[44] said about everything roaming between life and death, wandering in being and not-being.

As I argued before, *waka* is not a product conveying any religious or philosophical thought. It does not go beyond simply stating that I am moved by the moon, I am moved by the cherry blossoms, I long for my beloved. What we should call the marrow of *waka* does not exceed the single notion of "pathos" *(aware)*. Although it is not easy to explain what this notion of "pathos" is about, if we analyze it we will notice that it is made of two elements. The first is the element of love for beauty; the other is grief over the ephemerality of beauty. Water, the moon, flowers, the grass, birds, insects— each of them has beauty, not to mention the most outstanding among all creatures, the human being. Although everything in the world is endowed with beauty, beauty itself does not last. Consider the poem:

Utsusemi no	Do not they look like this world of ours—
Yo ni mo nitaru ka	A cast-off shell?
Sakurabana	Cherry blossoms,
Saku to mishima ni	As soon as we see them blooming
Katsu chirinikeri	They immediately scatter.[45]

This poem well represents the prosperity and decline of all things. The poets of our country viewed the entire world with this feeling of *aware*.

As I mentioned before, *waka* poetry is truly deficient from the religious point of view. And neither Shintoism nor Buddhism, which are so common in our country, has made up for this deficiency. The reintroduction of Christianity, together with the recent importation to our country of Western culture and institutions, are on the verge of effecting great changes. Will Christianity remedy this lack that we find in *waka*? Will Christianity provide religious life to our national literature? Will Christianity, as a result, renew our society? This is a problem that belongs to the future history of Japanese literature. We

---

43. *Kokinshū* 18:942; Okumura, *Kokin Waka Shū*, p. 320.

44. Heraclitus of Ephesus (fl. 500 B.C.), a philosopher who maintained that all things are in a state of flux (Gk.: *panta rhei*).

45. *Kokinshū* 2:73; Okumura, *Kokin Waka Shū*, p. 49.

are not yet in a position to judge it. Perhaps our descendants will be able to decide. But is there no sign at the present time that would allow us to predict the future?

Waka should not only reform its spirit, but also renew its form. What can you say in the small frame of thirty-one syllables divided into verses of five and seven syllables each? We should say that *waka* is a kind of old-fashioned poetic form. Authentic poetic thought (poetry) is not found in *waka*, but rather in the fashionable tunes of the city. Nowadays, the genuine poets of our country are not the national scholars who string particles together, but those authors of folk songs and limericks who delight men and women, young and old, with their poetic eulogies of the streets.

The field of national literature has been waiting a long time for a natural talent in poetry who is able to devise new directions. I do not care a hang, of course, for those who, like our antiquated national scholars, strictly adhere to the styles of the *Collection of Ten Thousand Leaves* and the *Collection of Ancient and Modern Times*. Yet I do not dare to say that the study of native *waka* is useless. On the contrary, I lament the fact that scholars of today are getting estranged from *waka*. Would it be possible for a dignified university graduate not to have read the *Collection of Ancient and Modern Times*?

I cannot consider the idea of discarding endeavors such as poetry on the grounds that the world is pursuing a utilitarian path. Rarely do the values of today's society extend to poetical taste. Generally speaking, they are rather prosaic. Not even the countries of Europe and America, which fight for the beauty of culture, can escape this unfortunate situation. In a poem lamenting the conventions of his time, Wordsworth says:

> The world is too much with us; late and soon,
> Getting and spending, we lay waste our powers:
> Little we see in Nature that is ours;
> We have given our hearts away, a sordid boon!
> The sea that bares her bosom to the moon;
> The winds that will be howling at all hours,
> And are up-gathered now like sleeping flowers;
> For this, for everything, we are out of tune;
> It moves us not.—Great God! I'd rather be
> A Pagan suckled in a creed outworn;
> So might I, standing on this pleasant lea,
> Have glimpses that would make me less forlorn;
> Have sight of Proteus rising from the sea;
> Or hear old Triton blow his wreathed horn.[46]

---

46. Ōnishi provides a Japanese version of "The World Is Too Much with Us; Late and Soon" by William Wordsworth. See Paul D. Sheats, ed., *The Poetical Works of Wordsworth* (Boston: Houghton Mifflin, 1982), p. 349.

Every time I read this outstanding poem, a flood of emotions gushes forth in my chest. Every time I read this poem, I reflect upon the present circumstances of our nation, and at the bottom of my heart I am overwhelmed by deep emotions. Isn't the life of businessmen and politicians poor in aesthetic values? Shouldn't scholars and educators, who are responsible for this deficiency, share some of the same deep feelings of Wordsworth? I cannot but criticize present-day education and say how unreasonably tasteless it is. [*Rikugo Zasshi* 76, April 1887]

FIVE

The Aesthetics of the Nation
Takayama Chogyū

THE YEAR 1899 was momentous for the field of Japanese aesthetics. In June, Mori Ōgai published his translation of Eduard von Hartmann's *Philosophy of Art (Shinbiron)*. Six months later, Takayama Chogyū (or Rinjirō, 1871–1902) published his *Modern Aesthetics (Kinsei Bigaku),* soon to become a best-seller in Japan. Based on the work of von Hartmann, the *Critical History of Aesthetics (Kritische Geschichte der Ästhetik)* of Max Schasler (1819–1879), and the *History of Aesthetics as Philosophical Science (Geschichte der Ästhetik als Philosophischer Wissenschaft)* of Robert Zimmermann (1824–1898), Chogyū's work convinced Japanese readers of the need to set up a field of aesthetics independent from the commonly known field of art criticism.

With Fenollosa, for example, knowledge of the philosophy of art was deemed necessary for the actual practice of art criticism. Ernest Fenollosa and Okakura Kakuzō were instrumental in giving the field of art autonomy with respect to the pragmatic views of art prior to the Meiji period. They did not, however, keep the field of aesthetics separate from the pragmatics of aesthetic judgment applied to concrete forms of art. A more academic approach to aesthetics—in which the subject was studied for the sake of aesthetics itself rather than as a means toward something else—started only with the institutionalization of aesthetics in the academic world with the appointments of Ōtsuka Yasuji at Tokyo Imperial University in 1900 and Fukada Yasukazu at Kyoto Imperial University in 1910. Chogyū's work freed the aesthetic field from the anxiety of having to come up with standards of value immediately applicable to specific works of art.

Chogyū's interest in aesthetics can already be seen from the topic of his research as a graduate student at Tokyo Imperial University: "aesthetics in general and the position of Japan, with regard to the literature on the arts, as compared to the world." In April 1898, he replaced Ōnishi Ha-

jime as a lecturer in aesthetics at Waseda University after Ōnishi's departure for Europe. Chogyū was chosen by the Ministry of Education to travel to Europe in order to further his knowledge of the discipline, but he
was forced to decline on account of poor health. Instead he lectured, in
1901, at Tokyo Imperial University on "the value of Japanese art." In the
same year he received his doctorate with a dissertation on the art of the
Nara period.[1]

The literary historian Hijikata Teiichi has divided the writings of Takayama Chogyū into three periods: during the years 1891–1896, Chogyū
devoted his energies mainly to subjects of an ethical nature, inquiring as to
how to fulfill the good while searching for people's happiness; between
1897 and 1900, he concentrated on articles on nationalism and the need
for the formation of a national spirit for the ultimate benefit of the state;
after 1901 he wrote about his religious awakening, a trend that continued
until his death. The last period corresponds mainly to the time of his production of articles on aesthetics under the strong influence of Nietzsche's
philosophy.[2]

This interest in aesthetics led Chogyū to write a series of articles on the
philosophy of art in which he pointed out that aesthetics was less a science
to be mastered than an art to be lived. This is the topic of one of his major
essays, "A Debate on the Aesthetic Life" (Biteki Seikatsu wo Ronzu), which
he published in the journal Taiyō in June 1901. In it Chogyū argued that
the purpose of life is happiness—a fulfillment of the instincts to be reached
by living aesthetically and independently from the value of moral judgment. As he put it at the beginning of the essay: "If someone should approach me and ask what I mean by 'aesthetic life,' I would answer that it
is service to life and body, which are far superior to food and clothing."[3]
Such a fulfillment of instinctual desires, however, requires the overcoming
of all moral standards, whether past or present, as Chogyū pointed out in
his total relativization of traditional moral values. See, for example, the following lengthy quotation:

> Morality foresees the highest good. The "highest good" is my ideal notion
> of what is the highest purpose of human behavior. The action that is of

1. Watanabe Kazuyasu, *Meiji Shisō Shi: Jukyōteki Dentō to Kindai Ninshiki Ron* (Tokyo: Perikansha, 1978), pp. 210–211.

2. Hijikata Teiichi, *Kindai Nihon Bungaku Hyōron Shi* (Tokyo: Hōsei Daigaku Shuppankyoku, 1973), p. 22.

3. *Takayama Chogyū Shū, Anezaki Chōfū Shū, Sasakawa Rinpū Shū, GNBZ* 13 (Tokyo: Kaizōsha, 1956), p. 206.

much benefit to the realization of the highest good is called "good." The action that hinders it is called "evil." Although scholars have advanced different theories regarding the content of the highest good, there is one thing that is shared by all ages and has never changed: Moral judgment is based on this foundation. Therefore, we can say that all different kinds of moral systems, as far as their formation is concerned, inevitably are provided with at least two requirements. What are these requirements? One is the awareness of the idea of the highest good. The other is the matching of the action's purpose with the action's external manifestation, following this awareness. If there is a will to realize the highest good, how can this not be accompanied by a corresponding action? Or if the action truly fulfills the good, how can there not be a heart actually doing good? Shouldn't we be calling moral values the perfection of intention and action?

If I put it in these terms, I am confronted with a doubt. If we take as an example the loyal samurai of the past who commits suicide for his lord and his country, or the filial son and faithful wife who devote themselves to father and husband, do their acts of loyalty contain the idea of the highest good? Does their behavior conform to that idea? To put it differently, did they think that to act for lord and country was the ideal and to die was a means to achieve that ideal? Or did they believe that the resulting benefit to father and husband was the highest good and that devotion was their duty? Or should we take this to mean that beside the concrete concepts of lord, country, father, and husband, they recognized abstract moral principles such as filial piety and chastity, and that they abode by these principles? If we are not allowed this interpretation, is it not pointless to speak of loyalty, filial piety, and chastity in terms of moral values?

I do not wish to pursue this interpretation. What notion of "highest good" was there in Nankō[4] when he died on the battlefield at Minatogawa? Why was there a distinction in his mind between purpose and means? He was simply carried away with emotion for one who once had been his lord and emperor, the forever humble and loyal servant who laid down his life for his lord! To die for his lord was for that general the supreme fulfillment of his life. To talk about this fulfillment, however, is not to talk about ethics; it was simply the general's private state of mind.

What notion of "highest good" was in Lord Sugawara,[5] when he wor-

---

4. Honorific name of Kusunoki Masashige (1294–1336), a loyalist general and supporter of Emperor Go-Daigo during the fights against the Kamakura shogunate. A hero of the Kemmu imperial restoration, he was eventually defeated by the troops of the shogun Ashikaga Takauji and lost his life at the battle of Minatogawa.

5. Sugawara no Michizane (845–903) was the minister of the right during the reign of Emperor Daigo. He died in exile after being slandered by Fujiwara no Tokihira.

shiped the robe of his emperor in his house of exile? Why should we think
that he behaved out of gratefulness for his lord's benevolence and fulfilled
the duty of a loyal retainer? After all, the real purpose behind Lord Sugawara's behavior was simply self-gratification. How could Lord Michizane
explain his true purpose in terms of good reason and justice? I will save
you many more anecdotes of soldiers in time of war. Let me just tell you of
those who, inspired by a brave warrior, spare each other's life; or, although
popularity is very ephemeral, they die to make themselves known to others. Where is the highest good in examples like these? What is the purpose and what are the means? I certainly do not approve of the understanding that those teachers of the way[6] have of these people's loyalty and
sense of duty.

They say, for example, that the realization of beauty takes place spontaneously, without the intervention of the mind, like the song of birds and
the flowing of water. We might think of the following statement from the
past: "Take the lily that blooms in the fields. Without laboring, without
spinning, not even the height of Solomon's[7] prosperity compares with the
beauty of this flower." How can you compare a lily to the beauty of human
behavior? If you look with the eyes of morality—without a previous understanding of the highest good and therefore lacking the motive of making the highest good a reality—how can you say that your behavior has
moral value? Moral behavior requires the presence of consciousness; it demands study and cooperation.

For those scholars, behavior is like a cloud that comes out from a cave in
the mountain without any real intention; like a reindeer instinctively approaching a mountain stream. For them, to die for lord and country, or to
devote oneself to father and husband, is the same thing as for a baby to yearn
for his mother. They do not introduce an analysis of people's state of mind
and the whole notion of reason and justice. The baby's yearning after his
mother is grounded in the instinct of human nature. If we argue that his behavior follows the same rules, then we should conclude that, after all, the
baby lacks moral values.[8]

The absoluteness and interiorization of the aesthetic life was, according
to Chogyū, a way to overcome the relativity and exteriority of morality and
reason. Profoundly influenced by his reading of Nietzsche, Chogyū
preached the strong individuality of the overman—which he saw in medieval historical figures such as the military leader Taira no Kiyomori

---

6. A term that includes Confucians, Taoists, and Buddhists.
7. Solomon (fl. 928 B.C.), son of David, king of Israel and Judah (ca. 967–928 B.C.).
8. *Takayama Chogyū Shū, Anezaki Chōfū Shū, Sasakawa Rinpū Shū*, pp. 206–207.

(1118–1181) and the religious leader Nichiren (1222–1282). Chogyū's involvement with nationalistic propaganda was directly related to his positions in the aesthetic field.[9]

Chogyū's study of aesthetics led him to defend the subject's role in the formulation of aesthetic judgment in a famous dispute he had with Tsubouchi Shōyō. Centered on the topic of paintings representing historical subjects, this controversy, which filled the pages of the journal *Taiyō* between 1898 and 1900, was prompted by Tsubouchi's privileging the historical fact over its artistic representation, so that a painting would be a simple means *(hōben)* to describe history and bring it to life. Chogyū, however, argued that beauty was inherent to the painting and not to the historical event portrayed in it. He stated that the act of artistic creation was free and independent from external reality. The latter was simply a pretext for artistic expression. Chogyū reminded Tsubouchi of the need to pay attention to the role played by the consciousness of the subject in the formulation of artistic truth. The artist was not a simple mirror reflecting the alleged beauty of an external reality. Chogyū denied the existence of what Tsubouchi had called "historical beauty," since beauty was prompted less by the appreciation of a past event or a historical figure than by a process brought into motion by the artist's imagination. Should art be subjected to historical contingency, Chogyū concluded, art would lose its freedom.[10]

By advocating the freedom of artistic expression, Chogyū launched a critique of civilization that involved the reconciliation of the scientific realm of reason with the aesthetic realm of the passions: the reconciliation of truth and beauty.[11] The reduction of truth to the contingency of reality, as advocated by Shōyō, was depriving humanity of the metaphysical dimension of Being that was the basic condition for liberation from the grip of an oppressive reality. Artistic beauty was an expression of Being and of the potential for social improvement—a notion that the Japanese romantics developed around the image of the ideal nation at the beginning of the twentieth century. For Chogyū the realm of aesthetics stood as the last bulwark against the "realists'" apologia of existence.

---

9. See Chogyū's essay "Japanism" (Nihon Shugi) in *Takayama Chogyū Shū, Anezaki Chōfū Shū, Sasakawa Rinpū Shū,* pp. 202–205.

10. Chogyū's articles on this subject are collected in Takayama Rinjirō, *Chogyū Zenshū,* vol. 1: *Bigaku Oyobi Bijutsu Shi* (Tokyo: Hakubunkan, 1914), pp. 32–110. For a discussion of the controversy see Watanabe, *Meiji Shisō Shi,* pp. 211–218.

11. See Chogyū's essay "The Scholar as a Critic of Civilization" (Bunmei Hihyōka to Shite no Bungakusha, 1901) in *Takayama Chogyū Shū, Anezaki Chōfū Shū, Sasakawa Rinpū Shū,* pp. 260–266.

Observations on Aesthetic Pleasure
by Takayama Chogyū

1. Aesthetic Consciousness
and the Consciousness of Truth

A SCHOLAR OF AESTHETICS must recognize two facts at the start of his research.[12] From the point of view of the subject, beauty is "the passions" as well as the feeling of pleasure derived from those passions. I shall begin my discussion from these points.

No one will object to the fact that the human mind is divided in two major parts, one related to knowledge, the other related to passions. With regard to knowledge, the mind sets up a standard that is acknowledged by the majority of educated people. It compares the matter in hand with this standard, concluding whether the one conforms to the other. With regard to passions, there is no such thing as a standard. The mind limits itself to judge whether the matter at hand is pleasant or not. Namely, the operating sphere of the passions is bound by agreeableness and disagreeableness. Of course, so long as the charm of agreeableness and nonagreeableness exists even in the workings of knowledge, we should say that knowledge is accompanied by the workings of the passions. Likewise, so far as positive and negative judgments mingle in the workings of the passions, we should say that the passions play a role in knowledge as well. And yet if we talk about their inner properties, then we should recognize a difference among the two: knowledge aims at truth, while the passions culminate in beauty (agreeableness). Here I shall call the first "the consciousness of truth" and the latter "aesthetic consciousness."

People with an underdeveloped intellect might think that something untrue is true. Yet it is not hard to discern the mistake. For example, it must be hard for an uneducated person to believe that the earth moves. But who with a proper education and a sincere heart will not understand this principle? That is to say, it is easy to teach the truth. The person who, no matter how much he has been taught, still does not understand is not serious. It is only natural to conclude, looking from the outside, that such a mistaken thought is a fallacy. This is a distinctive feature of the consciousness of truth.

Aesthetic judgment, however, does not work in the same manner. Since beauty is feelings, it is an absolute truth for the person who is experiencing those feelings. Although everyone in the land might argue that something is not beautiful, if at least I feel the presence of beauty, then there is absolutely

---

12. The original text of this essay, "Bikan ni Tsuite no Kansatsu," appears in Takayama Rinjirō, *Chogyū Zenshū*, vol. 1: *Bigaku Oyobi Bijutsu Shi* (Tokyo: Hakubunkan, 1914), pp. 267–290.

no way to avoid saying that this is beautiful. We should avoid concluding that what either someone in the land or myself might consider beautiful is actually ugly. The reason why beauty is an absolute truth for the person experiencing it is, after all, because the taste in charge of judgment seldom changes by itself, and it is rarely made to change. Taste is not something that can be easily nurtured by scholarship. Grounded in the a priori of human nature, taste is extremely profound. We should compare this difficulty and profundity to the shallowness of science that illuminates the intellect for a short day. Namely, it is difficult to teach beauty. It is difficult to reject as fallacious even those tastes that refuse to change, no matter how hard you try to instill them. Beauty is the beauty of what you feel. No external judgment has the power to change it. This is the main point where aesthetic consciousness differs from the consciousness of truth.

2. Aesthetic Consciousness and Moral Consciousness

According to what I mentioned earlier, the relationship between aesthetic consciousness and the consciousness of truth should be clear. I also explained the difference between science and the arts on this point. Here I would like to add a third kind of consciousness, which I will call "the consciousness of good" (moral consciousness). What is the relationship between this consciousness and aesthetic consciousness?

Moral consciousness is based on fixed standards in the light of which are decided the good and evil of human behavior: namely, moral judgment. These standards are not the same for all ages, nor do they remain identical for all people living in the same age. Generally speaking, however, standards exist in certain places at certain times. Every country in every period has its own constitution, laws, manners, and customs that bring coherence to each and every human society. These are nothing but the standards I am talking about. Seen from the viewpoint of the fixity of standards that become the yardstick for objectively judging good and evil, moral consciousness is similar to the consciousness of truth. To be a little more accurate, it is similar inasmuch as the consciousness of truth sets up objective standards of truth according to which it discriminates truth from fallacy.

Those who are intrinsically without conscience, however, or whose conscience is different from the conscience of the age to which they belong, or from the conscience of the majority of people, will not easily agree, in their inmost feelings, with the social sanctions against their personal behavior. For example, if public opinion judges someone's personal behavior to be evil, it might well happen that he will not acknowledge the reason why his behavior is considered evil. There are plenty of examples that would prove my point— examples of people from the past who rebelled against the disposition of the age and refused to bend their conscience. Inasmuch as it has an awareness of the self, making it an absolute reality, moral consciousness is close to aesthetic consciousness. In short, so far as the act of judging according to objective standards is concerned, moral consciousness is close to the consciousness of truth. So far as it makes the awareness of the self an absolute reality, it is similar to aesthetic consciousness.

The formalistic difference between these three kinds of consciousness is after all based on the ebb and flow of subjectivity and objectivity. The consciousness of truth has the highest degree of objectivity and the lowest degree of subjectivity, while aesthetic consciousness has the highest degree of subjectivity and the lowest degree of objectivity. Moral consciousness occupies the middle position. Subjectivity reaches its height in the emotions; objectivity is at its best in the intellect. Knowledge must be mutually exchanged. That is why it is so easy to pass it on to somebody else. This is explained by the fact that knowledge is regulated by objective standards. On the other hand, it is difficult to explain one's passions to others and, therefore, these are hard to transmit, since self-consciousness is an absolute reality.

Moral consciousness appears to join together subjectivity and objectivity and then to divide them into two halves. It is hard to explain the passionate side of morality, in the same way that it is difficult to express the perception of beauty. But with reference to the act of arguing according to the logic of judgment, moral consciousness is close to the consciousness of truth. Then, although moral consciousness does not change as easily as the consciousness of truth, to make it change is not so difficult as with aesthetic consciousness. While at the same time feeling the absoluteness of its own consciousness when facing its innerside, moral consciousness recognizes the objective standards to be obeyed when looking at the outside. Therefore, we should be able to see that moral consciousness includes two principles—subjectivity and objectivity—that are opposed to each other. Equality and discrimination, nation and individual, heteronomy and autonomy, are simply the expressions of the source of these two opposite principles. To worry about, to feel reverence for, and to cooperate toward the unification and harmonization of both, this is the moral activity of humanity.

3. Aesthetic Pleasure and Pleasures of Sense

Earlier I mentioned the differences between moral consciousness, the consciousness of truth, and aesthetic consciousness. This is not sufficient, however, to clarify the nature of aesthetic pleasure. Since we must discuss in its entirety the workings of the passions—as I noted earlier in discussing moral consciousness—I must now proceed to problematize the differences between pleasures in general and aesthetic pleasure.

The first thing I should affirm with regard to this problem is that aesthetic pleasure is the pleasure of the senses par excellence. Beauty should provide you always and on all occasions with a pleasurable experience and leave you satisfied. Beauty is something everyone should yearn after. To argue that beauty brings anguish and dissatisfaction is self-contradictory. Aesthetic pleasure is consistently a sensuous pleasure.

Although aesthetic pleasure is always a pleasurable feeling, not all pleasures of sense are necessarily aesthetic. Therefore, we must ask: What is the particular nature of that pleasure within the category of pleasures of sense that is called aesthetic pleasure? This is a problem I shall consider later on. After all, the answer to this question comes from the many theories on the notion of aesthetic pleasure that aestheticians have devised since ancient times. Let me summarize my observations as follows.

4. Disinterestedness of Aesthetic Pleasure

The explanation of the characteristics of aesthetic pleasure in terms of disinterestedness (or *interesselos* in German), is not a recent one in the history of aesthetics. Not only, as everybody knows, philosophers of the school of pure reason since Kant,[13] but also realist philosophers such as Kirchman,[14] have laid particular emphasis on this concept. British scholars as well approved of the general outline of this theory, though with a few variations. I remember that a few years ago Mr. Ōnishi Hajime explained this in detail in an article published in the journal *Waseda Literature* with the title "An Outline of Modern Aesthetic Thought."[15] Although to repeat it here is somewhat annoying, let me summarize it briefly in what follows.

Mr. Bain,[16] whom we should consider the most representative psychologist of England, defined aesthetic pleasure as a passion outside pleasures of sense,

---

13. Immanuel Kant (1724–1804), German philosopher, is the author of *Observations on the Feeling of the Sublime and the Beautiful* (1764) and the *Critique of Judgment* (1790). In Kant, "the distinguishing feature of the judgement of taste is that the satisfaction it reports is 'disinterested.' Kant adapts this important concept from the empiricists, to make it the cornerstone of his aesthetic system. When the satisfaction we get from an object is bound up with a desire that it exist, or a desire to possess it, that satisfaction is called 'interest'. . . . In this important respect, judgements of taste are entirely different from judgements of pleasurableness and judgements of the good, for pleasure excites an inclination, and the good involves the concept of a purpose, of what the object judged good ought to be, while when we find an object beautiful we need have no definite concept of it. The judgement of taste, Kant insists, is 'merely contemplative'; it is not a cognitive judgement, for it does not formulate or connect concepts at all. The satisfaction in the beautiful 'is alone a disinterested and *free* satisfaction.'" See Monroe C. Beardsley, *Aesthetics from Classical Greece to the Present: A Short History* (University: University of Alabama Press, 1982; 1st ed., 1966), p. 212.

14. Julius Heinrich von Kirchman (1802–1884), German philosopher, "while freely drawing on idealistic esthetics, tried to supplant the idealist basis by an uninspired sensationalism and so-called realism" (*Ästhetik auf realistischer Grundlage*, 2 vols., 1868). See Katharine Everett Gilbert and Helmut Kuhn, *A History of Esthetics* (Bloomington: Indiana University Press, 1954), p. 516, n. 37.

15. Ōnishi Hajime (1864–1900) published the first part of "Kinsei Bigaku Shisō Ippan" in *Waseda Bungaku* 25, January 1897. The second installment appeared in *Waseda Bungaku* 26, January 1897. The third and final part was published in *Waseda Bungaku* 28, February 1897.

16. The British scholar Alexander Bain (1818–1903), author of *Mental and Moral Science* (1872) and *Education as a Science* (1879), defended the theory of art as a kind of play.

with no direct connection with any object, completely disjoined from interest in the realities of life. He explained the characteristics of aesthetic consciousness as the fruition of beauty per se. I believe that this thought derives from the same view as Spencer's play theory.[17] Grant Allen[18] has espoused Spencer's theory, too, and expressed the same views. All these opinions work in the same way as the disinterestedness theory of German aestheticians.

Recently the American Santayana[19] has denied this theory, however, arguing that, on the contrary, there is a fine relationship between aesthetic pleasure and interest inasmuch as the former should be seen as the forerunner of the latter. After seeing beauty, who does not desire to possess it? Although people say there is no idea of competition in aesthetic enjoyment, when a rare art object disappears after a while, don't people strive to be the first to get close to that object?[20]

The Frenchman Guyau[21] also shared with Santayana the same opposition to the theory of disinterestedness. Guyau argues that not only is there not a very big difference between utility and beauty, but that what is most useful goes hand in hand with what I perceive to be the most beautiful. In other words, where there are great profits in life, aesthetic consciousness is active

---

17. Herbert Spencer (1820–1903), English philosopher. "His theory was that human beings develop a surplus of energy in their struggle to survive, and this energy can be expended (indeed, must be expended, to preserve equilibrium) in the form of play. Artistic activity is simply play, though of a specially valuable sort, for in beauty we enjoy the greatest quantity and intensity of stimuli with the least effort, because of their integration into orderly patterns. Beauty follows the principle of economy. The advance of industrialism consists in transforming human life so that useful labor, work, makes room more and more for play; and the arts are destined to take a larger and larger place in the inherent satisfaction of life." See Beardsley, *Aesthetics*, p. 379.

18. Grant Allen (1848–1899) is the author of *Physiological Aesthetics* (1877), from which comes the following well-known quotation: "The esthetically beautiful is that which affords the maximum of stimulation with the minimum of fatigue or waste." See Gilbert and Kuhn, *History of Esthetics*, p. 542.

19. George Santayana (1863–1952) is the author of *The Sense of Beauty* (1896) in which he argues that beauty is a value that can exist only in perception. His formula is that "beauty is pleasure regarded as the quality of a thing," or "pleasure objectified." See Beardsley, *Aesthetics*, p. 330.

20. "The supposed disinterestedness of aesthetic delights is not truly fundamental. Appreciation of a picture is not identical with the desire to buy it, but it is, or ought to be, closely related and preliminary to that desire. The beauties of nature and of the plastic arts are not consumed by being enjoyed; they retain all the efficacy to impress a second beholder. But this circumstance is accidental, and those aesthetic objects which depend upon change and are exhausted in time, as are all performances, are things the enjoyment of which is an object of rivalry and is coveted as much as any other pleasure. And even plastic beauties can often not be enjoyed except by a few, on account of the necessity of travel or other difficulties of access, and then this aesthetic enjoyment is as selfishly pursued as the rest." See George Santayana, *The Sense of Beauty: Being the Outlines of Aesthetic Theory* (Cambridge, Mass.: MIT Press, 1988), p. 27.

21. Jean-Marie Guyau (1854–1888) is the author of *L'Esthétique Contemporaine* (1884) and *L'Art au Point de Vue Sociologique* (1887), in which he "tried to break down separation of art from other aspects of culture. He emphasized, especially, the connection and continuities of beauty with utility, for example, in architecture and practical objects. And he denied any essential difference between aesthetic emotions and other emotions that bring men together. Art is essentially social." See Beardsley, *Aesthetics*, p. 301.

in its highest degree. With the opening of the world, increase in specialization forces people to be one-sided. Beauty functions to mitigate the vice of onesidedness, compensating for this defect. There will come a time in the distant, distant future when people will need beauty like they need their daily bread.

The way I see it, however, the theories of these two gentlemen do not necessarily deny the theory of disinterestedness advanced by the German aestheticians. That is, when the German aestheticians and Spencer talk about the disinterestedness of the sense of beauty, they refer to the consciousness at the time of perceiving beauty. They are not concerned as to whether beauty exerts any influence on body and mind or in people's life. If you ask them what is the utility of beauty, these scholars would answer that it is absolutely nothing. When people like Spencer say that beauty is unrelated to the vital functions of life, they clearly remind us that they do not reject at all the notion of indirect utility.

But when I look at the countertheories of Santayana and Guyau, they both speak of the indirect utility of beauty or the indirect desire for this beauty. They do not say that inside aesthetic pleasure there is the idea of utility or the desire for private ownership. I do not see any place where they collide with the theory of disinterestedness. After all, the theory of disinterestedness talks about sensations at the time of the perception of beauty. The theories of people like Guyau, who are said to oppose disinterestedness, exclude from their remarks sensation in favor of influence. Each group starts from a different position. They are certainly not conflicting and mutually exclusive views.

In any event, will it be safe to state that, up to now, scholars have not made any objection to the theory of disinterestedness—namely, the view that characterizes aesthetic pleasure as separate from a utilitarian consciousness? From actual experience I personally recognize the difficulty of denying this theory. But does not the reason why sometimes people misunderstand the notion of disinterestedness depend on the excessively narrow meaning with which German aestheticians explain this notion? They often argue that beauty is something that rejects the working of the intellect, something that annihilates the working of the will, complete freedom from ideas and thoughts, something that draws your heart into the state of the nirvana of nondifferentiation. This seems to me an exaggeration. These statements indicate the highest effect of beauty. I do not wish to argue about the high admiration they have for beauty, but my ordinary notion of beauty includes things that have nothing to do with these exaggerations. A person's state of mind when he praises the beauty of the cherry blossoms should not necessarily be free from ideas and thoughts. A part of the will joins in the working. He should not be prevented from the selfish desire of breaking off a branch. German scholars carry the concept of beauty to an exaggeratedly lofty frontier.

From the point of view of common experience, I will say that "aesthetic pleasure is the pleasure of sense that guides me to a state of relative disinterestedness." What do you think about this definition? (By interest, however, I mean actual profit. When I say it idealistically, even aesthetic pleasure should not be without interest. If there were not even a slight interest, why then should we look for beauty and yearn after it?)

Scholars have talked about the disinterestedness of aesthetic pleasure; poets have sung of it. No one has ever mentioned someone's beauty without first beginning to talk about the notion of aesthetic disinterestedness, so it is pointless for me to repeat it here. Who among those who are chasing after fame and gain, to the point that time is never enough, will not have their distressed heart lightened by the view of the beauty of the setting sun while hurrying home at dusk? Who will not remember having had his sensual desire repressed when faced with a superb beauty? The one who gazes in rapture at the lilies blooming in the field will certainly lament that the height of Solomon's prosperity does not even amount to the efflorescence of just one of those flowers!

Who, reflecting upon himself, will not hate the vanity of a life spent chasing after fame and gain upon listening to the delicate sound of a flute on a crimson night lit by the moon? Mind and body will never forget majestic scenery or a delicate poem. As for our thoughts floating between heaven and earth as in a dream, logic should not be discriminating, names should not designate. Where do you find the concept of utility? In short, if you have the strength to mitigate the idea of benefit, or to erase it, then the nature of aesthetic pleasure should become all the more clear.

5. The Resounding of Aesthetic Pleasure in Body and Mind

Next, as one remarkable quality of aesthetic pleasure, we should pay attention to the fact that it does not show partiality to any particular section of either body or mind but affects the entire body equally. This has been best clarified by Guyau. No aesthetician from the past has failed to notice this fact. This can be easily grasped when we think of pleasures of sense that are not aesthetic pleasures. It is difficult to call beautiful the pleasure of getting close to the fireside on a winter night. This specific pleasure derives mainly from the warming up of the skin. Namely, this pleasure leans toward the sense in question without equally involving the entire body and mind. Likewise, we should call pleasurable the sensation we feel when savoring delicious meat, but it would be hard to call it beautiful. We see that, in this case, pleasures of sense are biased mainly toward those organs which are related to the alimentary system. It is the same with smell.

Of course, I cannot state that the pleasures felt when putting on warm clothes, or tasting delicious meat, or sniffing a fragrant perfume, involve *only* the sense in charge of that particular feeling and have no influence whatsoever on other parts of the body. I am only saying that, although pleasurable feelings do have to a certain degree an effect on the entire body, pleasures of sense that are not aesthetic pleasure tend essentially to privilege a particular sense. In other words, I am saying that in the case of pleasures of sense that are not aesthetic pleasures, there is a remarkable difference in the degree of strength with which those feelings are felt in the specific sense and in the rest of the body.

In the case of aesthetic pleasure, however, the difference is not so significant. The significance is so slight that we almost fail to feel any difference. Pleasures of sense related to hearing and sight are usually called aesthetic pleasures. The pleasure of listening to delicate music does not appeal primarily and exclusively to the sense of hearing. The pleasure of admiring a lovely landscape is not particularly remarkable for the sight. In cases such as these, I experience pleasure equally, with all my body and mind, even before I forget the existence of my senses—or, to put it a different way, even before I forget that I am listening with my ears and seeing with my eyes. At that time, I feel as if my body and mind are made up, as a whole, of all my senses. This is the kind of pleasure that is usually referred to as aesthetic pleasure.

We should not reject the idea that at the root of aesthetic pleasure there are pleasures of sense which are related to the senses. But as soon as they turn into aesthetic pleasures, they should not be felt any longer as pleasures of sense deriving from the senses. To say it from the point of view of psychology, pleasures of sense adhere to the affected part of the body without being retained by it. Moving forward, they shake our entire nervous system and become an essential element of our ideas. They are a driving force behind our thoughts and emotions. The condition according to which pleasures of sense change into aesthetic pleasure is similar to the collection of many independent sounds into a single harmony.

So far I have discussed pleasures of sense. Although it is more difficult to indicate clearly, as I have done above, the working of the pleasurable feelings of the fancy, I will attempt to explain them using the same logic. The relationship between the pleasure of solving a difficult scientific problem and the enjoyment at reading the ingenuous *Book of Psalms* is similar to the connection between the pleasure derived from savoring delicious meat and the pleasure that comes from listening to delicate music. The pleasure following the solution of a scientific problem arises mainly from the working of the intellect. If the mind is provided with spatial qualities, pleasures of sense will lean in that direction. It is the same with pleasures deriving from morality.

With regard to aesthetic pleasure, however, similarly to the pleasures that are related to the senses resounding equally in the entire body, the pleasures that are related to the fancy reverberate in the entire spirit. After all, aesthetic pleasure derives from the harmonization of the senses, thought, and the emotions without ever privileging any of these essential elements. The pleasure of learning privileges knowledge; the pleasure of morality leans toward the will. Neither of them can be said to appeal equally to our entire mind. To make a comparison, can we say that aesthetic pleasure is like a republican government and that pleasures of sense which are not aesthetic are like a despotic government or a monarchy? With the latter, authority privileges a few citizens; with the former, power expands to everybody. Although the strength of the latter is superior to the former, the breadth of the former is superior to the latter.

If I am allowed another comparison, aesthetic pleasure is like striking a bell whereas pleasures of sense that are not aesthetic are like hitting a board. When striking a bell, although you concentrate on one particular spot, the sound reverberates equally all over the bell and not just on the spot that gets hit. When hitting the board, the sound concentrates particularly on the place that is hit without ever vibrating over the whole surface. This is exactly like the difference between pleasures of sense and aesthetic pleasure.

The fact that aesthetic pleasure possesses a charm that reverberates all over body and mind was pointed out not only by Guyau but by many other scholars as well. As when we talk about ideal aesthetic pleasure in opposition to actual pleasures, although the words are different, the meaning remains the same. Although it would be extremely interesting to make a comparison between the aesthetics of psychologists and the aesthetics of philosophers, there is no time here for a detailed explanation. I will simply call your attention to the fact that:

6. The Strength of Aesthetic Pleasure is Weaker Than Nonaesthetic Pleasures of Sense

I shall explain a few matters related to this topic. Not a few scholars have tried to explain the difference between aesthetic pleasure and normal pleasures of sense from the point of view of strength. After the German Kirchman had at one time clarified this idea, other scholars such as Hartmann[22] followed suit, making it a characteristic of aesthetic pleasure. I completely agree with them. On the whole, excess in the intensity of feelings—whether they are related to the senses or to fancy—has the tendency to make body and mind easily retain them, making them adhere to a particular spot of the body. This excess is not like the weaker intensity that reverberates equally in the entire body.

Therefore, although we call the eye and the ear aesthetic senses, if the sound is too loud it seldom becomes music; if colors are too bright, they only bring discomfort to the viewer. When you strike a bell, for example, if you put too little strength in it, then only the part inside the wooden bell hammer will vibrate intensely. If you put excessive strength into hitting it, the bell will break and its echo will not reverberate as much as if the bell had been struck with less strength. This can be applied to the senses of the same kind. Probably there is

---

22. Eduard von Hartmann (1842–1906), the author of *Philosophie des Schönen* (1887), was a "'concrete idealist,' who remained faithful to Hegel's view that any Idea is a beauty when it appears in sense." See Beardsley, *Aesthetics,* p. 240.

no difference with regard to the other senses either. Namely, the intensity of the so-called inferior senses—touch, taste, smell, and the like—should be stronger than the effect of the superior senses of sight and hearing. It is a very hard enterprise to bring a scientific proof to this. Although today psychologists have not yet succeeded in their undertakings, by analogy to other evidence we shall see that there is a strong basis allowing us to think in this manner.

I must now explain the different qualities inherent to aesthetic pleasure with regard to its relative weakness—namely, the low degree of its retention by the human body. When I read ten pages from a book of philosophy, for example, I feel quite fatigued and hardly feel fit to do anything else with ease. But when I enjoy a dramatic poem or a novel, I do not feel such a strong hardship. Two hours of a scholarly speech should make you much more tired than an entire day of theatergoing. Those who have experienced it know the great difference in levels of fatigue between walking in a specimen room doing research on natural history and touring an art exhibit to admire the display. Are these not exemplary proofs of the relative weakness of aesthetic pleasure?

Since pleasures of sense that are not aesthetic abound in the power of retention, people who amuse themselves with these pleasures do not easily turn their interest to a different object. This is comparatively rare with aesthetic pleasure. Don't readers of novels or theater viewers easily change their interests from their immediate object of appreciation after a short time?

As I mentioned earlier, the reason aesthetic pleasure can provide long-lasting enjoyment is also grounded in the weakness of its intensity. You can keep looking at a famous picture for ten years without ever getting tired of it— something you could never expect from nonaesthetic pleasures. The way I see it, nonaesthetic pleasures of sense, so long as they are pleasurable even in the slightest degree, constantly keep on growing. Those who like their food spicy will eventually stop feeling pleasure no matter how strong the spiciness becomes. Those who crave after profit, if they get one, they want ten; if they get ten, they want a hundred; they want billions and yet they will never be satisfied. It is the same thing with craving after knowledge.

For those who devote themselves to desire, there are only two destinies into which they eventually fall. Either the external reality is not enough for their strength, or their strength does not meet the external reality. For those who search for spicy food, either the world does not provide as much spiciness as we are looking for, or our own body has not enough strength to stand the taste. Either one or the other comes about. It is the same with searching for fame and gain or looking after knowledge. Only aesthetic feelings provide the knowledge of what is worthy in this world. Aesthetic pleasure acknowledges absolute value in its objects. Therefore, the pleasure aimed at beauty is indisputably permanent. Although this is an idealistic definition of aesthetic pleasure, it is an undisputable truth that aesthetic pleasure, generally speaking, when compared to nonaesthetic pleasures of sense, confers eternal enjoyment. The psychological explanation for this is that aesthetic pleasure is comparatively weak.

7. The Objectivity of the Pleasures of Sense and Their Perpetual Recurrence

Santayana has argued that the pleasures of sense which are perceived as the essence of the external object are aesthetic pleasures. The main point of his theory is that delicious taste inhabits one part of the nutrition organs. It is hard to think of it as of the essence of food. The same applies to the pleasures of sense derived from the lower sense organs. On the other hand, the pleasures of sense related to hearing and sight hit the perceiving subject and bring him to oblivion, just as if they were perceived as the objective nature of the external object. This is the unique characteristic of aesthetic pleasure.[23]

In my opinion, such an objective nature exists in aesthetic pleasure, and it is clear that comparatively speaking it exists in a particularly large amount in aesthetic pleasures. Yet I wonder from the several passages mentioned above whether the argument according to which this is a characteristic of aesthetic pleasure is particularly cogent. Actually, this objective nature is also remarkably present in the pleasures of sense outside of aesthetic pleasure. For example, don't we usually speak of "a tempting cake" or "warm clothes"? Isn't that because we think of the delicious taste as the nature of the cake? We should not consider it a casual choice of words. Doesn't this show how, without realizing it, we objectify all our pleasures of sense? Then the idea of making it a specific characteristic of aesthetic pleasures does not seem appropriate. At least we cannot say that the defense of this truth derives from a clever explanation.

But I think we should call quite appropriate the observations on the characteristics of aesthetic pleasure advanced by Marshall,[24] whose theory says that aesthetic pleasure is, comparatively speaking, an often recurring pleasure. The major point of this gentleman's theory is that instant appearance and disappearance is the normal condition of the pleasures of sense. Yet there are cases in which we should see the permanency of pleasures of sense. An object whose image is deep in our heart, for example, if only it is brought back to life in our

---

23. "Most of the pleasures which objects cause are easily distinguished and separated from the perception of the object: the object has to be applied to a particular organ, like the palate, or swallowed like wine, or used and operated upon in some way before the pleasure arises. The cohesion is therefore slight between the pleasure and the other associated elements of sense; the pleasure is separated in time from the perception, or it is localized in a different organ, and consequently is at once recognized as an effect and not as a quality of the object. But when the process of perception itself is pleasant, as it may easily be, when the intellectual operation, by which the elements of sense are associated and projected, and the concept of the form and substance of the thing produced, is naturally delightful, then we have a pleasure intimately bound up in the thing, inseparable from its character and constitution, the seat of which in us is the same as the seat of the perception. We naturally fail, under these circumstances, to separate the pleasure from the other objectified feelings. It becomes, like them, a quality of the object, which we distinguish from pleasures not so incorporated in the perception of things, by giving it the name of beauty." See Santayana, *Sense of Beauty*, pp. 32–33.

24. Henry R. Marshall (1852–1927) argues in his *Aesthetic Principles* (1895) that aesthetic pleasure is basically a stable pleasure.

memory, will make us remember the pleasures of sense. In case the image is brought back to life, it will always rouse the pleasures of sensation and will never produce a sense of unpleasantness.

If we remember a delightful view of a place formerly visited or recollect a theatrical performance seen a long time ago, for example, we should always feel a certain pleasure for those objects. The permanency of this feeling deriving from the recurrence of the pleasure of sense is seen only in the objects that we call aesthetic. Namely, the characteristic of aesthetic pleasure is permanence derived from recurrence. This is a theory upon which everybody should agree.

Now, if we consider the perception of the lower senses, it is difficult for touch, taste, and smell to recur as images. Even in occasional examples such as the quenching of thirst at the thought of a sour plum, this is nothing but an idea indirectly evoked by the actual form, color, and size of the plum through a visual reproduction. There is no way to reproduce abstractly the actual taste. The same goes for pleasures of sense related to fancy. There is no need for me to explain this in detail.

Although I fully endorse the theory about the remarkable nature of aesthetic pleasure as the reproduction of pleasures of sense, I wish to point out one further characteristic. Since this is something that scholars in the past have not clearly discussed, I shall mention it here. To be more specific, in aesthetic pleasure we bear witness to the:

8. Matching of Pleasures of Sense and Utility

When I talk about matching, I do not mean that this always takes place no matter what the circumstances, but that, compared to nonaesthetic pleasures of sense, there are remarkably many more cases in which this matching occurs.

It is a rather evident truth that in the lower senses there are several cases in which the matching does not appear. A soft fabric is pleasant to the skin, but not necessarily beneficial. Sometimes, in order to make our skin stronger, we wear coarse and stiff clothes and must endure the pain of a cold wind blowing. A sweet taste might be pleasing to me, but it might also damage my stomach. As they say, a good medicine generally tastes bitter. The scent of the apricot flower is fragrant, yet doctors say it is harmful to the human body. On the whole, cases like these in which pleasures of sense and utility run counter to each other are not unusual with regard to the lower senses.

On the contrary, in aesthetic pleasure what is unusual is actually this confrontation. No one will end up with an ulcer by listening to a sweet melody, and I do not think anyone will ever develop a headache while admiring beautiful scenery. Not only are beautiful objects seldom harmful to body and mind but, in most cases, they also refresh people's spirit and have a relaxing effect on the organism's activities. Beauty consoles the grieving person, softens the heart of the angry man, and doubles the pleasure of the happy man. If you like it, you can be absorbed in appreciation of the arts in an immoderate fashion and yet you will never suffer the considerable harm deriving from a wild life of debauchery. Although aesthetic pleasure has not the same strong effect as a drop of miraculous water that cures all kinds of distress, it is remarkable inasmuch as in most cases it is compatible with utility.

Clearly the same thing applies to the aesthetic pleasures related to fancy. To exert the intellect in scientific research, to discipline the will in moral training, not only are these often harmful to the body but they often lead to obstinacy, to bigotry, to depression, to a loss of common sense, and, eventually, in extreme cases, to madness. A scholar has said that those who are called moralists, no matter how high the level of their erudition and virtue, as human beings they are biased. The working of their heart leans either toward the intellect or toward the will. They cannot avoid behaving like despots with regard to the entire spirit. When Schiller[25] says that perfection resides only in play, he voices well the nature of aesthetic pleasure.

9. Obiter Dictum

I have described in the foregoing the most remarkable features of the nature of aesthetic pleasure. It would be a big mistake, however, to say that we do not find these features in nonaesthetic pleasures of sense, acknowledging them as forming the exclusive nature of aesthetic pleasure. No matter from which point of view we look at it, between general pleasures of sense and aesthetic pleasure we should see only a quantitative difference and not any qualitative distinction. Therefore, what I have been saying from the beginning of my comparative lecture is nothing but the acknowledgment that these particular features are especially marked in aesthetic pleasure. Moreover, all these features do not belong to different and separate categories. If we search for their psychological or physiological foundations, probably we would see that they all end up in the same reality. We should regard each of these features as an expression of one side of the same reality. I shall speak some other day on this particular matter.

Since ancient times, the three disciplines of religion, ethics, and the arts have been revered as the most precious treasures of humanity. Artless science, however, is ignorant of the art of kneeling in front of this altar. Just like a child

---

25. Friedrich Schiller (1759–1805), German poet and dramatist, according to whom the play impulse *(Spieltrieb)* overcomes, in a synthesis, both the sensuous impulse *(Stofftrieb)* and the formal impulse *(Formtrieb)*, thus restoring the unity of human nature. As he states in his *Letters on the Aesthetic Education of Man:* "How can we speak of *mere* play, when we know that it is precisely play and play *alone,* which of all man's states and conditions is the one that makes him whole and unfolds both sides of his nature at once? . . . For man only plays when he is in the fullest sense of the word a human being, and *he is only fully a human being when he plays.*" See Friedrich Schiller, *Essays* (New York: Continuum, 1993), pp. 130–131.

laughing at the naked body of a king wearing the mysterious robe of a sorcer-
er, it points at the truth of religion and teaches that it is nothing but illusion;
it says that morality follows the times and will surely change. The arts, which
we should see as the last refuge of those who hate smoke and the sound of gold,
are made into something suspicious. It now seems that the time of restoring
the privileges of beauty, which poets from the past sang of as sacred, has already gone.

That life is brief and art long lasting, however, remains the same today as
in the past. After all, the heart that searches for beauty chases after immortal-
ity. People in the past were tortured by such a heart, and yet they found happiness in this anguish. For them the blue sky was not empty; the stars shining in it were not a clod of earth. Alas, what unhappiness to have been born
in a world that does not praise the mysterious light of the sky as the breath of
god! Shall we compare it to the spite of the poet bewailing his inability to step
on the sea and listen to the sound of Triton's horn? [*Teikoku Bungaku,* May
1900]

AESTHETIC CATEGORIES

SIX

Ōnishi Yoshinori and the Category of the Aesthetic

Ōnishi Yoshinori (1888–1959) taught aesthetics at the University of Tokyo from 1922 until his retirement in 1949. In addition to his voluminous work on Western aesthetics in general and Kant in particular, Ōnishi applied his knowledge of Western philosophy to the elucidation of key concepts of Japanese aesthetics and poetics that had been used for centuries by Japanese poets and theorists. His efforts led to the publication of such books as *Yūgen and Aware* (*Yūgen to Aware,* 1939), *On Refinement: A Study on Sabi* (*Fūga Ron: Sabi no Kenkyū,* 1940), *Feelings Toward Nature in the Man'yōshū* (*Man'yōshū no Shizen Kanjō,* 1943), and a series of articles on the aesthetics of the Far East recently collected in the volume *The Artistic Spirit of the East* (*Tōyōteki Geijutsu Seishin,* 1988). His *Aesthetics (Bigaku)* in two volumes dedicates the first volume (1959) to the history of Western aesthetics while reserving the second (published posthumously in 1960) for the analysis and construction of Japanese aesthetic "categories" such as *yūgen, yūen, aware, kokkei,* and *sabi.*

According to Ōnishi, it was the responsibility of the aesthetician to deal in terms of "aesthetic categories" *(biteki hanchū)* when addressing traditional aesthetic terms, rather than confining them to the esoteric discourse of Japanese medieval poetics *(shigaku).*[1] Ōnishi followed this approach in his *Aesthetics* in an attempt to explain the notion of *aware* beyond the stages of linguistic and psychological analysis. As we can see from the excerpt translated here, Ōnishi felt that a psychologization of the term along the lines of Motoori Norinaga's (1730–1801) analysis of *aware* was only the first step in the process of grasping the objective potential of *aware* as the result of an aesthetic experience. Following a state of "contemplation" *(Betrachtung),* such experience is, first of all, an intellectual as well as an emotional response to an aesthetic object—a product of a process known

---

1. Ōnishi Yoshinori, *Bigaku,* vol. 2: *Biteki Hanchū Ron* (Tokyo: Kōbundō, 1960), pp. 176–177.

as "aesthetic consciousness." Motoori, according to Ōnishi, had already started to describe this process, for he was quite sensible of the universal power of *aware* in engendering a common experience of what modern aesthetics would call "empathy." Yet the "sorrow" of *aware* cannot be explained simply as a psychological movement of a subject that is involved in a situation of shareable experience. Ōnishi stressed the importance of an independent external reality—the *mono* (thing) of *mono no aware* (the pathos of things)—in the production of a "sorrow" which is already present in the external world (nature) and which the mind recovers as a sort of "world-weariness" *(Weltschmertz)*. The moving experience of *aware* is part of a metaphysical enterprise that recovers the presence of nature within the perceiving subject by letting the latter dip into the cosmic grief of "the ground of Being" *(Seinsgrund)*. Thus, a communication is created in which the subject (or "moment of artistic feeling") and the object (or "moment of natural feeling") come together.

Ōnishi's long essay on *aware* continues well beyond the excerpt translated here by addressing, first of all, the affinities that he argues are present between the notion of sorrow and "the aesthetic" *(das ästhetisch)*. He justifies his argument by mentioning the privileged status that sorrow and melancholy have in the romantic poetry of John Keats (1795–1821), Percy Bysshe Shelley (1792–1822), and Edgar Allan Poe (1809–1849), as well as in the satanic verses of Baudelaire. The sadness sung in poetry, however, elicits an aesthetic pleasure, as we see in the expressions "pleasure of grief" used by the French psychologist Théodule-Armand Ribot (1839–1916) and the Spenserian "luxury of pitty." The oxymoron implies a positivity of the aesthetic experience that overcomes both the positive meaning of pleasure and the negative meaning of sorrow—in the same way that "will to life" *(seimei ishiki)* encompasses the positive side of health and growth as well as the negative side of illness and death. This positive vitality of the aesthetic experience requires, however, a "motivation" *(motivieren)* which is grounded in the presence of an objective reality of metaphysical sorrow that liberates the subject from the subjective immediacy of positive (joy) and negative (grief) passions. Aesthetic "excitement" is nothing but the realization of this mental state that is brought about by the clear vision of, and therefore liberation from, the motivation of feelings—what Norinaga called "the meaning of events" *(koto no kokoro)* or "the meaning of things" *(mono no kokoro).*[2]

The experience of *aware*—Ōnishi continues—allows the perceiver to penetrate the metaphysical ground of Being by making him understand

2. Ibid., pp. 315–323.

the universality and objectivity of a cosmic sorrow he would otherwise construct as private and subjective. This corresponds to what Max Scheler (1874–1928) has called the moment of "reconciliation" *(Versöhnung)* of the tragic in which the origin of tragic sorrow must be searched in the "connections of Being" *(Seins-zusammenhang)*. The aesthetic pleasure of sorrow results from the understanding of the fact that the catastrophic element of the tragic is not grounded in a personal and subjective will. It is, rather, concealed in the "abyss" *(Abgrund)* of "nothingness" from which sorrow and pleasure originate. Aesthetics, then, fulfills the purpose of a religious system by making its audience sensitive to the phenomena of nature and life. Aesthetic intuition allows the penetration of the ground of Being, thus providing spiritual fulfillment and gratification—the oxymoronic pleasure of the encounter with sorrow. Ōnishi quotes the poet Yosa Buson (1716–1784) who, he argues, captured the nature of aesthetic experience in the following verses:

Sabishisa no	There is also happiness
Ureshiku mo ari	In loneliness:
Aki no kure	Autumn dusk.

According to Ōnishi, in this poem Buson highlights a major characteristic of beauty, which is the "fragility" *(Fragilität)* of Being as captured by a poet who finds fulfillment and pleasure in his awareness of the sorrowful nature of the world. An aesthetician of classicism would say that Buson has immortalized and purified in artistic beauty the potentially threatening elements of natural beauty, whose constant changes contain antiaesthetic elements as well. Sensitivity to the transformations of nature enhances the potential for aesthetic experience by nurturing an ability of taking pleasure from the awareness of the fragility of the aesthetic object. For Ōnishi this argument proves that the poet's closeness to "natural beauty" during the Heian period was a contributing factor to his development of "aesthetic sensibility."[3]

This explains Ōnishi's definition of the Heian period as an "aesthetic culture" *(biteki bunka)*—not in the sense of any particular development in the artistic life of the period (artistic life or *Kunstleben*), but in the sense of people's ability to transform life into an artistic object, making life beautiful (aesthetic life or *biteki seikatsu*). The aristocracy used the arts as a practical means to make their life aesthetic and ease their boredom (ennui). The aesthetic, in Ōnishi's opinion, replaced the intellectual side of Heian life, or "intellectual culture" *(chiteki bunka)*, which is the propensity for a philo-

---

3. Ibid., pp. 323–329.

sophical discourse that allegedly failed to take place at that time. Ōnishi
blames this lack of interest in logic as a major cause for the failure of the
development of science in the Heian period. A sustained concern for a successful show of aesthetic understanding eventually led to the concealment
of logical and rational situations that might conflict with an aesthetic vision of life. This explains—as Motoori Norinaga had already pointed out—
the erasure in Heian writings of the medical treatment of patients in favor
of lengthy descriptions of colorful religious rites that replace the more rational but aesthetically less acceptable scene of a doctor prescribing a medicine. The aesthetic took the place of science in providing people with con-
solation from the hardships of daily life.

The aesthetic, then, becomes a mask covering the world-weariness or
ennui that runs through the "feeling" *(Stimmung)* of the entire Heian period, which Ōnishi describes as an epoch of "decadence." The aesthetic displaces a truth that speaks more of colors, perfumes, and ritualized acts than
of the lethargy *(Schwächengefühl)* and the *taedium vitae (Langweile)*[4] of a social class that is unable or unwilling to react to the status quo. One would
think that the reaction which fails to take place at the political and social
levels is displaced to the aesthetic level. Ōnishi, however, underlines the
fact that, unlike the modern notion of decadence, which implies the presence of a strong reaction against the evils of life, decadence in the Heian
period was not characterized by any particular reaction, since life at the
time was relatively peaceful and easy. Ōnishi explains this harmonious portrait of Heian society with the argument of a lack of coordination between
an aestheticized behavior and a philosophical/ethical system that would
prohibit such behavior. The relative freedom of sexual customs in the *Tale
of Genji,* for example, was not constricted by any stringent moral code that
would explain a strong need for reaction against that system. The aesthetic, for Ōnishi, was more an answer to the general existential problem of
the *mal de vivre*—an attempt at understanding the ground of nothingness
upon which Being was standing—than a challenge of a particular social
or political system.[5]

According to Ōnishi, an aesthetic intuition of the phenomena of nature
was responsible for opening the doors to the basic ingredients of the tragedy
of life, such as the notions of time and change, rather than any particular
philosophical system, Buddhism included. The metaphorical reading of
the passing of the four seasons as a constant reminder of human mortality

---

4. Here Ōnishi uses the vocabulary employed by Eckard von Sydow (1885–1942) in his book on the
culture of decadence, *Die Kultur der Dekadenz* (Dresden: Sibyllen-verlag, 1921).

5. Ōnishi, *Bigaku*, vol. 2, pp. 329–340.

(memento mori)—as well as the tense relationship between the constancy of the natural laws that determine temporal progression and the cycles of change *(mujō)* that the seasons represent—are potent ingredients in the formation of the passive aesthetic experience of ennui.[6]

Ōnishi ends his essay by summarizing in five steps the meanings of *aware.* First: the "specifically psychological meaning" in which "sorrow" is understood as an emotion with a specific characteristic—for example, to be moved by the view of Genji playing his koto alone during his exile at Suma.

Second: the "inclusive psychological meaning" that explains *aware* as a general emotional experience going beyond the limitations of the specificity of the first step—for example, the general lack of sensitivity, participation, or compassion on the part of the oarsman who drinks alone on the boat despite the grief of the travelers journeying back to the capital in the *Tosa Diary (Tosa Nikki).*

Third: the "aesthetic meaning" in which an "aesthetic consciousness" is born with the addition of the intellectual intervention of "intuition" and "clear vision" in the understanding of the meaning of external reality. The reader or viewer is faced with an awareness of "Beauty" *(das Schöne)* that frees him from the purely emotional sense of "sadness" that *aware* still had in the first and second steps.

Fourth: the "specifically aesthetic meaning" in which the field of perception and clear vision overcome the immediacy of a specific object, becoming instead a metaphysical and mystical vision *(Einstellung)* of a general world-weariness informing the nature of existence or "Being"—for example, the reader's view of a Fujitsubo in *The Tale of Genji* who, after taking the tonsure, spends her days thinking exclusively of the afterlife, thus underscoring the metaphysical nature of an existence grounded on the absence of actual life. This is an overture toward the cosmic meaning of life that the reader perceives aesthetically through an aesthetic experience. The observation of the infinity of time and space in nature helps to bring about such an experience. As an example of the "specifically aesthetic meaning," Ōnishi mentions the "cosmic" *(kosmisches Gefühl)* poetry of Saigyō.

Fifth: *aware* seen as the "aesthetic category" of "the Beautiful," in which a specific "aesthetic content," made of the union of all kinds of "beauty," originates the specifically aesthetic experience of *aware.* In this step a symbolic and associative "empathy" *(Einfühlung)* takes place in which the essence of things is perceived intuitively through mental associations. The

---

6. Ibid., pp. 340–347.

examples provided by Ōnishi to explain this last step are all taken from situations dealing with the topics of death, demise, and disappearance as symbolic of the meaning of human life.[7]

To fully appreciate Ōnishi's commitment to give a philosophical foundation to a native concept that, with perhaps the exception of Motoori, was often dismissed as an untranslatable and undefinable feeling, we must remember the main purpose of his research, which he summarized in the preface to his first major book on the subject of *aware:*

> My original scientific concern was to include afresh all Japanese notions related to beauty in the logical network of discourses on aesthetic categories, as well as to further develop these debates from within the system of aesthetics in general.[8]

Modern critiques of Ōnishi's accomplishments, although they are reasonable reminders of the easy appropriation of the field of aesthetics by politicians in need of cultural justification for questionable practices, often overlook Ōnishi's sincere commitment to bring the best of philosophical speculation to the articulation of discourses that several Japanese scholars chose to keep shrouded in the mist of ineffability.[9] Such critiques would be more suited to the description that the philosopher Watsuji Tetsurō (1889–1960) gave of *mono no aware* in his *Study of the History of the Japanese Spirit* (*Nihon Seishin Shi Kenkyū,* 1940). Watsuji's reduction of the concept to a mystical experience can be glimpsed in his definition of *aware* as "yearning for the source of eternity" in which is allegedly rooted the human response to the awesomeness of external reality—humanity's reverent exclamation *(eitan)* when confronted by the mystery of the universe. Rely-

---

7. Ibid., pp. 347–367.

8. Ōnishi Yoshinori, *Yūgen to Aware* (Tokyo: Iwanami Shoten, 1939), p. 1.

9. See, for example, the following remarks by Minami Hiroshi in a recent publication that calls attention to how writings on aesthetics and the "Japanese spirit" informed Japan's fascist literature in the 1930s and 1940s: "An even more precise study of Japanese aesthetic consciousness is *Yūgen and Aware* by the aesthetician Ōnishi Yoshinori. Ōnishi took *'yūgen'* to mean 'not a disclosure of the path through the grasses' mist, not something clear, but something that is somehow hidden,' 'gloom, haziness, a twilight.' Moreover, he also used the expressions quietness, depth, fullness (the coagulation of infinity), mystery, and also supernaturalness. As for *'aware,'* he gives as its first meaning a specifically psychological sadness, as its second meaning a common psychological emotion, as its third meaning gentleness, loveliness, gracefulness, charm as general aesthetic consciousness. Similarly, in his 'Essay on Elegance' (*Fūga Ron,* 1940) he takes the notion of *'sabi'*—which treatises on *haikai* employ when they state that 'elegance is somehow sad'—not in its narrow sense of 'secluded quietness' but as an aesthetic concept specific to *haikai.* Moreover, he describes *'sabi'* as the age of a perpetually self-recreating nature from which the essence of things comes into being. He argues that the tearoom can be characterized as quietness, playfulness, freedom and that 'asymmetry,' its major characteristic feature, is at the root of the aesthetic consciousness of a people who is fond of irrationality." See Minami Hiroshi, *Nihonjin Ron: Meiji kara Kyō made* (Tokyo: Iwanami Shoten, 1994), p. 181.

ing on the vocabulary of idealism, Watsuji called *mono no aware* "the feeling of the infinite." He commented further as follows:

> By looking at the matter from this perspective, we can clearly understand why "the pathos of things" *(mono no aware)* had to be interpreted as a purified feeling. What we call *mono no aware* is the feeling of the infinite, which has in itself a tendency toward an unlimited purity. That is to say, *mono no aware* is inside ourselves, one of the mechanisms used by origin itself to make us return to the origin. The literary arts express it in a concrete form at a heightened level. Thanks to it, we come into contact with the light of eternal *things* that do not pass away, while we pass through things that pass away between things that pass away.[10]

The return of the Absolute Spirit to the original light was a lesson that Hegel had taught one hundred and twenty years earlier—a lesson perfectly mastered by a line of Japanese thinkers from Okakura Kakuzō to Watsuji Tetsurō. In 1941, one year after Watsuji's statement, Okazaki Yoshie (1892–1982), another major aesthetician and historian of the Japanese literary arts, made the following remarks on *aware:*

> Originally *aware* was an exclamatory particle. An exclamatory particle is the whole consciousness that defies analysis. It indicates the most basic form of expression. The way an expression such as *aware* works probably exists everywhere at the beginning of all races *(minzoku)*. In Japan, however, even after culture had developed to a high level, [*aware*] became, in a uniquely polished shape, the ground of our culture and the foundation for the adaptation of complicated foreign cultures. We can further speculate that the homogeneity of the Japanese people is reflected in *aware*.[11]

The following comments, made by Minami Hiroshi with regard to Okazaki Yoshie, could easily be applied to the mythologies of Watsuji Tetsurō:

> In *Forms of the Japanese Literary Arts (Nihon Bungei no Yōshiki)* Okazaki Yoshie, an advocate of the Japanese literary arts, argues that the substance of the Japanese literary arts privileges impression over thought, life's moods over conceptions of life, feelings over will. They are poor in intensity, vehemence, and depth while being rich in magnanimity, elegance, and refinement. Similar to the characteristics of our race, [the Japanese literary arts] are youthful and feminine. For example, the notions of *"sabi"* and *"shiori"* possess a touch of antiquity, and yet after all they are feminine.[12]

A lack of serious engagement with Western epistemological problems—an engagement that is constant in the work of Ōnishi Yoshinori—has

---

10. Watsuji Tetsurō, *Nihon Seishin Shi Kenkyū* (Tokyo: Iwanami Shoten, 1940), pp. 242–243.

11. Okazaki Yoshie, *Geijutsu Ron no Tankyū* (Tokyo: Kōbundō, 1941), p. 55.

12. Minami, *Nihonjin Ron,* pp. 181–182.

often led Japanese thinkers such as Watsuji and Okazaki to lose sight of the hermeneutical nature of aesthetic categories, which are then taken as a prioris to be entrusted with the explanation of historical becoming and the creation of a consoling but illusory strong subject. Like God in the metaphysical tradition, these categories act like principles outside history that legitimate the historical process from the loftiness of omniscience. This delusion is carried over in contemporary criticism in renewed efforts to provide readers with a strong sense of self-identity by calling their attention to the alleged continuity that notions such as *mono no aware* carry over from the past. We see it even in recent literary debates—a reminder of the need to resist the temptation of replacing theology with aesthetics:

> I have said at the outset that "mono no aware" was a sentiment of sadness, but in fact it is a sadness that is constantly evolving toward gaiety. I should be careful to note that this gaiety was nothing other than a sort of salvation for the urban citizen of the early modern period for whom a feeling of powerlessness was endemic. In this way, "mono no aware" becomes the basic principle of solidarity and of salvation in the godless cities of early modern Japan.[13]

Aware
by Ōnishi Yoshinori

AFTER ANALYZING gracefulness *(yūen)* or graceful beauty *(enbi)* as a special type deriving from "beauty" *(das Schöne)* seen as a basic aesthetic category, I will now turn from the same perspective of "basic category" to another new form of beauty branching off in a different direction: the notion of *aware*.[14] As most

---

13. Momokawa Takahito, "'Mono no Aware'—The Identity of the Japanese," *Kokubungaku Kenkyū Shiryōkan Kiyō* 13 (1987):11–12. For the Japanese version see Momokawa Takahito, "Kokugaku Ron no Kadai," in Saigō Nobutsuna, ed., *Nihon Bungaku Kōza*, vol. 1: *Hōhō to Shiten* (Tokyo: Nihon Bungaku Kyōkai, 1987), p. 157.

14. This essay is an excerpt from chapter 4 of Ōnishi's *Aesthetics*. See Ōnishi Yoshinori, *Bigaku*, vol. 2: *Biteki Hanchū Ron* (Tokyo: Kōbundō, 1960), pp. 288–368.

of my readers already know, this concept has been variously used by scholars of Japanese literature to indicate the content of the aesthetic consciousness of our people. I doubt, however, that it has ever been acknowledged as an "aesthetic category." Even if it has been acknowledged as such, I still wonder where can we find the aesthetic essence of *aware*. And in which sense can we ascribe it to the basic aesthetic category of beauty? Can we think of *aware* as a "special type" deriving from *das Schöne?*

It will be my work to answer these questions here, although I already foresee several problems from the very beginning. First of all, notwithstanding the fact that *aware* is a specific form of beauty, it developed completely among our own people, particularly in the spirit of the Heian period, and therefore contains a special, autonomous "aesthetic content" that is completely alien to the West. Not only is *aware* a topic that has never been treated in Western aesthetics, but in our country too we can safely state that there has never been an aesthetic study of it in the strict sense of the word. (Despite the efforts of, first of all, Motoori Norinaga and then more contemporary scholars of Japanese studies along similar lines, we cannot find an approach that can be defined as truly aesthetic.) As we have previously seen with regard to the concept of *yūgen,* when we confront Eastern and Japanese ideas from a genuinely aesthetic perspective, we are faced with a truly new topic of study.

We must also be alerted to problems posed to our study by the specific historical situation in which *aware* developed. Namely, when compared to notions such as *yūgen* and *sabi, aware* is historically more ancient and used in a much broader sense. It is true that the expression *"yūgen"* already appears in the Chinese preface of the *Kokinshū* (905) and, therefore, has been in use since ancient times. However, we can find the word *"aware"* used several times in the *Kojiki* and the *Nihongi* (712–720), while its meaning kept changing until the early modern time of the Edo period.

According to one theory, in ancient times prior to the Nara period the word *"aware"* mainly meant cute, dear, interesting, while in the Heian period it was used to indicate "the perception of a mood." During the Kamakura period, the meaning was twofold: on the one hand, *"aware"* indicated the glory *(appare)* of bravery; on the other it pointed at the softer feeling of sorrow *(aware)*. These two meanings were somehow combined in the Ashikaga/Muromachi period, while again during the Tokugawa period the word's meaning split into two, indicating both praise for the just winner *(appare)* and sympathy for the loser—a kind of compassion *(aware)*. When we consider this development, we realize how long the history of *aware* is.

Moreover, unlike technical expressions such as *yūgen,* which was used mainly with relation to the way of poetry, and *sabi,* which was mainly concerned with *haikai,* the use of *aware* was not limited to the specialists of Japanese literature but reached all corners of daily language, up to the present common idiom. Of course, the connotations of *aware* are much richer than the meanings of those other concepts, and much more difficult to grasp, especially in their original aesthetic meaning. The difficulty for an aesthetic study of *aware* is due not only to the word's polysemy; it is also related to the fact that, no matter whether it indicates praise and dearness or grief and compassion, *aware* always expresses a kind of "excitement" *(kandō)* or "emotion" *(kanjō)*, which are usually analyzed linguistically or in terms of content. When the research is of an aesthetic nature, its study stops at the level of "psychological" aesthetics. Research on *aware* never goes beyond this point, and we feel no necessity to exhaust this topic from a theoretical point of view. I do not deny that aesthetics can benefit from the study of psychology in developing a unique methodology. But research on *aware* that starts directly from the meaning of the concept, and is done from the perspective of aesthetics, always pulls in the direction of psychologism—with all the disastrous consequences that this tendency has when dealing with aesthetic categories, at least from my point of view.

First of all, according to the dictionary *(Daigenkai)*, the noun *"aware"* has two meanings, both nouns used as exclamatory particles indicating praise and pity. The first meaning of *aware* is explained as "something to be praised, excellence," and it is usually written with a character meaning "superiority" (優). From this derives the verb "to love" *(awaremu)*, which means "to treat someone tenderly." The latter meaning is explained as "something we should take pity of," "to grieve for," and it is written with a character meaning "sorrow" (哀). From this derives the verb "to feel for someone" *(awaremu)*. This became the ground for the interpretation of the exclamatory particle *"aware"* as the voice of all feelings of joy, anger, sorrow, and pleasure. Not only does the word *"aware"* possess a variety of meanings. It also includes in itself a connotation related to positive value—*aware* as "superiority"—as well as a connotation related to a negative value—*aware* as "sorrow" (two meanings seemingly contradictory).

But when we talk about value relationships in this case, we must pay attention to the following fact. Here, in terms of appropriate value relationships, we might think of three different meanings. The first value relationship concerns ourselves as subjects; the second is the value as perceived by other subjects that we actually see as objects; the third is the value relationship that is common to subject and object and, therefore, is universal and objective. There are remarkable differences in the nature and tone of the emotions that are engendered *(motivieren)* by these different meanings. When the value is denied and the meaning is "negative," our subjective response is mainly an emotion of repugnance and hatred. In the case of "positive" value, however, a feeling of passion is engendered—of "love" that includes "desire." If we think in terms of "positivity" and "negativity" with regard to the gain or loss of the value object, then our direct emotional response is mainly one of either "joy" or "sadness."

As for the second meaning of value relationships, since it is indirect, essentially it does not engender any direct emotional response of value in ourselves, neither a positive nor a negative one. Rather, it is the objectivity of the gain or loss of the value object on the part of the experiencing other that arouses our subjective response. This translates into positive feelings of "congratulations" as well as negative feelings of "compassion" and "pity."

As for the third meaning of objective value relationships, on the negative side feelings of "hatred" and "contempt" are aroused whereas on the positive side feelings such as "passion," "respect," and "admiration" are engendered.

But if we take as "life" the content of the value relationships of *aware,* this value content has such a vague form that, unlike the case of ideal and spiritual values, it becomes difficult to distinguish the first and third meanings discussed above and, moreover, it is often problematic to distinguish these two from the second. We might even think that it is meaningless to make these differentiations of value relationships. Or we might think it is actually appropriate to explain in these terms the value contents related to the concept of *aware.*

In fact, the word *"aware,"* as it is generally used, is equally inclusive of all the value relationships I have just mentioned. This explains why it is equally written in its positive meaning, with the characters indicating "praise," "love," "excellence," and in the negative one with the characters of "pity," "grief," and "sorrow." However, I personally think that in spite of this fact—or, better, because of this fact—we must analyze the various relationships of these "value meanings" if we want to proceed from the perspective of aesthetics.

When I relate the three value relationships that I have examined to the meaning of the word *"aware,"* I notice that they are almost always present whether *aware* implies praise, love, and excellence or pity, grief, and sorrow. To be more precise, it is difficult to acknowledge in *aware* the direct presence of the first relationship—that is, the meaning of the feeling of hatred *(hassen)* that comes from the negative pole of a subjective value. Similarly, it is also hard to see in it directly the passional meaning of "contempt" *(Verachtung)* that arises from the negativity of the third meaning. Since the use of words is established by habit, however, we find examples in which the word *"aware,"* originally used simply to express the form of "excitement," came to mean "hatred" and "contempt." Yet among the direct, essential meanings of *aware* indicating emotions, so far as I can tell, there is no "attitude" *(Stellungsnahme)* of rejecting or pressing the object in order to promote the self over it. When used with reference to an object that must be hated or despised, for example, *aware* is not a direct responsive emotion but rather a way of taking some distance from that object—a kind of indirect feeling or exclamation at the time of quiet resignation. To say it in a different way: The original meaning of *aware* is nothing but the expression of feelings of "sorrow" or "pity" that are somewhat charged with an objective quality.

Similarly, although we find the meaning of "love" in *aware,* in my opinion this is a "love" that is very close to the "aesthetic" meaning of the word—or, to say it differently, it is a feeling of love with a slightly objective quality. I think that the remarkably subjective meaning of "passion" or "attachment," as in opposition to "hatred," is very thin. (Therefore, we can also speak of a "love" whose connotation is close to the meaning of "adoration"—*Bewunderung.*)

This is why we must say that among the value relationships previously distinguished, the meaning of the emotions that are grounded in the first kind of relationship (namely, the relationship of subjective and direct value in which the object only exists in relation to the subject) is extremely rare in the original content of *aware,* although some might be included. Moreover, although the third meaning is certainly the most important with regard to the object of *aware,* this emotional meaning of negativity (for example, the feeling of contempt) becomes extremely thin in the concept of *aware.* Rather, as a variation of the "value emotions" of the first and second meanings, it is difficult to distinguish it from the slightly vague feelings of "pity," "sorrow," and so forth.

For those who are mainly concerned with a linguistic analysis of the problem of *aware,* what has been said so far might look like a useless search. And yet this is extremely meaningful to me. In fact, from the kinds of relationships described here I can draw the following conclusions. Namely, the premise that, despite the inclusion in the concept of *aware* of a large variety of emotional meaning contents, and despite the presence of both positivity and negativity in its value meaning, the spiritual attitude originally signifying the notion of *aware* is, generally speaking, an attitude *(Einstellung)* that we should call "contemplative" *(kontemplativ).* At the root of both the positive and negative emotions that *aware* contains within its "contemplative attitude," however, there is a condition producing "love" in its aesthetic sense: an "eros" that has an objective and universal quality. In sum, the concept of *aware* expresses an "emotional attitude" that is equipped with the general psychological condition of "aesthetic consciousness." It is what Moritz Geiger[15] has called "contemplation" *(Betrachtung)*—namely, "a keeping away from subject and object" *(Fernhaltung von Ich und Gegenstand),* or what we call in this country "exclamation" *(eitan).*

In the first and second roll of his *Jeweled Comb of The Tale of Genji (Genji Monogatari Tama no Ogushi),* Motoori Norinaga discussed the meaning and the spirit of the entire *Tale of Genji.* As many people know, Norinaga strongly opposed not only the views of those scholars influenced by Confucianism and

---

15. Moritz Geiger (1880–1937) developed a phenomenological aesthetics in *Phenomenology of Aesthetic Appreciation (Beiträge zur Phänomenologie des Ästhetischen Genusses,* 1922). According to Geiger, aesthetic appreciation is autonomous with respect to the aesthetic object—the result of intuition and insight rather than of induction. Appreciation is a kind of disinterested contemplation that separates the subject from the object. All aesthetic appreciations are contemplative ones. This does not mean that the observer lacks interest in the aesthetic object *(Interesselosigkeit)* but, rather, that the attitude in approaching an aesthetic object is not dictated by a specific interest for a specific object *(Uninteressiertheit).* Geiger also wrote *The Psychic Meaning of the Arts (Die Psychische Bedeutung der Kunst,* 1928).

Buddhism, according to which the meaning of the work lies in its ability to promote good and to punish evil *(kanzen chōaku)*, but also those views that see in the *Tale of Genji* a parable *(hōben)* devised in order to teach the Buddhist way. Instead, he stressed the aesthetic autonomy of the tale that should be read as "literature," arguing that the expression *"mono no aware"* (the pathos of things) was actually the purpose and the spirit behind the work. At the same time, he developed a detailed discussion of the concept of *mono no aware*. Since his theories on this subject are at the basis of all studies on *aware,* I will be quoting the most telling passages:

> What does "to know *mono no aware*" mean? *Aware* is the voice of sorrow that comes out when the heart feels after seeing, hearing, or touching something. Today we would use the exclamations "Ah!" *(aa)* and "Oh!" *(hare)*. Looking at the moon or at the cherry blossoms, for example, we are deeply impressed and say: "Ah, these splendid flowers!" or "Oh, what a beautiful moon!" The word *"aware"* is the combination of *"aa"* and *"hare."* This is the same as the Chinese exclamation *"Wu hu"* that in *kanbun* reads *"Aa."* . . . Later on, *aware* was given the character meaning "sorrow," making us believe that the word simply meant grief. But *aware* is not limited to the expression of sorrow. It also applies to the state of being happy, interesting, pleasant, and funny. Therefore, we have the expressions "to be movingly funny" and "to be movingly happy." Whenever we feel *aware,* whether in a funny or a happy circumstance, the expression *"aware"* is used. True, there are many cases in which *aware* is used in opposition to "funny" and "happy." Since human passions vary, when the excitement over something funny or over joy is not very deep, or when our heart is deeply moved by sorrow, anxiety, longing, or some other unfulfilled desire, that depth is specifically known as *aware*—which explains why in our daily usage we associate *aware* only with sorrow. . . . It is the same with the expression *"mono no aware."* To say *(iu)* something *(mono)* is called *monoiu. Mono* is often added to words as in "to tell" *(monokataru),* "sightseeing" *(monomi),* "confinement on unlucky days" *(monoimi).* Whenever we meet with a situation in which we should be feeling something, the feeling of knowing that the heart should be moved by that something is called "to know *mono no aware.*" Of course, the fact that the heart is not moved on occasions when it should actually be feeling something, such an inability to feel is called "ignorance of *mono no aware*" and such a person is known as "a heartless man."[16]

Here I would like to pay attention to the end of the quotation, where it says: "the feeling of knowing that the heart should be moved by that something." This passage deserves special attention from an aesthetic point of view. It should become clear when this is read in conjunction with another famous ex-

---

16. *Genji Monogatari Tama no Ogushi,* roll 2. See Ishikawa Jun, ed., *Motoori Norinaga,* Nihon no Meicho 21 (Tokyo: Chūō Kōron Sha, 1984), pp. 406–408.

planation by Norinaga. He formulated the same question—"What does 'to know *mono no aware*' mean?"—in the first roll of *Poetic Whisperings (Isonokami no Sasamegoto),* in which he discussed the essence of poetry. Norinaga answers as follows:

> We read in the preface to the *Kokinshū:* "The poetry of this Yamato land takes one heart as its seed that grows into myriad leaves." This is the heart that knows *mono no aware.* . . . All beings living in this world have a heart. . . . Men are exposed to more complex experiences than beasts, and since many are the things they must deal with, numerous are their thoughts. Therefore, men cannot do without poetry. As to what is so very deep in their thoughts, that is the knowledge of *mono no aware.* Since our experiences are so complex, whenever we come into contact with external reality we are moved emotionally, and we are never silent. . . . There are differences among people with regard to the depth or shallowness of their ability to understand and to discern the heart of things. Since the ability of beasts is shallow compared to people, it seems that they do not discern things. Being superior to things, human beings discern well the heart of things and know *mono no aware.* Because of this difference in the depth of human perception, relative to those who have a deep understanding of *mono no aware,* some people seem to be completely ignorant of *mono no aware.* Because of this big difference in human nature, ordinarily there are many people who do not know *mono no aware.* Actually, it is not that they do not know it. It is only a matter of difference between depth and shallowness.[17]

Motoori explained the notion of *aware* in another theoretical work that shares the same content as *The Jeweled Comb* and actually antedates it: *The Essentials of Murasaki's Work (Shibun Yōryō).* Although the essential thought about *aware* remains unchanged, it is worth noticing Motoori's further emphasis on the intellectual and objective moments of the consciousness of *aware.* In this later work Motoori more intimately ties the act of "knowing the heart/meaning of things" and the act of "knowing the pathos of things." In fact, the basic structure (as far as this topic is concerned) that appears in *The Jeweled Comb* and in *Poetic Whisperings* is expressed more clearly in *The Essentials,* in which the real meaning of *aware* is all the more deeply understood. For example, in this work Norinaga states: "The ability to feel the presence of good in the portrayal of a character of lowly disposition in his moments of goodness is to understand the meaning of things, to know their pathos. It is the same with everything." He also says: "A man who thinks longingly of a woman's beautiful features shows his knowledge of the heart and pathos of things. The reason is that to think that something is good when you see something good is to understand the meaning of things and to know their pathos."[18]

---

17. Hino Tatsuo, ed., *Motoori Norinaga Shū, SNKS* 60 (Tokyo: Shinchōsha, 1983), pp. 280–283.
18. The original text appears in Hino, *Motoori Norinaga Shū,* p. 88.

From the following quotation we understand even more how the notion of *mono no aware* in *The Essentials of Murasaki's Work*—the combination of "the knowledge of the meaning of things" and "the knowledge of the pathos of things"—is close to the general idea of "aesthetic consciousness" seen as the harmonious union of what we call in aesthetics "perception" *(schauen)* and "excitement/sensation" *(fühlen)*:

> We could summarize the entire fifty-four rolls of this story in one phrase: "to know the pathos of things." Step by step I have previously shown the meaning of *mono no aware*. To be even more detailed, I would say that to savor in our hearts all those things in the world that we see with our eyes, hear with our ears, and touch with our body, and to ponder deeply in our hearts over the nature of all those things, is to understand the meaning of events, to understand the meaning of things, to understand the pathos of things. To subdivide the topic even further, the act of understanding by distinguishing is to know the meaning of things, to know the meaning of events. *Mono no aware* is the feeling that is appropriate to the type of thing that we have understood. To perceive as beautiful flowers the view of extremely beautiful cherry blossoms at their height, for example, is to understand the meaning of things. It is the feeling at the thought of how beautiful the cherry blossoms are after actually understanding and distinguishing the beauty of those flowers. This is precisely what *mono no aware* is about.[19]

The meaning of *aware* should be clear enough from Norinaga's explanation. Yet we must admit that the distinction between "perception" and "intellectual judgment" remains quite vague in his use of the phrase "to know and distinguish." While this is a simple introduction, if we keep reading the extremely detailed yet slightly verbose explanation that follows, we cannot overlook the remarkable closeness that this concept has with the so-called notion of empathy *(Einfühlung)* of modern Western aesthetics. For example:

> When someone sees or hears of a person who is grieving after meeting with heavy sorrow, his fathoming the degree of the other person's grief depends on the fact that he knows that the other person is certainly grieving. This is to know the meaning of events. Knowing the fact that the other person is certainly grieving, the feeling that follows the fathoming of the degree of that person's grief is *mono no aware*. When we know the reason for the other person's certain grief, no matter how hard we try to repress that feeling, we will be naturally unable to contain grief and will feel as if we were forced to feel: this is what is called "human feelings" *(ninjō)*.[20]

---

19. Ibid., pp. 124–125.
20. Ibid., p. 126.

These words correspond to the so-called "intrinsic empathy" *(eigentlich Ein-fühlung)*. In the same work, Norinaga also talks about something corresponding to "symbolic empathy" *(symbolisch Einfühlung):*[21]

> We read in the "Paulownia Court" chapter that "everything, the moaning of the wind, the humming of autumn insects, added to the sadness. . . ."[22] This is to know the pathos of things by transferring it to the scenery according to the occasion. The way of perceiving things changes according to the mood of the time. . . . Since what we see and what we hear do not have a mind of their own, although the external appearance of things does not change according to the viewer, the perception of that thing as a sad or an interesting object varies according to the viewer's mood.[23]

According to the theory that Norinaga presents in *The Jeweled Comb,* a prerequisite for *aware* is the presence of *deep* feelings. Yet we must inquire about the meaning of "deep" in the preceding sentence. Here we do have a problem. Basically the notion of the "depth" *(Tiefe)* of feelings is one fraught with an ambiguous multiplicity of meanings open to a variety of interpretations. (On this topic there are original interpretations on the part of aestheticians such as Lipps[24] and Geiger.) Leaving aside for the moment the general debate on "em-

---

21. "Empathy means the projection of human feelings, emotions, and attitudes into inanimate objects. The fact itself was already familiar to Aristotle who deals with it in connection with the problem of the metaphor. The modern term *Einfühlung* was first used by Robert Vischer. His suggestions were taken up and developed in Germany by Theodor Lipps, and Johannes Volkelt, and Karl Groos, in France by Victor Basch, in England by Vernon Lee. . . . The phenomenon under consideration stretches further than esthetics. Social intercourse as a whole is based on the understanding of expressive attitudes, gestures, and words. Myth and religious symbols are vehicles of expression. The empathy theorists were not blind to these facts. But the animation of the lifeless, they believed, attains to consummation in the esthetic act. A sympathetic generosity, prompting us to lend a human soul to inanimate objects and to unite us with the universe, accounts for the depth and power of the esthetic enjoyment. Thus the idea of sympathy as developed by Lord Kames and other eighteenth century writers reentered the esthetic discussion. Victor Basch rendered the term *Einfühlung* by 'sympathetic symbolism' or 'symbolic sympathy.'" See Katharine Everett Gilbert and Helmut Kuhn, *A History of Esthetics* (Bloomington: Indiana University Press, 1954), pp. 537–538.

22. Edward G. Seidensticker, transl., *The Tale of Genji* (New York: Knopf, 1976), p. 12.

23. Hino, *Motoori Norinaga Shū,* p. 129.

24. Theodor Lipps (1851–1914) is the author of a *Guide of Psychology* (*Leitfaden der Psychologie,* 1903) and a famous *Aesthetics* (*Ästhetik,* 1903–1906), in which he discusses the notion of empathy. "There is a tacit presupposition underlying the arguments of the empathy psychologists. Experience appeared to them to offer facts and objects originally alien to man. Hence the occurrence of anything like expression, a human feature in non-human reality, was to be marvelled at, and the hypothesis of a hidden psychic mechanism was needed to account for it. This hypothetical act, occult in itself though manifest by its result, was called 'empathy.' An emotional state is infused into and merged with some object, so as to penetrate and mold it to its own image. All this goes on in subconsciousness. The conscious self, knowing nothing of this loan made to the external thing, encounters the manifestation of itself without necessarily recognizing it. We find things talking to us in our own language and we are unaware that their voice is merely the echo of our own. On the other hand, the responsive power in the object may persist after we become conscious of this fact. It is the latter possibility on which art rests. Art is the persistence of illusion in a disillusioned world.

pathy," I wish to concentrate on what is relevant for us here. In my interpretation, in order to problematize Norinaga's theory, we should divide the meaning of "depth" into two. One meaning refers to the feelings' overwhelming intensity that strongly shakes the "self" during the experience. The other involves the continuous absorption of the "self" in these feelings and in their drives *(Motiv)* during the emotional experience. It is *depth* in an introverted sense in which the self clearly sees and reflects upon these feelings. The first meaning simply privileges the strength and depths of feelings; the second implies that, together with the emotional experience, the attitude of the "self" itself has wholly deepened. Because of this whole deepening, we are no longer dealing just with the depth of emotions: a new depth is remarkably added that is related to the intellectual and reflective spirit. Of course, we cannot deny that in actual emotional experiences—especially in the experience of *mono no aware*—both "intellectual" and "emotional" sides are strictly fused with each other. Yet I believe that it is not only possible but necessary to emphasize and differentiate, at least theoretically, all the meanings of "depth."

Norinaga says in his *Jeweled Comb:* "Feeling is movement, and since it is the movement of the heart . . ." Likewise, in his *Poetic Whisperings* he says: "Whenever we come into contact with external reality, we are moved emotionally, and we are never silent." His own etymology of *aware* as the combination of "Ah!" and "Oh!" reinforces his interpretation of the word's meaning as the voicing of exclamation and excitement. It is clear that in all these instances Norinaga privileges the meaning of *aware* as a moment of strong emotions that deeply moves the "self." In this sense, independently from the content of the emotions, the development of each of them in the form of excitement transforms these emotions into *aware.* Based on the etymological meaning of *aware,* Norinaga pointed out that, first of all, the general meaning of this notion applies *(gelten)* to all kinds of emotions. But if we think in terms of the psychological difference between emotions *(Gefühl)* and affects *(Affekt),* Norinaga privileges the passive sense of the body in his definition of excitement as emotional movement, leaving aside all kinds of emotions that are related to the instinctual, active movement of volition such as, for example, "anger."

We must pay particular attention to the passage in *The Jeweled Comb* that says, "when the excitement over something funny or over joy is not very deep, or when our heart is deeply moved by sorrow, anxiety, longing, or some other unfulfilled desire." To interpret this passage we must ponder over Norinaga's thought in order to grasp what he really meant. Here I believe that we should provide an interpretation of the word "depth" slightly different from the one

---

Wordsworth pictures daffodils and waves 'dancing in glee.' Yet he does not expect us to ascribe in full earnest any mood to waves and flowers; or if he did so, this wish should have nothing to do with the beauty of his verse. Reality may be dumb, unfeeling, utterly estranged from us. Yet we are in possession of a device which reawakens it to temporary life and responsiveness, and the psychological mechanism which works this transformation is designated 'empathy.'" See Gilbert and Kuhn, *History of Esthetics,* pp. 538–539.

previously given. As Norinaga had previously noted, it is clear that we can consider "depth" in the sense of a development of the intensity of simple emotions—whether they are related to joy or to interest—into the form of "excitement." Therefore, *aware* would be the voicing of this excitement. If we understand Norinaga superficially, we might say that there is continuity in his explanation of the "depth" of emotions and that the only difference can be found in the degree and frequency of that intensity. In fact, it is possible to say that, for example, although at times feelings of joy can reach the degree of "excitement" known as *aware*, this case is, generally speaking, rare when compared to feelings of sadness, which in most cases involve "a special intensity of feelings." Perhaps this is actually what Norinaga thought when he was writing the last passage just quoted. But when I compare it to other detailed explanations that Norinaga gave of *aware*, I feel that a different meaning of "depth" was creeping into his mind, perhaps without his knowledge—namely, the second meaning of "depth" I distinguished earlier, the one that, at the same time as being an emotional experience, bursts forth from a combination of perception and clear vision, a spiritual "depth."

The method used by Norinaga to explain *aware* in *The Jeweled Comb* transformed a very general approach, considering this concept in its large sense, to a more specific and narrow definition. But beyond questions of broadness and narrowness, it seems to me that he actually laid the foundation for the development of a theory that moves away from a psychological interpretation of *aware* and approaches an aesthetic interpretation. If we approach the problem from an exclusively linguistic perspective and focus on the etymology of the word, then our explanation would be reductionist and narrow. It would be like saying that among many flowers, the "cherry blossom" is the one called "flower" and nothing more. A narrow definition of *aware* points, however, at a relationship that takes us from the fields of linguistics and psychology to literature and aesthetics.

As I have pointed out, although we talk in terms of feelings of "sadness," "alienation," and "longing" as opposed to "joy" and "fun," if we think of "longing" alone we understand the complexity of its structure in terms of experience. It would be unthinkable to stop our analysis at the intensity of simple feelings in looking at the "depth" of emotional experience. In addition to the problem of intensity, when we compare feelings of "joy" and "delight" that are part of positive "life feelings" *(Lebensgefühl)* with the negative emotions of "sadness" and "alienation," we are drawn into the motivations and the foundation of such experiences. We feel increasingly inclined to see clearly the metaphysical universality of humanity and the world—in other words, we must acknowledge the psychological reality common to all human beings about the easiness with which the "depth" of emotional experience (our second meaning of "feelings") comes to life. As for the explanation of how such reality takes place, this is related to the philosophical problem of visions of the world and human nature—a topic I do not intend to discuss here. I only wish to point out the undeniable influence that, either directly or indirectly, Buddhism has had on the spiritual life of peoples and ages, although it might not always have been acknowledged.

In *Poetic Whisperings,* the participation of intellect and perception is considered an important condition of the emotional experience of knowing *mono no aware.* Namely, "the discernment of the meaning of things" is vital to the experience. The previous quotations particularly emphasize the importance of differences of degree. Therefore, the original meaning of feeling *deeply* and the *depth* of feelings—as the word *"aware"* indicates in tales from the Heian period—is related to overwhelming meditation and vision. "Depth" here suggests an emotional experience that permeates the entirety of the "self." The structure of such an experience—perception and sensation—penetrates the innermost "self," making it an essential condition for aesthetic consciousness.

As I have pointed out, I think that this meaning of *aware* is particularly clear in the explanation that Norinaga gives of the word in *The Essentials of Murasaki's Work.* Here the appreciation of workmanship in the production of objects is considered to be "the knowledge of the meaning of things, an example of knowing the pathos of things." Then we can say that aesthetic consciousness in genuine art appreciation is the quintessence of knowing *mono no aware.* Of course, Norinaga does not put the problem in terms of contemporary aesthetics, such as the aesthetic consciousness of art. But when he talks about the consciousness of appreciating "beauty" at the view of the splendid cherry blossoms in full bloom and states that this is what *mono no aware* is about, thus fusing together "the knowledge of the meaning of things" (perception) and "the knowledge of the pathos of things" (excitement), he actually paves the way to the development of the notion of pure aesthetic consciousness.

When we ask ourselves about the meaning of all this, we find in Norinaga's thought, though in a still underdeveloped fashion, an inclusive way of formulating the experience of *aware* as a form of aesthetic consciousness—one that cannot be interpreted exclusively from a subjective point of view that is one-sided and biased toward emotional principles. In short, Norinaga's debate on *aware* approaches the problem from different perspectives that include linguistic, psychological, and aesthetic analyses never before attempted. In *The Essentials* he emphasizes the objective side of "the knowledge of the meaning of things" and privileges the aesthetic meaning of *aware,* thus introducing elements worthy of further scrutiny. Yet I believe there is no fault in stating that Norinaga stopped at the threshold of "psychological aesthetics" and the counterpart of what we would today call "empathy."

As we know from dictionaries, the word *"aware"* includes both a positive meaning, when written with the characters for "praise" and " excellence," and a negative one in which case *aware* is given the characters for "sorrow" and "pity." But when we try to apply this psychological interpretation of the concept to all occasions in which apparently contrary emotions are involved, we run in a series of difficulties. As Norinaga pointed out, when we deal with this problem from a simple linguistic point of view, since this word originally indicates the voicing of "excitement," it should not be surprising to see it equally used with regard to the content of disparate emotions that inevitably go in opposite directions. At the same time, when seen as a special "aesthetic category," whenever we address the problem of "aesthetic content" we are not bound to problematize one after another things such as, for example, the meaning of *aware* as "glory" (*appare*) or, in a strict sense, as "pity." Rather, we should concentrate only on the internal relationships in which the meanings of positive and negative emotions are integrated in the word "*aware*" as an aesthetic concept in the new dimension of the "aesthetic meaning." I will be talking about this problem in the following section.

From what I have said here, we know that two problems can be introduced with regard to the conceptual content of *aware* as an aesthetic category. First is the relationship between the general, psychological meaning of the concept *aware* and its specific, aesthetic meaning. Second, we are faced with the problem of the relationship between the larger meaning of the word, with the connotation of passions at large, and its narrower meaning of sorrow and pity that appeals directly to the linguistic sense of the word as we use it today. Although from a logical point of view these two problems cannot be reduced to one, such a tendency already appears in the theories by Norinaga that I have mentioned: by dealing with the problem of *aware* in the literature of *monogatari,* the two problems are constantly interrelated to the point where it becomes hard to avoid collapsing them naturally into one. I myself, for the sake of discussion, will consider these problems together and attempt to use them as our ground in inquiring about the development of *aware* in the special meaning that we attribute to the word as a derivative, aesthetic category.

Earlier I offered my interpretation of Norinaga's explanation of *mono no aware* as "the depth of feelings." In that instance we paid attention to the two meanings of "depth" and saw how Norinaga used it. On the one hand, he used it to indicate the depth of pure passions—namely the degree of "excitement"—while grounding his explanation in the etymological meaning of *aware.* On the other, in his explanation of a type of *aware* "that does not match what one feels in the heart," he included in the meaning of "depth" the intellectual and objective connotations of perception and clear vision. Once we put the two series of meanings together, Norinaga's concept of *aware* comes closer to the general meaning of aesthetic consciousness as the fusion of "perception" and "excitement." We could abbreviate it with the word "excitement" within a "contemplative attitude" (or "an attitude of serene contemplation").

Therefore, if we borrow for a moment the aesthetic vocabulary of Geiger, instances that lack the contemplative condition known as "uninterested" (*uninteressiert*)—as in the case of the jealous heart of a Lady Kokiden in the *Tale of Genji* mentioned by Norinaga—are beyond the boundaries of the problem of *aware.* The same can be said with regard to instances such as those portraying the religious feelings of monks struggling after liberation from all desires and worldly passions—cases that are unfit to the conditions of "aesthetic appreciation" by being excessively "indifferent" *(interesselos).* (These are cases that lack a motive for "excitement.")

In short, we cannot help admiring and respecting the excellent insights of Norinaga that provided him with a correct understanding of the psychological and aesthetic essence of *aware.* But when we think about the same issues from an aesthetic point of view, we cannot help feeling a sense of incompleteness with regard to an aesthetic analysis of *aware* that is still too generally defined. Although there is no doubt that the "excitement" within a "contemplative attitude" or the fusion of "perception" and "excitement" are indispensable elements of the aesthetic of *aware,* we cannot regard them as the only necessary conditions for the formation of *aware.* To which conditions, then, should we turn our attention?

To answer this question, I think it would be useful to rearrange here all the various meanings of the concept of *aware* along the stages of the word's development from the psychological to the aesthetic. As I have pointed out, the most direct meaning that this word has for us today indicates the content of peculiarly definite passions such as "sorrow," "grief," or "pity." I will call this kind of meaning the peculiarly psychological connotation of the concept of *aware.* Since this, after all, indicates the name of a specific feeling, it is only natural to conclude that such meaning is not yet related to any "aesthetic meaning."

Once we disengage *aware* from the limited passional content of "sorrow," the word expands to include the notion of "excitement" in general or the universality of "feeling." In this sense, *aware* applies to a variety of emotions, not only to "sad things," as Norinaga pointed out, but also to "happy events" and "funny situations." I will call this kind of *aware* its inclusively psychological meaning.

When we proceed to the third step, a new moment of "perception" is added to the general meaning of "excitement," such as we find in the knowledge of the "meaning of events" and the "meaning of things." In this case, not only does consciousness take "an attitude of serene contemplation" but *aware* takes its first step as "aesthetic feeling." For the sake of differentiations, I will call this last meaning of *aware* the universally aesthetic. (Or, to be a little more precise, I should call it the universally psychological/aesthetic meaning.) But this way of framing the issue eventually reduces the problem of *aware* to a general "aesthetic consciousness" without yet addressing problems of an exclusive aesthetic nature—or, to say it differently, the meaning of problems such as "aesthetic category" and "aesthetic types."

How, then, can we further proceed from all the steps of the meanings of *aware* analyzed here to order to reach the level of its peculiarly aesthetic meaning? Before entering this topic, I should be specific about what I actually mean by these differentiations in order to make our aesthetic analysis complete. First of all I must address the differences and relationships between Norinaga's way of dealing with the problem of *aware* and the way we do it today from the perspective of aesthetics, with particular regard to what we have called the "aesthetic meaning" of *aware*.

Norinaga problematized the notion of *mono no aware* by mainly inquiring about its meaning. This mode of approach necessarily corresponds to what I have previously called the universally aesthetic meaning of *aware*. Of course, when we talk about "the pathos of things," there is also a problem with the concept of "things." I do not want to enter into this matter here, however. I will simply follow Norinaga's explanation, taking it to mean the unstipulated external object. Therefore, if we analyze *mono no aware* as a formal expression, the "thing" or "external object" cannot be acknowledged to be a primary factor in the establishment of the meaning of *aware*. "Thing" is a "universal thing" fit to elicit an experience of *aware*. Although, formalistically speaking, "thing" is followed by "the pathos of," in terms of content this is nothing but the articulation of the sentence, "the pathos of things with pathos" *(awarenaru mono no aware)*. (This is what Norinaga meant by this last expression of his.) Here we must regard the general concept of "thing" regulated in terms of content by "the pathos" *(aware)* and not vice versa.

If we take it the opposite way, however, and actually consider the "thing" to be an a priori of *aware*, then the "thing" takes on a new and important content, such as "universal thing" or "universal Being" in its philosophical sense. Then "the pathos of things" becomes an experience that is regulated by a concrete, objective, primary factor. Here again we have a ground for the appearance of a new and different problem. Nothing is said about this last problem in the work of Norinaga, however. After all, Norinaga problematized *mono no aware* on a subjective level of consciousness, analyzing it from a psychological point of view, seeing it, at best, in its universally aesthetic meaning. Our aesthetic analysis, however, is different from Norinaga's approach. We must grasp the problem from the side that shows the special "form" of *aware* as an "aesthetic category" that somehow differs from the general notion of "beauty." Ultimately we must search for the ground regulating such "peculiarities" in the direction of the subject's perception of external reality—namely, into the side of "intuitive content."

To understand the path leading to the specifically aesthetic meaning of *aware*, it is now necessary to think about the following relationships. It is the relationship—which also regulates their content—between the passional direction of sorrow and grief as the "specifically psychological meaning," or first step in our analysis of *aware*, and the new, specific direction toward *aware* as "excitement" that finds its amplification in the second and third moments: "the inclusive, psychological meaning" and the "aesthetic meaning." To say it in further detail: From the "sorrow" that initially meant a specific, passional content is removed first of all the "specific, psychological meaning" or, better, the latter is overcome. When the *aware* that had become the "universally psychological meaning" of the second step ("universal excitement") and the meaning of "universal, aesthetic excitement" of the third step (as Norinaga had thought) reaches the fourth step, then it takes a turn toward the passional direction of a specific "sorrow" with a new metaphysical (worldview) meaning. By being established in this new moment, here, for the first time, a special "content of aesthetic meaning" is born from inside the concept of *aware*. As a result, the essence of *aware* as the "aesthetic category" we are searching for— or the experience of *mono no aware* that has overcome the "pathos" in its narrow, experiential, and psychological meaning—is absorbed into and permeated by the aesthetic excitement and by intuition to the very metaphysical bottom of the "universal thing" and the "universal Being." From there it widens into something like the meaning of a worldview, and it is universalized into a kind of world-weariness *(Weltschmerz)*. We may then think that *aware* exists in something that tries to metamorphosize into a special passional experience of "sorrow."

When we consider it from the general structure of "aesthetic experience," we can say that the main motive and ground of this special kind of sorrowful feeling lies in the side of what we call a natural aesthetic moment. Perhaps in our daily life, the so-called experience of *mono no aware* increases the depth of the immersion into it and widens the field of clear vision. It is a dipping into a kind of continuous grief, taking from what we could call "the ground of Being" *(Seinsgrund)* possessed by all things in the world. Like the special experience of, for example, mysticism, this is easily caused by a contemplative attitude toward a great "nature" that lies in the background of human activities. Actually we can explain all this when we think not only of the influence that Buddhist thought probably had on this attitude, but also when we ponder the lifestyle of the Japanese during the Heian period and the spirit of the time.

Yet this simply indicates the basic and general path of the development of the special meaning of *aware* as "aesthetic category." As we can see from the literature of the Heian period, when we look at the special structure of the "aesthetic experience" of *aware,* several other relationships mingle with the basic relationship described here, creating a concrete "form." I will try to give a couple of examples to which we should turn our attention.

As I mentioned earlier, the perception and excitement through which we realize *mono no aware* is an experience that is deepened by a special feeling of aesthetic sorrow. This, to a certain extent, is similar to world-weariness. It is like a dark and secluded depth that lies equally, togetherly, and basically in the innermost of *mono no aware* that the phenomena of the present world occasionally recall to our memory. No matter whether the concrete content of *mono no aware* is related to a "happy event" or a "funny one," a "joyous occasion" or an "outstanding one," in the innermost of the individual, positive "passions of life" it is always concealed as a background: a layer of such a dark, secluded, and deep passional experience. As a result, this deep background emotion, although it must be—to say it from the tone of feelings *(Gefühlston)*—a kind of pathos, floats in the foreground, conjoining with the positive emotions of fluttering "joy" and "fun." From there it appears a peculiar, subtle mood or sentiment that we should not explain conceptually. When we think of the "life emotions" on the flashy surface of the nobility, we can say that a uniqueness that we should explain according to this structure is included in *aware* as the special "aesthetic emotion" of the Heian period. I shall talk about this on some other occasion.

Next, when we think of the developmental ground of aesthetic *aware,* despite the basic truth behind the relationships examined here, fundamentally speaking, the concrete aesthetic consciousness is always the result of the fusion between a subjective and an objective side—or between the "moment of artistic feeling" and "moment of natural feeling," whatever the occasion on which it arises. Therefore, we will have to ponder over the conditions of subjective attitude *(Einstellung)* in aesthetic consciousness when dealing with the formation of *aware* as an aesthetic category. I have previously treated *mono no aware* along Norinaga's lines in its "comprehensive psychological meaning" and, at best, in its "universal aesthetic meaning." Then I have problematized these approaches as a path leading to the specific aesthetic meaning. When I look at the subjective attitude of *aware* as aesthetic consciousness, I see that it corresponds to, or runs parallel to, the development described above, being strictly related to it.

As we have seen, such a development, when it pursues the course of the content of objective meaning, starts from *aware* in its "special psychological meaning." It then proceeds toward a "comprehensive psychological meaning," as if it were in search of an emotional content, and toward the "universal aesthetic meaning," finally reaching the content of *aware* in its meaning of world-weariness. We have seen that within this process, in the second step of *aware* in its "comprehensive psychological meaning," the workings of our subject overcomes the specific emotion content of "sorrow," "grief," and "pity." In the third step, the moments of contemplation and exclamation are added, and the "attitude," as consciousness, becomes closer to the universal aesthetic consciousness. At this point we are temporarily standing in the viewpoint of subjectivism. The subjective "attitude" in the experience of *aware* in its "general aesthetic meaning" is again overturned, leading us to consider the relationship with a special object or situation that calls to mind "sorrow," "grief," and "pity" as special emotions.

Although here the object is the same, it goes without saying that our "experience" does not return to the initial type of *aware* as "special psychological meaning." Namely, it is not a "sorrow" that is felt in the practical consciousness of everyday life. The act of being moved, even with regard to a heartbreaking situation, is a special experience—as if you were feeling a sort of aesthetic satisfaction. This is because such experience is related to a special attitude *(Einstellung)* that is present in consciousness. Although, as I have pointed out, this experience belongs to the meaning of *aware* in its third step, we must acknowledge a unique characteristic to the concrete nature of such experience. Just as in Western aesthetics, we must think of this experience as something that gives us a special aesthetic satisfaction or pleasure, such as the "Tragic" and the "Melancholic." In the same manner, the experience of *aware* is nothing but the production of a complex and special aesthetic experience because of the unique nature of the external situation. In sum, then, even with regard to my previous observations on the basic relationships leading to the formation of the special meaning of *aware* as an aesthetic category, once we see it from the position of an actual subject, it is possible to add the special tone of aesthetic pleasure and satisfaction.

Yet it is hard to believe that we can exhaust our explanation of the essence of *aware* as an aesthetic category solely by looking at the peculiarities of the subjective meaning (the peculiarities of the psychological, subjective attitude). This is a side that has been stressed whenever one lists all the examples of *aware* that actually appear as aesthetic objects in the literature of the Heian period. Whenever a sad case is presented that elicits sympathy on the reader's part, for example, the word *"aware"* is generally employed. (This is similar to what in Western aesthetics is called the "cute," *das Niedliche.*) In such instances, the examples are related not only to a reality of "natural beauty" but also to the "beauty" of a reality that is produced in the human world. These are the instances that Norinaga calls "sad things" or "melancholic things." If we accept the idea that the "depth" of feeling discussed by Norinaga necessarily produces a kind of aesthetic pleasure or satisfaction, then we can probably conclude that his discussion of *aware* was concerned not only with the concept's universal, aesthetic meaning but also with the special aesthetic meaning of *aware* as "aesthetic emotion," which is a characteristic of *The Tale of Genji*. Today, however, it is inevitable to feel that his explanation is not sufficient from the point of view of aesthetics.

I personally believe there are two ways for *aware* in its aesthetic meaning to overcome the limitations of the emotional content of *aware* in its psychological meaning. One is the way that brings to life the special meaning of *aware* as an aesthetic category from the general "excitement" of *mono no aware,* by having the cause of psychological *aware* widened and deepened metaphysically. The other is the overcoming of the negative, special feelings by the attitude of consciousness on the level of external reality that elicits *aware* in its narrow sense of sorrow and pity, thus making you directly feel a special "aesthetic satisfaction." In fact, these two ways are always intertwined, originating the special structure of the experience of aesthetic *aware* as we find it in the Heian period. When we approach the problem theoretically, however, I think we should essentially follow the first path.

Therefore, not only it is hard to provide an exhaustive aesthetic explanation of the final value ground of *aware* as aesthetic form by simply concentrating on mental processes such as satisfaction and pleasure. Even when we follow the two paths described here, the latter is inherently limited. It is extremely hard to believe that when the external object of *aware* calls to mind excessively strong passions—such as "wretchedness" or "special sorrow"—the average person can expect to go though an "aesthetic experience" or assume that he is feeling an "aesthetic satisfaction." I believe that we cannot exhaust the problem theoretically unless we stand on a very special ground—such as the aestheticism or satanism of the type of Baudelaire or Oscar Wilde in the modern history of letters in the West. When we think of the main spiritual direction or the worldview of the Heian period, I believe there is a thread uniting the ground of the consciousness of *aware* with such an aestheticism. However, I will defer this problem to some other time. . . .

SEVEN

The Creation of Aesthetic Categories

THE WORK of Ōnishi Yoshinori had a profound impact on Japanese literary critics who adopted the notion of "aesthetic category" to explain the literary values of specific ages of Japanese history. Hisamatsu Sen'ichi (1894–1976), for example, probably the most influential scholar of premodern Japanese literature in the twentieth century, clearly refers to Ōnishi's work in "Patterns of Beauty in Ancient Japanese Literature" (Nihon Kodai Bungaku ni Okeru Bi no Ruikei, 1953), in which he explains the development of Japanese literary history in terms of the changes that occurred at the level of aesthetic discourse.[1]

Hisamatsu adopted the same scheme in his later *History of Japanese Literature* in six volumes (*Nihon Bungakushi*, 1955–1960), an abridged part of which appeared in English as *The Vocabulary of Japanese Literary Aesthetics* (1963). Here the author divides the history of Japanese literature into five ages,[2] explaining each of them according to representative works that fall into the three categories originally devised by Ōnishi: humor *(kokkei)*, sublimity *(sōbi)*, and elegance *(yūbi)*. The author then identifies aesthetic discourses or "patterns" that apply to each of these three major rubrics. As we can see from Table 1, most of the names used to define the patterns were taken from the vocabulary of classical Japanese poetics.

Hisamatsu was very attentive to the problem of philology. He had been introduced to the German brand by Haga Yaichi (1867–1927) while studying at Tokyo University. He paid considerable attention to the views and theories on literature developed by the major philologists of the Edo period, such as Keichū (1640–1701)[3] and Fujitani Mitsue (1768–1823), whose

---

1. This topic is discussed in Shida Nobuyoshi, "Hisamatsu Sen'ichi: Bungaku Shi to Bungaku Hyōron Shi," *Kokubungaku: Kaishaku to Kanshō* 57(8) (1992):100.

2. Antiquity (Jōdai, eighth century), Middle Antiquity (Chūko, 794–1156), Medieval (Chūsei, 1156–1560), Early Modern (Kinsei, 1560–1868), and Modern (Kindai, 1868–1912).

3. Hisamatsu graduated from Tokyo University in 1919 with a thesis on the philology of Keichū ("Keichū no Bunkengaku"). See Shida, "Hisamatsu Sen'ichi," p. 96.

Table 1. Japanese Literary Categories

Period	Humor	Sublimity	Elegance
Antiquity	*choku* (uprightness)	*mei* (brightness)	*sei* (purity)
Middle Antiquity	*okashi* (comic)	*taketakashi* (sublimity)	*aware* (sensitivity)
Medieval	*mushin* (witty)	*yūgen* (profundity)	*ushin* (discriminating)
Early Modern	*kokkei* (comic)	*sabi, karumi* (tranquility, lightness)	*sui, tsū, iki* (knowing, connoisseurship, chic)
Modern	—	*shajitsu* (realism)	*rōman* (romanticism)[a]

[a] Hisamatsu Sen'ichi, *The Vocabulary of Japanese Literary Aesthetics* (Tokyo: Centre for East Asian Culture Studies, 1963), p. 9.

suggestions Hisamatsu often combined with the philosophical material he assimilated from his reading of the aestheticians.[4] Aestheticians, on the other hand, being mostly concerned with the field of philosophy, were more interested in explaining local aesthetic categories in terms of the philosophical systems with which they were most acquainted. A good knowledge of Western epistemology could inspire Japanese scholars to reconstruct an entire epoch of their land's history in the spirit of a meticulous geometry—al-

4. See, for example, the following statement on a major Japanese theorist who is to this day considerably neglected even in Japan: "In *Makoto-ben,* Fujitani Mitsue establishes the four categories *henshin, ikkōshin, kōshin,* and *magokoro,* terms which mean, respectively, a biased spirit, a singleminded spirit, a rational spirit, and a spirit in which emotion and reason have achieved a natural state of equilibrium. When these mentalities manifest themselves in actions, the results are selfish deeds, rational deeds, 'pure-hearted' deeds, etc. Speaking in Mitsue's terms, we may say that *makoto,* a natural union of emotion, reason, and will, is the essential human quality, and that the same quality underlies all literature." See Hisamatsu, *Vocabulary of Japanese Literary Aesthetics,* pp. 10–11.

though at times questionable on philological grounds. This was the case, for example, of Kuki Shūzō (1888–1941), whose original and thought-provoking reading of the Edo period was informed by the aesthetic category of *iki* (chic) in his *Structure of Iki (Iki no Kōzō,* 1926, but not published until 1930).[5]

After examining the genealogy of major terms taken from the vocabulary of premodern poetics, Japanese aestheticians aimed at constructing them as aesthetic categories and providing new readings in the light of contemporary philosophy. As the reader will see from the essay translated here, Kusanagi Masao (b. 1900) followed this procedure in his analysis of a major poetic term very popular in Japan during the Middle Ages: *yojō,* the "surplus of meaning" that lingers after one has finished reading a poem, mainly because of the richness of its unstated implications. The following is a standard explanation of *yojō:* "remaining feeling, after-meaning, the affective and cognitive richness lingering after one has finished reading or reciting a poem, often because a poem is taken to imply more than its surface statement, predication."[6]

After interrogating what the classics had to say with regard to this concept, Kusanagi, who was a major scholar and Japanese translator of the German philosopher Karl Jaspers (1883–1969), worked Jaspers' metaphysics into his explanation of the overtones implied by the notion of *yojō.* At the same time, he provided a definition of the work of art that resisted the notion of closure and was grounded in the perfection of incompleteness. To avoid reducing the problem of incompleteness to mystical experience, however, Kusanagi strove to explain it in logical terms—thus creating his oxymoronic notion of a "logic of feelings" or, to use the title of his 1972 essay, "The Logic of Passional Surplus" (Yojō no Ronri). Kusanagi's project is faithful to Jaspers' "philosophy of reason," a philosophy centered on a universal will to communicate. This is realized by uncovering the "ciphers" *(Chiffreschriften)* and "symbols" of which the world is made—the only way for Jaspers to grasp the infinity of a transcendence that cannot be brought to closure. Applied to the work of art, this reasoning led Kusanagi to write an apologia of incompleteness in the artistic object—particularly when the incompleteness is not the result of an author's inability to bring his work to a closure but is originally planned by the author.

---

5. See Kuki Shūzō, *Iki no Kōzō* (Tokyo: Iwanami Shoten, 1979). See also the fascinating discussion between Martin Heidegger (1889–1976) and Kuki during the latter's studies in Germany, fictionalized by Heidegger himself in his "Dialogue on Language Between a Japanese and an Inquirer." See Martin Heidegger, *On the Way to Language* (New York: Harper & Row, 1971; German ed., 1959), pp. 1–54.

6. Earl Miner, Hiroko Odagiri, and Robert E. Morrell, *The Princeton Companion to Classical Japanese Literature* (Princeton: Princeton University Press, 1985), p. 304.

As "ciphers of transcendence," poetry and art enable transcendence to reveal itself within the "border situation" *(Grenzsituation)* of human existence—or, to use another expression employed by Jaspers, in "being-in-situation" *(in-der-Situation-Sein).*[7] Jaspers' authentic being can only be found in its transcendence which, in its turn, is related to existence.[8] After all, existence as presence and as possibility is the starting and ending point of all existential projects, since metaphysics makes the self return to himself so that to be oneself clarifies the meaning of being for transcendence.[9] By getting closer to existence we might avoid being trapped in the unauthentic

---

7. "In philosophizing we use the phenomena to touch being in our interpretation of *ciphers of transcendence,* and in the thinking that *appeals to Existenz.*" See Karl Jaspers, *Philosophy,* vol. 1, trans. E. B. Ashton (Chicago: University of Chicago Press, 1969), pp. 60–61. See also the following statement: "What was a mere function in the existential relation to transcendence becomes an object of contemplation in *reading ciphers.* There is no object that might not become transparent, none that might not in such visibility come to be more than it is as mere existence. The contemplation that reveals the world as a world of transcendence may be existential in character, but it may also decline into purely esthetic observation without efficacy in self-being. Metaphysics lets us read the ciphers consciously. It lets us understand mythology, poetry, and art as revelations of transcendence; it enables us to recognize their superiority and to adopt them with this understanding. Philosophical metaphysics has a creativeness of its own in its conceptual constructions of the cipher writing of mundane existence. Its conception comes to be an element of mythology. Such thoughts stand beside the true myths, and beside the artists' and poets' visions, as something different and yet analogous. Though incomparably less impressive, they are singularly, irreplaceably illustrative. As arguments they have no cogency at all. They are far from any hypothesis about extant being. From the point of view of logic, they are circles and paradoxes, and in the end they founder as all thought disappears." Ibid., pp. 94–95. And also: "Existenz, acting unconditionally in boundary situations will get its bearings from the ciphers of transcendence that fill its consciousness as *absolute objectivities,* as objects in the world fill consciousness at large. But in metaphysics, if we seek a *direct* approach to the absolute objectivity of a cipher of transcendence, it will elude our grasp. We must attempt to touch its existential roots, rather. If we succeed, by illuminating our own boundary situations and unconditional actions, the contact will validate the objectivity of the symbols because their content will have been felt." Ibid., p. 72. Furthermore, we read: "When we are truly ourselves, when our disquiet ceases for a moment, existence becomes transparent. Time stands still. Recollection uplifts us to being. The knowledge of what was makes the past an eternal present. This is not existence any more, nor anything that can be found in existence as such. It is the transcendence of existence; it is being as it appears to itself in existence." Ibid., p. 78.

8. "True being cannot be found in a sense that we might know. It is to be sought in its *transcendence,* to which only Existenz, not consciousness at large, can ever relate." Ibid., p. 63.

9. "The pivot of this movement, the junction and crossroads of whatever has absolute relevance for us, is Existenz. Without the presence or the possibility of Existenz we lose our way of thinking and our way of life in an endless, senseless waste. If I deny the being of Existenz not just conversationally but really, if I turn objective being into being as such, my existence will be void and dreary throughout the endlessness of things, with the rest an unexistential hustle and bustle impelled by the remaining, pointlike Existenz that leaves me no peace, demanding substance and fulfillment. And those are found nowhere but in the incomprehensible absolute certainty of an Existenz bent upon philosophical self-elucidation." Ibid., p. 66. See also the following statement: "Aiming at the universe, I lose my way in its inconclusiveness and am flung back upon myself; in this repulsion the stress is not on existence—I would be sliding down into that from the universe—but on myself in my freedom. And when metaphysics has put me through the experience of finding none of its objectivities valid for everyone, the recoil will again be on myself, and being myself will illuminate my relation to transcendence." Ibid., pp. 71–72.

discourse of subject and object, finding in what is not objective—and therefore not reducible to a mediated presence—the truth of our being as existence.[10]

In an essay on "The Concept of Japanese Art" (Nihon Geijutsu no Rinen),[11] Kusanagi analyzes the concept of *yūgen* (profundity)—first in the light of Japanese medieval theorists, such as the poets Fujiwara Shunzei (1114–1204) and Teika (1162–1241), as well as the playwright Zeami (1364?–1443). He then links the theoretical works of these classical thinkers to the existential philosophies of Heidegger and Jaspers, concentrating on the existential implications of the notion of "depth" contained in the concept of *yūgen*. Kusanagi locates *yūgen* within a metaphysical discourse, not by imposing piecemeal Western philosophy upon the concept, but by searching for traces of this metaphysical discourse in those Taoist and Buddhist texts where the word *"yūgen"* appears to indicate the profundity of a Taoist/Buddhist truth. He sees in a notion such as profundity the equivalent of Jaspers' "transcendence," which, unlike the metaphysical idea of a rational and objectifiable transcendence, can only be grasped in the empiricism of existence *(Dasein)*. Jaspers called his version of transcendence the "Being in the Comprehensiveness of Its Determinations" *(das Umgreifende)*. Kusanagi sees in Jaspers' ontology a parallel to the Japanese idea of transcendence that is usually caught in the act of its immanence—the Shinto presence of the sacred in the natural world (which for Kusanagi and other apologists of the Japanese "myth of immanence"[12] constitutes Japan's metaphysical world) and the presence of Buddhahood in the immediacy of the present body *(sokushin jōbutsu,* to become enlightened in the present life). As in Jaspers' case, Kusanagi argues, Japanese transcendence refuses to be made into an abstract concept and subjected to an absolute reason.

From what with the benefit of hindsight could be called "the myth of immanence" Kusanagi then turns to "the myth of seasonal determinism," according to which the Japanese mild climate and ordered seasonal cycle determine the Japanese closeness, admiration, and love for nature as seen in the vast local poetic production.[13] Since nature is for Kusanagi the

---

10. "Not until we approach Existenz do we come close to something absolutely nonobjective—and yet its self-certainty is the center of our existence, the wellspring of the search for being, and the spark that lights the *essentiality* of all objectiveness." Ibid., p. 66.

11. The article first appeared in *Bungaku* 11–12 (1967) and is now included in Kusanagi Masao, *Yūgenbi no Bigaku* (Tokyo: Hanawa Shobō, 1973), pp. 61–116.

12. This myth was particularly reinforced by the popularity of Nakamura Hajime's work, especially his *Ways of Thinking of Eastern Peoples: India, China, Tibet, Japan* (Honolulu: University of Hawai'i Press, 1964).

13. The myth of geographic determinism was particularly revived by Watsuji Tetsurō's book titled *Climate and Culture: A Philosophical Study* (New York: Greenwood Press, 1961).

original form of beauty and the center of Japan's metaphysical world, nature never becomes the object of mimesis or re-presentation and, therefore, is never re-created or given life by art. Nature is rather the source of life so that, instead of talking of "empathy" or art's tendency to provide nature with human feelings, as theorized by Theodor Lipps in his empathy theory *(Einfühlungstheorie),* the reader is encouraged to apply to Japanese art the word "anapathy" *(Zurückfühlung):* the return to the original ground of nature by entering into nature itself, or, to use another word, *yūgen.* Then, Kusanagi concludes, the Japanese work of art inspired by the metaphysics of *yūgen* works exactly as Martin Heidegger had described in "The Origin of the Work of Art"—by letting "something emerge as a thing that has been brought forth. The work's becoming a work is a way in which truth becomes and happens."[14] It works as one of Jaspers' "ciphers" that brings into visibility the invisibility of transcendence.

Kusanagi adopted Jaspers' vocabulary in defining Being as world, existence, and transcendence. Whereas world indicates man as an empirical and objectifiable reality, existence can only be made present to the existing self. The less objectifiable reality, transcendence, can only be perceived by existence in the objectified form of the cipher.[15] The latter, however, is not the object of empirical knowledge since the being of existence is freedom and not stability or duration.[16] While being the source of freedom, the truth of impermanence—which is at the very heart of existence—produces an anxiety out of which our confrontation with transcendence is born.[17] In the his-

---

14. Martin Heidegger, *Basic Writings from Being and Time (1927) to The Task of Thinking (1964)* (New York: HarperCollins, 1993), p. 185.

15. "The *world* is what exists, what occurs to me as the being of specific objects, and what I am as empirical existence. My cognition of the world is objective, concerned with things I have before my eyes as objects; but the world itself, the universe, is neither an object nor a whole. Of being—nonobjective as such—I can attempt only an illustrative, inadequately objectified ascertainment. This nonobjective being is *Existenz* if it can originally manifest itself to me in my own being; we call it *transcendence* if it is being in the objective form of a cipher but conceivable for Existenz alone." See Jaspers, *Philosophy,* vol. 1, p. 68.

16. "The intellect puts weight and emphasis upon successes due to visible causes and effects. What Existenz rates most highly seems most feeble to the intellect. The quietude of existential communication is inaccessible to mundane knowledge, except where it has grown superficial. But that the power of ideas is nonobjective—that in the honest view of empirical knowledge they are indeed wholly powerless—is the very sign that they concern being as freedom, not being as duration. A matter of freedom cannot possibly be turned into a knowledge of processes." Ibid., p. 70.

17. "It can indeed only be shown, not proven, that the world is not self-sustaining but perishing all the time. This aspect will be as self-evident and ever-present to one man as the statement will seem senseless to another—too senseless for him to know what to make of the words, he will say. The source of transcending is an otherwise irremediable disquiet about the impermanence of all existence." Ibid., p. 79.

toricity of its finitude, the self experiences the manifestation of the essential Being when the self comes to its authentic self.[18]

No matter how loudly we may hear theological and metaphysical resonances in Jaspers' notion of transcendence, his philosophy of existence starts from the premise and returns to the premise that such transcendence can only be fulfilled within the limitation of existence. After all, existence (and death) are the only verifiable truths upon which we can rely. It would be absurd to try and overcome the boundaries of this very existence in order to find authenticity in a transcendental world located outside the human condition. At the very best the authenticity of transcendence can be found in the form of traces—Jaspers' "ciphers"—to be fulfilled within the limits of border situations.

By following Jaspers' thought, Kusanagi argues that if Being is brought into existence by the work of art and the work of art is a historical product of human time, the truth of Being can only be captured in the fragmentariness of an empirical artistic expression. Traces of Being are brought into vision within the framework of human time, which is in constant flux *(mujō)* and refuses to provide the work of art with the possibility of closure. Here Kusanagi calls the reader's attention to the many medieval Japanese literary works that are informed by the Buddhist doctrine of impermanence. Foremost among them stands Kenkō's (1283–1350) *Essays in Idleness (Tsurezuregusa),* celebrated for these words: "Are we to look at cherry blossoms only in full bloom, the moon only when it is cloudless? To long for the moon while looking on the rain, to lower the blinds and be unaware of the passing of the spring—these are even more deeply moving."[19]

---

18. "The more substantial my theoretical and practical world experience, the more lucid my faculty of transcending the world. Without the world there is not transcendence." Ibid., p. 83. See also the following statement: "When I transcend to my intrinsic self, I am Existenz with other Existenz; but I cannot—as this statement tempts me to try—watch the several selves as an aloof consciousness at large. Consciousness at large, an objective observer, cannot see any Existenz. Existenz is real only for Existenz, in communication. Philosophizing to elucidate it does not mean getting to know something else; it means to reveal essential being as I come to myself. It is the self-being that cannot once more confront itself. A philosophy of Existenz as a pseudoknowledge of myself would tempt me to evade reality. Instead of really being myself, I would merely lay claim to self-being." Ibid., pp. 85–86. And also: "Without Existenz, world orientation would be senseless, and transcendence would become superstition. Without world orientation Existenz would be pointlessly pointlike, and transcendence would remain without a voice. Without transcendence Existenz would lose its proper self-being, and world orientation, its possible depth. It takes all three to make a human being, a possible Existenz that takes its bearings in the world as consciousness at large and relates, through the world, to its transcendence. Factuality, self-being, and the reading of ciphers, are only with one another, and by one another." Ibid., p. 89.

19. Donald Keene, trans., *Essays in Idleness: The Tsurezuregusa of Kenkō* (New York: Columbia University Press, 1967), p. 137.

The notion of incompleteness provides Kusanagi with the necessary link to discuss the concept of *yojō* in another famous essay, "The Logic of Passional Surplus," which is translated here.

The Logic of Passional Surplus
by Kusanagi Masao

1

How can we explain the beauty of mystery and depth *(yūgenbi)* that constituted the aesthetic ideal of the Japanese fine arts during the Middle Ages?[20] We cannot deny that *yūgen*, which was originally endowed with a metaphysical meaning, is an artistic concept born from its combination with the grace and refinement that the Japanese people felt as their innate and simple sense of beauty. There the beauty of mystery and depth is related to metaphysical Being (in the Japanese case, Nature)—a Being that is not closed into an object but is infinitely open. So long as we use the vocabulary of Jaspers[21] and define *yūgen* as the "Being in the Comprehensiveness of Its Determinations" *(das Umgreifende),* it is only natural that we cannot represent *(repräsentieren)* in a real sense the artistic concept of the beauty of mystery and depth in an objective and thorough manner.

As I have briefly mentioned in a previous chapter, the beauty of passional surplus *(yojōbi)* that, since the Middle Ages, has, together with the beauty of mystery and depth, been made into the traditional aesthetic essence of the Japanese arts is related to the metaphysical ground in the same capacity of the beauty of mystery and depth. The reason is that the beauty of passional surplus cannot be directly expressed—that is, with regard to what is left unsaid by the aesthetic object, it is similar in nature to the beauty of mystery and

---

20. The original text of this essay, "Yojō no Ronri," first appeared in the March 1972 issue of the journal *Bigaku.* It is now included in Kusanagi Masao, *Yūgenbi no Bigaku* (Tokyo: Hanawa Shobō, 1973), pp. 117–146. The word *"yojō"* literally means "an excess of feelings" or "overtones." It was used in medieval poetic treatises to indicate the overtones deriving from the poetic use of allusion to ancient poems or the use of conventional diction.

21. Karl Jaspers (1883–1969), a specialist in psychology and psychiatry, taught philosophy at the Universities of Heidelberg and Basel.

depth. This becomes all the more clear when we look at the following rule on *yūgen* by Kamo no Chōmei,[22] who in his essays on poetry particularly emphasized the passional surplus and can be said to be the first person who noticed the identity of *yojō* and *yūgen:*

> *Yojō,* which is not stated in words and an atmosphere that is not revealed through the form of the poem. [*Mumyōshō*][23]

Such an equalization of *yūgen* and *yojō,* or this grounding of *yūgen* in *yojō,* plays an important role in our examination of the essential meaning of *yojō.* Shōtetsu,[24] however, distinguishes *yojō* from *yūgen* and says:

---

22. Kamo no Chōmei (1153–1216) is the author of a famous theoretical work on poetry, *The Nameless Treatise (Mumyōshō).*

23. This quotation comes from Chōmei's famous definition of *yūgen:* "All aspects of form in poetry are difficult to understand. Although the old collections of oral traditions and guides to composition teach the reader thoroughly in difficult points by leading him along, when it comes to formal aspects we find nothing at all precise. This is particularly true of the style of *yūgen,* whose very name is enough to confuse one. Since I do not understand it very well myself, I am at a loss as to how to describe it in a satisfactory manner, but according to the views of those who have penetrated into the realm of *yūgen,* the importance lies in *yojō,* which is not stated in words and an atmosphere that is not revealed through the form of the poem. When the content rests on a sound basis and the diction excels in lavish beauty, these other virtues will be supplied naturally. On an autumn evening, for example, there is no color in the sky, nor any sound, and although we cannot give a definite reason for it, we are somehow moved to tears. A person lacking in sensitivity finds nothing particular in such a sight, he just admires the cherry blossoms and scarlet autumn leaves that he can see with his own eyes. Again it may be likened to the looks and bearings of a fine lady who has some grievance, does not however, express it in words, but suffers secretly and gives only a faint clue as to her situation; this has a stronger appeal to one's compassion than if she were exhausting her vocabulary with complaints and made a show of herself wringing out her sleeves. A child, on the other hand—how could it understand this just by seeing her looks and bearing, unless the meaning is explained in detail in proper words? By these two analogies it should be evident that this is a matter impossible to understand for people of little sensibility and shallow heart. Again I would like to compare this style to the speech of a lovely child, awkwardly and without clear perception, but lovable in all its helplessness and worth listening to. How can such things be easily learned or stated precisely in words? You can only comprehend them for yourself. Again, if you look at the autumn hills through a rift in the mist, you catch only a glimpse, and, unsatisfied, try to figure out freely in your imagination how pleasing it might be to see the whole of those scarlet leaves—this is almost better than saying it clearly. Completely to display your feelings in words by saying of the moon that it is bright, or by praising the cherry blossoms, declaring that they are pretty, how can that be difficult? Where would there be the virtue of the *uta,* which is to be more than an ordinary statement? Only when many ideas are compressed in one word, when without displaying it you exhaust your mind in all its depth and you imagine the imperceptible, when commonplace things are used to display beauty and in a style of naïveté an idea is developed to the limit, only then, when thinking does not lead anywhere and words are inadequate, would you express your feelings by this method which has the capacity to move heaven and earth and the power to touch the gods and spirits." See Hilda Katō, "The *Mumyōshō* of Kamo no Chōmei and Its Significance in Japanese Literature," *Monumenta Nipponica* 23(3–4) (1968): 408–409. For the original text see Hisamatsu Sen'ichi and Nishio Minoru, eds., *Karonshū, Nōgakuronshū, NKBT* 65 (Tokyo: Iwanami Shoten, 1961), pp. 86–88.

24. Shōtetsu (1381–1459), poet of the Muromachi period, supported the revival of the poetic style of the famous poet Fujiwara Teika (1162–1241) in a poetic treatise called *Conversations with Shōtetsu (Shōtetsu Monogatari).*

What most people seem to understand by mystery and depth is simply the style of overtones, which is not mystery and depth *(yojō no tei)* at all. Some people call the style of the sad beauty of things *(mono aware tei)* mystery and depth, and so on. But the style of overtones and the style of mystery and depth are completely different from each other. [*Shōtetsu Monogatari*][25]

This distinction does not clarify the substance of the matter. We may think that in setting up such a distinction, Shōtetsu probably did not accurately grasp the metaphysical meaning of *yūgen* and *yojō*. However, this might be related to differences in the interpretation of the meaning of *yūgen*. As a genuine poet, Shōtetsu took the meaning of *yūgen* entirely in the direction of grace and refinement. For example, Shōtetsu classified the following poem "among those written in the style of mystery and depth":

Sakeba chiru	In my dream
Yo no ma no hana no	Of cherry blossoms that in a night span
Yume no uchi ni	Fall as soon as they bloom,
Yagate magirenu	The white clouds on the peak
Mine no shirakumo	Alone are not confused.[26]

He then explains the meaning of *yūgen* as "something that is in the heart but is not expressed in words. The moon veiled in thin clouds, or the bright foliage on the mountains concealed by autumn mist—such poetic conceptions are regarded as having the effect of mystery and depth. But if one asks in which particular feature the mystery and depth are to be found, it is difficult to specify exactly. A person who failed to comprehend this fact would argue that the moon is at its most enchanting when it is glittering brightly in a clear sky with not a cloud in sight."[27] By interpreting the poem in this manner, what becomes the aesthetic object ceases to appear to our eyes in its reality and objectivity.

25. The quotation comes from *Shōtetsu Monogatari* 1:82: "The style of mystery and depth can perhaps be only understood by those who have actually reached that level of accomplishment. What most people seem to understand by mystery and depth is simply the style of overtones, which is not mystery and depth at all. Some people call the style of the sad beauty of things mystery and depth, and so on. But the style of overtones and the style of mystery and depth are completely different from each other even though everyone thinks they are the same. Lord Teika wrote, 'The poet Tsurayuki, in ancient times, composed in a style of strength *(mono tsuyoki tai)*, but he did not compose in the ultimate style of mystery and depth.' The style of the sad beauty of things is favored by poets." See Robert H. Brower, trans., *Conversations with Shōtetsu (Shōtetsu Monogatari)* (Ann Arbor: Center for Japanese Studies, University of Michigan, 1992), p. 98. The original text appears in Hisamatsu and Nishio, *Karonshū, Nōgakuronshū*, pp. 189–190.

26. The poet argues that the ephemeral nature of the cherry blossom is such that he cannot see them even in his dreams. The only reminder of such a fleeting existence is the white clouds that stand out distinctively in the poet's memory. The poem appears as number 3098 in a poetry collection compiled by Shōtetsu and supplemented by his disciple Shōkō (1412–1494), titled *Grass Roots (Sōkonshū)*. Shōtetsu discusses this poem in *Shōtetsu Monogatari* 2:77.

27. Brower, *Conversations with Shōtetsu*, p. 150. For the original text see Hisamatsu and Nishio, *Karonshū, Nōgakuronshū*, p. 224.

Its concealment behind "thin clouds" and "the autumn mist" entrusts the poem to the free imagination of the reader—or, to use Shōtetsu's own words, "it is hazy, shimmering delicacy, about which nothing can be said," "it is impossible to say just what it is that is enchanting or lovely." As a result, a sentiment of profound mystery and depth arises.

But if we were to limit our inquiry on *yūgen* to Shōtetsu's explanation, we would not be thinking of the metaphysical meaning in which *yūgen* and *yojō* are originally grounded. According to him—to overstate it a little—the beauty of mystery and depth simply means a mystical and visionary, genuine aesthetic feeling. In a different section, however, Shōtetsu states that "good is the poem that leaves something to be said," and even in his previously mentioned explanation of *yūgen* he explains it as "something that is in the heart but is not expressed in words." Here we can say that even Shōtetsu inherited the meaning of *yūgen* = *yojō* that we find in Chōmei. Yet his distinction of *yojō* and *yūgen* indicates that he did not sufficiently realize the metaphysical implications of the two concepts. So long as *yūgen* and *yojō* are related together to a metaphysical Being, their essence cannot differ.

For a genuine poet like Shōtetsu who was influenced by Teika and accepted the latter's "overtones and ethereal charm" *(yojō yōen)*[28] as a valuable principle for poetry, it was probably only natural that he would hold charm and grace in high regard in his poetic treatises. The treatise of Shinkei,[29] however, Shōtetsu's disciple in the way of poetry and a high-ranking monk who later became an adjunct chief abbot, is far more stern in stressing the metaphysical meaning of *yūgen*. This might be due to the remarkable influence that Buddhism, particularly Zen thought, had on him. In Shinkei *yūgen* and *yojō* are clearly seen as identical:

You find mystery and depth as well as the sad beauty of things where things are left to be said and logic is absent. [*Sasamegoto*][30]

In Teika and Shōtetsu's interpretation of the surplus of feeling as "overtones and ethereal charm," the tie between the surplus of feelings and a metaphysical sentiment is not yet clearly realized. More than the metaphysical side, it is

---

28. The aesthetic ideal of *yōen* (ethereal charm) became particularly dominant in the age of the *Shinkokin-shū* (1205), thanks to the poetic practice of Fujiwara Teika. Brower and Miner explain *yōen* as follows: "Basically, *yōen* was the romantic idealization of a delicate, dreamlike beauty—the beauty of a peony or of an exquisite heavenly maiden descending to earth on a hazy spring night. Such beauty was elusive, ephemeral, the stuff that dreams are made of, and while the typical imagery of *yōen* had the delicate lightness of cherry petals, it was often used to convey a tone of sadness—of lovers parting or of nostalgia for the vision of a beauty not of this world." See Robert H. Brower and Earl Miner, *Japanese Court Poetry* (Stanford: Stanford University Press, 1961), p. 262.

29. Shinkei (1406–1475), a poet and a master of linked verse *(renga)*, is the author of the poetic treatise *Whisperings (Sasasamegoto)*.

30. For the original text see Ijichi Tetsuo, Omote Akira, and Kuriyama Riichi, eds., *Rengaronshū, Nōgakuronshū, Haironshū*, NKBZ 51 (Tokyo: Shōgakukan, 1973), p. 88.

clearly the pure aesthetic component (grace) that constitutes one pole of "the beauty of mystery and depth" as an artistic concept. Episodes from *Conversations with Shōtetsu* such as the following, however, speak of a tendency directed toward the metaphysical nature of *yūgen* that constitutes the other pole. According to what is reported in *Conversations with Shōtetsu,* Shunzei,[31] who in his old age was distressed with the inconsistency between his lifestyle as poet and artist and also a seeker after the Buddhist truth, undertook a retreat of seven days at the Sumiyoshi Shrine vowing: "If poetry is a purposeless activity, I will give up this art from now on and devote myself wholeheartedly to religious preparations for the life to come." Shunzei himself felt that his creative life as an artist was a game disengaged from an active spiritual life—or, to use an expression borrowed from existential philosophy, an irresponsible and nonexistential aesthetic behavior. On the night of the seventh day of his vow, however, the god appeared to him in a dream announcing: "Japanese poetry and the way of the Buddha are one whole, not two." Realizing that the way of the Buddha did not exist apart from the way of poetry, Shunzei devoted himself to poetry more fervently than ever. The same event is reported with regard to Teika *(Shōtetsu Monogatari).*[32]

In this manner came into existence a philosophy of art peculiar to the Japanese Middle Ages, known as the oneness of the way of poetry and the Buddhist way. You find a direct indication in Shinkei's statement: "The lofty verse rich in depth and profundity, and free of intellectualism, is equivalent to the Dharma Body."[33] According to Shinkei's *Whisperings,* Shōtetsu had previously called the way of poetry "the direct path to sudden realization." For Saigyō[34] it was "a wholehearted endeavor in contemplative practice." Moreover, the words of Minamoto no Tsunenobu[35]—"*Waka* is the fountainhead of the life of seclusion; it is the direct path that leads to enlightenment. The true reality

---

31. Fujiwara no Shunzei (1114–1204), father of Teika, is the compiler of the imperial collection *Senzaishū* (Collection of a Thousand Years) and a proponent of the "style of mystery and depth" (*yūgentai*) in the composition of poetry. He had more than four hundred poems collected in imperial anthologies. Shunzei is the author of a major poetic treatise, the *Korai Fūteishō* (Notes on Poetic Styles Through the Ages).

32. *Shōtetsu Monogatari* 1:58; Brower, *Conversations with Shōtetsu,* p. 89; Hisamatsu and Nishio, *Karonshū, Nōgakuronshū,* p. 184.

33. Ijichi et al., *Rengaronshū, Nōgakuronshū, Haironshū,* p. 156. Shinkei refers to the Buddhist doctrine of the Three Bodies *(Trikāya),* according to which the Dharma Body *(Dharmakāya)* is the absolute reality, beside which there is no other reality; the Body of Bliss *(Sambhogakāya)* is shared by all transcendent buddhas, such as, for example, Amida Buddha; the Body of Manifest Beings *(Nirmānakāya)* belongs to all buddhas who appear in the world in physical form, such as the historical Buddha Gautama. See Hans Wolfgang Schumann, *Buddhism: An Outline of Its Teachings and Schools* (Wheaton, Ill.: Theosophical Publishing House, 1974), pp. 101–109.

34. Saigyō (1118–1190), with ninety-four compositions, is the best-represented poet in the *Shinkokinshū.* He is the author of a private poetic collection, as well, *Cottage on the Mountains (Sankashū).*

35. Minamoto no Tsunenobu (1016–1097), poet of the late Heian period, is the father of the famous poet Shunrai.

of the suchness of all things is comprehended in the thirty-one syllables of *waka*"—clearly indicate the religious and metaphysical nature of Japanese poetry.[36]

Thereby Shinkei says that superb poetry does not exist in "verses of weighty and saucy form"—that is, verses embellished by rhetorical flourishes and polished expression. You find it, rather, in those "chilly and slim verses with a reduced degree of content and diction." When he admonishes "to turn at heart to what is unspoken and awaken to and grasp the chill and desolate" *(Sasamegoto),*[37] the surplus of feeling is remarkably charged with a Zen-like, metaphysical nature. Moreover, the standard for excellence in poetry here privileges the philosophical meaning of *yūgen,* which constitutes the other pole of the notion of the beauty of mystery and depth.

So far I have examined the apodictic relationship between *yūgen* and *yojō*—that is, the fact that the beauty of passional surplus and the beauty of mystery and depth both share the Buddhist = metaphysical characteristics inherent to the medieval Japanese arts. This means that the arts become a stage where the aesthetic Being and the transcendental, metaphysical Being confront each other.

Far from being limited to the way of poetry, this literary thought was particular to and common to all artistic expressions since the Middle Ages, such as the fine arts, music, or, more broadly, to all the arts in general. For example, the famous quote from Tosa Mitsuoki,[38] "even an empty space within a pattern will fill you up with feelings" *(Honchō Gahō Taiden),* refers to passional surplus in painting. As for the reason behind it, Mitsuoki provides the following concrete explanation:

> Good is the artist who detests painting anything without leaving a sufficient amount unsaid—an artist full of inspiration but somber in representation. The unskilled painter is the one whose painting, on account of the artist's poor inspiration, lacks something despite a sufficient amount of drawing. The skilled painter is the one whose surplus of inspiration flows over the somberness of representation.
>
> It is good not to set a pattern and to leave about one-third of the painting open to additions. You won't be able to express all the feelings contained in a poem unless you search deep in your heart and include it in your painting. [*Honchō Gahō Taiden*][39]

---

36. *Sasamegoto* 1:20. See Dennis Hirota, *Wind in the Pines: Classic Writings of the Way of Tea as a Buddhist Path* (Fremont, Calif.: Asian Humanities Press, 1995), p. 157; Ijichi et al., *Rengaronshū, Nōgakuronshū, Haironshū,* p. 96.

37. Hirota, *Wind in the Pines,* p. 151; Ijichi et al., *Rengaronshū, Nōgakuronshū, Haironshū,* p. 124.

38. Tosa Mitsuoki (1617–1691) was a famous painter in the Yamato style and a revivalist of the Tosa school of painting in the early Edo period. He wrote the *Honchō Gahō Taiden* in 1690.

39. The original text appears in Sakazaki Shizuka, *Nihonga no Seishin* (Tokyo: Tōkyōdō, 1942), pp. 31–63.

The painter Nakabayashi Chikutō of the late Edo period[40] also admonishes us "to reach the interesting space of graceful and deep resonances that is located outside the work, outside brush and ink" *(Gadō Kongō Sho)*.[41] Moreover, the painter Nakayama Kōyō of mid-Edo[42] says: "Awesome is the eternal elegance of landscape painting" *(Gadan Keiroku)*.[43] This last sentence apparently derives from the words of Hsüeh Kang of the Ming dynasty: "It is because among paintings, only landscape paintings are endowed with such a profound meaning and such an eternal elegance that the literati have painted so many of them." Even Kuwayama Gyokushū[44] quoted Hsüeh Kang's words and highly praised the merits of *nanga* paintings, the paintings of the literati:[45] "It is in the heart of the literati to toy with the mysterious elegance of mountains and rivers." Acknowledging that poetry and painting shared the common purpose of expressing the mysterious sentiment of nature, Gyokushū said: "People who paint this sentiment must necessarily be men of letters."

The reason why Gyokushū, who was a painter of the Southern school, rejected the works of the Northern school as the product of "a rustic style" lies in the fact that the latter emphasized realistic paintings and held in light esteem the expression of the mysterious and deep passional surplus:

> The paintings of the Northern school make the imitation of forms the whole purpose of art, taking for artistic skill the use of ink to color in detail. . . . Since many of these painters served at the imperial court, their style has been named the court style. It has also been called the style of the specialists, a rustic style.

On the opposite side, the Southern school "is the place where the nobility and men of great taste and refinement toy with the arts in their moments of leisure. Their paintings aim at recapturing ancient refinement and look after superb beauty, while their heart overflows dampening the form of things" *(Kaiji Higen)*.[46]

---

40. Nakabayashi Chikutō (1776–1853) defended the Chinese and Japanese ink landscape paintings *(nanga)* from the spread of Western styles. He wrote the *Gadō Kongō Sho* in 1802.

41. The original text appears in Sakazaki Shizuka, ed., *Nihon Garon Taikan,* vol. 1 (Tokyo: Arusu, 1927), pp. 171–185.

42. Nakayama Kōyō (1717–1780) painted figure subjects more frequently than landscapes. He wrote the *Gadan Keiroku* in 1775.

43. The original text appears in Sakazaki, *Nihon Garon Taikan,* vol. 1, pp. 841–876.

44. Kuwayama Gyokushū (1737–1812) was a pupil of Ike no Taiga (1722–1776). He wrote the *Kaiji Higen* in 1799.

45. "Nanga, meaning 'Southern School painting' reflects the taste of Chinese scholar-painters as interpreted by Japanese artists. Another name for this art is *Bunjinga,* or 'literati painting.' The paintings by such Chinese literati as Mi Fu, Ni Tsan, and Huang Kung-wang had been classified as 'Southern School' by the Ming painter, calligrapher and theorist Tung Ch'i-ch'ang, as opposed to the works of professional and court artists which he called 'Northern School.' Tung thus established a new orthodoxy based on the art of scholars and poets. In like manner, the Nanga painters Gyokushū and Chikutō also wrote theoretical works trying to give a history and rationale for Bunjinga in Japan." See Stephen Addiss, *Zenga and Nanga: Paintings by Japanese Monks and Scholars* (New Orleans: Museum of Art, 1976), pp. 11–12.

46. The original text appears in Sakazaki, *Nihon Garon Taikan,* vol. 1, pp. 135–153.

Even if we admit the influence of Chinese ink painting, in light of the fact that the representation of sentiment at the expense of pure imitation was the original purpose of ink painting, particularly since the time of the Japanese Middle Ages, landscape painting became quite popular on account of its appeal grounded in the beauty of mystery and depth. As I mentioned earlier, the reason for such popularity was "because among paintings, only landscape paintings are endowed with such a profound meaning and such an eternal elegance." This came about as a result of the peculiar meaning of Chinese perspective. Western perspective aims at portraying objects in the world three-dimensionally within a well-defined and limited space to convey a feeling of the object's visual existence. In opposition to this, Chinese perspective was a device used to elicit a mysterious and deep aesthetic sentiment from the portrayal of nature's magnificence and profundity. The result was the same whether artists used the triple perspective of Kuo Hsi[47] (height, depth, and horizontal dimension)[48] or the six-dimensional perspective of Han Cho,[49] who added the three dimensions of wideness, dimness, and mysteriousness. The aim was not to provide the object with a feeling of visual reality.

The fact that the Southern school and the literati privileged ink paintings and took nature as the object of their representations, and the fact that most of Teika's poems sang of nature, show how *yūgen* and *yojō* were regarded as the essential value of works of art both in China and in Japan. This also means that the formation of *yūgen* and *yojō* was related to transcendence (in the Japanese case: Nature).

2

In the formation of works such as those mentioned here, we must anticipate a confrontation between author and transcendence. In these instances, to use the appropriate vocabulary of Jaspers, the so-called transcendence is a nonobjectifiable Being known as "Being in the Comprehensiveness of Its Determinations"—namely, a place that cannot be grasped directly and objectively as com-

---

47. Kuo Hsi was born in Henan province in 1020 and acquired great fame as a landscape painter. He is the author of an influential treatise, *An Essay on Landscape Painting (Lin Ch'üan Kao Chih),* of which an English translation by Shio Nakanishi is available (London: John Murray, 1935).

48. "A mountain has three dimensions: looking up to the top from below gives the dimension called height; looking toward the back from the front gives the dimension called depth; looking across at a mountain from an opposite height gives the horizontal dimension. The tone of the distance of height is clear and bright; that of depth, heavy and gloomy; that of the horizontal plane is sometimes clear and sometimes dark. Height is obtained by expressing an upward force. Depth is obtained by piling layer upon layer. The effect of distance is obtained by the use of misty lines which gradually disappear. In painting human figures in these three dimensions those of the heights must be clear and distinct; those in the depths detailed and fine; those in the distance dreamy and tranquil. Clear and distinct figures should not be short; fine and detailed ones not too tall; mild and dreamy ones not too large. These are the laws of the three dimensions." See Kuo Hsi, *Essay on Landscape Painting,* p. 46.

49. Han Cho (fl. 1119–1125), Chinese painter.

pletion or as a "closed" *(geschlossen)* totality. Moreover, for Jaspers such a transcendence exists in a subjective way only for sake of being-there. This institutes a relationship between existence and transcendence. Being-there gains reality only within this relationship with transcendence; transcendence acquires meaning as the reality of existence only within its relationship with being-there.

But since human beings live only a finite actual existence, notwithstanding the fact that for them transcendence appears with the meaning of reality, this is actually so only with regard to the "I" (potential being-there) as finite, potential being. For an author who is a finite, potential being-there, however, transcendence, when it appears, can only be read each time instantaneously within historical time as—to use Jaspers' technical language again—a "cipher" *(Chiffreschrift)* or a "symbol" *(Symbol).* Therefore, the work of art as well is nothing but a (second) cipher written by an author who is a potential being-there. This means that, so far as the form of the work is concerned, you have fragmentariness and incompletion.

In an analogous way, even to those works of art that make the beauty of mystery and depth their aesthetic ideal, *yojō* necessarily brings the quality of incompleteness. To say it differently: The work of the artist as potential being-there—if he performs his creative activity through his relationship with transcendence and instantaneously meets with the depth of existence within historical time by writing a cipher—while being incomplete, must be called the expressive form of *yojō* as an "appeal" moved by the will of art. Since this *yojō,* as I have mentioned, developed within the sentiment of an existential world and against the background of "the philosophy of impermanence" that we could also define as the Buddhist expression of such a world sentiment, we can classify the Japanese traditional arts since the Middle Ages as existential arts.

As we have seen with regard to the Japanese traditional arts since the Middle Ages, the beauty of passional surplus was stressed in relation to the incompleteness of the work of art. It is of great interest to us to see how incompleteness in art has been considered a new topic of discussion in German aesthetics. Following the importance this topic has achieved in essays on art, starting in this century, famous contemporary aestheticians and art critics such as Joseph Gantner,[50] Dagobert Frey,[51] and Herbert von Einem[52] have drawn at-

---

50. Joseph Gantner (1896–1988) was an art historian who specialized in the works of the Renaissance. He wrote major works on Leonardo (*Lionardo da Vinci,* 1954; *Lionardos Visionen von der Sintflut und vom Untergang der Welt,* 1958), on Michelangelo (*Rodin und Michelangelo,* 1953), and on Rembrandt (*Rembrandt und die Verwandlung Klassischer Formen,* 1964).

51. Dagobert Frey (1883–1962) analyzed human spatial and temporal power of representation in the work *Gotik und Renaissance als Grundlagen der Modernen Weltanschauung* (1929). In English see his *Architecture of the Renaissance from Brunelleschi to Michael Angelo* (The Hague: G. Naeff, 1925).

52. Herbert von Einem (1905–1983) was an art historian whose book on Michelangelo is available in English. See Herbert von Einem, *Michelangelo* (London: Methuen, 1973), especially the conclusion, "The Incomplete and the Uncompletable," pp. 256–265.

tention to the incompleteness of the arts. Let me explore this subject a little.

Broadly speaking, the work of art, so long as it is seen objectively, is usually regarded as something that has been completed. According to the most commonsensical view, at the time when an author puts the brush down after having first taken it up, the work is accomplished. In this case, however, the appreciation, criticism, and reflection upon the work of art are limited to the process of composition. This might seem natural when we think that the work of art is constructed within a set form that is usually limited. But if that is the case, the artist is destined to be spellbound by this limited, set form—for example, in the case of the *waka*, the thirty-one-syllable structure. On the other hand, he struggles to set himself free from these boundaries. For example, the explanation that Nijō Yoshimoto[53] gives of the origin of long poems *(chōka)* attests exactly to this:

> In ancient times poets sang many long poems. They did so because they could not exhaust in thirty-one syllables the deep feelings that were welling up in their hearts. [*Gumon Kenchū*]

It was only natural for artists struggling after self-liberation to feel dissatisfied with an imitationist and realist art that contented itself with an expression limited by a set form. Would it be unfair to consider *yojō* as well partly related to a similar dissatisfaction and to a desire for self-liberation? If works of art come into existence as a demand for self-expansion, for overcoming the limited boundaries of the self, it would be inadequate to think of works of art as something simply limited to the exterior form as it appears in reality.

Seen from this point of view, and with the use of the idea of "prefiguration" *(Präfiguration),* people such as Gantner have for the first time in the field of aesthetics attempted to explain the process of artistic production as a total process that is not limited to the objective form observable in reality but goes beyond this limitation to what is included within the process of artistic creation as an objective form:

> The use of this idea brings a complete and essential expansion to what has been known until now with the word "the nonfinished" *(non-finito),* or the incomplete work of art. [Gantner, *Formen des Unvollendeten in Neuren Kunst*]

First of all, Gantner called "figurations" *(Figurationen)* the formation process of real, objective works of art, while providing a detailed analysis of incomplete works by Leonardo da Vinci and Michelangelo. Since sketching, drawing, and the fragment are the first steps in the creative process that precedes

---

53. Nijō Yoshimoto (1320–1388) had a distinguished political career and played a major role in the codification of linked poetry *(renga).* He is the author of a major poetic treatise, the *Gumon Kenchū,* in which the poet Ton'a answers several questions formulated by Yoshimoto on the way of poetry.

these *Figurationen,* and since these all come prior to the work that is perceived in its materiality, they are nothing but the condition preceding "figuration," which is the accomplished work of art. Therefore, seen in its constitutive elements, the work of art is seen as incomplete. But Gantner calls *Präfigurationen* the whole inclusion of the invisible (immaterial, spiritual) dimension that shapes the artistic enterprise. He then analyzes the total process of artistic production, grounding the work of art in the existential basis of incompleteness.

What particularly draws our attention to this theory is the fact that in Gantner the incomplete work of art seen as *Präfiguration* is taken as a positively independent artistic form. Gantner's study starts from an actual analysis of the incomplete works of Leonardo and Michelangelo that survive unfinished to this day. The problem of incompleteness in Japanese art, however, is not related to incomplete works that are left unfinished. Incompleteness in this case was planned intentionally as the essential artistic form of a completed work of art. In this regard the case of Japanese art differs from the case suggested by Gantner. But if we focus on Gantner's view of the independent and discrete state of the unfinished work of art, we can relate our concept of *yojō,* in which we found the nature of incompleteness, to Gantner's study—particularly his conclusions. Namely, in Gantner the incomplete work of art as the material *Präfigurationen* of sketch, drawing, and fragment is not simply incomplete, but it signifies completeness. While quoting Condivi[54] that "the rough form never hinders the work's completeness and beauty," he further explains—and we can see this clearly in the confrontational relationship between *Präfigurationen* and *Figurationen:*

> The material *Präfiguration* becomes independent and, as a result, starts losing its *präfigural* nature. It is not that it aims at coming to the rescue of what later will become the completed work of art. Rather, from a pure joy within its own form and for its own sake, the created sketch is not in a strict sense some kind of *Präfiguration.* To say it differently: The apparently incomplete work becomes increasingly complete. Moreover, *Präfigurationen* move more and more within the role of *Figurationen.*

The following words that Gantner quotes from the contemporary poet Charles Morgan[55] apply as well to this concept: "The essence of art is the genius lost in deep thoughts; it is not to write a poem, to paint a picture, or to compose music. . . . The work might follow this, or it might not." The reason is that "a work may be complete in conception without being complete in execution" (H. v. Einem, *Unvollendetes und Unvollendbares im Werk Michelangelos*). The reason why artists left works not completed is because "their vision was completed, and this completion was incomplete."

54. Ascanio Condivi (b. ca. 1520) was a disciple of Michelangelo and the author of *Vita di Michelangelo Buonarroti.*

55. Charles Langbridge Morgan (1894–1958), novelist and dramatist, was dramatic critic of *The Times* (1926–1939).

Moreover, according to Gantner, *Präfiguration* develops where the creative impulse confronts the worldly object (nature). Following this confrontation, whenever the artist's personality is dominant, he always expresses himself in this *Präfiguration*. As a result, completeness, that is, *Figurationen*, already ceases to be a problem. Not only does it "not become an obstacle for the incomplete work," but a positive meaning is born: that the very nature of incompleteness is the original essence of the work of art. Incompleteness "is the artistic form freely planned by the artist" (Gantner, *Rodin und Michelangelo*). We can call it the completeness of incompleteness. As Einem argues: "Incompleteness always follows a priori the reality of art." When we convert these words to the positive meaning that the essence of the work of art is incompleteness, we meet with the positive meaning of our *yojō* as incompleteness. This is because real completeness is rejected in the highest degree.

As we can see in the concept of passional surplus and the notion of the beauty of mystery and depth, from the numerous essays on poetry and paintings written during or after the Middle Ages, as we have noticed—for example, the opening paragraph of chapter 137 from Kenkō's *Essays in Idleness*,[56] "are we to look at cherry blossoms only in full bloom, the moon only when it is cloudless?";[57] or the passage referring to those people who, rather than paying attention to the festival, "look at the avenues of the city and understand the pathos of the festival;"[58] or "what is harmonious is bad" and "to leave something un-

---

56. Yoshida Kenkō (1283–1350) was a famous poet and the author of *Tsurezuregusa* (Essays in Idleness), a series of 243 essays written over thirty years of Kenkō's life.

57. "Are we to look at cherry blossoms only in full bloom, the moon only when it is cloudless? To long for the moon while looking on the rain, to lower the blinds and be unaware of the passing of the spring—these are even more deeply moving. Branches about to blossom or gardens strewn with faded flowers are worthier of our admiration. Are poems written on such themes as 'Going to view the cherry blossoms only to find they have scattered' or 'On being prevented from visiting the blossoms' inferior to those on 'Seeing the blossoms'? People commonly regret that the cherry blossoms scatter or that the moon sinks in the sky, and this is natural; but only an exceptionally insensitive man would say, 'This branch and that branch have lost their blossoms. There is nothing worth seeing now.'" See Donald Keene, trans., *Essays in Idleness: The Tsurezuregusa of Kenkō* (New York: Columbia University Press, 1967), p. 115. For the original text see Kidō Saizō, ed., *Tsurezuregusa, SNKS* 10 (Tokyo: Shinchōsha, 1977), pp. 153–154.

58. "Such people have a very peculiar manner of watching the Kamo Festival. 'The procession's awfully late,' they say. 'There is no point waiting in the stands for it to come.' They go off then to a shack behind the stands where they drink and eat, play *go* or backgammon, leaving somebody in the stands to warn them. When he cries, 'It's passing now!' each of them dashes out in wild consternation, struggling to be first back into the stands. They all but fall from their perches as they push out the blinds and press against one another for a better look, staring at the scene, determined not to miss a thing. They comment on everything that goes by, with cries of 'Look at this! Look at that!' When the procession has passed, they scramble down, saying, 'We'll be back for the next one.' All they are interested in is what they can see. . . . I never weary of watching the different carriages going back and forth, some delightfully unpretentious, others magnificent. By the time it is growing dark you wonder where the rows of carriages and the dense crowds of spectators have disappeared to. Before you know it, hardly a soul is left, and the congestion of returning carriages is over. Then they start removing the blinds and matting from the stands, and the place, even as you watch, begins to look desolate. You realize with a pang of grief that life is like this. If you have seen the avenues of the city, you have seen the festival." See Keene, *Essays in Idleness*, pp. 119–120; Kidō, *Tsurezuregusa*, pp. 115–156.

done is a way to prolong your life;" or, as Shinkei said, "wherever you leave something unsaid and whenever you are beyond logic, you will find mystery and depth, as well as the moving pathos of things"[59]—works that apparently have already been completed are actually works that were planned as incomplete works in "leaving something to do" or "leaving something unsaid" or "leaving something to be painted." In this case, it is probably fit to use the expression "incompleteness is completeness or completeness is incompleteness."

We all know that in ancient times, the Japanese philosophy of art consciously dealt with the positive meaning of incompleteness. As I have mentioned, famous aestheticians and art historians starting from Gantner began with the study of actual works left unfinished by Leonardo and Michelangelo. On the other hand, Japanese essays on the arts started from an essential examination of art. Although on this point the two approaches differ, the conclusion that in art "incompleteness is completeness and completeness is incompleteness" remains equally valid for both.

3

Now I will be taking a look at two essays on the development of the philosophy of art that are mentioned in an earlier collection of essays entitled *Incompleteness as Artistic Form:*[60] H. von Einem's *The Incomplete and the Uncompletable in the Works of Michelangelo (Unvollendetes und Unvollenbares im Werk Michelangelos)* and D. Frey's *Fragmentariness as Variability in Rembrandt (Das Fragmentarische als das Wandelbare bei Rembrandt)*. I believe that the major characteristic of both essays lies in the explanation of the philosophical and, particularly, existential ground of the formation of incomplete works seen according to the notion of *Präfiguration* advocated by Gantner.

Namely, Einem sees the worldview of Plotinus[61] behind the creative activity of Michelangelo and its incompleteness:

> As a disciple of Dante and Petrarch, Michelangelo, in his interpretation of the possibilities and limits of art, was influenced by Plotinus' thought—that art is not simply an imitation of nature, but is an actualization of an inner idea.

---

59. Ijichi et al., *Rengaronshū, Nōgakuronshū, Haironshū*, p. 88.

60. *Geijutsu Keishiki to Shite no Mikanseiteki na Mono.* This is the name of a symposium held in Saarbrücken from 28 May to 30 May 1956. It is also the title of the conference papers edited by J. A. Schmoll Eisenwerth, *Das Unvollendete als Künstlerische Form* (Bern and Munich: Francke AG Verlag, 1959). The Japanese translation, *Geijutsu ni Okeru Mikansei* (Incompleteness in Art), appeared in 1971 (Tokyo: Iwazaki Bijutsu Sha).

61. "Plotinus (c. 203–262), Greek philosopher, the chief exponent of Neoplatonism. His *Enneads* did much to shape Christian theology in the 4th cent., and also exercised a wide influence on Renaissance thought through Ficino's translation (1492). They were studied by the Cambridge Platonists. The concept of the Chain of Being which Plotinus elaborated was generally accepted until the end of the 18th cent., as was the principle, which Sidney learned from Scaliger, that a poet is a second creator, Art re-ascending to the Ideas from which Nature is derived." See Margaret Drabble and Jenny Stringer, *The Concise Oxford Companion to English Literature* (Oxford: Oxford University Press, 1987), pp. 444–445.

Moreover, Einem argues that the fact that in Michelangelo "what was not completed, as a matter of fact, could not be completed" bespeaks a general view of art's possibilities and limits that was under the influence of Plotinus' philosophy of art.

The reason is that, as mentioned earlier, so long as we give the idea of Being the meaning of Comprehensiveness of Its Determinations, in no way can we define it as something that is objectively completed. So long as what the artist struggles to represent—that is, what he plans to complete in actuality—is not an imitation of nature but an inner idea, to be "incomplete" is the inevitable destiny of the work of art. But unlike the conscious affirmation of incompleteness that we find in the Japanese artists of the Middle Ages, "Michelangelo never purposively planned incompleteness." Although, generally speaking, "incompleteness is usually disavowed by artists," the unfinished works of Michelangelo could not be brought to completion "because he despaired of finishing them." For Michelangelo, "completion and finitude meant limitation and powerlessness against the infinite." That is to say: Incompleteness is a breakdown *(Scheitern)* in the process in which the artist approaches the plastic actualization of the idea. This explains why in Michelangelo's case, according to Einem,

> the incomplete work of art is a tragic proof of a heroic fight to make the idea visible. This becomes clear when we think of Neoplatonism in Michelangelo's background. This also explains very eloquently how, even in the sixteenth century, the purpose of art was sought in making visible the idea.

With regard to the fact that Michelangelo dared to leave unfinished his incomplete works, Einem speculates that "by entering too deeply into reality, he might have feared to lose ideality in the process of freezing reality into form. Wasn't his hesitation the product of such—metaphysical—anxiety *(Sorge)*?"

The metaphysical meaning of incompleteness becomes all the more clear in Frey's essay. In it Frey considers the opposite concepts of completeness and incompleteness as a conflict between fragmentariness and totality, variability and constancy. Of course for Frey fragmentariness means everything that is incomplete—including Gantner's *Präfiguration.* This is not all, however, since fragmentariness aims necessarily at a totality of a higher order. Within this relationship, the complete work of art can well be fragmentary. "In itself, the complete work is fragmentary in relation to a general totality." Therefore, in a work of art fragmentariness and totality stand in a reciprocal relationship:

> If unchangeability, hence also a supra-time, exists in the essence of the icon, on the other hand, time and variability with it are linked to the fragment—no matter how we grasp its meaning. The problematic of the Western plastic arts is mainly contained in the following truth: the truth that in the basic nature of the figurative arts, seen as constancy and unchangeability, glitters the experience of time and, hence, variability.

Yet even here, as in the case with Einem, what is called totality, the ultratemporal, the unchangeable, is essentially unregulated; it means a comprehensive, infinitely open totality. Nevertheless, the fragment still presents the impossibility of representation; it is the expressive form of what cannot be articulated in words. However, a tragic relationship arises between the two:

> Although, overcoming the limits set up by itself, the fragment aspires toward Totality, this Totality unfolds without rules. Exactly because of this unregulation as well as the original impossibility of regulation, a unique, tense relationship is born between the fragment and Totality.

This tense relationship is nothing but Michelangelo's tragic despair. Borrowing the philosophical terminology of Jaspers, Frey explains this tension as follows:

> Here communication with the other is cut off and the creator is thrown back to himself. The impossibility of expressing oneself, of making oneself understood, signifies his existential loneliness. . . . This, in the matter of the "border situation" *(Grenzsituation),* is the mark of his meeting with the ultimate boundary within the expressive possibility conditioned by time.

According to Frey, the confrontation of man with this border situation is a problem related to one kind of ethos.[62] Namely, man might meet with his downfall in this border situation or, taking the task upon himself, he can assert himself in his own humanness as an undertaking imposed on him. "The latter is the stand taken by Rembrandt in his late work."

What this means for Frey is that art, while being related to being-there, is affirmed in the fragmentariness and incompleteness of the art objects that Michelangelo disavowed. This means that an independent meaning is granted to the fragmentary and incomplete work of art. "The artist sees in incompleteness *(non-finito)* its ultimate determination." Then what is the content of the independent meaning of such an incomplete work of art?

If the fragment is a fragment because of its being included in totality, the relationship between the two is of a necessary nature and, therefore, fragmentariness necessarily anticipates totality. But for Frey the fragment does not show itself as totality. As I mentioned earlier, their relationship does not exceed a peculiar tension. In this Frey sees a decisive difference between fragmentariness and the symbol. Namely:

> According to this meaning, the symbol is by no means fragmentary. The reason is that the symbol itself is one plastic totality and, as such, it represents *(repräsentieren)* an ideal totality with which the symbol essentially shares a relationship of sameness.

---

62. *Ethos* as the opposite of *pathos* or, to use *Webster's* definition of the term, "the moral, ideal, or universal element in a work of art as distinguished from that which is emotional in its appeal or subjective."

Here Frey bids farewell to the theory of imitation in whatever form it might come. Frey's distinction of fragmentariness and symbol is fundamental to determining the independent meaning of the incomplete work of art. The relationship of fragmentariness and totality is not a symbolic relationship—that is, the tension between the two is not related to the expressive content of the idea of totality. This existential tension attaches a deep significance to the "richness" and "extensiveness" of the work of art. (I would also add its "depth.") It would be a big mistake to use the word "symbol" in talking about the philosophical nature of art and to think that art expresses symbolically some kind of metaphysical truth. For Frey, what caused the tension between totality and fragment in Michelangelo was his tragic despair. On the other hand:

> By virtue of the direct experience of variability in the process of the creation of a fragment, and by virtue of the fact that this variability hints at an inclusive and transcendental totality, the work of art becomes richer, more extensive.

This means, not that the purpose of the fragmentary work of art is to hint at an inclusive and transcendental totality, but that such hinting is a device to make the work of art "richer, more extensive."

In a previous article,[63] I pointed out that the meaning of the beauty of mystery and depth, which is the artistic ideal of the medieval Japanese arts, does not lie in showing any specific aesthetic content but in providing the work of art with depth and intensity. If we follow Frey's claim that the meaning of the work of art as incompletion and fragmentariness does not lie in the representation of an idea, but in its richness, extensiveness, and depth, we might be entitled to say that the beauty of mystery and depth, incompletion, and the fragment are actually tied together in a chain of necessity.

When we voice the paradoxical possibility that, in order to be rich and extensive, the work of art must be increasingly fragmentary and incomplete, for the first time we can truthfully say that the fragment cannot be disavowed as simple incompletion but acquires the positive meaning of the complete perfection of incompletion. Therefore, as Gantner pointed out in *Rodin and Michelangelo,* incompletion is for the artist a freely planned art form. Between *Präfiguration* and the completed work of art or *Figuration,* there is only a difference of degree, not a fundamental one.

When Shinkei talks about "slim verses with few words" and admonishes us "to turn at heart to what is unspoken and awaken to and grasp the chill and desolate," so long as what is left unsaid means incompleteness, he really hits at the heart of the positive essence of such an incomplete and fragmentary work of art. The reason is that in the chilly and desolate verse the formation of a richer passional surplus is by design.

---

63. See Kusanagi's "The Concept of Japanese Art" (Nihon Geijutsu no Rinen), in Kusanagi, *Yūgenbi no Bigaku,* pp. 61–116.

4

When we take incompleteness to be completion within incompleteness, completion keeps on retreating in its course toward completion and is always left
behind. This is what is meant by completion is incompleteness. This is the
border situation of artistic creation. Here passional surplus escapes the author
as completion that has been left behind, and it must be entrusted to the appreciator. If completion is possible in a work of art, as Sartre has pointed out,[64]
such completion must be achieved by the reader or the appreciator. Passional
surplus is the form of completion that is left behind by the appreciator. On
this relationship Frey makes the following remarks to which we should pay attention:

> As Gantner has pointed out, the fragment plays a major role also in the rela-
> tionship with the appreciator of plastic works of arts as the "you" that has been
> engaged in a dialogue. The experience of figuration as a second creation on the
> part of the appreciator guides and provides direction. In this sense, it is neces-
> sary. Or, again, the supplementation on the appreciator's part and his freedom
> of interpretation open widely to the fragment—or, more than this, they demand
> the presence of the fragment, even calling and waking up the appreciator. Thus
> the fragment stimulates the creative activity of the appreciator. . . . As a result,
> fragmentary expressions gain in richness and extensiveness thanks to their mul-
> tiplicity of meaning. Now, the possibility of variation arises in the subjective
> experience of the appreciator—namely, the possibility of variation with regard
> to the object's interpretation, the temporal extension of the occurrence that is
> portrayed, and the emotional response. This is basically what differentiates each
> age that has a tendency for fragmentation from classical ages endowed with a
> form that is definitely completed.

Namely, the fragmentary work of art is itself a *non-finito;* its completion is entrusted to the appreciator. In the classical work of art that brings itself to a closure, the artistic experience is seized by the author; in the fragmentary work
of art, however, the same experience is in the hands of the appreciator himself.
Sartre expresses the same concept when he entrusts to the appreciator the completion of the work of art:

> Since the creation can find its fulfillment only in reading, since the artist must
> entrust to another the job of carrying out what he has begun, since it is only
> through the consciousness of the reader that he can regard himself as essential
> to his work, all literary work is an appeal *(appel).* To write is to make an appeal
> to the reader that he lead into objective existence the revelation which I have
> undertaken by means of language. And if it should be asked *to what* the writer
> is appealing, the answer is simple. As the sufficient reason for the appearance of

---

64. Jean-Paul Sartre (1905–1980), philosopher, critic, novelist, and dramatist, was a major representative of existential philosophy in the twentieth century.

the aesthetic object is never found in the book (where we find merely solicitations to produce the object) but in the writer's appeal to the reader's freedom to collaborate in the production of his work. . . . Thus, the author writes in order to address himself to the freedom of readers, and he requires it in order to make his work exist.

Kant believed that the work first of all existed as fact to be seen, however, later. As a matter of fact, the work exists only when someone takes notice of it; it is the purest form of appeal, a demand for pure existence. [Sartre, *What Is literature?*][65]

As against Gantner's *Präfigurationen,* I believe that I am justified in calling Metafigurations *(Metafigurationen)*—I use the word "meta" to include the meaning of both "post" and "trans"—this search for the work of art's completion in what follows the actual, objective process of the work's formation, that is, in the freedom of the reader that makes such true completion exist, namely in the reader's "recreation." Thus this meaning of art clearly indicates the nature of art as being-there. The reason is that the meaning of art's closure of incompletion starts out as an existential intercourse between the incomplete work and the appreciator, and each time it reaches closure. Moreover, such existential intercourse does not take place in between aesthetic consciousnesses that are common to everybody, but between an author who is a historical, specifically free, and potential existence and an appreciator who is equally an existence of possibility.

Jaspers argues that a philosophical work is nothing but a half. Therefore, it requires the supplementation of its other half by the reader in order to become truth. To achieve such supplementation, it is not sufficient for the reader to think the work only in terms of thought. He must make it historical through his own thought and in his own being-there (Jaspers, *Der Philosophische Glaube,* 1948). We might apply the same explanation to artistic truth. That is, passional surplus as incompletion demands supplementation on the part of the appreciator as Metafiguration in its existential intercourse. This thought is deeply related to the important topic of "heart" *(kokoro),* or "debates on the intensity of feeling" *(ushinron),*[66] which have characterized the Japanese philos-

---

65. Jean-Paul Sartre, *What Is Literature?,* trans. Bernard Frechtman (New York: Harper & Row, 1965), p. 40 and p. 45.

66. "Among the ideals inherited from Shunzei, *ushin* became crucial for Teika, who further developed and elaborated upon it in ways important for theory and practice alike. In the *Maigetsushō,* the most important of his extant writings, Teika insists upon the supreme importance of what he calls the 'style of intense feeling.' He uses the term in both a narrow and a broad sense—as a separate category among the ten styles which he codifies ('the style of intense feeling') and as an element essential to all ('a conviction of feeling')—an overlapping system of classification which, together with the lack of specific examples of poems in the various styles named, has given rise to several different interpretations of what he actually meant by the terms. Teika's dual usage of the term *ushin* and the high estimation he gave the concept can best be illustrated by a crucial passage from the *Maigetsushō.*

ophy of art since the Middle Ages. I am not going to deal further with this problem, however.

In any event, the passional surplus develops in the space of artistic intercourse as the existential Metafiguration of incompletion's closure. Thus, as Gantner also points out, incompletion acquires the positive meaning of the artistic form that is freely planned by the artist. But as I have mentioned, for people like Gantner the reason for dealing with artistic incompleteness as an

---

Among the ten styles there is not one in which the true nature of poetry resides more wholly than in the style of intense feeling. It is extremely difficult to create, for it cannot by any means be put together at random in any of a variety of ways. Only when one has composed one's thoughts and entered into the unique realm of this style is it possible to compose in it, and even at that success is rare. It must be for this reason that great poetry has been said to be possible only when every poem is suffused with deep feeling. However, if one goes through excessive contortions in the effort to instill even greater feeling into it, the poem will be overdone and overcomplicated, and such defective, imperfect, and incomprehensible poems are even more distasteful and ugly than those which lack feeling. The borderline between success and failure is of supreme importance and must constantly be given the most careful thought. Those who are serious about this art must not even occasionally compose in an easygoing manner without concentrating their minds. To produce a faultily constructed poem not only becomes a source of embarrassment by inviting the adverse criticism of one's detractors, but also leads to the debilitation of one's artistic powers. Thus one hears of people who, having brought criticism upon themselves, have pined away and died of chagrin, or who, having had a fine poem expropriated by someone else, have after death appeared in dreams weeping and lamenting and demanding the return of their poems, with the result that these have been expunged from the imperial anthologies. Instances of this kind are not limited to the ones I have cited, and I find them most affecting.

One must take pains, both on the days of preparation for a poetry meeting or competition, and on informal occasions, to compose one's poems with great care, reciting them over and over to oneself. Carelessness will inevitably give rise to adverse criticism later on. You, my lord, should continually have your mind fixed upon poems that are in the style of intense feeling. However, there are times when it is quite impossible to compose in this style. When one feels ill at ease and the depths of one's heart are in turmoil, no amount of effort will succeed in producing a poem in the style of intense feeling. If one persists in trying to produce such a poem under such conditions, one's artistic powers will weaken and the result will be a faultily constructed poem. At such times one should compose 'lively' poems, that is, poems whose style and phrasing are light and easy, and whose overall effect, though lacking in any deep emotion, is somehow pleasing to the ear. This advice should be especially borne in mind on informal occasions when the topics are not given out in advance, for even such trivial poems as these will, when one has composed four or five or as many as ten of them, disperse one's heavy spirits and quicken one's sensibilities so that one can compose with assurance. On the other hand, I feel that when one is assigned such topics as 'Love' or 'Expressing Personal Grievances,' the style of intense feeling must be used exclusively. I do not mean to say that unless it is in this style a poem cannot possibly be good. Nevertheless, this style of intense feeling must extend over the other nine styles for the reason that the style of mystery and depth must possess conviction of feeling—so must the lofty style, and so must all of the others. It is indeed true that no matter what style it may be in, a poem which lacks conviction of feeling is bad. Among the examples of the ten styles which I have chosen, and sent to you previously, those which were grouped under the heading the 'style of intense feeling' were not poems in the other styles which also possessed conviction of feeling, but rather only those poems composed in the attempt to produce the single effect of intense feeling. Whatever the style may be, however, it must possess conviction of feeling." [Brower and Miner, *Japanese Court Poetry,* pp. 258–259]

independent art form originated in their meeting with unfinished works of art that were actually left by such artistic giants as Leonardo and Michelangelo. This situation was different from the Japanese case during the Middle Ages when the problem of incompleteness was grounded in the true nature of art. We must acknowledge, however, the fundamental meaning that we find in the possibility of discovering a common ground of mutual hermeneutics and mutual influence between the Japanese (broadly speaking, the Eastern) and the Western arts, which are diametrically opposed in terms of form.

Since I do not have the space to enumerate all the many examples I might be able to find on this topic, I will conclude with a single quotation from Hermann Hesse.[67] It is related to the following story from *Gossips at the Teahouse (Kissa Zatsuwa)* by Chachiku Shi:[68]

> He did not like to see both the lotus and the camellia in the same picture. It showed that this was a story from a different land. Then he wrote a poem: "The forest hidden in front of me in the deep snow. / Last night several branches bloomed." One of his artist friends said: "It would have been more correct had you said, 'One branch.'" The poet invited that friend, called him "the master of the word '*ume* flower,'" and paid homage to him. He called that verse the blood vessel of the Way of Poetry.[69]

On what occasion did Hermann Hesse learn about this story? He provides the following explanation in his *How to Read World Literature:*

> Japanese lyrical poetry also fascinated me very much, especially its effort toward an extreme simplicity and brevity—you should not read contemporary German lyrical poetry immediately after reading the lyrical poetry from Japan. Otherwise you will find our poetry unbearably bulging and dull. The Japanese thought that something like a seventeen-syllable verse must be admired. The Japanese always knew that art does not become good by making it easy, but that the opposite is true. For example, at one time, a Japanese poet composed two lines. They say that two or three branches of the *ume* tree bloomed in a grove that was still buried under the snow. He had his poem read to a colleague poet. Then the colleague said: "One branch of *ume* is enough." The author felt that the words of his colleague were very reasonable, and he realized how far he still was from true simplicity. Therefore, he followed his friend's suggestion. To this day I cannot forget that poem.

---

67. Hermann Hesse (1877–1962), German-born novelist and poet, won the Nobel Prize in literature in 1946.

68. A Zen monk who admired the tea master Murata Jukō (1422–1502). He wrote the *Kissa Zatsuwa* in 1620.

69. The original text appears in Hanawa Hokinoichi, ed., *Zoku Gunsho Ruijū*, vol. 19, *ge* (Tokyo: Zoku Gunsho Ruijū Kanseikai, 1912), p. 523.

POETIC
EXPRESSION

EIGHT

The Space of Poetry
The Kyoto School and Nishitani Keiji

TO APPRECIATE the work of the philosopher Nishitani Keiji (1900–1990), we must understand the background of the philosophical school within which he operated. The Kyoto school developed in the department of philosophy and religion of Kyoto University around the figure of the leading Japanese philosopher, Nishida Kitarō (1870–1945). One of the major characteristics of the school was a direct engagement with Western epistemology in order to create a Japanese philosophical subjectivity that would incorporate traits of both the Western and the Eastern traditions. The conceptualization of the Kyoto school's philosophical system, therefore, developed around definitions of two cultural blocs that were respectively centered on the German idealist tradition and the Buddhist notion of emptiness. The school's search for a synthesis of the two blocs led to what has been called "a crude sort of syncretism."[1]

In talking about aesthetics, the Kyoto school grounded the arts in a privileged space of "emptiness," or "nothingness," which was understood to provide man with a complement to the limited faculty of reason in grasping a complex reality to which logic alone could hardly do justice. This empty of nothingness *(mu)* was seen by Nishida and his followers as a kind of metaphysical ground that is alleged to explain the specificity of Eastern culture and, consequently, its differences from Western thought. In one of his major essays on comparative cultures—"The Forms of Culture of the Classical Periods of East and West Seen from a Metaphysical Perspective" (Keijijōgakuteki Tachiba kara Mita Tōzai Kodai no Bunka Keitai)—Nishida Kitarō locates the central difference between Western and Eastern cultures in the space used by their respective metaphysical systems to ground, justify, and explain their notions of truth. Nishida argued

---

1. Jan Van Bragt, "Translator's Introduction," in Keiji Nishitani, *Religion and Nothingness* (Berkeley: University of California Press, 1982), p. xxix.

that while the West depended on a "strong" metaphysical apparatus that was based on the presence of "being" *(yū)*, Japan, like China, rooted the explanation of reality in the formlessness of a less strong but otherwise effective notion of nothingness *(mu).* [2]

By taking the Greek world of art and philosophy to characterize the cultural roots of the West, Nishida reduced Western philosophy to a strong notion of presence: the ultimate Being of Parmenides, the discursive reality *(logos)* of Heraclitus, the plasticity of artistic intuition and expression. Nishida, however, did not deny that a philosophy of nothingness also developed in the West. He mentioned the tendency in Christian culture to depict the supreme Being as what because of the limitations of human knowledge cannot be named or fathomed. As an example, he pointed to the negative theology of Dionysius the Areopagite, according to whom God could only be described in negative terms, with the inevitable consequence that God could never become the object of scientific inquiry.

According to Nishida, however, the Western idea of nothingness is still marred by the resilience of the concept of presence that simply refuses to die. The God of the Judeo-Christian tradition is still profoundly anchored by a strong concept of personhood, whose perfection requires the presence of a free will that works within a structure of self-conscious self-determination. As soon as the concept of nothingness is introduced in the West in the description of the idea of transcendence, the West celebrates its death by personalizing it into a concrete essence. Therefore, the West inevitably fails to achieve a true negation-qua-affirmation—the ideal paradigm of nothingness discovered by Mahāyāna Buddhist thinkers, who asserted the identity of being and nonbeing: "The phenomenal being is emptiness; emptiness is the phenomenal being" *(shiki soku zekū, kū soku zeshiki).*

In Nishida's opinion, China does not fare any better with regard to the metaphysics of nothingness. He noticed the stiffness that the concept of *mu* suffered at the hand of what he saw as an immanent metaphysics crystallizing in the Confucian notion of "heaven" and the Taoist idea of "nonbeing," or "the form of the formless." The immanent aspect of Chinese metaphysics derives from the strong ethical connotation of the Chinese religio/philosophical system that, no matter how negative in its definition of truth, undermines the credibility of the local notion of nothingness by underlining the centrality occupied by rites and ceremonial propriety.

---

2. The essay appears in Nishida Kitarō, *Nishida Kitarō Zenshū,* vol. 7 (Tokyo: Iwanami Shoten, 1965), pp. 429–453. An English version appears in David A. Dilworth, trans., *Nishida Kitarō's Fundamental Problems of Philosophy: The World of Action and the Dialectical World* (Tokyo: Sophia University, 1970), pp. 237–254.

Nishida saw in Japanese Buddhism, and in the Mahāyāna tradition in particular, the seeds for overcoming both Western and Chinese metaphysics—seeds that the Russian brand of nihilism attempted to plant in the West, Dostoevski before anyone else. Nishida's culture of nothingness is a contemporaneity of presence and absence, a dialectical movement of being and nonbeing that sees the world as being-qua-nonbeing and nonbeing-qua-being *(yū soku mu, mu soku yū)*. Reality is the self-identity of the opposed poles of subject and object that we perceive through action. Differences, however, are not denied in the philosophy of nothingness; they are transcended in a dialectical process.

In order for an individual to determine itself, Nishida Kitarō argued, there must be a determination of what he called "a place" *(basho)*, "the unity of absolute contradictories," "an absolute negation-qua-affirmation," "the continuity of discontinuity." The determination of the individual by the absolute occurs through the mediation of absolute negation. Being is what exists by not-being—as in the case of an existence whose life is defined by its death, which is the continuity of discontinuity. As the place where the unattainable is grasped, the space of nothingness is where the existence of the self-determining individual takes place, and the unity of contradictories comes into being in an infinite dialectical process.[3]

Nishida's idea of *basho* has been seen as a privileging of space in an attempt to remedy the overestimation of time in Western epistemology.[4] He gave analytic consistency to the theme of spatiality that found a strenuous defender in the works of Watsuji Tetsurō (1889–1960). We might think of Watsuji's definition of person as what lives in a definite, spatial "place," or *topos,* or field *(basho),* as a being interconnected with other beings—*ningen* (person) literally means "between man and man." The primary significance of being human is to exist in space as the "betweenness" of extended embodied subjects *(shutai)* that communicate through the intersubjectivity of space. It is no accident that Watsuji used the category of "climate" *(fūdo)* to describe the peculiarities of cultures, whose essential meaning derived from the location of people in nature as the space of the life-world.[5]

In addition to being used to describe the workings of human society, the notion of interconnectedness also found favor in the definition of discrete human beings, since it provided Nishida and Watsuji with a solution to

3. Nishida Kitarō, "A Preface to Metaphysics," in Dilworth, *Nishida Kitarō's Fundamental Problems of Philosophy,* pp. 1–42.

4. See Yuasa Yasuo, *The Body: Toward an Eastern Mind-Body Theory* (Albany: SUNY Press, 1987), pp. 41–46.

5. Watsuji Tetsurō, *Climate and Culture: A Philosophical Study* (New York: Greenwood Press, 1961).

the problem of the dichotomy of body and mind. Watsuji simply used the Buddhist idea of the unity of body and mind *(shinjin ichinyo)* to overcome the Cartesian dualism of subject and object. Nishida worked out a scheme of bodily consciousness that deprived the mind/body difference of its justificational ground: the subject that sees cannot live apart from its being an object that is seen, so the mental (subjective) and corporeal (objective) dimensions depend on each other by both belonging to a field of communal, interconnected meanings.[6]

The field of nothingness *(mu no basho)* is the ground for the realization of the self as authenticity, the possibility for the self to escape the everyday finitude to which the field of presence *(yū no basho)* restricts it. In nothingness the ego consciousness of the human subject is discarded because of what the contemporary philosopher Yuasa Yasuo calls "the acting intuition in the self as *basho*." In this intuition the strong self disappears "in the bottom of consciousness," in a world of "pure experience" whose immediacy precedes any articulation on the part of the mind.[7] We might think of the great pianist whose flawless execution is the result of his fingers' and mind's immediate presence to themselves, as if the artist had suspended the articulation of thoughts (judgment) and confined them to a parenthesis—the Husserlian *epoche*—in order to attain immediate apodicticity. In the field of nothingness the mind becomes one with the body.

The intuition that allows us to uncover the field of nothingness is not intellectual in the sense that it employs inferential judgments. It is, rather, creative, as in the act of artistic composition in which, as Nishida argues in his *Study of Good (Zen no Kenkyū)*, "the self and things are mutually responsive to each other; things do not move the self nor vice versa. There is only one world, one scene."[8] The "lightening" of the body deprives itself of the heaviness of objectivity, while at the same time allowing the mind to discard its ego consciousness that originally derived from its own construction of itself as a subject opposed to an object. All this disappears in a philosophy that grounds the materiality of reality and the ideality of its perception in the field of nothingness.

Japanese philosophers in the twentieth century, particularly those associated with the Kyoto school, have challenged the stiffness of Western metaphysical theories by trying to (un)ground the concept of nihility from its still strong metaphysical connotations and replace it with the idea of

---

6. Yuasa, *The Body,* pp. 50–52.

7. Nishida developed his notion of "pure experience" in his *Inquiry into the Good,* trans. Masao Abe and Christopher Ives (New Haven: Yale University Press, 1990).

8. Ibid., p. 32.

emptiness (Skt. *śūnyatā;* Jpn. *kū*). On the ground of this weakened nihilism, which reinterprets the most central notion of Mahāyāna Buddhism, Nishitani Keiji based his epistemology of difference, continuing Nishida's work by discussing Japanese philosophy in Western terms in order to accelerate its acceptance in the West and make local epistemology a truly universal system.

The target of Nishitani's criticism is what he calls the Western brand of "old metaphysics": the one-dimensional relationship of correspondence that Western epistemology has devised in relating thing to concept. For Nishitani, the West either conceptualized reality as a thing-in-itself, a substance, according to the Aristotelian model, or, following Kant, as a representation of the subject. A negation of either the idealistic or the materialistic view of reality that would attempt to explain the world on the ground of (Western) nihility would simply deprive things and self from being objects of cognition, thus making them utterly incomprehensible.[9]

The philosophy of nothingness, according to Nishitani, transforms a negative negativity into a positive one. Rather than defining the self as something that is not, as we would expect from a nihilist perspective, the self should be seen as emptiness itself. Then the question is: What is emptiness? Nishitani defines it as "the *original* mode of being of things as they are in themselves and as they in fact actually exist." It is neither phenomenal as what appears to us; nor is it noumenal as what is unknowable to us. It is the "suchness" of the property that is expected from beings—such as, for example, the "like" in the sentence, "the flying bird that looks *like* a bird." Such "likeness" is the bird's mode of being in its own "home ground" or its "middle position." Emptiness is the contemporaneity of manifestation and apprehension of the thing itself, before reality is prehended either by sensation or by reason. It is a taking hold of things as they are, pulling away from an understanding that is biased by "our ordinary self-centered mode of being." Being is in unison with emptiness: a presence to itself that maintains its autonomy while, at the same time, avoiding separation and alienation from other beings, as in the case of Western nihility.

This organization and ordering of beings derives from the fact that they are subordinated to other beings, inasmuch as, in order for beings to be what they are, beings must be emptied of their own being. In order for a thing to be, it must not be itself since, while continuing to be itself, being must be in the home ground of everything else. Beings are related to each

---

9. See Nishitani's article "The Standpoint of Sūnyatā," in Nishitani, *Religion and Nothingness,* pp. 119–167.

other by a mutual reciprocity in emptiness that Nishitani calls "revolvingly reciprocal" *(egoteki)*. Things are in the world in a field of emptiness where beings are seen as being-qua-nothingness and nothingness-qua-being. The original self of being has its home in the ground of emptiness, thus being "an original self in itself."

Nishitani provides a concrete example of the negation process in emptiness by remarking that the being of the eye lies in the necessity of not seeing in order to see. In order for the eye to be recognized as an eye, it must see things. The eye does not see itself, however, so that in the home ground of the eye there is an essential nonseeing. Seeing is possible through an essential nonseeing: "Not being an eye (not-seeing) constitutes the possibility of being an eye (seeing)." The basic structure of emptiness, therefore, is as follows: "The eye is an eye because it is not an eye." And yet the blindness of the emptied eye is not what in Western nihilism would simply become sightlessness. The affirmation that the eye does not see itself means that the sensation or perception of seeing, consciousness, is essentially empty. The saying that the eye does not see the eye means to affirm the self-identity of the eye, which is located not in the substance of the eye, nor in the act of seeing, but in the home ground of the eye: in the eye itself.[10]

According to Nishitani, the space of the concept of emptiness is better located once the character for emptiness *(kū)* is dissociated from its Buddhist implications and understood in its original etymological sense of "the empty space," "the empty sky" *(kokū)*. Nishitani's argument goes as follows: Once the concept is made concrete in the immediacy of the original phenomenon from which it derives, the Buddhist idea of emptiness assumes the depth of eternity and immutability. The infinitude of emptiness is finally caught in an image, the sky, whose finitude allows one to grasp the notion of the unseen. The infinite is brought to a graspable reality by the image of a concrete sky that makes infinity a manifestation of the concrete. "Manifestation of the concrete" is the etymological meaning of the

---

10. Ibid., pp. 152–153. In the essay "Nihility and Śūnyatā," Nishitani gives the example of fire, whose selfness derives from its own negation, the fact that the fire does not burn itself: "If we suppose that the natural, essential quality *(physis)*—or, in Buddhist terms, 'self-nature'—resides in the power and work of combustion, then the selfness of fire resides at the point of its so-called *non*-self-nature. In contrast to the notion of substance which comprehends the selfness of fire in its fire-nature (and thus as *being*), the true selfness of fire is in its non-fire-nature. The selfness of fire lies in non-combustion. Of course, this non-combustion is not something apart from combustion: fire is non-combustive in its very act of combustion. It does not burn itself. To withdraw the non-combustion of fire from the discussion is to make combustion in truth unthinkable. That a fire sustains itself while it is in the act of burning means precisely that it does not burn itself. Combustion has its ground in non-combustion. Because of non-combustion, combustion is combustion. The non-self-nature of fire is its home-ground of being. The same could be said of water: it washes because it does not wash itself." See Nishitani, *Religion and Nothingness,* p. 117.

Japanese word for "reality, actuality" (genjitsu). The mediation between the graspability of the mind (the infinite) and the graspability of the eye (the phenomenon) takes place at the level of poetic language through the metaphorical power that language has to say the unsayable. Poetic language gives form to the formlessness of the infinite. Poetry reduces to immediacy a link between mortality and the infinite—a linkage that the logic of an alleged rational language, the language of Western philosophy, is forced to describe in analogical terms.

The translation into rationality of what cannot be caught rationally is, therefore, mediated by the aesthetic act that articulates in the language of emotions, such as poetry, the rationality of an order that, in the case of "sky" and "emptiness," is essentially Buddhist. The contiguity of the infinite space of the Buddhist law, on the one hand, and the space of purity of the human heart, on the other, is immortalized in the poetry of reclusion, in which a geography of emptiness reveals itself in the quietness of the surroundings as well as in the heart of the monk absorbed in meditation. The infinity of the outside world—the "deep valleys, mountains, and forests" in which the recluse confronts in solitude the depth of his heart—translates into the finitude of feelings and mortality, whose overcoming is the major goal of the Buddhist practitioner. The achievement occurs through an act of positive denial: finitude positively does not exist. The result is the poetry and poetics of "intransience" (mujō) in which the space of emptiness is present to the space of the purified heart.[11]

According to Nishitani, the articulation of the space of nothingness in poetry takes place by having the logic of grammar (bunpō) replaced by poetic "grams" (aya) that do not conform to an organization of reality based on subjects and objects. He gives as an example the following haikai:

Sabishisa no	The bottom of loneliness
Soko nukete furu	Falls off:
Mizore kana	Oh, the falling sleet!

Rather than addressing the problem of loneliness and sadness from an epistemological perspective, as a philosopher would do, the poet avoids being entrapped in the sphere of knowledge and chooses to capture the immediacy of experience. Is the falling sleet (subject) seizing and pulling the "bottom" (soko) of loneliness (object), making the pains of sadness even more poignant? Or is it that the "bottom" of the human heart (subject) simply

---

11. Nishitani Keiji makes this argument in his article "Kū to Soku" (Emptiness and Sameness), which is translated later in the chapter. See Nishitani Keiji, Nishitani Keiji Chosaku Shū, vol. 13 (Tokyo: Sōbunsha, 1987), pp. 111–118.

quits, independently of the presence of the winter scenery? What then is the relation between the heart, sadness, and sleet? Two actions take place in the poem, one internal, the other external: first, the heart that was able to contain its sadness has eventually lost its ability to do so and is now sinking into a deeper state of loneliness; second, the sleet keeps falling outside. How do the two actions come together, if indeed they do come together? They seem to be collapsed into a single sentence, thus confusing the reader as to the grammatical relation between words. There is no direct relationship between the two actions—only a prosaic paraphrase by introducing a particle indicating either temporality or causality could logically tie them together. Because (or at the same time that) the sleet started falling outside, my sadness deepened inside. By taking the space of nothingness to be the location of the articulation of poetry, the poet is confronted with one space and one space only, whether it be occupied by sleet or by sadness. The revelation of this space does not occur at the level of words or verbs, but at the level of "particles" *(teniwoha)* that precede the unfolding of the action and work as an a priori of the poetic composition.[12]

Rather than tying the word "sadness" *(sabishisa)* to the specificity of the experience of the human heart, as a modern reading of the genitive particle *"no"* would have us believe, the use of *"no"* at the beginning of the poem as a subject clause—a synonym of *"ga"*—separates "sadness" from the rest of the poem, thus tying it to both actions, without forcing the poet to introduce analogical explanations in an attempt to unite human perception and natural phenomenon. Nishitani refers to the term "equalogical" *(soku)* to indicate the relationship between the two actions/parts of the poem. Yet a problem still remains with the expression "equalogical," since it implies the presence of a *logos* from whose rationality poetry is actually free. The presence-to-itself of poetry resists thematization and all other rationalizing—and therefore reductivist—techniques. The "continuity" of the structure of poetic expression is a "noncontinuity" *(hirenzoku)* that the poet achieves by employing all sorts of "cuts" *(kireji),* which impede the logical progression of poetic expression. The abundant use in Japanese poetry of exclamations (which are hardly a pleasure for "logical" readers, above all translators) contributes to the expression of an experiential knowledge that, unlike a logical one, precedes the act of discernment and discrimination. In poetry, Nishitani argues, the reader perceives the sound of a crying ci-

---

12. The Edo scholar Fujitani Mitsue used to teach his students how to write poetry by indicating the infinite combinations of particles used to string together nouns, adverbs, and verbs. The nouns, adverbs, and verbs were indicated with circles to stress their subordination to the primacy of *ga, wa, no, ni, wo,* and all other exclamatory particles.

cada before he has had the time mentally to associate the sound with the insect's physical image. There is an immediacy between sound and perception that does away with the presence of a perceiving subject and a perceived object. The poetic voice brings into the space of nothingness this dreamlike state of immediacy.[13] Now let us listen to Nishitani's words.

Emptiness and Sameness
by Nishitani Keiji

THE WORDS "sameness" (soku)[14] and "emptiness" (kū) are usually encountered in the domain of Buddhist doctrinal investigation as specialized terms used in Buddhist thought.[15] The countless results of the research by Buddhologists on these categories is such that we can probably say there is nothing more to add. Therefore, I wish to problematize these concepts from a slightly different angle.

1. "Emptiness" in Poetry

To begin, the first problem is that the words "emptiness" and "sameness" were not originally coined within Buddhism; they were, and still are today, widely used common words. This can be clearly seen even among the usages that appear in various Chinese Buddhist dictionaries. For example, the character for "emptiness/sky" (kū) is often used in combination with the character "void" (ko). However, the compound in this case indicates the "sky" one sees with one's eyes (kokū = empty sky).[16] The sky is an eternally constant empty space

---

13. Nishitani, "Kū to Soku," pp. 118–130.

14. "Soku," which I have translated as "sameness," also includes the meanings "namely," "=," "that is," "qua," "in other words," and "is."

15. This article, titled "Kū to Soku," appears in Nishitani Keiji, *Nishitani Keiji Chosaku Shū*, vol. 13 (Tokyo: Sōbunsha, 1987), pp. 111–160.

16. "Kū," or "emptiness," also has the connotation of sky and can be read as "sky." Throughout this chapter, the reader should keep in mind both these meanings as the connection is lost in English.

with unlimited depth and endless width. It is the only "eternal thing" we can see with our eyes. The sky of the visible world has been used in scriptures as an image *(Bild)* to indicate eternally unlimited things that cannot be seen with the eye, or eternal limitlessness. With that meaning, the words "sky" and "empty sky" can be seen fundamentally as metaphors, although there is something that cannot be reduced to a simple metaphor. The empty sky, to the extant that one can see it with the eye, is a given fact and a reality. Even if it is supposed to indicate the limitless eternity that one cannot see with the eye, there is a much more strict relationship than a metaphorical link between the visible phenomenon and the invisible thing indicated by those words. Earlier I used the word "image," but actually the empty sky visible to the eye has no form, and, in a strict sense, one cannot say it is a figure or image. Rather, one should say that it is a visible image without form. In this case, the relationship between the visible and the invisible thing is not clearly defined. Insofar as the word "analogy," which has been used from ancient times in Western philosophy, comes under the heading of ontology and is related to ontological discourse, it is not clear whether or not it can be applied to the relationship we are problematizing. This is because this word is altogether too vague to regulate the relationship logically. We can only say that this relationship has an intimacy that exceeds logic.

Secondly, the words "sky/emptiness" and "empty sky," along with permeating Buddhism and being used as Buddhist terms in scripture, have come to be used to express a Buddhist-like feeling. Rather than being a logical expression of Buddhist dharma, these are sensory expressions of those principles. Even in this case, these words could be interpreted as being metaphors used in a sensory world concerning laws that exceed simple sentiment. But again a strict relationship appears that goes beyond the simple level of metaphoricity. The empty space that phenomenologically signifies the sky reflects itself as a visible reality in the emptiness of the sensory world, and the relationship between the two is much more pronounced than a simple metaphor. And even in the case when the sensory emptiness is tied to pure principles, it is in excess of metaphor and analogy. The form in which emptiness as a Buddhist doctrine has permeated the sensory world is Chinese and Japanese art. Particularly this permeation appears in painting and poetry. Although this was quite a universal phenomenon, I will choose for my quotations the *Selections from Tang Poetry* that received the most diffusion. For example, Meng Haoran's "At the Retreat of Monk Yi Gong":

> Monk Yi Gong makes it a practice to meditate
> Here in the hut he has built in the empty forest.
> Outside his door is a towering mountain peak.
> In front of his step crowd many deep valleys.
> The rays of the setting sun shine through a passing shower
> And cast the shadow of the empty verdure on the yard.

When I see the pure lotus blossoms,
More fully I understand his unstained heart.[17]

Here emptiness appears twice: in "empty forest" and "empty verdure." On the whole, the poem is evoking the atmosphere of the cell of Yi Gong (a Zen priest), so the word "emptiness" also expresses that atmosphere. This word is not expressing the empty space of the sky but has become a word to indicate the presence of stillness in the monk's quarters. Yet one could say that it expresses a certain kind of limitless and formless mood that lies within the connections between empty space, as emptiness, and sensory intimacy. At the same time, the reference to the purity of the lotus blossom and to the unstained heart at the end of the poem show the strict connection between sensory emptiness and the notion of emptiness in the Buddhist doctrine. The metaphorical use of the lotus flower growing out of the mud to indicate the pure heart of the Buddhist is well known. In the *Selections from Tang Poetry,* this poem is joined by the one that follows it, "Passing by the Xiang Ji Temple" by Wang Wei:

Without knowing the whereabouts of the Xiang Ji Temple,
I advance many leagues into the cloud-covered peaks.
Among the old trees there are no footpaths.
Faintly you hear the sound of a bell somewhere deep in the mountains.
Spring water murmurs over jutting rocks.
Sunlight passing through the green pines sets a chilly mood.
In the twilight, by a deserted [empty] pool,
I control the poison dragons in my heart through meditation.[18]

Although the empty pool here expresses the hollow empty interval of the valley, generally speaking the poem talks about the sequestered tenor of a temple in the Junan mountains. The place of the pool is also part of this landscape. Here also controlling of the "poison dragon" through meditation at the end of the poem means meditating by the pool and washing and purifying one's heart from the carnal desires that have stained it. When one compares this poem with the previous one, a further interiorization occurs that includes the meaning of the mental state during meditation. What remains the same is the direct tie between the sensory emptiness of the refreshing atmosphere among the mountains and the notion of emptiness in the Buddhist doctrine. The next poem, also by Wang Wei, is "Climbing to Bian Jiao Temple":

The path through the bamboo goes from the first step
Until it gives out onto the Conjured City at the top of Mount Lotus.
From a window one can see the three states of Chu,

---

17. Meng Haoran (689–740). For an explanation of the poem see Mekada Makoto, *Tōshisen, SKT* 19 (Tokyo: Meiji Shoin, 1988), pp. 331–332.
18. Wang Wei (699–761). For an explanation of the poem see Mekada, *Tōshisen,* pp. 334–335.

And beyond the treetops, the nine rivers are spread out.
Young foliage supports those sitting cross-legged.
The sounds of Sanskrit chants reverberate among the tall pines.
By living here in the sky of emptiness beyond the clouds of dharma
One sees the world and comprehends its unborn nature.[19]

Like the previous poem, this poem expresses the viewpoint of sitting in the meditative position in the middle of the mountains. In the final two lines, however, the level of "meditation" of the Buddhist doctrine has deepened further. Moreover, doctrinal words are frequently used. For example, there are the expressions "first step" *(shōji)* and "dharma clouds" *(hōunji),* which are part of the notion of the "ten stages" *(jūji),*[20] as well as the Conjured City *(Kejō)*[21] and nonbirth *(mushō),* which refer to "illusion" and "nirvana" respectively. On the other hand, the empty space of interiority has increasingly broadened, coming quite close to the feeling of empty space in the natural world. This is also the case with the whole of the Chu states that can be seen from the window and the nine rivers that are spread out broadly beyond the tops of the trees as we see in the second verse. Such an empty space can particularly be seen in the poet's living in the sky of emptiness beyond the clouds of dharma. The observation of the world and the attaining of the unlimited nonbirth of nirvana make one feel as if the emptiness within the poet has become the Buddhist emptiness of the thing-in-itself.

As one can see from these examples, the word "emptiness" is tied to our everyday feelings of futility and hollowness. It is particularly used time and again in connection with the feeling of impermanence *(mujō)* in the realm of world affairs. Moreover, within Buddhism this usage is included in the doctrine as the principle of the impermanence of all things. From there, what we could call the negativity of the word has progressed in its thoroughness until it has turned into the meditative practice of contemplation of the void and has

---

19. For an explanation of the poem see Mekada, *Tōshisen,* pp. 335–336.

20. The ten stages of a bodhisattva, according to the *Kegon-gyō,* are the stage of joy, the stage of freedom from defilement, the stage of the emission of the light of wisdom, the stage of glowing wisdom, the stage of difficulty in overcoming, the stage of the manifestation of reality, the stage of going far toward the ultimate reality, the immovable stage, the stage of wondrous wisdom, and the stage of dharma cloud, which is the ability to spread the teachings over the world as clouds overspread the sky. See Hisao Inagaki, *A Dictionary of Japanese Buddhist Terms* (Union City, Calif.: Heian International, 1989), pp. 150–151; and see *Japanese-English Buddhist Dictionary* (Tokyo: Daitō Shuppansha, 1991), p. 165.

21. The parable of the transformed city is one of the seven parables of the *Lotus Sutra.* "A group of people were making a journey to reach some jeweled city, but became exhausted along the way. A wise man, through his magical powers, created a jeweled city for the people to rest in. Once they had recovered from their exhaustion, he allowed the mirage of the jeweled city to fade away so the people could once again resume their journey to the real city. So it is with the *Hīnayāna Nirvāna,* which is just a temporary resting place on the road to the ultimate goal of *Mahāyāna. Hīnayāna Nirvāna,* like the transformed city, is merely a skillful device *(upāya)* to lead the person to a higher end." See *Japanese-English Buddhist Dictionary,* p. 188.

reached the point of expressing a positive meaning as the fundamental self-consciousness of Buddhism. Even in that case, the standpoint of self-consciousness as a standpoint of the mind comes forth through, for example, the poets' sentiment and advances to the degree where it becomes the mental state floating in the poets' poetry. That there are varying degrees of depth and differing shades permeating the Buddhist contemplative state among the poets can be seen by looking at the two or three examples I have given.

It goes without saying that the same tendency can be seen in the poetry of Japan after Buddhism permeated the country. Consider, for example, the following poem by Saigyō:

Kaze ni nabiku	The smoke of Mount Fuji
Fuji no keburi no	Trailing in the wind
Sora ni kiete	Disappears in the sky:
Yukue mo shiranu	Are they my thoughts
Waga omohi kana	Which do not know their destination?[22]

While the sky means both the "firmament" that one can see with the eye, and also the emptiness of the smoke disappearing in the sky without a trace, at the same time it also signifies the emptiness that is invisible to the eye of one's own inner consciousness, continually disappearing, as well as the emptiness within one's own self. We can say that this is a kind of metaphor, but in actuality it is also an experience beyond metaphor. We have just seen the mountain smoke disappearing into the sky as a fact that is present before our eyes. The sky in which the smoke disappears is also present in the poet's mind as an empty space. The transfer of the sky into the space of the transient impermanence of the poet's heart is not a metaphor but, rather, ought to be a more direct relationship. This is why we can say that this particular poem is the product of the poet Saigyō, who wrote it as a Buddhist.

To give another example: in Myōe Shōnin's anthology of poems there is the verse "the pure heart lives only in emptiness."[23] There is an interesting anecdote that goes along with this poem. Hōjō Yasutoki, who highly esteemed

---

22. Saigyō (1118–1180) was a poet recluse and the author of the *Sankashū*. The poem in question is a love poem that appears in the *Sankashū Shūi*. See Oyama Tokujirō, ed., *Saigyō Zenshū* (Tokyo: Gogatsu Shobō, 1978), p. 242.

23. Myōe Shōnin (1173–1232), monk of the Kegon school, is the founder of the Kōsanji temple on Mount Toganoo. The poem in question appears in the *Myōe Shōnin Kashū* (poem 131):

Kami wo tsugu	Why should I desire
Sokuhi mo nanika	Some rice paste
Hoshikaramu	To hold paper together?
Kiyoki kokoro wa	The pure heart
Sora ni koso sume	Resides in emptiness.

See Higuchi Yoshimaro et al., eds., *Chūsei Waka Shū: Kamakura Hen*, SNKBT 46 (Tokyo: Iwanami Shoten, 1991), p. 256.

Myōe, at the time of sending him a letter also appended a poem. It was a poem wondering why even though I spend all my time thinking of you and communicating with you in my heart, either you are unaware of it or you refuse to send me even the slightest message. A reply came from Myōe saying:

Hito shirezu	Isn't there any sign
Omofu kokoro no	Superior to words to show that
Kayofu koso	My heart that thinks of you
Ifu ni masareru	Unknown to others
Shirube narurame	Calls forth response in your heart?[24]

The subject of this poem is "communication of the heart." The expression "thinking of you unknown to others" is all the time present in love poetry. In this poem, however, it does not mean that the poet hides his heart in order to remain unknown to others. It means that although he intends to convey what is in his longing heart, the poet has no way to do it. The thoughts deep in one's heart are beyond words. He says that heart communication is "the sign superior to words." Direct communication from heart to heart is the sign (indicator, marker) that is superior to any other signs, such as words written in a letter or spoken words. To say it in modern terms, this is the problem of I and Thou. Yet it also means that the original locus of the problem is beyond words and understanding.

Refusing Yasutoki's offer of alms, Myōe sent him the following poem in reply:

Chigiri araba	If it is in our destiny,
Shōjō seze mo	We will meet again
Mumare awamu	In a future life,
Kami tsugu yō ni	Certainly not because of some offerings
Sokuhi ni wa yoraji	Such as paste gluing the paper.[25]

The destiny spoken of here is the same as the communication of the heart spoken of in the previous poem. Both stress the deep relationship between heart and heart that goes beyond words and concepts. Through this kind of deep association, two hearts can understand each other. Hearts that communicate so deeply can truly interact. Moreover, this communication is an unchanging phenomenon that overcomes the various changes in the world and even the transformations of the world itself. It is because of this that the poem says they will meet again in a future life. This is different from the gluing together of scraps of paper. There is no need for rice paste. This explains Myōe's humorous rejection of the offerings (his material means of survival). In return, Yasutoki replies wondering why should you dislike the

---

24. *Myōe Shōnin Kashū* (poem 128); Higuchi et al., *Chūsei Waka Shū*, p. 255.
25. *Myōe Shōnin Kashū* (poem 129); Higuchi et al., *Chūsei Waka Shū*, p. 255.

rice paste that holds paper together, although you might think that you do not eat pheasant and such, on account of your state of purity. Myōe responds by making the following poem:

Kami wo tsugu	Why should I desire
Sokuhi mo nanika	Some rice paste
Hoshikaramu	To hold paper together?
Kiyoki kokoro wa	The pure heart
Sora ni koso sume	Resides in emptiness.[26]

If we place this exchange in its proper background, then we clearly understand the meaning of the line "the pure heart resides in emptiness." Emptiness is the place where the heart "resides" (lives and clears itself)[27] in purity, separate from the dirty dust of the world. To settle in emptiness is to become clear in the pure clearness of emptiness, so that "to clear oneself" is in itself "to reside." The use of the moon residing in the sky as a religious metaphor and symbol for the pure heart has become, particularly in Buddhism, quite customary. Emptiness is the place far beyond all the words and concepts of earthly life, where "a door" opens for the first time to a true communication of the heart. It is the space where the "solidarity" of reciprocal connection is truly possible, the space where the heart remains eternally unchanged, no matter into which life it is reborn, and no matter into which world it transits during rebirth. As is well known, among the metaphors used in the *Lotus Sutra,* this world (the three worlds)[28] is often likened to a burning house, and one metaphor also depicts the story of saving the frolicking children from the midst of the raging fire.[29] The place to where they are saved is said to be an empty ground apart from the pain of desire. The empty ground is a space in which emptiness exists. Emptiness is judged in comparison to both heaven and earth.

As one can see from the few examples I have given, the notion of "emptiness" appears in the literature of China and Japan and includes many different meanings. As I have mentioned, emptiness appears as a chance to regulate the sensations, perceptions, emotions, and moods occurring in the experiences of everyday life. Emptiness has come to impart to sensibility and feelings a special characteristic. What exactly is this sensory and emotional emptiness? In order to progress somewhat into this problem, I will present an example from *haikai* as a clue.

---

26. See note 23.

27. In Japanese, *"sumu"* means both "to live" and "to become clear."

28. Sangai: the three worlds or the world of unenlightened men. "It is divided into three: 1. The world of desire, whose inhabitants have appetite and sexual desire. 2. The world of form, whose inhabitants have neither appetite nor sexual desire. 3. The formless world, whose inhabitants have no physical forms." See *Japanese-English Buddhist Dictionary,* p. 279.

29. The parable of the burning house is one of seven parables of the *Hokkekyō* or *Lotus Sutra.* The suffering of sentient beings is likened to a burning house. This parable is found in the chapter titled "Parables." See Leon Hurvitz, trans., *Scripture of the Lotus Blossom of the Fine Dharma* (New York: Columbia University Press, 1976), pp. 58–61.

2. An Example from Bashō

Sabishisa no	The bottom of loneliness
Soko nukete furu	Falls off:
Mizore kana	Oh, the falling sleet!

[Jōsō]

Chirachira mekaru	Buried embers of rice bran
Nuka no uzumibi	Glitter.

[Kyorai]

Kujira hiku	All in the offing
Oki ni hitohama	Pulling the whales:
Ie akete	The houses on the beach are empty.

[The Master][30]

These are three stanzas at the beginning of a poetic sequence (1690). The central mood appears in the opening verse, which regulates the entire exchange: "the bottom of loneliness falls off." We can say that it shows the place where the action of the poem occurs—the falling of sleet that is the subject of this verse—as well as the way in which the falling takes place. In both cases, we are witness to the presentation of the "place" where the phenomenon reveals itself in the world of nature and the "way" in which this revelation takes place, as the same mood of "loneliness." The sadness of the falling off of time in the verse "the bottom of loneliness falls off" is also directly the place where the sleet falls, as well as the manner in which it falls.

Generally speaking, it is a very common matter of daily experience for all natural phenomena to take form in connection with the "moods" (which we variously call emotions, sentiments, feelings, passions, and so forth) through sensorial perceptions like sight and hearing. At the same time, however, when we address the matter by problematizing the relation and combination of external and internal worlds, then a web of complexities challenges our understanding. There is no need for me to remind you that in the realm of problems known as ontology or epistemology this became the biggest aporia in the history of Western philosophy. Poetry, however, differs completely from the tendency in philosophy of stopping at a cognition that objectifies everyday experience, or at objectifying cognition, searching for it in the realm of "knowledge" as cognition. This poetic approach implies a course of inquiry that never departs from experience but penetrates the source of experience. Such a course shares the same standpoint with religion. While digging into the ground of knowledge, religion also includes a tendency to overcome the standpoint of "knowledge." Poetry, or more generally the arts, acknowledges

---

30. See Nakamura Toshisada, ed., *Kōhon Bashō Zenshū*, vol. 5: *Renku Hen, Ge* (Tokyo: Kadokawa Shoten, 1968), p. 320.

sense and perception, as well as emotion and sentiment, to be the most important moments of experience. The arts rotate around them, trying to penetrate the emotions in their innermost parts. To say it with the example I presented earlier, the mood of "loneliness" becomes the center that makes the entire poem live. The poem's purport is located in the "falling off" of loneliness' bottom.

When we try to paraphrase this verse in prose, the words "the bottom of loneliness falls off" are not very clear from a grammatical point of view. They are far from being distinct and explicit. In the sentence "loneliness falls off," it is clear that "loneliness" is the subject while "to fall off" is the verb, so that it means that the bottom of loneliness has fallen off or is falling off. The verse continues, however, saying: "the bottom has fallen off, falls." In that case, it is not that the working of the sleet, which "falls," causes the bottom of loneliness to fall off. It is the bottom that falls off. Yet at the same time we must acknowledge the presence of a hidden meaning according to which the sleet falls by going through and coming out from the bottom of loneliness. As I mentioned earlier, the continuation of the verse, "the bottom falling off: falling sleet," indicates that the sleet falls in the place where the bottom of loneliness has fallen off, or in a way that the bottom of loneliness falls off. But if the poem does not say that the falling off of the bottom is the direct result of the falling sleet, then two actions that would be two propositions in prose appear in this verse as one single pattern. Here we have two actions that should become two propositions with separate subjects: the bottom of loneliness has fallen off, and the sleet falls. On the one hand, we have the inner event of the author Jōsō; on the other, we witness an occurrence related to the external world. But in this poem the two facts are collapsed into one pattern. Interiority and exteriority are linked together; they become one single event. This linkage is not a direct "relationship" such as the inner is reflected in the outer or the outer affects the inner. Although the heart which was originally sad has become bottomlessly lonely because of the falling of sleet, at the same time this bottomless loneliness is also the place where the sleet falls. The sleet is "the bottom of loneliness falls off, falling sleet."

Are we not witnessing here the history of a sentence becoming "poetry"? In this instance, what allows the formation of poetry is probably the strength that is hidden in the particle *"no"* following "loneliness." We can see here Bashō's belief that the life of Japanese poetry was in its particles. To sum it up, this poem talks about a situation prior to the split between interiority and exteriority. Or such a "space" is disclosed. The "bottom's falling off" indicates such space.

The sleet falls on a place where the mood is loneliness, and this loneliness becomes a bottomless loneliness. This bottomless place becomes a space where the sleet now keeps falling. The situation in this case is different from the usual instance—such as, for example, "For a mountain village / Winter is the season / When loneliness excels." In the latter case, the deep emotion born out of the time when one looks at the form of a mountain village in winter—or the impression that it is always a sad mountain village but particularly sad in winter—are projected onto and qualified by the form itself. A subjective emotion is easily transferred onto an objective form. In the previous instance, however, loneliness is not a simple adjective modifying sleet. It is, rather, the actual place where the actually falling sleet is produced. Inasmuch as it overcomes the judgment of "this sleet is sad" and goes beyond the realm of the cognitive discernment that is found in consciousness, the reality of the falling sleet is a place which is cast as an absolute reality in itself. Such a place is also an opening to the bottomless loneliness. We could call it a straightforward expression of direct experience. Such a place is in itself neither subjective nor objective. Rather, it is a basic space that is made possible the first time by standing on it and seeing it as both a place of subjective emotion and a place of objective reality or description. This "loneliness" shows such a "place." Until now, this place has been called with various names such as "mental state," "mind," "stage." If I had to use such a word here just for a moment, I would not use "mind" in the sense of a subjective condition existing within the mind. Nor would I use the word "boundary" as a realm of something that has happened in the external world. What, then, is the nature of the place of the "mind" or "boundary" that appears in the verse, "The bottom of loneliness / Falls off: / Oh, the falling sleet"?

3. "Gram" and Grammar

The problem lies in the fact that *haiku* is a form of poetry, and "language" remains at the root of the problem.[31] Therefore, so long as I want to explain the "boundary" from which poetry comes, and so long as I want to be instrumental in pursuing what I previously called "emptiness in emotion," I must deal with the problem of language.

If I take the *haiku* that I introduced earlier, as I have noted, what should have been expressed as the content of two topics—that is, a reality represented as a double object—comes together in the form of poetry as an indivisible, single "gram." Usually sentences such as "the bottom of loneliness has fallen off" and "the sleet is falling" are tied together by a conjunction. In the resulting compound proposition, moreover, the "psychological" reality created by the subjective mood of interiority and the general reality of the natural world are expressed as the representation of a single object. (There are various ways to connect these two realities. In the present instance, one can use different conjunctions depending on whether we have a causal or a fortuitous relation-

---

31. In the title of this section I am translating *"aya"* (文, or *bun*)—which literally means "pattern"—as "gram" in order to retain in the English translation the presence of the same character *bun* 文, which also appears in the Japanese word for "grammar" (*bunpō* 文法).

ship.) What is thus expressed is arranged according to experiential categories or it is grasped with pure categories, finally leading to the area of the basic problem ("general rule"). The logic *(logos)* behind this situation is presented as the object of either "knowledge" as logical cognition or "cognition" as scientific knowledge. The given situation is provided with a direction of investigation that from the beginning is based on the light of the intellect and on logical thinking. This remains the same whether the two realities tied together (different from the sleet and from loneliness) are both part of a psychological process or whether they are both phenomena of the external world.

But is logic enough in this case to exhaust the grasping of the entire given reality? To say it with a generalization by borrowing a Buddhist compound: How far should we pursue the "logic" at the bottom of "things" in order to reach the point of perfect fit between "thing" and "logical principle" without allowing for any separation between the two? It is a well-known fact that this question has been problematized since ancient times, both in the East and in the West, as a basic doubt in "ontology." At the source of this problem lies an extremely simple fact. The sleet that keeps falling, for example, or the lonely mood, no matter how ordinary these phenomena might be, as far as the actual place in which they are experienced is concerned, they appear as *this* actual sleet, *this* loneliness—that is, a unique, specific, and original reality. At their source, realities are directly "given." We cannot call this "something given directly to consciousness," let alone consider it a material that is provided by "knowledge" as a variegated "representation" of consciousness. The experience of such a reality is a direct experience—a "bodily experience" *(taiken)* in the word's literal sense. Such an event occurs in the realm of the original "thing."

Accordingly, a relationship is established between two realities. When this relationship appears in actuality as one reality, the place of this appearance belongs to the realm of the same basic "thing." In this place, such a reality is directly experienced. To use once again the example of the previous haiku, an interpretation along the lines of "loneliness has deepened *as a result* of the falling of the sleet," or "by chance the sleet started falling *while* I was feeling down," departs from the actual place of the original "thing," transferring (and reflecting) the original reality into the realm of "logical thinking," which is dominated by mechanisms such as causality and contingency. Yet even when we avoid binding sentences with connective particles such as "because" or "when," and try to express the entire concept in one expression, as in the case of the sentence "the sleet falls onto the bottomless loneliness," we still do not express the "thing" of falling sleet and loneliness in the wholeness of direct experience. The word "onto," which in this case is the center of the entire sentence, works as its fulcrum, logically sustaining the structures of the sentence's meaning. It plays the role of a rivet that nails down the surface of cognition. Whether this shows some kind of "thing" within the original reality directly experienced is a different problem. How does it come about that different realities which, according to the rules of logical "grammar," should be indicated by two propositions can be expressed in that verse as a single "thing" and within a single "gram"?

All poems possess a specific rhythm that is peculiar to this kind of composition. In the tradition of haiku, the rhythm is established by the cuts of verses of five, seven, five syllables out of a total of seventeen syllables. In the previous verse, the first five syllables, "loneliness" *(sabishisa no),* are linked to the following seven syllables, "the bottom falls off, falling" *(soko nukete furu).* But grammatically speaking, there is a caesura between "the bottom of loneliness falls off" *(sabishisa no soko nukete)* and "the sleet falls down" *(furu mizore).* The two propositions—"the bottom of loneliness falls off" and "the sleet falls down"—are linked by this caesura. In this case, the auxiliary word "of" *(no)* in "of loneliness" *(sabishisa no)* indicates the genitive case, linking "loneliness" to "bottom" *(no soko).* That is to say, the logical subject is "bottom," while "of loneliness" is an appended word. In the case of our verse, however, thanks to the appearance of the cut word "of" *(no),* loneliness is stressed as the subject and the deriving mood includes "the bottom's falling off." Moreover, grammatically speaking, the simple possessive "of" *(no)* also plays the role of the subject particle, *"ga."* The image of the situation in which loneliness has become bottomless is simultaneously superimposed by the particle "of" *(no)* on the figure *(Bild)* or image of the movement of the falling off of loneliness' bottom—thus originating a compound image of loneliness that defies analysis. This is the strength of poetic "grams."

Moreover, "the bottom falls off" is immediately followed by "falling," thus becoming a part of the seven-syllable verse that comes after and centers on the conjunction "and" (*-te* of *soko nukete*). Through this conjunction, the image of loneliness that previously centered on the particle "of" *(no)* transmits an echo to the entire seven-syllable verse. Or, rather, the images of bottomless sadness and the falling sleet are superimposed into one image by the conjunction "and." The two images mutually reverberate with each other. Within this reverberation, the expression "the bottom is falling off, falling" is permeated by loneliness, becoming the poetic language that is specific to poetry. Logically or grammatically speaking, an expression such as "the bottom has fallen off, falling" does not correspond to any objective reality and is meaningless. In poems like this one, however, the appearance of a reality originally "given" and the actual space of direct experience open up to the reader.

Here we can also recognize the reason why Bashō stressed the "reverberation" of words. The possibility for all words to reverberate in such a way, as well as to reverberate with each other, is brought about by the caesuras between the five- and seven-syllable verses. These cuts make links more profound. Poetic profundity depends on the strength of these interruptions. This strength opens up the "place" where the context, which we should call discontinuous continuity, is made possible. From within this space that has been opened up, a complex superimposition of images arises. Images permeate each other, and the resulting comprehensive image overlaps again another similar image. The breath and depth included in the links of images are an unlimited, subtle movement, like the weather that sometimes changes in the open sky.

In any event, the verse ends with five syllables: "oh, it is sleet!" (*mizore kana*). All the linkages of the image that are contained in all the words up to "falling" are compressed into the sleet which in this verse is the only concrete image. This is made possible by the caesura between "falling" and "sleet," thus bringing to the surface the image of "sleet," which is the subject of this poem, and making it reverberate all the other images represented up to that point. (This is what is meant by the "reverberation" of words.) And then, from this mutual reverberation, comes the spontaneous exclamation: "oh" (*kana*), the sleet! In this poem, the entire reverberation of words is concentrated in this exclamation. At the same time that the source of the author's excitement appears straightforwardly in a simple form, the place of the original appearance of the reality of sleet—which this poem expresses in its wholeness—is brought into view. In a simple word, this is the direct expression of the "mental boundary" in the meaning of mind = border that I examined earlier.

When I speak of the reverberation of words, I do not mean the simple reverberation produced by the words' sound and pitch as they are caught by the sense of hearing. The sound that is heard by the ear is essentially important for music to whose specific field it belongs. For the specific field of poetry, however, which is the art of words, the most important element is the image (form and mental picture) that words bring about. Things such as the linkage of images contained in the words of poetry, and the meteorology of the heart, provide poetic language with a contextual coherence known as "grams."

But what usually provides spoken and written words with a basic structure and gives them an order is called "grammar." All kinds of specific linguistic systems have their own peculiar grammar—a basic logical foundation that we should call the law of language in general and that is at the basis of all languages, a logical foundation contained in the general notion of "grammar." An intensive representative of this thought is *logos* as seen in this sentence: "A human being is a living being endowed with *logos*." *Logos* means words (*koto*) and thing (*koto*) at the same time. Moreover, since the mechanism of saying with words some thing—or according to which mechanism the content of some thing is expressed in words—is basically linked to the mechanism of "thinking" in its broadest sense, we cannot separate language from thought. As a result, because the law regulating things and the law regulating thoughts correspond to each other, they are both expressed by the word *"logos."* Eventually the union of this correspondence comes into actuality, and the faculty of self-consciousness that by materializing itself knows itself—that is, "reason" (*nous*)—enters into the category of *logos*. "Reason" is the faculty that reaches the point at which to see the law regulating external things—or, as it was called later on, "mental intuition"—is to speak (*legein*) oneself, and to see oneself is to speak the law regulating external things. (This corresponds to what in Buddhism is called "the eye of the law"—*hōgen*.)

The meaning of *logos* had gone a long way by the time it came to be used to define man as an animal endowed with *logos*. Along that way several concepts developed, such as the intuition of ideas, the system of "dialectics," the grasping of the essence of things as "categories" *(logos)* through judgment (reason or *kotowake*), and thereby the system of "analytics" that explains the law (reason or *kotowari*) sustaining external reality. It goes without saying that all these concepts became the foundation of the Western philosophical tradition. We can say that even the development of linguistic theories (philology and linguistics) was basically premised on these systems. But with the coming of the modern age, with more attention drawn to the foundation of epistemologies based on mathematics and natural sciences, new fields within the realm of "logic" opened. Starting from "mathematical" logic and "semiotic" logic, several new types of logic were constructed, so that the realm of logic broadened conspicuously. We could call these changes a kind of diastrophism that potently influenced views on language. I do not have time now, however, to proceed in this new direction. What I would like to problematize here actually takes the opposite route. I would like to go back to a more pristine place from which a traditional logic based on pure "reason" came, a logic that is linked to metaphysics, as "first philosophy," and to epistemology. By "pristine place" I mean, at the same time, the place in actual experience as well as in history. In both instances, the problem is related not only to the fact that words become poetry but also to the formation of poetry and to the process of poetic composition.

With regard to the pristine field in actual experience, as I mentioned earlier, for us the experienced reality of actuality is originally always "something directly given." Yet it is not given to our "consciousness" as a "representation." Reality "is given" experientially to ourselves as one body and mind. When we say that a cicada is singing, for example, or that we hear the cicada's voice, what is originally given is not the link between the representation of a general "voice" and the representation of a general "cicada"; it is the voice of the cicada that is actually given to our sense of hearing. *This* voice is nothing but the cicada's voice. By listening to the voice we hear this *cicada.* Of course, the cicada's shape and color are not included in the voice. What is heard in the cicada's voice is the image of the cicada. In any event, when we hear the cicada's voice, the image of the cicada is given together with the sound. This place is what I previously called the actual place of the becoming of the original "thing." This is an opening that precedes the consciousness of "I." There is no "I" in the direct "thing" of the coming into being as hearing of the cicada's voice alone. In the instant that the voice is heard, I "am forgetting the I." That is the place where the "sense" of voice = hearing comes into being. But because at that moment the cicada is heard in the voice, at the same time the sense of hearing also includes the cicada's image. All sensations, not hearing alone, always come into being in this manner as concrete experience. In this sense, hearing hears originally "all sounds." It does not hear an abstract voice in general but a voice that is limited to "something concrete." Within the qualification of sound, the pristine, germinative image which produces that sound is included. That is to say, this is not the mental image that has been imagined through the personal activity of the faculty known as imagination. I mean the mental image that is the result of the power of image formation included in the strength of "passive" sensations (passive faculty)—like an embryo within the germ of a seed.

Not only that, but in sensations as concrete experiences is originally included a pristine discrimination within the "thingly" limitations of a concrete sensation—that is, a seedily perception. This is not a distinct judgment of self-awareness, although it includes cognitive discrimination that perceives the concrete "thing" in its pristine form, a kind of "dream viewing" judgment. Imagination and judgment lie hidden in a state of nondifferentiation and as a single body in the power of "sensations" as "things." This wholeness becomes the power of "perception."

If we think of poetry as belonging to the spiritual culture known as the arts—and if we believe that poetry is rooted in the deepest foundation of existence known as man, being the self-expression of man—the transformation of words into poetry has an important meaning that we cannot ignore once we problematize the essence of language. Even if we inquire into the law implied in the words, taking words as *logos*, and introspectively reflecting this law onto the standpoint of reason (understanding or also *nous*), would the only correct path be to reduce all this to the logical system known as "grammar"? In the case of this logicization, the cognitive discrimination that divides subject and predicate and unites them with a copula (is)—that is, "judgment" as a mental activity known as "predication"—becomes the center of the entire operation. This judgment is ordered into a proposition, however, and by adding various words it becomes a complex proposition, until the logical structure of the (prosaic) sentence is investigated. At that point, the entire language is for the first time atomized as "words" and the whole text is regarded a relationship between word and word. Each word is divided into "parts of speech" such as nouns, verbs, adjectives, and the like according to the different function performed. Basing its principles on this logical premise, the law of language is arranged and "grammar" comes into being. At the root of all this movement is the intellect—particularly the mechanism of discriminating intellect—which arranges the *logos* of language along the path of logic.

I do not intend to deny the broad and general meaning possessed by the operation of the discriminating intellect, particularly in relation to language. Earlier, however, I took a completely different direction with regard to poetic language. Rather than making language the object of cognitive reflection, my direction goes back to the place where reality comes into being as something "given" in the first place: a place where reality is original, taking precedence over reflection; an actual place where reality is experienced as the "thing" in itself. If language is the expression of reality, then the place in question where reality reveals itself in the original form of the "thing" must be the place where language reveals its pristine form.

Earlier we saw how, by taking a haiku as our clue, the *logos* of language shows a completely different kind of texture from the logical structure that we find in prosaic sentences (or propositions). There, rather than having a texture in which words are continuously connected as figures of speech, we have cuts between verses. And the connection is of discontinuous continuity, so that verses and words "reverberate" each other. The texture is literally the thread connecting the "text"; it is not a logical structure. When I speak of the thread connecting the text, by "text" I mean words that are the original form of self-expression of living human beings who are endowed not only with intellect but also with emotions. That is to say, it means that in addition to words, the breathing of man, his ardor, his long breath, and his sigh also come with the "text." For example, we have the following verse by Bashō:

Ide ya ware	Oh, my!
Yoki nuno kitari	What a beautiful dress I am wearing:
Semigoromo	The cicada's shell.[32]

This is the verse that Bashō wrote when his disciple Sanpū sent him a hemp garment for summer. The ardor of the verse, "Oh, my!," the strong emphasis in "what a beautiful dress I am wearing," and the weight placed on "the cicada's shell"—all show the emotions inside the author's heart. Such a thread of words is the thread of the "text." Let me quote one more famous verse:

Yagate shinu	Without in sight the view
Keshiki wa miezu	That soon she will die:
Semi no kowe	The cicada's voice.[33]

The preface tells us that the poem sings of "the swiftness of impermanence." And yet, at the same time, the cicada sings frantically, perhaps aware, or perhaps not, that its brief life is bound to end with summer. Somehow the reader secretly sympathizes with such earnestness. We might say that the poet has sung "the pathos of things" *(mono no aware)* in its deepest sense. We might say that the life of this poem lies in the continuation—"the cicada's voice" *(semi no kowe)*—immediately after the strong separating cut following "without in sight the view" *(keshiki wa miezu)*.

The *logos* of the language that appears in the thread of "gram" is not a reason in its logical sense. It is a "reason" that comes into being together with the "thing" in the pristine place where reality is given. It is a "reason" that is directly grasped in the place of the experience of reality—something that we could call the original form of "unhindered reason." In this kind of linguistic

---

32. Kon Eizō, ed., *Bashō Kushū, SNKS* 51 (Tokyo: Shinchōsha, 1982), p. 304.

33. Ibid., p. 229.

logos is included the moment of "silence" and "muteness" that play an important role in the world of passions. They are as important as words when they express something that cannot be said in words or would lose truth if stated in words. At the source of language, words and silence permeate each other. This is why words acquire the possibility of reverberation. Words such as "oh!" in "oh, the falling sleet!" or "oh, my!" in the last verse, logically speaking, are meaningless. And yet, within the thread of "gram" of living words, they play the most important role, which is the transformation in language of things that are hard to express. Linguistic *logos* is a law that is originally endowed with such peculiarities: a "law" *(hō)* appearing in the thread of "gram" *(bun)* that is different from the so-called "grammar" or "law of the text" *(bunpō)*. In the Japanese language, particles are especially powerful in expressing language and muteness, words and silences. They are a potent force in the linguistic arts of Japan.

4. The *Logos* of Unhindered Reason

Earlier I said that language was originally "unhindered reason" and that if it attempts to express reality in the original place in which reality is given and comes into being, then words become poetry of their own accord, showing the *logos* (law) as the thread of "grams." The composition of poetry investigates the pristine reality, keeping itself free from the obstacles of rationality as much as possible. It is an operation that brings reality to expression. Basically such an operation is the deepening of the poet's actual experiences—that is, it cannot be separated from the fact that the study of his actual experiences are investigated within himself. The deeper the investigation, the closer the expressive language of poetry composition approaches the source of reality. I think that this is, broadly speaking, a matter that is generally included in the original makeup of what we call poetry.

In that case, however, one cannot help thinking that there remains one more issue we should explore further. How far can we go to exhaust our investigation of the original process of poetry making, which I just mentioned? What are we going to find? What kind of problems are we bound to encounter? We can look at this from two sides. One side is the experiential investigation of the fact; the other is linguistic expression. In the first case, once we have reached the place of reality's source, reality must come into being simply as reality, in the "thing" itself, that is, as reality as it is. Isn't the poet's experience—which is formed from "the freedom from the obstacles of rationality" and originally linked to linguistic *logos*—faced with the disappearance of "logic" at the extremity of the investigation of reason? There, along with being absorbed in its own wholeness, reason is absorbed into the "thing." Moreover, with the opening of a place that has overcome the entire "reason," in that place the "thing" shows itself as only a "thing," in its truly original ground.

If we look at the same phenomenon from the side of linguistic expression, in the situation I called reciprocal permeation of word and silence within living words, things that are difficult to express in words gradually spring up from the bottom of reality and "silence" predominates—faced at the extreme end of the process with a place where words are consumed and powerless. What remains is the standpoint of what is called "silent mediation" and "silent envisioning." Now, if we put the two sides together, the thoroughness of the ground known as "unhindered reason" corresponds to what leads to the ground of "unhindered things"—of course, such a correspondence occurs at the level of ground as a pristine form. If we speak in terms of the present problem, poetry as the art of language faces an extreme condition. This condition is the appearance of the limits binding the possibility of linguistic arts, as well as the fact that the impossibility of art becomes a possibility. In theory, and as a rule, the ground known as the "arts" is faced with the limits of its possibilities. Even arts such as painting and music, so long as they express something through drawings and melodies, "say" something. But when the limits of "art" appear in such a way, the opening far in the distance of such limits is, to say it simply, the horizon of "religion." The appearance of reality as simply "reality," beyond language and all its *logos* and reason, is the end of the way known as art and the beginning of the new way of religion. I cannot go into detail here, but the ground of "unhindered things" is included in the root of religion. In any event, there are probably not a few artists who realized deep in their hearts the presence of these limits and were deeply distressed by the divergence of "art" and "religion."

We can think of three directions we might take when faced with this problem. The first is to leave the way of the arts and enter the path of religion; in the past there have been many practitioners of religion who adopted this route. The second is clearly to recognize the fundamental limits of art as a normative standard of life but choose to stop within those limits. In that case, a light projects in various ways and degrees from the horizon of religion onto both the artist's life and his work. This happens quite often in the case of people known as great artists. There are not a few cases of people who started living a half-religious and a half-worldly life. The third attitude is that of a religious person who creates works of art as a hobby. In this case, if the hobby assumes the depth of something like a true skill and the "gram" opening on the horizon of art projects its light on the life of the religious man, then he becomes half a poet. Both the second and third attitudes indicate the possibility of reciprocal permeation of religion and art from both sides. Paradoxically, through a clear division, the line that partitions the realm of the arts from the religious realm makes a mutual permeation possible.

The boundary line resembles a plank that partitions two rooms. Side x of the plank that faces room A represents room B, as the thing which indicates the limit of room A. We can say that side x, in its essence, is the expression of room B that is shown to room A. At the same time, however, the side x that expresses room B, being one part of room A, belongs to room A. So far as it appears to room A as a "phenomenon," it is of room A, an element of room A's structure. We can say all the same things about side *y* that faces room *B*. Side *y* belongs to room *B* as part of room *B*'s structure. "Phenomenologically," it is one part of the phenomenon known as *B*. At the same time, however, side *y*, as that which sets the limits of *B* from *A*, essentially represents room *A* in *B*. It is the expression of room *A* that appears in room *B*.

In general, a "boundary" implies that a division is also a joining. This joining comes into being as a relationship that I have called reciprocal permeation and mutual projection among differentiated things. If we call this structure "revolvingly reciprocal,"[34] the most important thing for a revolvingly reciprocal relationship is, first of all, the fact that, when something belonging essentially to *A* is a phenomenon reflecting itself (moving toward) or projecting itself onto *B*, it does not phenomenologize itself as *A* in *B* but, rather, appears as part of *B*. Said differently: When body *A* transmits itself as body *B*, it does not transfer itself in the "form" of *A* but in the "form" of *B*. Body *A* communicates (*mitteilen*) itself to *B* in the form of *B*, while *B* also partakes (*teilhaben*) in the form of *B* of what it has received from *A*. This is the "function" of *A* known as self-transmission to *B*. The same thing happens when the transmission occurs from *B* to *A*.

The point I have raised here relates to the problem of the image mentioned earlier. The issue of the image is a problem that always occurs in ontology and epistemology whenever we theorize about "essence" and "phenomena." In those cases, it is not enough to frame the problem of the image by starting, as is usually done, from the standpoint of divergence and discrimination in which we first think of the essence or phenomenon of a "certain thing" called *A* and then, after thinking in the same manner with regard to *B*, we ponder over the "reciprocal operations" of the two. In that case, after all, one comes to rely on the operational judgment of the discerning intellect and seeks to theorize the thing. But under these conditions one ought not to be able to think really of the problem of image and, by extension, the problem of art and religion as well. Rather, a viewpoint comes to be required where it is as if we can see, at the same time, both divergence and discrimination, or essential connection/affiliation and nondiscrimination, as one. In that case *A*, taking the form of *B*, is reflected onto the completely other *B*. To borrow the words of Eckhard,[35] *A*'s "thinking itself toward" (*hineinbilden*) *B* is nothing other than the making of *A* into an image. In the realm of humans, for example, things like the "im-

---

34. Jan Van Bragt translates the term *"egoteki"* as "circuminsessional" and provides the following explanation: "I have chosen the term 'circuminsession' to translate this notion because the relationship it refers to seems to me to imply such a reciprocity that nothing in Western thought can approximate it except this term used to describe the relationship between the divine persons of the Trinity. I do not suggest that the Japanese word and the English word are exact equivalents." See Nishitani, *Religion and Nothingness*, pp. 294–295.

35. Johannes Eckhard (?1260–1327), a German Dominican known as "Meister Eckhard," was regarded as the founder and one of the greatest exponents of German mysticism.

age of God" *(imago Dei)* or "Buddha nature" informing all creatures are first understood in this sense.

The second point of which we should be aware in the revolving reciprocal connections is that these relationships are not limited to the space between two things. In the previous example of the room, in the case that the room was triangular, three divisions would make one whole in which three of those connections were compounded. So also with four corners: the more corners the room has, the more complex things become. If this is the case with an extremely simple structure such as a section of a room, how much more complex is the concrete reality of the actual world! No matter which of the innumerable laws, innumerable images, innumerable things one takes, or whatever corner of the world one seizes, a limitless complexity of connections is included that is beyond analysis by the logic of discerning intellect. The phenomena of this physical world, as small as dust dancing in the wind, not to mention the living creatures in the world of life, the life force, and all the phenomena that manifest themselves in life, including what is directly beneath our own daily life in which we actually live, all relationships that we might find in all laws and all creations, they all come into being together. In other words, the world itself comes into being. Or, we could say, the world "worlds." If we say that the world worlds, the "thing" of the world becomes the most simple and straightforwardly peculiar phenomenon. But at the same time this "thing" is the dynamism of the limitless and complex body of linkages, the appearance of life. If we consider the "world" along these lines, then I wonder whether the revolving reciprocal linkage that I mentioned earlier, with regard to the division of the partitioning of the room, is not the basic form of the linkages of the "world" seen as a limitless and complex whole.

In the connections that we call the "world," there are partitions, divisions, and limits everywhere. Pine trees are pine trees and they are not cedar trees; this pine tree is *this* pine tree and not that pine tree. In the various dimensions of "being," being always includes a sense of self-sameness that is itself and is not the same as any other thing. Insofar as one piece of dust, or even the individual atoms inside the particle of dust, are existing "beings," they possess self-sameness. In whichever dimensions they come to stand, the various self-samenesses include essential (that is, peculiar to "being") partitions and boundaries between them and all the infinite other possible things. If, for example, one is a human, this is so in the dimension of *humans* and in the dimension of *this* human. Infinite boundary settings are included both in the dimension of "being," seen in general as the specific "human being," and in the "human being" qualified as "this" specific human being seen in his individuality. (This is what Spinoza means by "limitation is denial.") All specific people and individual people are localized in their various self-samenesses and in their various "beings" through the so-called *extensive setting of boundaries.* That A is A and cannot be B or C, or that B is B and cannot be A or C, is an indication of a kind of self-enclosedness that encounters barriers wherever it turns.

Because this means that the self can never venture out of itself, all other things become obstacles to the self. And the fact that all things in the world are able to exist only as varied selves, with various boundaries on all sides, indicates that the world of connections includes a system of thorough ramifications and discriminations. Yet a diametrically opposed situation also appears with regard to the connections of the world—that is, nondiscrimination and equality, or oneness and unhinderedness, on all sides. These connections are simultaneously and necessarily accompanied by separation and equality, discrimination and nondiscrimination, closedness and oneness, obstacles and unhinderedness. At this point, the diametrically opposed directions I just cited are linked together. In other words, they are "fused together" into a sameness. But what is this "sameness"?

When a certain A is in the world, it is given its own "place" among the various other things $(B, C, \ldots)$. This is not merely the locus of phenomenological being; rather, it is the place that signifies the essential field of being itself—the "purportedly innate field" of that materialization. When among all things A "achieves its possible being" as A (in short, when A is A as A), A has "achieved its place" in the world. Earlier I said that the self-sameness of A $(A=A)$ indicates thorough boundary settings as individualistic restrictions. But we might now also say that A has an innate field given to it in the world: a "place" peculiar to itself. Although that "place belongs to the "world" and is one of the "local fields" of the world itself, at the same time it is also a "place" peculiar to A. (In Christianity, this is probably the position that A should occupy in the system of the world, the place that was prearranged at the time of God's creation of the world.)

It is fundamental that within the world, each of all the varied things has its own "place." In olden times, people called it "the universe" or "the cosmos." In more modern times, Ch'eng Ming-tao[36] says that "all things realize themselves," for example, and Leibniz[37] calls it "the prearranged order and harmony of the universe." This distinct "order" is what caused all things to exist as themselves, but it is no different from the many-sided partitions of the divided room I mentioned earlier. The "self-enclosedness," in which all things are mutually and wholly divided, also implies the meaning of their being distinct things that are not "other things" (Cusano),[38] with a proper individuality and independence, that is, also "self-sufficiency." In their foundational "being," all

---

36. Ch'eng Ming-tao (1032–1085), Chinese philosopher of the Sung dynasty.

37. Gottfried Wilhelm Leibniz (1646–1716), German philosopher and mathematician, was known for his "optimistic" philosophy of eternal harmony.

38. Niccolò da Cusa (1400–1464) is the author of works on politics, philosophy, theology, science, and mathematics. His doctrine states that the Absolute is one, infinite, and indivisible. Being God or the center of all oppositions *(coincidentia oppositorum)*, the Absolute can only be known by the spirit *(intelligentia)* or pure intuition. The latter is superior to rational thought *(ratio)*, which in turn is far superior to the perceptions of the senses *(sensus)*.

things originally possess the characteristic of self-sufficiency. Moreover, if indeed all things "achieve their own place" by being "sufficient in themselves," by "achieving themselves," and by being "fit to themselves," this "place," while being the thorough compartmentalization of the "being" of the various things, at the same time is also the direct local field of the "world" itself. Which is to say that it is self-expression as self-compartmentalization of the "world." The limitlessly complex structure of the mutual limits existing between things brings compartmentalization everywhere into the world. This simply means that everything is within the world and "achieves its place" in the world. This is what is meant by the fact that we live in the world as independent beings, each endowed with his own body and mind. The fact that within their being all things include a continually diversifying discrimination comes about only because "the world is one," and only within the world's linkages. This is why it is said: "When one particle of dust rises, the world calms down; when one flower opens, the world occurs." In other words, along with the motion of one particle of dust being blown and dancing on the wind, the world in which everything has achieved its place appears in the form of a quietness composed of a distinct "order." This is the world worlding in a "contented" form. Along with a single flower quietly opening, the world manifests itself in the form of a new liveliness. This is the world worlding in the appearance of "occurring." All movement and quiet are as one. Even the world that appears as nothing but limits and obstacles from the perspective of "all things and all laws" appears, in general, from the perspective of the "world" itself, only as the all-encompassing world worlding. In this case, simply "worlding" is only the taking shape of the unlimited compartmentalization of the whole surface of the world. The absolute closedness in which everything appears in the universe, and the absolute openness in which the world is one, naturally call each other, they become the same thing, and by so doing they create the linkages of the world.

We can call this mutual fusion the equality of absolute discrimination and absolute nondiscrimination or perhaps the fusion of absolute confrontation/diversification and absolute normalcy/equality. Moreover, the arising of this mutual fusion, opening of the field, is the "place" of "being," as I mentioned earlier. This is the "place" of "innate" meaning. This "place" where the existing thing "achieves the possibility of being" is the immediate "being" itself. Just as it is said that being is time and time is being, so also "place" is being and being is "place." The "achievement of the place" is the ability of a certain thing to exist innately (in the ontological sense of the word). Moreover, this place is, originally, one aspect of the world worlding and none other than one compartment of the "world" itself. In short, we can say that such a "place" indicates the characteristic of compartmentalization that is essential to individual "beings" materializing in the world.

If one tries to fit such a structure of world linkages into the form of one = many, many = one, the one = many corresponds to the case of seeing all things from the world's viewpoint. In that case, "one" corresponds to the world that is the opening of the space where everything comes into being: the world seen as its own ultimate "place." "Many" indicates the many compartmentalizations that are included in the world's worlding (that is, the opening up of the world's opening). On the other hand, many = one corresponds to the perspective from the side of all things. Then "many" expresses the ultimate individuality or personality of all things that come into being. "One" is seen as the "place" achieved by the various things. It is made transparent as the localized "place" where "beings" endowed with their own personality dwell. We can also say that in one = many, "place" is "being" whereas in many = one, "being" is "place." Now, both one = many and many = one stand in a relationship of equality between one and many. But as I just noted, the world linkages themselves are a relationship of equality of two relationships of equality. As I said earlier, these connections are infinitely complex. If we try to grasp the makeup of the structure of these linkages using logical schemes such as "one" and "many," and express this in the *logos* of language, then we evoke the standpoint of "scientific" knowledge—and such a standpoint will lead us from "scientific" considerations to "philosophical" speculations. This mental procedure will not exhaust our thoughts on these relationships, however. Those speculations will clarify the linkages in a world of "theory" but will be unable to deal with the reality that is actually given to things—a world of "things" that can only be experienced by the emotions. This is due to the fact that apart from the "theoretical world," the solid "universe of actual things" remains. Therefore, a form like one = many and many = one is necessary in order to grasp these connections in their structure. This is the *logos* of the law I earlier labeled unhindered reason. In this case, "unhindered" indicates the form of the structural relationship known as "sameness" *(soku)*.

What exactly is this unhinderedness? Adding to what I have said before, we can first think of unhinderedness in the opening of the world as the "one" in the expression "one = many" or in the world as "opening." No matter what kind of thing we are talking about, inasmuch as that thing exists, that "being" exists in the world. Yet the only place about which we can say this is only the single opening known as the "world." Accordingly, this opening is absolute. This means that a place of transmission opens where "all relations" that come into being between different things somehow mutually communicate back and forth partaking of each other. Although it is an opening of a revolvingly reciprocal relativity, the opening known as the world is nothing but the original opening where all openings as "relationships" come into being. This relativity is made up of several dimensions, levels, and steps, each of which is in its turn mutually relative. Opening as such relativity—the opening of place in the form of "connections"—is reduced to what I have called "the many compartmentalizations" (the compartmentalization of the entire surface of the world's opening, in other words, or the occurring of compartmentalization as far as the opening reaches) that are included in the world's worlding. The opening of the world itself does not include any kind of relativity, however, being an absolute "one." It does not include in any way the meaning of opening of place as a relationship between things. It surpasses the "dialectical" relativity accompanying all reciprocal denials that include the notions of reciprocity and equality. As an absolute one, it is a nonrevolving reciprocity. Thus the world-ing of the world is a pure and simple, unique thing that overcomes compart-mentalization. The opening of the world is equal to "emptiness," and it is non-adherent.[39] In this sense it is totally "unhindered." Unhinderedness can be seen in the opening of the world.

Yet we cannot say that the opening of the world—spoken of from the to-tality of the world's connections and as the thing that creates the extremity of those connections as the "one" in one = many—is an unhindered opening un-less there is no obstacle on the other side. The other extremity of the world's connections is the place I called earlier the "many" of many = one. In other words, it is the place where everything that comes to being in the world is en-dowed with extreme personality and individuality. Over there, all things ma-terialize in their naked reality in which they are given. That place cannot ab-sorb all the light coming from the outside. The external light, whether it be the light of the senses or the light of the intellect, merely touches the outside of that place and is reflected away. Reality is the "stubborn reality." When re-ality comes into being as reality—in other words, when reality is in the place originally "given" to it—it is given as a stubborn reality. It follows that the only way to reach that reality is to experience it from within.

Now, what does it mean to return to the original place of reality and look at it "from within"? Although this is a problem I should confront later, let me spend a few words here with regard to the issue that I have been raising. Look-ing at reality "from within" is connected to the opening of the surface where reality originally "is." The coming into being of a "thing" as reality occurs within the opening of the world. All this is "given" since it takes place in the world. Within that world, it obtains its own "place" among all other things, and in that place it actually exists. That "place" is one with the "being," but at the same time it is also a compartment of the world. Each thing, in its giv-en nature, shows a "stubborn" self-sameness that makes that thing absolutely itself. To that extent, this "being" is a thoroughly limited being, limited on all sides, and closed within itself. As an absolute one, each being is beyond all relativities and surpasses "revolving reciprocities" such as mutual permeation and equality with others. It is similar to the previously mentioned opening of the world as an absolute one. It is a completely "nonrevolving reciprocity."

This being is one "place" in the world, however, and when the "limits" of being come to mean one "compartment" in the world, then being does not stop

---

39. Nishitani uses the Buddhist expression *"muichimotsu,"* or "nothing to cling to," a term used to in-dicate the lack of substance in all things.

at nonrevolving reciprocity-qua-itself. But, rather, by departing from itself within itself, it comes to stand within the world's connections. Said in a different way: The boundary wall of individuality (or personality) that closed it off becomes transparent, and being enters into a revolving reciprocal relationship with other beings within the perspective of the world connections. The absolute self-sameness of the being itself comes to include within itself the opening of the place of relativity. Being showing the meaning of "place" is being showing the meaning of one compartment of the world. It takes one step toward the opening of the world, entering into a relationship with other things that are similarly compartments of the world. Through this, being begins the process of becoming transparent from within itself. Even if we say that "being" and "place" are innately one, between the space of the "being" of stubborn reality and its "place" there is a fundamental dislocation along with an innate sameness. This is the development of an inner view that is concealed within being. This view is the ground for looking at reality "from within." This dislocation is essentially a transference from the actual "reality" to its image. Within "reality," the image that has become one with reality appears as the distinctive form of the image itself. The power that becomes one with reality as "common sense" within each of the five senses, moreover, appears as the imagination. I will not go into this any further, however. Our original problem was the two extremities of the world's relationships as a whole as they are tied to unhinderedness—that is, the opening of the world on the one hand and the actual reality of all things on the other. I must now return to that problem.

5. Unhindered Things and the World of Faith

All things as a whole form one linkage, thus creating the varieties of objects, phenomena, and laws known as "the world." This is an extremely complex linkage that we cannot address with any other name than "living linkage." If we think of its structure in the form of one = many, many = one, however, then at the two extremities of this linkage we have, on the one hand, the problem of the one without many and, on the other, the straightforward many without one. At one extremity, the whole known as the "world" is absolutely one as an "opening." This "one" appears in places such as "the empty space" where the world is nonadherent. At the other extreme, the various things are completely differentiated as actual reality and the world that is made of their gathering is absolutely "many." This "many" appears where the world is "a myriad of things," "a myriad phenomena," "a myriad of laws." Yet the absolute "one" and the absolute "many" have one logical contradiction. The notion of one without many and many without one—both as an abstract concept of formal logic and as a concrete concept of ontological logic—suffers from the logical contradiction between the "hollow space" of openness, where no "thing" exists, and the "actuality" where all sorts of things exist. The opening forms the ultimate ground of the world's wholeness as one "world." This opening is limitless, however, since it is not limited by anything and does not limit anything. On the other hand, the things that come into being in the world are thoroughly limited in their "being," and their totality signifies the world as "all existences," "all nature." The extensive limit of all existence and the limitlessness of the opening is another contradiction. Nevertheless, since both the world as opening and all existences that come into being there belong to the "thing" of actuality, this contradiction defies ontological logic. On the one hand, the sphere of the "thing" also extends over the realm of the experience of the senses. So long as it includes the certainty of the senses (for example, the actual hearing of the cicada's voice), this "thing" is prior to all "logics" that belong to the realm of the intellect and pure thought. On the other hand, the "opening" of the world, as I will be mentioning later, is also the place where religious reality (in the different forms of mythology, revelation, mysticism, enlightenment, and so forth) "is given" as well as experienced. To this extent, it "goes beyond" the intellectual power of reason and comes after all logics.

Between these two extremities, the whole revolvingly reciprocal and concrete linkages of the world stipulated as one = many, many = one, develop. Here many laws and *logos* must be included as routes of these linkages. These laws are not something that must be thought apart from reality, however. The linkages making up the "world" were not set up to make us think of the separate realms (or "the universe")[40] of "thing" and "law." There "law" and "thing" were originally one. This is what I mean by "unhindered reason." Within the concrete world's connections, which constitute the middle space between the two extremities, we might think of ethics and the arts as fundamentally important realms. But the "principles" and "obligations" that sustain the praxis and action in human relationships, as well as the *logos* sustaining the arts (for example, the linguistic *logos* in poetry), differ from the logic that belongs exclusively to the working of pure intellect. This is a law that belongs to "will" and "emotions" as well as to the intellect—something like what was once called "the logic of feelings" (Ribot, *La Logique des Sentiments*). But this world's connections—something we could also call the "universe" of unhindered reason—possess both extremes that set limits to the controlling power of the *logos* of unhindered reason. These two extremities—the "law" of the absolute one and the absolute many and the "thing" (false and true) as the world's opening, which includes the world's worlding, and as the coming into being of all nature, all existences, and all things—are in an absolute, contradictory position.

At the same time, however, this absolute contradiction does not end as a

---

40. Here Nishitani uses the Buddhist word *"hokkai,"* or *dharma-dhātu. Hokkai* means (1) the realm of cosmic law; (2) the phenomenal world; (3) the whole universe; (4) the absolute; (5) the realm in which the law of cause and effect is operative; (6) one of the eighteen realms; or (7) the realm as an object of the mind. See *Japanese-English Buddhist Dictionary,* p. 120.

contradiction. This is because all existence, all things in the world, are the world's opening. Conversely, the world opens because all nature comes into being there. Without the materialization of all things, the nonadherent "opening" would not be actualized—and without actualization it would not be the opening of the actual world. On the other hand, the actualization of all things depends on the fact that the world's opening actually opens. Therefore, the two extremities are the two faces of the same coin, and these faces are mutually contradictory. This is not a "revolvingly reciprocal" relationship in which self-sameness is a "sameness" as self-sameness. Moreover, it is not sustained by a logic of unhindered reason. The self-sameness of the absolute one and the absolute many is not one = many nor many = one. And it is not the equality of equality. If we really want to talk about equality, then we should say one = zero, zero = one, and then call it the equality of these two "equals" (=). But by no means can we talk about a *logos* or a "law" here. It is rather a lack of logic, or a "nonlogic." Moreover, by doing away with the absolute one and the absolute many, there is no one nor many in one = many, many = one; nor is there any equality between the two equals. In short, there is no revolvingly reciprocal world relationship. The concrete, actual "world" as the world's relationships is possible only because the contradictory extremities, as absolute non-revolving reciprocity, are the same thing. This sameness must overcome all "equalities" and also the "logic" of equality. This is nothing but the universe of "unhindered things" mentioned earlier. This makes possible the formation as world of the actual "world" as the universe of "unhindered things." What makes the "world" possible as all nature, all existences, and all things (potentially the whole, limitless cosmos) is the "world" as opening of the place where everything is potentially coming into being. The absolute opening that makes the world's opening possible, however, is the "world" as unhindered things. Of course, it is not that another world different from the world as "opening" exists somewhere outside reality. The absolute opening is the "worldliness" of the world itself as opening. This is what I mean by making the world possible. Conversely, what makes the world's opening actually open is nothing but the "world" known as unhindered things, the absolute "thing" that makes all things possible as nonrevolvingly reciprocal "thing," as a "stubborn reality" that brings all things into being. Yet even in this case we are not talking about a separate world, but of "wholeness" in all things (the wholeness of everything). In this sense all nature is made possible.

Unhindered things are a place beyond all logical routes. Over there, both contradictory extremities become one thing. On the one hand, this is an absolute opening, a totally nonadherent, empty space. On the other, it escapes the framework of reason that limits and connects all things within the order of "cosmos," appearing in the form of primeval chaos. However, here chaos as well becomes one thing with emptiness, following the world's linkages of unhindered things. This is nothing but the universe of unhindered things, the place of selfless self-awareness characterizing the universe of unhindered things, where the universe steps out by itself into the outside and returns to its own "origin," located at the extremity of the "logic" of philosophical ontology and epistemology—that is on the extreme side of the "universe" of unhindered things that include being and nothingness, knowledge and ignorance, and equalizes law and thing in a revolvingly reciprocity. In the Kegon school of Chinese Buddhism, several names were devised to indicate this universe. But one of its patriarchs (Tu-shun)[41] called the unhindered things—to use examples from contemporary life—the getting drunk of Mr. B when Mr. A drinks or the receiving of an injection by a shepherd who happens to be near a sick man who called a doctor. The dullness shown in these expressions is not a relative dullness due to an insufficiency of intelligence or logic. Moreover, it is not a simple fallacy. Rather, it is something that has overcome both intelligence and logic—a relative illogicality which, in that sense, might be called absurd (silly). While the relationship (for example, causality) between reality and reality (for example, drinking and getting drunk) is illogical, the situation's ability to make sense, as noted earlier, lies in the religious dimension. "Faith," which is the key opening this dimension, is only a belief in the religious sense. The fact that a reality which is not of the religious type is believed depends on the evidence presented to sustain the reliability of such a reality, based on unquestionable proofs, systematically reasoned analysis, or intuitive insight. In the case of religious belief, however, the given reality is absolutely illogical and the ground on which such reality lies is also completely beyond reason. Religious belief is actually the fact of believing in spite of illogicality, or rather because of it. I think that this is a basic fact common to all "religions" no matter what the circumstances—a fact that becomes particularly clear when, during its development, a religion reaches the level of self-consciousness as "religion."

Now, the expression "I believe because it is illogical" *(credo quia absurdum)* is a famous sentence that is attributed to a Church Father (Tertullian)[42] at the beginning of Christianity. At that time, in the Christian world, a faction of people who were influenced by the theories of Greek philosophy became prosperous. Tertullian's words originated from within a debate against these people. The reality of his object of faith was the son of God, Christ, who was sent as Lord to save this world, was crucified together with robbers, died on the cross, was resurrected after being buried, and ascended to the sky. The content of this reality—the crucifixion of the Savior, the death of a God who is supposed to be immortal, and the resurrection after death—is simply and absolutely impossible to understand. In this case, proofs are the eyewitnesses who actually saw these facts—particularly the statements by the apostles. There is

---

41. Known also as Fa-shun, Tu-shun was the founder in China of the Hua-yen (Jpn. Kegon) school of Buddhism in the late sixth to seventh centuries.

42. Tertullian (b. ca. 150), a major early Christian writer in Latin, composed the *Apologeticus* (197), an appeal to Roman governors on behalf of the Christians.

no other choice but to believe these facts as reality. To attempt making them philosophically logical, and changing them into theory, is actually considered a heresy. Within this "faith," belief in God also includes faith in the absolute existence of God, which forms the ground of faith, as well as belief in his omnipotent will and providence (ability to see ahead). From an intellectual standpoint, it is incomprehensible and ungraspable. Yet this reality should be believed in absolute terms exactly because it is absolutely illogical to the human intellect.

But if the death of a God who is supposed to be immortal is absurd, the "language" of a God who is supposed to remain eternally a God and is born taking a human body is also absurd. When God emanated words that were within himself, these words became "embodied." The act of "speaking" for a God comes into being by actualizing itself. In the case of Christ, God spoke about God himself. But when he spoke of the "thing," "let the light be," for example, the thing known as the "light" came from nowhere. All existences in this world are "creations from nothing." The fact of making "things" materialize by saying those "things" in words is not only incomprehensible for the human intellect but illogical. For the *nous* of science, it is nothing but the superstition of an uncivilized age. But from a religious standpoint, it is made into an object of belief beyond the discernment of reason. By calling this mystery a "miracle," we see that miracles are hidden at the source of the being of all existences.

In earlier ages known as primitive societies, the standpoint of archaic religious "beliefs" supported the entire surface of human life. Various kinds of "belief"—what the later science of religion distinguished from true religions as "magic"—flourished in different forms, producing magicians who recited spells and performed incantations. No matter what, people must have felt directly connected to the mystery that was originally part of the natural phenomena surrounding them, as well as in the human affairs of daily life. For example: the sunlight, the darkness of the night, thunder, lightning, volcanoes and earthquakes, the harvest of grains, the sprouting of grasses and trees, as well as the birth of children, illness and death, fire and water, the sky, the earth, and the breadth of the sea, the objects of their dreams and their hallucinations, the list goes on forever. The numinous power and actions emanating from these things and phenomena were taken to be directly related to the possibility and impossibility of their life and existence. Whenever they feared that power, of course, they took various precautions to appease it and calm it down. Whenever they desired something, they started praising, since they needed to cope with those powers and actions. Such behavior related to one's personal life and existence is, generally speaking, a basic pattern of human behavior—the most primeval expression of "will to life." This behavior, to divide it roughly, is comprised of two directions. On the one hand, by believing in and faithfully following that power, human beings empty themselves of their thoughts and desires, and in that emptied space they return to the source of the possibility of their life. This view sees one's personal life bestowed by those powers upon himself. In this case, for a human being to live is to become completely a "thing" of those powers. The fact that one exists means that those powers "have spoken."

On the other hand, while emptying himself, one draws those powers near that empty space, making those powers move him from within that space. In this case, the fact that those powers move through a space which is in himself means that those powers are his "thing" and that he "has spoken." In the previous case, the articulation of language on the part of those powers appears as a "confession of faith" on the part of man. This "confession" is a basic self-expression of his existence. But here, just as in the situation of hearing the words "let the light be" in the reality of the actual being of light, man listens to the word "Be!" in the source of his actual being. His life and life power are nothing but this faithful listening to the gracious command of a benevolent power. In the latter case, man's "act of talking" summons those powers through the strength of the spells that he utters, so that he moves the powers in the direction of his prayers. Here "let the light be" is an expression of human desire. Religiously speaking, the desires that are related to his life and his existence, are, as I have mentioned, a basic moment of man's primeval life: a prayer for future security. A prayer—such as, for example, asking for rain, or praying for a good harvest and a bountiful catch, or praying for the happiness of the dead in the other world—gathers within the praying person the numinous powers who are at the root of all human affairs, turning those gathered primeval powers toward the source of being, thanks to one's own personal strength (as a personal "meritorious deed"), and thus controlling the movement of those powers that lie in the original place. In this prayer is hidden an imperative nature in the sense that an invocation is made to those powers in the direction of one's personal desires. To address the eight-headed dragon at the time of heavy rainfall in order to ask for an end to the rain is a kind of order: "Stop the rain!" In this case, however, unlike the previous case of faith, the "order" is given to the numinous powers by the praying person.

The latter behavior, which appears in the realm of religion, is generally called "magic" and at the present time is mentioned in a disparaging sense. Especially in the European countries that were Christianized—since the object of the Christian religion was "faith" in a God with an absolute character—everything that smelled of magic was vehemently rejected as heresy against the orthodox "belief." It was a matter of common practice to eliminate as paganism whatever belonged to "non-Christian religions." Magical practices such as sorcery and witchcraft, as well as their practitioners, were put in a completely different category from the reverence that was felt for faith in God and the sacred. As a result, when in modern times the fields of the history of religions, the science of religion, and religious philosophy were created in the West, faith and magic were separated in the realm of religion as two completely opposite attitudes. Religion was interpreted as a totally different phenomenon from magic. In its own way, there might have been a reason. But here I want to concentrate on the two moments at the basis of religious "faith" on which the religious field is grounded. In this case, what I have called "moments" are the united body made of the direction and the pattern of the workings of "faith." Direction is where the workings aim. Position is the mechanism behind the way in which the direction comes about—the pattern or topology of this mechanism. These two moments are one—as in the expression *"kata,"* which means both "direction" and "pattern." The direction of this mechanism is related to temporality; the pattern is concerned with space. When the two come together, we might want to think of the nature of a vector and perhaps call it "vectorial." When we say "horizontal," "vertical," or "diagonal," or when we mention the four, eight, or ten cardinal points, we think of direction and pattern coming together into one.

When we interpret the two moments that are included in the basic attitude of "faith," it is important to notice that they oppose each other and, if we inquire further, they show an incompatible contradiction. And yet, despite this opposition, they permeate each other and basically speaking form one single body. The basic place where the two are actually one is the standpoint where "faith" comes into existence in its religious meaning—the position taken by Tertullian when he says "I believe because it is absurd." This is the only position that makes it possible for a meeting with the absolutely mysterious and ungraspable. By comparison with Christianity, Buddhism made the direction of self-awareness the basis of its philosophy from the beginning. The link of logic and intellect with the wisdom of self-awareness was also profound. Yet even Nāgārjuna[43] himself, who more than anyone else exhausted the intellectual path, remarked that you can enter the vast sea of the Buddhist law by faith. To state that the narrowest faith is the only entrance to the vast sea of the Buddhist law means that in any event we must proceed step by step toward the place where we come to meet the "enlightened"—this place being faith in the "Buddha" who is the source of all "laws." In Buddhism this movement is called the arousal of single thought, the awakening of faith, or the awakening of the aspiration to enlightenment. Faith in its religious sense—movement into "vast faith"—means, to use Buddhist terms, that the self has awakened to enlightenment (correct perception) for the first time, or that this aspiration to enlightenment has occurred from within itself in a self-aware and experiential manner as "one single thought." In this sense, the possibility of entering is the opening of our heart, as well as, at the same time, the opening in front of our eyes of the vast sea of the Buddhist law. We could compare it to the heart standing on the wharf or on the beach of the vast sea—an expanse where sky and water merge into each other. If we use the metaphor of the two rivers and the

43. A preeminent Mahāyāna philosopher, Nāgārjuna (ca. 150–ca. 250) is revered in Japan as a major patriarch by all schools of the Great Vehicle.

white road,[44] I would say that it is like seeing the white road from the midst of the world of suffering while listening to Buddha's summons. It would be like coming out through that way to the beach of the sea of Amida's Original Vow.

Moses heard the voice of God coming from the brushwood and calling his name on the top of Mount Horeb. At the Jordan River, Jesus saw the sky open and the Holy Spirit come down to him in the shape of a dove, and then he heard a voice from the sky saying: "You are my beloved son." The Bible says: "And so the Spirit drove at once Jesus to the desert." Paul also talks about the "Revelation of Christ" that happened to him, in which God said: "I will make my son appear to him, and make him spread the Gospel of Christ among the gentiles." We should call these episodes the most decisive moments of the entire history that developed between Christianity and the previous historical age. And yet the decisions brought about by those moments are not conclusions based on reasoning. Of course it is not a conclusion based on an abstract, theoretical logic as in science. But it is not even a conclusion based on the concrete logic of philosophy (such as an ontological or an epistemological logic). It is rather a determination based on a "thing" that comes when we wake up for the first time. As I mentioned earlier, this is nothing but "faith" in its religious sense. The opening of the religious world is a turning toward the original place where the opening of the "world" is an absolute opening, and it is the opening of man's heart. Such a meaning of "awakening" must be included in the "great faith" of the religious type. I think that this meaning of "awakening" is also included in what is called "belief" in Christianity. On the other hand, "faith" as stressed by Nāgārjuna, who saw it as a primeval awakening of his own heart, should be at the core of the development of Buddhism, actually becoming the prime mover of all teachings, practices, and evidence in the later development of Mahāyāna Buddhism that originated with Nāgārjuna himself.

In the history of the development of world religions, however, each religion came to establish different and specific understandings of "faith." The different attitude that was taken with respect to magic should serve as a clue when analyzing the differences between such understandings. But since I cannot go into details here, I will stop with an example.

Monk Yün-men[45] walked with a staff, and, while showing it to the people, he said: "This staff became a dragon and ended up by drinking the entire universe. From where can we now bring mountains and rivers and all the land?" The staff this monk used was often employed by magicians in their walks, and

---

44. A reference to the narrow path between the river of fire and the river of water—symbols of human suffering—leading to the Amida's Pure Land. This image originally appeared in the work of Shan Tao (613–681), the founder of the Zendō school of the Chinese Pure Land. See Yamaori Tetsuo, *Sei to Shi no Kosumogurafī* (Kyoto: Hōzōkan, 1993), pp. 101–108.

45. Yün-men Wen-yen (864–949) was the founder of the Yün-men sect of Chinese Buddhism.

it was known as "the magic wand." The miracle of having water springing from the ground where the wand was violently thrust is not an uncommon magical practice in religions. Several monks showed their staffs at the place where they were preaching, saying things such as the sun and the moon rotate on the top of this staff; or all buddhas, demons, mountains, waters, and the earth come from and return to the tip of this staff; or they play and fight on the tip of the staff. Sometimes the monk hits members of the audience with his staff, driving them away, and saying that now that they are gone he feels much better. Or even when they do not use a staff, these preachers talk about white waves bubbling up from the top of a high mountain or the sun shining at the bottom of the deep sea. Events that are absolutely absurd and defy all kinds of logic are presented as a matter of everyday life. These are all super-natural changes that fill the Buddhist scriptures from beginning to end and probably have a magical nature.

For the monks, however, these were not particularly magical events sepa-rated from the actual world, as the magicians were claiming, but a matter of normalcy. But this was neither the standpoint of a faith required to become an absolute believer in the *kami* and the buddhas. From the standpoint of belief—for a country controlled by the power of the gods and the Shinto and Buddhist laws—everything is truly, actually existent. A world like ours, which is dom-inated by crimes and desires, is a world of illusions and irrelevant thoughts de-prived of any reality. For those monks, however, the sacred things that are seen as real, as well as the sacred world, are all in their own way illusions. In short, no place is sacred and nothing is there to cling to. Instead everything—in-cluding images that are like simple absurdities—is simply an image.

Take, for example, the sentence quoted at the beginning of the chapter on "Being Time" from *The Eye and Treasure of the True Law:* "An ancient Buddha said, At a time of being, standing on the summit of the highest peak; at a time of being, walking on the bottom of the deepest ocean; at a time of be-ing, three-headed and eight-armed; at a time of being, sixteen feet and eight feet; at a time of being, staff and whisk; at a time of being, pillar and lamp; at a time of being, the average man; at a time of being, earth and sky." (The sentence continues: "So-called time of being means time is already being; all being is time.")[46] The place given in this example is the place of "unhindered things," which has overcome the place of "unhindered reason." Moreover, in this place the grounds of magic and belief, which are usually seen as oppo-sites, are included together and overcome. The problem here is to define the meaning of image at the place of unhindrance known as "unhindered things." I must now return to this problem, which I have reserved for the end of my discussion.

---

46. This is the beginning of the "Uji" chapter from Dōgen's (1200–1253) *Shōbōgenzō.* The translation is by Thomas Cleary, trans., *Shōbōgenzō: Zen Essays by Dōgen* (Honolulu: University of Hawai'i Press, 1986), p. 104.

6. On Elemental Imagination

Here I will be talking about the imagination, although I will not be able to deal with all the complex aspects of the problem as they have been discussed by many scholars from ancient times up to the present (for example, Bergson[47] and Sartre[48]). In any event, things such as "the cicada's voice can be heard" (I hear the cicada's voice), or "the mountain comes into view," or "a cool wind rubs my cheek" are a reality of the experience of the human senses—at this early stage we could also include animals. We can say that at the place of this original reality, all human faculties become one, appearing in the working of the senses. In this sense we can say that imagination and judgment are included in the senses in the form of an original "seed."

The person who has heard the crying voice of a cicada comes near the tree, for example, and acknowledges the form of the cicada. The sense of hearing hears the cicada's voice but, while the voice opens as nothing but the cicada's voice, its shape can only be included as an image. On the opposite side, the sense of sight can distinguish a cicada by seeing its shape and the flapping of its wings, but the voice can only be imagined in that visible shape. But in this case, since both are given at the same time, "the crying form" of the cicada is experienced sensorially thanks to the complementary union of hearing and sight. This experience becomes possible thanks to the mutual supplementation, by other sensorial contents, of the image included in the sense of hearing and the image included in the sense of sight. A link between these images is established through which the union of the two senses becomes a possibility. Generally speaking, such a complementary union does not occur only between hearing and sight, but in all other kinds of senses and sensations, as well, so that we can acknowledge this fact to be basic to our daily life experience. (We could also widen it to the life world of animals.) On which ground, however, does this fact come to being?

Briefly stated, this ground is located in the partaking of all sensations—whose different types are made specific by their going through the five senses—in the "functions" of all sensations, as well as in the nature of the "power" that makes one feel. In the past this was called "common sense" *(sensus communis),* which creates the ground for the complementary union of all sensations, as I noted earlier. To say it from the perspective of original nature of sensations, common sense is the a priori nondetermination prior to the senses' receiving specific qualifications. It is nothing but the original "power" *(physis)* that makes one feel where all sensations dwell: the "prime mover" in all sensations. At the same time, on the other hand, this same common sense departs from the specific nature of sight, hearing, and so forth by maintaining the innate function of universality that is peculiar to itself. This function is the

---

47. Henri-Louis Bergson (1859–1941), French philosopher.
48. Jean-Paul Sartre (1905–1980), French philosopher.

production of what is called image (both material and mental) and, seen from this perspective, the common sense is called imagination. On the one hand, what is known as image is deeply tied to the sensations from which it can hardly be cut. To this extent, imagination also belongs to the realm of the senses, and the "world of the senses" is the place where it operates. On the other hand, an image is essentially different from the specific content of a particularized sensation ("color, sound, smell, taste, and touch"). The imagined cicada and its imagined voice possess an unqualified universality that differs from the form of *this* cicada or the crying voice of *that* cicada. To this extent, the working of the imagination includes a "perception" and an "intellectual discernment" that are located in the "seedily" pristine form mentioned earlier. This does not belong to the realm of pure intellect, but it is characterized by what we could call the projection of the intellectual realm onto the realm of the senses. The peculiar realm of the imagination is an intermediate zone where the senses and the intellect are blended—a mediatory realm where each draws mutually apart from the other and, by drawing apart, they get tied to each other.

In our daily conversation, for example, we use the word "round"—as in a round full moon, a round face, a round column, a round dish, the earth is round, to settle a thing in a round manner or amicably, a well-rounded person, and so on and so on. When we hear these expressions, we are immediately reminded of a round figure. Yet even the roundest thing among all the round objects visible in this world does not show a perfectly round shape. Even a circle drawn with the most precise tool is not perfectly round. A true circle cannot appear in the "round things" that are the objects of sensations. A true circle, in the true meaning of the word "round," can only be grasped in the realm of the intellect overcoming the realm of the senses by a thought process that has been purified into the "science" known as geometry. When the circle is defined in this science as the locus that is equidistant from a point on the same surface, such a definition is a pure conceptual stipulation. The definition indicates the pure concept of the "circle." There is no figure in it. The distance from the center is simply conditioned by equidistance without being defined within any concrete numerical value. This distance is simply indicated by an unqualified n that indicates a general numerical value. But since it is the indicator of a universal able to catch any numerical value, this unqualified n allows, by being given a numerical value, various large or small circular figures to be drawn freely. At that point the circle is perfect, but it is not something visible to the eye. It is a pure image produced by the imagination.

In order to learn geometry, when we draw a circle on the board or on paper (or a line or a triangle), we see a round image, which is actually invisible to the eye, through a visible circle. Moreover, through that image we pursue knowledge as a formless and purely conceptual science. At the same time and in the opposite direction, the information that is obtained in science is "applied" through technology. In the case of the circle, the concept of the circle is drawn as the circle's image in the realm of the imagination, and then it is put to a "practical use" in the realm of the senses through the production of various utensils and machines such as dishes and wheels. With the preceding example I have given a rough sketch of the opening of the space where the senses and the intellect blend: the space mediating the working of both through the production of images. However, I have eliminated many details from my discussion. I still have a few things to add with regard to the imagination—particularly from the perspective of its relationship with "the emptiness in emotional situations," which is the original topic of my discussion.

The imagination opens the mediatory zone where the senses and the intellect mix, getting itself intertwined with both of them. The respective irreversibility is the sign that the imagination is a kind of individual faculty different from both the senses and the intellect—a faculty that is provided with a specific ground within itself. Several words indicate this faculty: form, shape, mode, type, model, pattern, figure, in short, the realm of image. Since originally they cannot be separated from what is visible to the eye, we can say that the imagination belongs to the side of sensations (if we clearly cut the sides of the senses and the intellect). However, I said earlier that the image as image is not directly felt by the five senses. Of course, the tea bowl in front of my eyes, so long as it is actually seen by the eyes, appears only as directly given to the senses, and its form, color, and brilliance are seen as one thing. Its shape is the basic factor behind the coming into being of the "reality" of the tea bowl actually existing and appearing in front of me—one part of the directly given. The sensorial intuition at seeing this tea bowl does not come into being without the bowl's shape. On the other hand, it is also a fact that the shape *as* shape is distinguished and can be differentiated from the color. Briefly put: The shape is the factor that gives the tea bowl the name "tea bowl." It has the form of a utensil made to drink hot and cold water, with a hollow and an opening to contain water and other liquids. As for the color, it can be white, blue, or any other color. If it is white, it is a white bowl; if it is blue, it is a blue bowl. The form, however, no matter which one among the infinite variety of possibilities, must be the form of a tea bowl. Our sensorial perception discerns the object in front of us as a tea bowl by its shape. In our daily experience, the object in front of us receives the connotation of the general concept known as "tea bowl" by its form. The shape is a clue for the intellect at the time of the experiential recognition of the object.

Going even further, when we problematize philosophically the "being" of things, shape becomes a clue to think about "form" *(eidos),* "substance" *(substantia),* "form of being" *(Seinsform),* and so forth, as well as a handhold in pondering over "form" and "matter" when dealing with the problem of cognition. There are cases, for example, in which Kant talks about "intuitive form" and "formal intuition." We might be able to say the same thing in science with regard to geometric figures and models in physics. So long as the act of "seeing" is involved, can't we say that everywhere, and at all levels, at the beginning was the "form"? No matter what the intellectual science, the reality that things actually exist in the "world" would not have occurred without the experience of seeing and knowing through the "shape" of things by intuition and perception that are located in the senses—that is, *within* intuition and perception and *qua* them. The shape of things is the way by which the thing "is seen" or "appears"—the actual form or the visible form of the thing in strict conformity with the thing itself—and to that extent it belongs to the realm of the senses. But at the same time it is also the starting point of the action of seeing things. It is the clue for the thing to be seen as a tea bowl, a pine tree, a bamboo, a dog, a cat, to be called by its name, to be classified conceptually. In this sense, it contains a link with the realm of the intellect. If to see intellectually is represented by the word "to reflect," the image of things is always *prior* to reflection; but at the same time, we can also say that it is prior to *reflection.* As mentioned earlier, the realm of the image comes into being in the middle zone between the two completely different spheres of the senses and the intellect, continuing to be linked to both of them in an inseparable fashion. It is tied to these two spheres by separating them. In this case, as I noted earlier with regard to "limits," the image stubbornly expresses in the realm of the senses the concept of intellect as the sensorial shape of the thing while, at the same time, stubbornly expressing in the intellectual realm the form or "actual aspect" of the senses as intellectual forms. What unites these two aspects together is the so-called image (or the "bodily form" of the image).

Therefore, the image has its own autonomous way of being, and it must have its own specific ground. This ground is nothing but the source of the power known as the "imagination." What brings this power directly into view, however, is the mechanism usually called "fancy" or "fantasy." Here the imagination is not caught in the form of the thing as given in the realm of the senses, and it is not bound by any qualification by concepts in the intellectual realm. A completely unreal, surreal, irrational, hyperrational image is freely produced. Sometimes this image has a perfect will, and it is imagined as the most unexpected fancy. This kind of mechanism behind the imagination also appears as technical "discovery" and as scientific "concept." But more than anything else, its most central role takes place in all fields of the arts. The problem of "abstraction" in modern art (especially in painting and poetry) is essentially a problem of the image. In religion, too, the fancy plays a basic role in the entire course of its development. This is easily understood when we think, for example, of the "mythology" that is an ingredient of all religions. The problem of mythology is not simply a fact related to "primitive religions," but it is present even in the most developed religions of our day. At the time of their historical inception, moreover, technology, science, the arts, and religion all form an undifferentiated unity that we could say is regulated by the activity of the imagination as it appears in mythology. All human actions, all their "doing," is grounded in the relationship between god and man *(religio)* as *poiesis,* and in this relationship the imagination rules as an elemental power. All arts originated from this power when they were not yet separated from religion. It is a well-known fact that it also penetrated the political and economic systems and ideas. In these cases, however, as in the case of the arts and religion, it is not only a problem of a past, known in history as an archaism. Even in today's political and economic word, several political and economic doctrines support, as ideologies, the structure of the nation and international relationships, hardening people's passions and intellect into beliefs and causing anxieties and crises throughout the entire world. We cannot deny that at the root of this situation lurks the motion of the imagination—including fancy and fantasy—in the shape of "evil."

Although I should be more detailed on the foregoing points, I must limit my discussion to this rough sketch for lack of time. Here it is sufficient for me to say that the imagination is a faculty that has its own specific ground and that its working extends to several fields. I want to point out that while mediating and intervening in both realms of the senses and the intellect, the imagination is basically different from both. It is always linked to will and passions, from which it freely creates images. The life of the physical and mental figure as image lies in this sensorial world, thanks to which sensorial intuition and perception create a nongiven figure. Moreover, those things that materialize in the realm of sensations, as well as the mental images and concepts that are thought in the intellectual sphere, are endowed with sensorial elements. The creation of the artist and the faith of the religious person can be conveyed from heart to heart, thanks to the working of the imagination. There is no need for me to give examples here of works of art or religious visions demonstrating this last point.

At the beginning of the Meiji era, a monk by the name of Tairyū[49] burned some incense at the Shōgenji of Ibuka[50] during the festival commemorating the enlightenment of Śākyamuni,[51] and he composed the following poem:

With the pupils of my eyes blinded, I look at the universe.
The frosty wind pierces my bones: how cold!
Dust on the path back to my house.
In the snow the fragrance of the plum blossoms hits the tip of my nose.

We do not know whether he composed this poem at that time or some other time. Previously, however, he had prepared a verse singing of a blizzard in the sky—only to find on that day fine weather with no wind or snow. In any event, the monk calmly recited the poem on the blizzard. Later another monk, who was in the habit of finding fault with him, told him what a big snowstorm they were having that day. The first monk answered by asking whether he had seen the blizzard. To the eyes of the first monk, the image of the blizzard on

---

49. Tairyū (1827–1880) took the tonsure in 1884, becoming a monk of the Rinzai school.
50. In Gifu prefecture.
51. The Jōdōe festival was celebrated on the eighth day of the Twelfth Month.

the clear day actually existed. But in order to see it as an actual reality, you needed the eyes to see it. The place where one opens the eyes is the place where "with the pupils of my eyes blinded, I look at the universe." It is also the place where you find the "dust on the path back to my house." This explains why the first monk teases the second by asking him whether he actually saw the blizzard with his own eyes. When earlier I spoke of Yün-men, Yüeh-shan,[52] and the other monks, I mentioned several images that by today's standards would be called nonsensical—giving examples of "extended nonsacredness" and "original nonadherence." These examples are identical to the episode of priest Tairyū that I just mentioned. These are all cases related to the elemental movement of the imagination, working from "the universe of unhindered things."

There are differences in the realm of the arts, even in the field of *haikai*, when we compare Bashō's poetry to the poetry of his disciples, as we saw at the beginning of this essay. But I think that they share a common ground. *Haikai* poets have lifted image and its place to the heights of "gram" through training in the realm of linguistic "connections" and by transferring (reflecting) into their will and passions the ground of the monks. Kyorai's verse, "Buried embers of rice bran / Glitter," receives the previous verse, "The bottom of loneliness / Falls off," singing of the buried embers that become the focus at the center of a dimly lit, quiet house and its empty space. While the scene of the image changes, the basic ground is taken over from the previous verse. Then the same ground goes into Bashō's verse, "All in the offing / Pulling the whales: / The houses on the beach are empty," where the scene is once more transformed into the setting of a large village on the beach. On this delicate ground, the lively image of the pulling of the whales in the offing, and the tranquil image of the empty houses on the beach, are integrated together. This ground runs through all the verses—we could call it "emptiness within the sensorial world"—and becomes the place of the deep mobility of the imagination in poetry.

---

52. Yüeh-shan Wei-yen (d. 828) inhabited the homonymous mountain in China during the Tang dynasty.

NINE

The Calonology of
Imamichi Tomonobu

IMAMICHI TOMONOBU (b. 1922), professor of aesthetics at the University of
Tokyo from 1968 until his retirement in 1983, has distinguished himself as
an original thinker and the author of a metaphysics of beauty known as
"calonology," in which he argues for the privileged status of the senses *(ais-thesis)*. Imamichi addresses the problem of the subordinate position in which
the senses were kept in the *Aesthetics* (1750) of Alexander Gottlieb Baum-garten (1714–1762), where they were described as an "inferior form of
knowledge" *(ratio inferior)* analogous to the superior intellect *(analogon ratio-nis)*.[1] "Calonology" is meant to be a process of ascent from the work of art, as
being, to beauty—from the ontic world to metaontological transcendence—
in which beauty *(kalon)* is prior to being *(on)* and both require the mediat-ing presence of the intellect *(nous)*. "Calonology," therefore, as the combina-tion of the four Greek words *"kalon," "on," "nous,"* and *"logos"* attests, is the
discourse on the *logos* of beauty, being, and mind. The study of "calonology,"
then, is an inquiry into the realms of beauty, existence, reason, and science.[2]

Imamichi first introduced this word in 1956, during the Third Interna-tional Conference of Aesthetics held in Venice, Italy, where he gave his de-finition of aesthetics as the science that must clarify intellectually the exis-tence known as beauty. But, he continued, beauty is not simply existence
but is prior to it and goes beyond it. Imamichi distinguishes different kinds
of beauty according to what he calls "the subjective vectors of intentionali-ty." If the vector goes from the specificity and dispersion of the present to
the unity of concentration, we are faced with natural beauty. If the intention
proceeds from this unified necessity to the specific target of use, we have the
beauty of technology. The beauty of art is the result of an intention that goes

---

1. Alexander Gottlieb Baumgarten, *Aesthetica* (Frankfurt: Johann Christian Kleyb, 1750).

2. Imamichi Tomonobu, "Karonorojia," in Imamichi Tomonobu, ed., *Kōza Bigaku*, vol. 3: *Bigaku no Hōhō* (Tokyo: Tokyo Daigaku Shuppan Kai, 1984), pp. 313–334.

from unified necessity to liberty and free decision. If the vector turns from that liberty to devotion and pure love, we are faced with moral beauty.[3]

Imamichi has also produced several studies on comparative aesthetics in which he focuses on the formation of Eastern and Western subjectivities with reference to issues of ethics and aesthetics. As for the former, Imamichi argues that whereas ancient Far Eastern cultures addressed the idea of responsibility as a kind of intersubjectivity governing human relationships, while ignoring the notion of "personhood," the West tackled the same problem in an inverted order. Until the eighteenth century Western thought developed philosophies of "personhood" while ignoring the issue of responsibility. Imamichi's conclusion is an invitation to take notice of the complementary nature of Eastern and Western humanisms.[4] With regard to the latter, the reader is referred to the essay "Expression and Its Logical Foundation," which is translated here. In this essay Imamichi argues about the absence of the notion of "expression" in ancient Western aesthetics, which instead developed the ideas of "representation" and "imitation" or mimesis, allegedly because of the Western dichotomy between subject and object. In the East, Imamichi continues, the situation was reversed in favor of a strong expressive presence, due to the "rhythm of the live spirit of the universe" that informs everything in the world, standing against the division of spirit and matter, body and soul, immanence and transcendence. In this essay, therefore, Imamichi seems to perpetuate "the myth of Otherness" that grew out of a need for the creation of an independent state during the Meiji period—a myth that still plays a role today, although in a minor tone, as part of the strong ideology of Japanese uniqueness.

Imamichi's dedication to the study of the relationships between ethics and aesthetics is at the core of the system that he called "eco-ethica"—"a new ethics inter homines and ethics ad res" in the technologically systematized environment.[5] As a result of the infringement of technology upon the temporality of human consciousness, whose time duration is continuously challenged by the mechanization of the world, the process of dehumanization and loss of spirituality has reached a speed that is threatening human survival if measures are not taken to counterbalance the process. In Imamichi's opinion, art can help to recover this loss of temporality. The

3. Imamichi Tomonobu, *Bi ni Tsuite* (Tokyo: Kōdansha, 1973). See also Noriko Hashimoto, "A New Perspective of Aesthetics: Outline of Calonology of Prof. Imamichi," in Editorial Committee of Festschrift for Tomonobu Imamichi, ed., *Aesthetica et Calonologia* (Tokyo: Bunkensha, 1988), pp. xix–xxiv.

4. See on this point Nicolae Tertulian, "Des Livres de M. Imamichi," in Editorial Committee of Festschrift for Tomonobu Imamichi, *Aesthetica et Calonologia,* pp. xvi–xvii.

5. Imamichi Tomonobu, "Toshi no Bigaku," in Imamichi Tomonobu, ed., *Kōza Bigaku,* vol. 5: *Bigaku no Shōrai* (Tokyo: Tokyo Daigaku Shuppan Kai, 1985), pp. 52–54.

depth and profundity of the work of art, its verticality, counterbalances the horizontal structure of ordinary time extension, making the appreciator ascend to absolute values. The Beautiful faces the Useful, having the spirit of the single individual purified through the aesthetic experience, while the world is automatically controlled by an impersonal plurality of people.[6]

Imamichi's reflections on technology prompted him to reexamine the notion of intersubjectivity at a time that mourns personhood as the impersonal abstraction of letters on a computer screen. Imamichi, therefore, devised his new eco-ethical system. Now that our relationship with the external environment has changed from contact with a physical world (nature and the physical neighbor) to absorption into a technological network (the phone, e-mail, and an absent, impersonal neighbor), the rules that were once good for interpersonal communication must be revised and restudied. If, in the past, thinkers developed "metaphysics" as a transcendental ground for the natural world of "physics" *(physis),* a philosophy of the new city (or "urbanica")—Imamichi argues—must find in a "metatechnica" the ground to explain and justify the existence of our "technical" world. A redefinition of the *oikos* (house), or sphere of livability, is what Imamichi attempts in his recent eco-ethical project.[7]

Expression and Its Logical Foundation
by Imamichi Tomonobu

The Prehistory of Expression

THE WORD "expression" does not have a univocal meaning in our daily language.[8] It is employed to indicate the face or the appearance of a person or an animal, with reference to language, to show an action expressing sentiments,

---

6. See Noriko Hashimoto, "Eco-Aesthetica," in Editorial Committee of Festschrift for Tomonobu Imamichi, *Aesthetica et Calonologia,* pp. 87–88.

7. Imamichi Tomonobu, *Eco-Ethica: Seiken Rinrigaku Nyūmon* (Tokyo: Kōdansha, 1990).

8. The original text of this essay, "L'Expression et Son Fondement Logique," appears in Editorial Committee of Festschrift for Tomonobu Imamichi, *Aesthetica et Calonologia,* pp. xxv–xxxvi. Originally this was a lecture read in Paris in 1962 and later published in *Revue International de Philosophie* in 1964.

to indicate an artistic activity, and so on. All these usages are identical in one respect, however, which is that they all signify the presentation of interiority. To express is—as the word's etymology suggests—a blossoming in the interiority's phenomenal domain of what one has inside the innerside. Because of the orientation of interiority's intention toward the outside world, expression in its aesthetic meaning is squarely opposed to representation, by which I mean the artistic description of things. This is because in the latter the theme is not the interiority of the self, but the exteriority outside the self.

The idea of representation is therefore the correct description of the object, which is to say, the imitation—in the sense of mimesis—of the object. This has been the classical concept of art since a long time ago. But why do representation and imitation have such an important meaning in the domain of classical aesthetics? There are several reasons that can easily be listed. The main reasons are, in my opinion, defects of classical times: one spiritual, the other mechanical. The first is, from the point of view of the human formation, the lack of an individual consciousness. In fact, the real object that is given to the common consciousness has directly become, without any personal deformation, the matter of artistic production. Here it is not the matter of a specifically personal image, but only a common image. It is nothing but a common given that is evident to the average consciousness of a closed society. It is the task of technique to expose the common image that consciousness receives as the objective form of an external thing. Now, this problem of technique is related to the second defect mentioned earlier. In antiquity the machine did not have the ability to represent *(Darstellungmöglichkeit)* that it has today. Even superficial reproduction did not depend on the mechanical functions of a machine but, rather, depended on the skills of the human hand. For this reason, in classical times it was mainly a matter of a technical capability of imitation within the different realms of the arts; in other words, people paid attention only to the artifice of realist imitation. Theoretically we cannot find here any difference between the artist and the artisan even though there were, in antiquity, many eminent artists who differed completely from artisans.

The discovery of the individual person by the religious conscience during the Middle Ages, however, and its affirmation during the Renaissance have gradually freed the images of their function as mirrors reflecting the external world, making them a projection of the self. That is: It made these images change from belonging to the domain of the common consciousness of man in general to the domain of the originality of the individual person. As a result, next to the problem of representation, there appeared necessarily an interest in the personal image that is totally crystallized toward its inside. This tendency was gradually reinforced by the rapid progress of the mimetic faculty of machines, which profoundly changed as a result of the innovations of the natural sciences and industry. The superficially correct imitation of a scene, for example, is meaningless in painting, since this is almost perfectly realized by photography. It is the same thing with musical instruments, where the mechanical function has become so subtle and so refined that it overcomes the level of nature on which it had previously depended. Therefore, art must now search for its proper ideal elsewhere than it did during the classical age—thus renouncing the rigorous representation ensured by the techniques of modern times. This new ideal of the arts, then, is the blossoming of personal images, the explosion of the inner self in the phenomenal world, that is, the expression that has recently become a primary theme of aesthetic thought.

This transition of the artistic idea just mentioned corresponds slightly to the transformation of the meaning of the word "expression." We cannot find a Greek word that corresponds to our term "expression" in any Greek classical literature nor, even more so, the form of the substantive *"expressio"* in any classical book in Latin. This is a post-Augustinian word. Among classical Latin writers—for example in Cicero—we have the verbal form *"exprimo,"* which always means "to imitate" or "to display the objective image of a thing," which in no way has a similar meaning to our phrase "to express." It means "to represent."[9] Even the post-Augustinian *"expressio"* and its French derivative *"expression"* did not at first have the meaning in question. Originally they both only meant, as is well known, "to extract the juice from a fruit" and such. As I mentioned at the beginning, today it is used metaphorically in different ways. In any event, we must note that the word in question is of recent origin. In fact, in the history of the European fine arts, this expression is a very modern concept that shows itself on the aesthetic scene as a modern provoker against classical representation. It is true, generally speaking, that only in modern works can we notice the artist's effort to emphasize, not the entire harmony of an object, but an interesting phase of what allows him to show his subjective consciousness through deformation as well as through ellipsis *(non-finito)* and the like. Especially in the case of modern art in its strict sense, it directly faces, independently of the objective world, anguish and joy, an almost metaphysical weltanschauung and the idea of beauty, and so forth, of an artist—in a word, the interiority of the author, his self.[10]

Therefore, we must notice that this expression is, both theoretically and practically, a very modern idea with regard to European aesthetics.

Expression in the East

The problem of expression does not present itself in the East in the same manner that I described with regard to the West. In the West it is after the appearance of the idea of expression—which is to say after 1900—that drawing has been given a meaning not simply of study or rough outlining but an independent status as a genre of painting. In the East, however, since antiquity

---

9. Original note: "Ex. gr. Cicero, *Leg.,* 2, 5, 13; *de Orat,* 3, 12, 47, etc."

10. Original note: "Cf. T. Imamichi, 'Gegenwärtige Aufgaben der Aesthetik,' in L. Pareyson, ed., *Atti del III Congresso Internazionale di Estetica,* pp. 39–43."

there have been many independent works that correspond to modern European sketching. On a large piece of paper, for example, we see only a branch of bamboo and the wide white margin left by the artist. It is not a *non-finito* at all but actually a *finitissimo,* since the artist here—by annihilating all the objective images he sees and by simply lighting one single important phase of only one thing that is necessary and sufficient to the interest of his soul—perfectly shows his interpretation of the universe. To achieve such a manifestation, he must first of all feel the rhythm of the living spirit of the universe behind things. He must plunge himself into a mystical contemplation. In the book *Chuang Tzu,*[11] which was edited no later than the end of the second century B.C., we find the following thought: A true painter is not attached to the details of matter but eagerly devotes himself to ascetic meditation.[12] Through this meditation, the human spirit penetrates the essence beyond the corporeal world. If you want to draw such a horizon, you cannot adhere to the phenomenal forms; on the contrary, you must build a contour of the essence by destroying those forms. This is why in the East, since antiquity, painting as well as the other arts are never representations but symbols. In fifth-century China, a great painter who was at the same time a great aesthetician, Xie He,[13] has listed six hierarchical aesthetic norms in his book, *Qualities of Painting:* (1) the living rhythm of the spirit of Nature; (2) the essential contour by the brush; (3) the realist representation of bodily forms; (4) the realist representation of color; (5) composition; and (6) the copy of the masterpiece.[14] The first two qualities are undoubtedly the most important categories in the Eastern tradition to perfect one's attitude toward beauty. To achieve the two qualities in question, we should not be satisfied with the imitation of the outside; rather, we must pay attention to the dynamics of the soul and express this consciousness. This is expression in the strict sense of the word. Certainly in the aesthetic literatures of China during the twelfth or thirteenth centuries, we often encounter the word "hsieh-i",[15] a compound word made of *hsieh* (to copy) and *i* (conscience or will). In French we would say "to copy his conscience" *(copier sa conscience)* or "to draw his innerside" *(dessiner son intérieur)* or "to express the self" *(exprimer le moi).* Then we can say that the classical idea of art in the East is never representation but, as a matter of fact, expression. Since the human sense cannot draw anything without a phenomenal form, however, the East has not completely scorned representation. This is clear if we look at some of the

---

11. Chinese classic bearing the name of its principal author, Chuang Tzu, who flourished in the fourth century B.C.

12. Original note: "*Tschangtse,* Chapter *Dientsepao* (in Chinese)."

13. Active in China during the years 500–535.

14. Original note: "Quoted in Tschang Huen Yeng, *The Critique of the Historical Masterpiece,* 9th c. (in Chinese), p. 10."

15. Original note: "Tang Khuo, 'Treatise on Painting,' in T. Imaseki, *Oriental Treatises of Painting,* vol. 1, p. 131."

six norms just listed. Actually we often find, in Chinese ink paintings of land-scapes, a kind of perspective and contrast between shade and light, as in West-ern painting after Apollodorus.[16] In the East, however, these are only prepara-tory stages on the path to the attainment of expression. They are not major means. Painting has always remained here essentially bidimensional, since the essence, likewise the original theme of art, is never corporeal and therefore nev-er tridimensional. We can say without fear of exaggeration that realist repre-sentation is a recent idea in the East. At the present time, under the influence of European painting, people here paint more and more paintings in the spir-it of scientific, realist imitation without paying any attention to traditional Eastern thought. What I have shown here with regard to paintings works for all the other arts as well. To take an example from the realm of literature, I could quote the case of tanka, one of the classical genres of Japanese poetry. As is well known, the tanka is composed of only thirty-one syllables—which is to say, only a few words. Within these limits, it is absolutely impossible to rep-resent the polyphase structure of phenomenal occurrence. The poet shows in tanka only the soul of the atmosphere—which is to say, the self lighted by the real fact. This is completely different from the epic poem, since we never meet with heroes in tanka. And in the *haikai* with only seventeen syllables, such an epic representation would be especially impossible. The latter is truly a typi-cal example of expression.

Thus we can note that in the East the expression is classic whereas the rep-resentation is modern. It is exactly the opposite case for the West. What are the reasons behind such a reversal in the development of aesthetic thought in the East and the West? This is not only a very interesting problem but also a very important one for human philosophy.

Comparison

Representation is not possible without an objective thought. Since Greek an-tiquity, this objective thought developed in the West in all domains of human life. This thought presupposes a "subject-object constellation." Thus people came to consider expression as an extreme subjectivism, the means to reach the true way of the self. At the beginning of this study I mentioned the same thing in a different manner. Originally in the West expression was nothing but the representation of the "self-nature": objective thought was opposed to interior-ity. Since then, in the West, the passage from representation to expression has simply been a reversal of the direction of objective thought.

In the East, however, the spiritual situation is completely different. Objec-tive thought in a strict sense, of which the typical form is the natural sciences,

---

16. Apollodorus (fl. fifth century B.C.), Athenian painter, is thought to have been the first to shade his paintings by graduating light and color. This explains why his contemporaries called him "Sciagraphos" ("Shadow Painter").

was not known in the East until modern times. Therefore, conditions here have not favored the birth of the idea of representation. The lack of an objective thought explains why its correlative, the subject, is also weak. Or, as we have seen with regard to the West, the appearance of expression was mainly caused by the awakening of the self. If I am correct, we would need to conceive the idea that the self has been established in the East since antiquity, since expression had already been established. Nevertheless, in the East we cannot find the distinct concept of person before the sixteenth century. Consequently, the question of a personal self was not posed. As we have seen, it is true that the *hsieh-i*, "to copy one's conscience," is certainly a kind of self-expression. But this self is not the self-nature that is the correlative of the object. It is never the self-nature that lives freely or suffers desperately in the phenomenal world, but the "I-sharp" *(moi-dièse)* that, by harmonizing with the dynamic rhythm of the universe, is intimately blended with the essence of the fact. This I-sharp is not the self individually awakened. At most, it is a subject without subjectivity—an I crystallized as nothingness by being absorbed into the essence. In other words, this I-sharp is the intermediary at the limit of objectivity and subjectivity.

So far we have noted from the beginning a contrast between East and West with regard to the artistic idea and next, by analyzing this contrast, we have discovered two fundamental facts: First, representation is linked to objective thought; second, expression is linked to the heterogeneity of the I. Now we must search for the sources from which these two facts derive. There we will find the radical difference between Eastern and Western thoughts.

Two Aspects of Truth

The artistic idea has not always been discovered by the efforts of a philosopher. But since it is a human idea, it is certainly one of those intellectual problems with which philosophy must engage itself in order to understand at least its logical structure. And now we must search for the logical reason behind the reversed difference between the West and the East with regard to the idea "expression." Therefore, from now on we shall be concerned with a purely philosophical reflection on the problem. Let us begin with the most fundamental question.

What is the most important thing for philosophy? Without any doubt, it is the truth. And what is the most useful instrument for the philosopher to search for the truth? Socrates said: "The *logoi* are the most important tools for the philosopher."[17] Now, what are these *logoi?* They are the name, the concept of an object, the logic operation, reason, relation, proposition (definition), the main normative being, and the truth. Such a series of meanings suggests a very

---

17. Original note: "Plato, *Politeia,* 582 d, 9. In this text we must interpret it as *ratiocinatio.* But here in my study, I use the word freely."

important fact. They essentially refer to each other—which is to say that all the meanings of *logoi* have the only nature that equally gives them the name *logoi*. The nature in question is their participation in the fundamental Logos, which is eternal and the dominant norm for all appearances. Then each Logos, such as word, reason, concept, and so forth, is a phenomenal phase of the fundamental Logos. Why are the *logoi* mentioned here the most useful tools for a philosopher who is searching for truth?

Or how is truth understood by the human spirit? In order to perfect philosophical knowledge—or, to say it differently, in order to obtain the *truth*—we must clarify the *concept* of an object with *words,* that is, in the form of *definition* (proposition). Through the *logical operation of reason,* we must clarify both the *norms* that dominate the object in question and their *relation.* Here again we must think of the series of meanings of *logoi.* All the italicized words are phenomenal phases of the fundamental Logos. Thus we can say that truth is entirely made when all forms under which Logos appears, all *logoi,* are unified in the form of definitions at the horizon of the human spirit. What does this mean? It means that truth announces itself to us by unifying each phase of Logos. Which is to say: For the human spirit the main identity of the Logos is obtained in the human spirit. This means that knowledge, by taking the subject-object constellation as its basic assumption, consists in the reunion of all objects with the subject in the form of the unifying movement of Logos. Said otherwise: Philosophical knowledge consists in searching the place of such movement in the horizon of reason. In this relation of the phases of Logos we perceive three important facts: (1) It is the authentic form of Western thought; (2) it is a movement of Logos; (3) truth is realized in the form of an explicit proposition. Then we can say by way of summary that in the West truth is realized by the human spirit in an abstract proposition. The fundamental identity of Logos is linked by man to the word. Therefore, thought is the expression of Logos in the human spirit. As a result, the expression of Logos is the movement that Logos impresses on the human spirit, that is, the impression. The objective expression of Logos is for the subject an impression. Or philosophical thought is the pure form of human thought in general. We can assert that all forms are analogical to that one. And the same can be said for artistic activity. Beauty expresses itself in the human spirit, and its expression is for the self an impression. If we want to state it in such a logical structure, all this comes about through the representation of an impression. In the West, where the expression of Logos is the human impression, there is no human expression in the strict sense of the word. There is only the representation of the impression.

Now what is the situation in the East? The series of words corresponding to one of *logoi* is found in the East in the Japanese word *"koto."* "Koto" means the fact. *"Kotowari"* means theory. Translated literally, it means: the analysis of the fact or the division of the fact. *"Kotoba"* means word or language but, in a more literal translation, it means a particle of fact. Thus we can map out the relation of the three elements mentioned earlier in the following manner: *koto* > *kotowari* > *kotoba*. What does this scheme mean? It means that we cannot clarify the rich reality of fact with its particle; in other words, we cannot express reality with words. Does this mean that we cannot achieve truth? But, then, what is truth in Japanese? It is *"makoto."* What is the literal meaning of *"makoto"?* Here *"ma"* means beautiful or perfect. Therefore, the word *"makoto,"* truth, means the perfection of the fact. What does this mean? It is the perfect reality as the effect of the elevation of the given fact. In order to obtain the truth, we want to use words and theory, but this is not sufficient. The richness, the polyphased structure, and the depth of fact are not exhausted by our intelligence. The fact *(koto)* does not announce itself at the horizon of reason. It dwells imperfectly on this side of truth *(makoto)* so long as it is not made perfect. Man is also the only key for the realization of truth. Therefore, this time, man is never the I-nature, which is only the horizon for the movement of Logos. He must be the I-sharp who, by being transfigured by the power of fact, lives at the limit between subjectivity and objectivity.

Actually, there is no fact that is isolated from the I—and, vice versa, there is no I that is isolated from the fact. There is only one reality, which contains both fact and I. There is only a given totality whose abstractly broken form is the subject-object constellation. Truth is never the announcement of an absolute object to the subject as human spirit. If there is truth, perfect fact *(makoto),* this is nothing but the elevation itself of this given totality, in which the given fact and the I are unified. This I is the I-sharp, since it is never an isolated subject like the I-nature. And this I-sharp is a real transformer in which the fact *(koto)* can perfect itself into truth *(makoto).* Then man is here the being who bestows *immanently* the perfect value on the given fact. Consequently, by going through human existence, which moves in the fact, this fact *(koto)* crystallizes itself into truth *(makoto).* It is also a movement of *Koto* itself. The fact *(koto)* expresses its movement toward truth in the form of human action. If man does not behave properly, the fact dwells on this side of its perfection, on this side of truth. The direction of its action must be chosen by the will, which can suppress all the other possible tendencies of the fact. We can well recognize here the relation of the fundamental words that belong to the series of *koto* corresponding to those of Logos. At the same time, in this relation we perceive three important facts:[18] (1) This is the authentic form of thought in the East; (2) it is a movement of the identity of *koto;* (3) truth is realized in the form of implicit silence. We can say, then, as a summary, that in the East truth, by starting from the word but nullifying it, is obtained by the human spirit in the concrete life. The direction of the movement of identity of *Koto* is sharply opposed to the one of the Logos in the West. The fundamental identity of *koto*

---

18. Original note: "Cf. T. Imamichi, 'Philosophical Reflection of the Logic of Natural Sciences' (in Japanese), in *Tetsugaku* (1960), pp. 22–45."

is linked not to the proposition but to the prominent act of man in order to perfect the fact. Here the expression itself of *Koto* is the moral blossoming that is realized by the suppression on the part of the I-sharp in order to find one direction only to the truth. The same thing happens in the artistic activity. If we want to express it, it will not be through a representation of what is suppressed to the I. We must suggest the suppression of the will itself, which has no represented form since, being incorporeal, it is never imprinted by the other. Therefore, expression in the East is always a symbolized suggestion. Here, in the East, we see the logical necessity for the paradox that expression must be suppression.

Expression for the Instant

Daily life develops in extended time. The object of representation is within this time. The phase of being that is in time is simply the average figure in each moment. It is never the true phase of being. The Eternal, or God, if he exists, is the farthest away from average value. If I am right, we cannot acquire what is the most important, in the case of the representation of temporal beings, since representation is only possible on the level of temporal beings. The most important appears only at the moment when we move beyond extended times. Such a moment is the blossoming of the identity where the Eternal and the I form a living unity. The manifestation of this moment is nothing but the true expression that is possible when we have seized two historical phases of expression or, in other words, the Eastern and Western types. In order to express the absolute moment in question, artists have made all kinds of efforts from antiquity to the present day, and there are certainly many masterpieces that touch us. Nevertheless, when we think of true expression we see that it does not yet realize itself, neither practically nor theoretically. We must wait for the future. I do not know whether this is a matter of hope or sadness for those who deal with beauty.

POSTMODERNISM
AND AESTHETICS

TEN

The Play of Mirrors
Sakabe Megumi

AMONG THE major books of the contemporary philosopher Sakabe Megumi (b. 1936), *The Hermeneutics of Masks* (*Kamen no Kaishakugaku,* 1976) and *Japanese Inside the Mirror* (*Kagami no Naka no Nihongo,* 1989) confront the subject of aesthetic experience. Both deal with the specificity of a Japanese subject that the author describes by resorting to the metaphor of the mask.

Sakabe argues that a mimetic view of reality provides a definition of "mask"—*kamen* literally means "a temporary frontside"—that emphasizes the characteristics of the object customarily taken to be different from "the true self" *(makoto no omote):* the "unpainted, unfeigned face" *(sugao)* of the person wearing the mask. He challenges the conceptual poverty of this definition of "reality" as the representation of an allegedly primordial appearance. Sakabe stresses instead the visual aspect of the perception of the self inasmuch as we see others as we see ourselves in the projection of a mirror. The frontside is simply a "sign" *(shirushi)* of refraction that can only be perceived in its moment of "re-presentation" *(saigenzenka).* The mirroring process questions the validity of the distinction between mask and face and challenges the possibility of positing a "true self." As Sakabe argues in the first essay translated here, the presence of a self as "surface" *(omote,* meaning both "mask" and "face") implies the existence of a structure of "reciprocity" *(sōgosei)* and "reversibility" *(kagyakusei)* that problematizes the visual self as "something that is seen by others, that sees itself, and that sees itself as other."[1] This latter definition applies to both the mask and the face, depriving them of the justificatory ground for positing any kind of differentiation.[2]

---

1. Sakabe Megumi, *Kagami no Naka no Nihongo: Sono Shikō no Shujusō, CR* 22 (Tokyo: Chikuma Shobō, 1989), p. 42.

2. Sakabe explains the Japanese use of the same word *"omote"* to indicate both "the mask" and "the face" according to the analogical structure of the two objects: "Inasmuch as the face manifests and hides something invisible or almost invisible that is known as 'the person' or 'the heart,' *omote* participates in the same

As a repository of pure difference, the mask is a metaphor of the human face—the metonymic representation of the person—in the same way that the face is a metaphor of the mask. Sakabe reminds us that the language of poetry has familiarized the reader with similar aporias when we think, for example, of the metaphorical reading of "farewell" as death and of death as "farewell." The reciprocity of the process of symbolization challenges the customary safety of categories such as "true" and "false" that do not take into due account the powerful working of difference.[3]

Sakabe gives the example of the nō actor who, before entering the scene, takes his mask to a room called the "Mirror Hall" (Kagami no Ma). The actor sees in the mirror his own face, as well as the mask, while at the same time being seen by his mask in the mirror and seeing himself transformed into the character he will be representing on stage—a god or a demon. The actor finds his presence in the metamorphosis of the other in himself or—which is the same—in the incarnation of the other into himself. The principles of "reciprocity" and "reversibility" explain, in Sakabe's view, the double signification of *omote*, paving the way to a softer model of subjectivity.[4]

> In the "Kagami no Ma," the actor puts on the mask; he sees in the mirror his own face or his own mask; at the same time, he is seen by his mask in the mirror and, finally, he sees himself transmogrified in some deity or demon. Afterward he walks onto the stage as an actor who has changed into a deity or demon or, which is to say the same thing, as a deity or demon who has taken the bodily form of this actor. To say it differently, the actor enters the stage as a self transmogrified into an other or as an other transmogrified into the self. Here we witness the typical manifestation of the structure of *omote* as I described it a while ago. What is important to notice now is the fact that the structure of *omote* is evidently the structure of the mask, as we have seen, but, at the same time, it is also the structure of the face. The reason is that the face also is what is seen by the other, what sees itself, and what sees itself as an other.[5]

The eclecticism of Sakabe's thought is particularly detectable in this passage. Here we see him invoking the name of the medieval playwright Zea-

---

double structure articulated in its meaning of mask." The self is separated from itself by the fact that the mask of the subject, the face, needs the presence of the mask of others in order to be made visible. Sakabe uses the metaphor of the "mirror stage" developed by Lacan to explain the psychology of children: "I cannot be a person *(hito)* unless I see myself as an other *(hito)* by locating myself ecstatically in the place of the other." In a footnote Sakabe reminds us that *hito* in Japanese indicates both "the person" and "the other." See Megumi Sakabe, "Le Masque, le Comportement et le Jeu," *Revue d'Esthétique* 21 (1992):101.

3. Sakabe develops this argument in the chapter "Mask and Person" (Kamen to Jinkaku) of *Kamen no Kaishakugaku* (Tokyo: Tokyo Daigaku Shuppan Kai, 1976), pp. 77–99.

4. Sakabe, *Kagami no Naka no Nihongo*, p. 44.

5. Ibid., pp. 44–45.

mi (?1364–1443) and his theory of "detached view" *(riken no ken),* according to which "the true actor must always see his own image from far away, even from behind, from his back," so as to be able "to see himself as the spectators do, grasp the logic of the fact that the eyes cannot see themselves, and find the skill to grasp the whole."[6] At the same time, however, Sakabe also relied on an array of Western thinkers, foremost among them Martin Heidegger, whose work on the ontological difference Nishitani Keiji summarizes as follows:

> The self who *actually* is has been thrown into the world and *is* in relation to the various things in it. To take this kind of actual existence as the clue to the human mode of being is to say that it is possible to question Being from within a mode of existence where the seeing self and seen self are truly one. In other words, it is to say that the ontological difference is understandable. This is the standpoint of Heidegger's existential philosophy.[7]

More directly, Sakabe was borrowing from the French philosopher Maurice Merleau-Ponty (1908–1961), whose influential article "Eye and Mind" of 1961 is dominated by the notion of the "reversibility" of subject and object. This, according to the French philosopher, is best seen in the painter who, caught in the midst of the visible, brings into vision a fundamental manifestation of Being in his paintings by showing that, in order to see, the seer must in turn be capable of being seen. This inversion, which for Merleau-Ponty is a doubling with difference and without fusion, is characterized as follows:

> Inevitably the roles between the painter and the visible switch. That is why so many painters have said that things look at them. As André Marchand says, after Klee: "In a forest, I have felt many times over that it was not I who looked at the forest. Some days I felt that the trees were looking at me, were speaking to me. . . . I was there, listening. . . . I think that the painter must be penetrated by the universe and not want to penetrate it. . . . I expect to be inwardly submerged, buried. Perhaps I paint to break out." . . . Depth is the experience of the reversibility of dimensions, of a global "locality" in which everything is in the same place at the same time, a locality from which height, width, and depth are abstracted, a voluminosity we express in a word when we say that a thing is *there.* In pursuing depth, what Cézanne is seeking is this deflagration of Being, and it is all in the mode of space, and in form as well. Cézanne already knew what cubism would restate: that the external form, the envelope, is secondary and derived, that it

---

6. Ibid., pp. 47–48.

7. Nishitani Keiji, *The Self-Overcoming of Nihilism,* trans. Graham Parkes with Setsuko Aihara (Albany: SUNY Press, 1990), p. 162.

is not what makes a thing to take form, that that shell of space must be shattered—the fruit bowl must be broken. But then what should be painted instead?[8]

According to Sakabe, the modernist construction of the self that splits and alienates the "subject" from the "object," as well as the enclosure of the self within its own hermeneutical horizon, deprive modern man of metaphorical and metaphysical explanations. This, according to him, indicates the demise from the contemporary philosophical scene of the belief in the existence of a "true self" that in order to exist must appeal to a theological grounding. The "true self" is nothing but the mask of god, the representation of a "full presence." The death of god signals in the modern age the darkening of godly refractions and the disclosure of an even, uniform, flattened light of human death.

An escape from the alienation following the realization of the absence of truth/meaning might rest with the identification of truth as a predicate (*jutsugo*) rather than as a subject (*shugo*): a dissemination of meaning that is displaced from the mask of a disposable subject to the underside of its being. Sakabe reminds the reader of Zeami's concept of "flower" (*hana*): the prerogative of the skillful actor whose credibility comes from the "depth and mystery" (*yūgen*) of symbolic/poetic forms rather than from his more or less—but in any event pointless—brilliant mimetic power (*monomane*). While losing his meaning as a subject, the persona retains it as a form upon which truth is predicated. Truth is production of meaning that cannot be meant. Rather than in a sign, truth can be recovered in the anxiety caused by the demise of meaning.

Omote—the surface of signification that translates into the metaphor of the human face—is etymologically associated with the idea of direction (*omotsuhe*) that leads from the anxiety of chaos to the cosmological—and tautological—tranquility of order. Following the lead of popular etymologies,[9] *omote* is also related to the totemic center (*omo*), the main wing (*omoya*) of the house (= center of the world), and the locale for the production of thought (*omofu*). The relationship between surface and thought is further strengthened by the fact that the classical past tense of the verb "to think" (*omoheri*) derives from the word "sympathy" (*omohiari*) that comes to the fore by appearing on the face of people sharing the same feelings. As Mo-

---

8. The essay appears in Galen A. Johnson, ed., *The Merleau-Ponty Aesthetics Reader: Philosophy and Painting* (Evanston, Ill.: Northwestern University Press, 1993), p. 129 and p. 140. See also, in the same book, Galen A. Johnson, "Ontology and Painting: 'Eye and Mind,'" pp. 44–55.

9. Sakabe himself acknowledges that his methodology is based on the wordplay of popular etymologies; Sakabe, *Kamen no Kaishakugaku*, p. 23, n. 2.

toori Norinaga had already argued in his *mono no aware* theory, people are predicated on other people rather than establishing themselves as discrete monads that reduce the world to binary categories (subjective/objective, internal/external). But in Sakabe's theory, unlike Motoori's, the reciprocity of the process of signification attempts to deconstruct the fixity of the nativist concepts of "frontside" *(omote)* and "underside" *(ura)*.

The voice *(koe)* emanating from the mask—Sakabe sees in the expression "per*son*a" the presence of the French word for sound, *"son"*—bridges the gap between the two. The musical moment of vocal expression that Nietzsche acknowledged to be the genealogical beginning of tragedy,[10] and Zeami called "the root of nō dance/performance,"[11] escapes facile classifications inasmuch as, while being uttered by the mask, the voice does not exclusively belong to it. By recuperating the sameness and difference of metaphoricity, the voice reacquaints us with the depth of meaning that has been lost since the eighteenth century. As a structure encompassing the voice *(kotoba/parole), langue* corresponds to the Japanese "act of narrating" *(kata-ri)*, whose symbolic power is underlined by being connected to the same realm of forms *(kata)* to which the Japanese expression "symbol" *(kata-dori)* is closely related. The proliferation of meaning returns to the idea of truth its fullest, deepest, and most meaningful presence. This takes place in "song" *(uta)*—that "verbal act of a higher degree . . . which corresponds rhythmically to the foundation of community and the universe."[12]

The dissolution of the subject in the quest for truth problematizes the provenance of the voice that can no longer be found in the objectivity of a third-person narrative voice. Instead the voice becomes the result of an anonymous dialogue between first ("I") and second ("you") personal pronouns—what the linguist Émile Benveniste has labeled "empty signs" *(signes vides)*. Their being empty derives from the fact that the voice of the dialogue can only be predicated on what is at the source of the difference between self and others. Sakabe calls it an "ur-pronoun" *(gen-ninshō)* that belongs to no one and everyone—like the voice emanating from the chorus in a Greek tragedy or a nō performance: the voice of the mask. Deprived of all objective specifications, such a voice plays out the dialogue between

---

10. Friedrich Nietzsche, *The Birth of Tragedy and The Genealogy of Morals* (New York: Doubleday, 1956), p. 101.

11. This appears in Zeami's *Mirror Held to the Flower (Kakyō);* see Tanaka Yutaka, ed., *Zeami Geijutsu Ronshū, SNKS* 4 (Tokyo: Shinchōsha, 1976), pp. 121–125. For an English translation see J. Thomas Rimer and Yamazaki Masakazu, trans., *On the Art of the Nō Drama: The Major Treatises of Zeami* (Princeton: Princeton University Press, 1984), pp. 77–82.

12. Sakabe, "Le Masque, le Comportement et le Jeu," p. 102.

sameness and difference, order and chaos, metamorphosis and metaphor. *Omote*—the mask—is then "the faceless form" *(katachinaki sugata)*, "the faceless space" *(katachinaki tokoro)*, to which Zeami referred in his definition of the "ineffable style" *(myōtai).*[13] Rather than being the simple ghost of the third-person pronoun, the mask "is exactly the place of emergence of the 'ur-pronoun' *(archi-personne, gen-ninshō)*."[14]

Sakabe points out that the voice plays a major role in the Greek word for "mask," *baskaino,* which means "to lay a curse on somebody" or "to shield oneself from someone else's curse."[15] In Japan, as well, the voice is an essential part of the mask inasmuch as the Japanese verb "to curse" *(norou)* is related to an act of proclamation *(noru)*—the announcement of the law *(nori)* in the primeval fight against chaos. To the question of who is in charge of this proclamation, Sakabe answers by indicating the etymological root of the Latin expression *"persona",* which is *personare,* meaning "to proclaim in a loud manner." The mask is then in charge of the announcement of the "divine voice," the *logos* that Sakabe translates as "the word of god" *(kotoba,* or "the Word"): an "ur-pronoun" *(gen-ninshō,* or *"archi-personne")* of infinite potentiality upon which difference is predicated.

Sakabe also argues that the poetic subject is the equivalent of a metaphorical structure, a transfer between two things, a communicative deferral. The specificity of a grammatical subject ("I," "you," and so forth) is replaced by a field of intersubjectivity at the bottom of which works what Sakabe calls "the anonymous or collective unifying function" *(mumei no shūgōteki na tōitsu no kinō).* This comes as the result of a tension between the individual subject/poet and the collective consciousness of the group that has gathered to compose, for example, linked verses *(renga).* The erasure of the self by the group empowers language to the point where the word eventually creates the subject. Language acts as the invisible unifying force that brings a subject to its signification. Following the linguistic tradition developed in the Edo period—Sakabe argues—the linguist Tokieda Motoki located the presence of the subject in particles *(ji),* by which he meant "particles" *(joshi)* and "auxiliary verbs" *(jodōshi),* found at the end of words. This was the result of Tokieda's effort to deprive the sentence of the presence of a specified subject and to reduce the subject to what the philosopher Nishi-

---

13. The source is Zeami's *Kakyō;* Tanaka, *Zeami Geijutsu Ronshū,* p. 144; Rimer and Yamazaki, *On the Art of the Nō Drama,* p. 98. Sakabe develops this argument in the first chapter of *Kamen no Kaishakugaku,* "The Boundary of Face" ("Omote no Kyōi"), pp. 3–23.

14. Sakabe, *Kagami no Naka no Nihongo,* p. 168. For a French version see Megumi Sakabe, "Dignité du Mot et Valeur de la Personne," *Acta Institutionis Philosophiae et Aestheticae* 1 (1983):26.

15. Sakabe mentions that the current expression "mask" (Ital. *"maschera,"* Fr. *"masque")* comes from the Arabian *"maskharah."*

da Kitarō has called "self-awareness" *(jikaku):* the subject's self-realization of its limitation that makes it part "of the place of void."[16]

Rather than a grammatical subject, the subject is in effect a sentence that accommodates what has yet to be coded: the transformative space—"the unifying force"—that acts from the outside upon the formation of the subject/sentence. Such an anonymous force brings to communication what is originally separated, thus originating what Rousseau had called "social affects" *(affections sociales)* and "pity" *(pitié)* and what Motoori Norinaga labeled *mono no aware.*[17] The subject is constituted metaphorically by the power of the other including, Sakabe adds, the metaphysical Other.[18]

Sakabe stresses the importance of the concepts of "transposition" *(ikō)* and "transfer" *(ten'i)* in the process of signification—the polysemic power that is mostly manifested in poetic discourse. In an article explaining the etymological meaning of four adjectives—*kanashi* (sad), *utsukushi* (beautiful), *yukashi* (refined), and *wokashi* (marvelous) which he takes to cover the entire gamut of the process of affectivity and "to determine the fundamental structure of intersubjectivity"—Sakabe derives *"utsukushi"* from the same root indicating "reflection" *(utsuru/utsusu).* In ancient times—Sakabe argues following the explanation of the *Iwanami Kogo Jiten*—far from having an aesthetic connotation, the adjective *"utsukushi"* indicated the "affection," "love," or "tenderness" felt between two members of the opposite sex. Once applied to the feeling of love, the concepts of "transposition" and "transfer" introduce an element of reciprocity between the subject expressing his love and the object receiving it: it then becomes impossible to distinguish the source of love from its reflections. Sakabe sees in poetry the expression of this ambiguity, as in the case of the following verse from the *Man'yōshū:*

Tachibana no	She must think of me,
Koba no hanari ga	That girl with the long,

16. Sakabe, *Kagami no Naka no Nihongo,* pp. 138–143. For a French version see Megumi Sakabe, "La Métaphore et le Problème du Sujet," *Journal of the Faculty of Letters, University of Tokyo (Aesthetics)* 5 (1980):86–88. Tokieda's theory appears in Tokieda Motoki, *Kokugogaku Genron: Gengo Kateisetsu no Seiritsu to Sono Tenkai* (Tokyo: Iwanami Shoten, 1941). For Nishida's definition of *jikaku* see Nishida Kitarō, *Ippansha no Jikakuteki Taikei* (Tokyo: Iwanami Shoten, 1929).

17. Rousseau argues that reflection makes intersubjectivity possible: "Comment souffrirais-je en voyant souffrir un autre, si ne je sais pas même qu'il souffre, si j'ignore ce qu'il y a de commun entre lui et moi? Celui qui n'a jamais réfléchi ne peut être ni clément, ni juste, ni pitoyable; il ne peut pas non plus être méchant et vindicatif. Celui qui n'imagine rien ne sent que lui-même; il est seule au milieu du genre humain." See Rousseau's *Essai sur l'Origine des Langues* in Antonio Verri, *Origine delle Lingue e Civiltà in Rousseau* (Ravenna: Edizioni A. Longo, 1970), p. 196.

18. Sakabe, *Kagami no Naka no Nihongo,* pp. 144–146; "La Métaphore et le Problème du Sujet," pp. 88–89.

Omofunamu	Young hair,
Kokoro utsukushi	Loving heart,
Ide are wa ikana	I will go and see her![19]

Sakabe's interpretation highlights the ambiguity of the expression "loving heart" with respect to the agency responsible for the act of loving. Although syntactically the heart belongs to the woman since it denotes the organ that is responsible for the woman's longing—the heart does the thinking— once the expression *"kokoro utsukushi"* is isolated, it could well become the "loving heart" of the man who then persuades himself to pay a visit to his beloved. The heart in question could easily belong to either the poem's subject or object, thus making a hermeneutics of identification pointless. What is left is a mutual feeling of affection that enchains the heart of the lover and the beloved, transposing a vertical relationship based on power and subjugation onto a horizontal model of intersubjectivity.[20]

Sakabe mentions a text by Watsuji Tetsurō titled "Mask and Person" (Men to Perusona) in which Watsuji philologically grasps the ambiguity of an undefinable subject by analyzing the changes that the Latin expression *"persona"* underwent through the centuries. A word originally employed to indicate a mask on stage, *"persona"* has come to connote in most Indo-European languages the idea of "a person," a subject with a "real" social status identifiable through a first, second, or third-person pronoun ("I," "you," "he/she")—*"personne"* in French. What was perceived as a fictional character performing on the stage of a theater has become a subject legitimated by rights who is now playing on the stage of life.

Sakabe then turns to a definition of "sign" *(shirushi),* which is located on the border *(sakai)* of such difference—an expression whose Japanese counterpart, *"kotonari/sa-i,"* also indicates the process of creation or coming into being *(kotonari).* A sign is the spatial difference between specification and presence, between the naming or vocal articulation of a table and the presence of the actual, physical table. The sign is posited in the differential degree of appearance *(araware)* that results from the indicative phenomenon of speech—"this is a table"—as it is predicated on absence

---

19. *Man'yōshū* 14:3496; Kojima Noriyuki et al., eds., *Man'yōshū* 3, p. 486.

20. Sakabe, *Kagami no Naka no Nihongo,* pp. 116–117. A French version appears in Megumi Sakabe, "Sur le Fondement Affectif de l'Éthique et de l'Esthétique dans la Tradition de la Pensée Japonaise," *Acta Institutionis Philosophiae et Aestheticae* 5 (1987):147. Notwithstanding repeated efforts to deconstruct the mirror image as a refractive device that transfers light without the need for a source of illumination, Sakabe eventually falls into the metaphysical trap of positing a principle of signification high in the sky. See the following statement, which concludes the explanation of the word *"utsukushi"*: "Would it be possible for a play of mirrors to take place without a light coming from high?" See Sakabe, *Kagami no Naka no Nihongo,* p. 122; "Sur le Fondement," p. 149.

(the vocal sign does not require the presence of the object named) combined with the sign of actuality—the table itself, whose presence as sign is different from the sign of its name "table." The sign, however, is not limited to the indication of the fractured "signifier"/"signified": it also denotes "the other" of the object, what is not visibly objectifiable by the object itself such as, for example, death in life, absence within presence, the process of becoming within difference. Sign is the marked *(shirushi)* trace *(sujime)* of difference.[21]

Several questions remain. What is our position with regard to the signification of signs? Where do we locate ourselves or where do others locate us within the space of difference? Sakabe finds an answer in the relationship between signs and the concepts of "mask" and "persona." The displacing activity of signs makes the "persona" a mark indicating *(shirushi)* his knowledge *(shiru)* of his being bound *(shime)* to relationships of power *(shiru)*. Sakabe provides an existential reading of "différence" by noticing that the Japanese character used to indicate "signs/marks" *(shirushi)* can also be read *"shime,"* which means "creating a boundary that indicates the presence of a specific possession." A shrine, for example, may be metonymically indicated by the presence of a rope *(shimenawa)* binding an area that the rope makes sacred. Such boundaries make one aware of being differentiated from others on the grounds of property (or lack thereof), social status, and all that is entailed in the subordination of subject to master *(kimi/hito)*. All these constrictive relationships make a person "an other" *(hito)* to himself, unrecognizable to himself, a mesh in a net lost on the sea of difference, alienated from himself and from others—including the transcendental Other—as a result of the fractured individualization *(kobetsuka)* that has been imposed upon him.

This is where Sakabe's thought becomes entrapped in the impossible task of sublating aesthetics to logic (or the logic of feelings to the logic of reason). His analysis develops the idea of a person whose subjectivity has always been nothing but a comforting illusion, knowing as he argues that the subject is constructed by its own displacement—the voice of a mask belonging to no one and everyone.[22] But his concern for the fate of humankind, and his faith in the voice of the unseen as a condition for the restoration of a new depth to human dimension, lead Sakabe to critique the very notion of difference that is basic to the development of his argument on the displaceable nature of masks. Despite its alleged displacement, the

---

21. For the definition of *"shirushi"* see Sakabe, *Kamen no Kaishakugaku*, pp. 159–187.

22. This issue has won Sakabe's philosophy the name of "weak thought" *(yawarakai tetsugaku)*. See Hirata Toshihiro, "Yawarakai Sakabe Tetsugaku," *Risō* 646 (1990):67–75.

"I" still rises *(tachiarawarete kuru)* as conscience *(ryōshin)* and as suffering *(itami)* at the thought of one's alienation from oneself and others. The "I" is still represented as a moment of needed reconstitution, following the decomposition of its alienated parts and the reunification *(ki-itsu)* of dispersion to the primeval law of divine proclamation *(nori)*. The reader constantly feels in Sakabe's pages the smile of a presence and the tears of its loss which, no matter how diluted or refracted in a play of mirrors, refuse to leave center stage.

Sakabe would argue, however, that such a presence simply cannot exist, since the Japanese language resists the very notion of "being as full presence" *(genzen)*. He proves that the Japanese expression customarily interpreted as "reality" *(utsutsu)* denotes a much more subtle phenomenon than the one of mere appearance opposed to the world of "dreams" *(yume)*. *Utsutsu* is the reflection *(utsuri)* of a movement *(utsuri)* of appearances *(utsushi)*, a drama played by the mythological deities of the *Kojiki* in their struggle to bring "reality" into being. By referring to the three cosmological planes described in mythological accounts—the High Plain of Heaven or "Takamanohara," the Middle Land of Reed Plain or "Ashihara no Nakatsukuni," and the Root Land/Underworld or "Nenokuni"—Sakabe describes the creation of the land as the formation of a neutral space never fully present to itself. This is because the land becomes the battleground for the deities of the highest and lowest plains, whose sustained tensions bring forth the ambiguity of the seen and the unseen, thus presenting "reality" as a surreal play of events. To fail to perceive these traces would flatten our vision of the world and make us take literally a reality whose literalness is constantly displaced by the refractions of the symbolic.

The problem of the concept of "reality" rests, after all, with language. Sakabe argues that an explanation of the Japanese language along the lines of Western "rationality" would require words to obey the law of noncontradiction and to find in them the alleged precision of metaphysical signification. This is a problem constantly confronted but rarely solved by translators and compilers of bilingual dictionaries. Sakabe finds in the desire to conform to the positivistic tenets of Western philological "science" the reason for the compilers of a major dictionary of classical Japanese, the *Iwanami Kogo Jiten,* to make a clear distinction between a conscious and an oneiric state of mind when discussing the word *"utsutsu."* According to the dictionary's gloss—explanation number three—the word indicates "a dreamlike state of mind *(yumegokochi)* as a result of a tendency since the age of the *Kokinshū* not to know whether one was dreaming or was awake, as attested in the expressions 'dream/reality' *(yumeutsutsu)* and 'dream or real-

ity?' *(yume ka utsutsu ka)*."[23] Sakabe faults the compilers for erasing the original ambiguity of a word that they reduce—explanation number one—to
mean simply "reality *(genjitsu)* as opposed to dreams, fiction, and death."
Sakabe's critique of formal logic in linguistics,[24] and his interpretation of
"reality" as the displaced space of the mask, deeply question the validity of
an explanation that neglects the presence of dreams, fiction, and death in
the alleged word for "reality." Sakabe concludes that a flattening of "reality" to the "precision and clarity" of incompleteness can hardly do justice
to the multivocal strength of the native voice.[25]

The key word in Sakabe's philosophy is "reflection." This term more
than any other captures the meaning of "thinking" as "the concentration
in the human mind of different surfaces *(omote)* and different beams of light
and shade *(kage)*." Once asked to identify the object of reflection, Sakabe
found the answer in the indirectness of metaphorical expression that Buddhist and Taoist philosophers call "void" *(kū)* and "nothingness" *(mu)*,
which Sakabe himself identifies as "what is experienced within silence." To
give a concrete example, Sakabe mentions the ritualized gestures of the female characters in the films of Ozu Yasujirō: the way they sit, rise, and
move, as if they had just come from the stage of nō.[26]

As the reader will see from the second essay by Sakabe translated here,
reality *(utsutsu)* is displaced in a play of mirrors in which the dispersive act
of reflection challenges theories of knowledge based on the concept of imitative reproduction. The appeal of etymological explanation prompted
Sakabe to construct philologically his philosophical reflections: as a derivative of the expression *"utsuutsu,"* indicating a gloomy state of mind that is
doubtful of its own conscious or unconscious status, the word *"utsutsu"* is
related both to the practice of "projecting" *(utsusu)* and to the act of "re-
flection/being reflected" *(utsuru)*. To limit the explanation of reality to the
one-sided signification of re-production, in which the subject construes as
"objective" the projection of himself onto the world, would lose sight of
the mirroring activity that occurs in the space between sameness (the sub-

---

23. Ono Susumu, Satake Akihiro, and Maeda Kingorō, eds., *Iwanami Kogo Jiten* (Tokyo: Iwanami Shoten, 1974), p. 174.

24. In a chapter titled "For Future Considerations on the Japanese Language: Logic and Thought in English and Japanese," Sakabe critiques the widespread tendency to define the Japanese language as "irra-tional and vague" on the basis of linguistic methods that are strongly bound to Western metaphysics. He notices how the ground for Orientalist practices in linguistics disappears once alternative methods such as semiotics are employed. See Sakabe, *Kamen no Kaishakugaku*, pp. 121–155.

25. For Sakabe's definition of "reality" *(utsushimi, or "body as presence")* see *Kamen no Kaishakugaku*, pp. 188–210.

26. Sakabe, *Kagami no Naka no Nihongo*, pp. 56–57.

ject) and difference (the other) at the moment of reality production. Rather than being the results of ideas, forms take and lose shape in a field of sunbeams that refuse to provide objects with determinate, objective forms. What is left is a shadow, a silhouette, a reflection, an image, a phantom, a sign, a trace resulting from the play of light *(kage)* and shade *(kage)*.[27]

Mask and Shadow in Japanese Culture: Implicit Ontology in Japanese Thought
by Sakabe Megumi

1

A FEW MONTHS ago in Paris I saw a movie by Ozu Yasujirō[28] titled *The Autumn of the Kohayagawa Family (Kohayagawa-ke no Aki).*[29] It is the story of three generations in a family of sake brewers in Osaka. As in most works by Ozu, you will not find a very dramatic plot or the description of a particularly tragic event. Even so, probably because I had been living alone in a foreign country for a while, I was deeply impressed by the constant lyricism and humor that characterize Ozu's work.

At the same time, the movie appeared to me to be a kind of a funeral hymn for Japan's traditional culture that nowadays is on the verge of disappearing

---

27. This argument is developed in chapter 2 of *Kamen no Kaishakugaku,* "A Rough Sketch on Shades" ("Kage ni Tsuite no Sobyō"), pp. 24–49.

28. Ozu Yasujirō (1903–1963), Japanese film director, was noted for his work on contemporary Japanese family life. Among his most famous movies are *Banshun* (Late Spring; 1949), *Bakushū* (Early Summer; 1951), and *Tokyo Monogatari* (Tokyo Story; 1951).

29. This essay was originally published in French as "Le Masque et l'Ombre dans la Culture Japonaise: Ontologie Implicite de la Pensée Japonaise," *Revue de Métaphysique et de Morale* 87(3) (July–September 1982):335–343. The author himself translated it into Japanese as "Nihon Bunka ni Okeru Kamen to Kage: Nihon no Shikō no Senzaiteki Sonzairon," and he included it in *Kagami no Naka no Nihongo,* pp. 37–58. My translation takes into account both versions. The Japanese version usually explains philosophical points that were obvious to Sakabe's specialized French audience. It also includes critiques of French thought that Sakabe decided to expunge from the French version.

from the world stage. Today it would be impossible to find anywhere in Japan, no matter how hard you search, the kind of typically Japanese lyricism of autumn that Ozu describes. This is because the traditional community and its customs are probably collapsing more rapidly in Japan than in any other part of the world.

Just a moment ago I said, "the typical Japanese lyricism of autumn." It goes without saying that I meant it metaphorically as well as in its literal sense. Each day the clear autumn scenes of nature disappear almost everywhere from the Japanese archipelago, particularly around the big cities. But in the domain of spiritual culture, as well, the lyricism of autumn is disappearing very quickly. Just like autumnal lyricism in the external world, every day, little by little, the lyricism of autumn degenerates in our heart: I mean the traditional feeling for the ephemeral nature of human beings and the feeling related to death.

It might well be that what I am going to say is nothing but the expression of nostalgia, a funeral hymn of the same type as Ozu's. And yet I hope to contribute something more by trying to extract some trait of Japanese culture, especially the modes of traditional thought that certainly survive in the works of Ozu. I would like to try to do this now by finding a leitmotif in Ozu's film.

What impressed me in the film is that some of the simple movements (such as sitting down or getting up) of the women (particularly the two daughters who are about twenty or thirty years of age) are very similar to those of nō theater. I do not know whether this is the result of Ozu's conscious planning, or whether it is due to the fact that, at least until the age of twenty or thirty, the movements of bourgeois or petit-bourgeois women in Japan are strongly influenced by the tea ceremony or by the traditional dance that originates from nō. We can say, however, that until the age of twenty or thirty it is a remarkable characteristic of Japanese culture that slightly ritualized movements penetrate daily life almost everywhere.

There is no need to repeat here contemporary psychoanalytical theories on the formation or acquisition of bodily schemes among children, or the sociological observations of M. Mauss[30] on human movements, in order to realize that the boundary between ritualized movement and the movement known as natural is, to a certain degree, always very ambiguous—indeed, ordinarily we cannot easily distinguish them. We always see in human movements a relationship with others: with other human beings, as well as, eventually, with an Other that is invisible and transcendent.

What is remarkable in Japanese culture is that precisely this boundary between the self and the other—and, therefore, as a result, between the natural movement and the ritualized movement—is always more ambiguous than in

---

30. Marcel Mauss (1872–1950), French sociologist and anthropologist. A nephew and disciple of Émile Durkheim, he became a professor at the Collège de France in 1931. Mauss is considered one of the architects of the structuralist school of French ethnology. Among his many works are *L'Essai sur le Don, Forme et Raison de l'Échange dans les Sociétés Archaiques* (1925) and *Sociologie et Anthropologie* (1950).

Western culture. With regard to this boundary or distinction between the self and the other, let us take as our example the problem of the mask.

2

First of all, we must notice the following peculiar fact related to Japanese: In the original language (the Yamato idiom) there is only one word to indicate mask as well as (the natural) face, *"omote."* Sometimes *"omote"* means mask (in nō and in the ancient court dances); sometimes it refers to the face. (I believe that the same thing happens with regard to the Greek word *"prosōpon,"* although I do not want to enter into the details of this issue at the present time.)

Let me return to the Japanese language. There is another very ancient expression, *"omozashi,"* which means the features, particularly of the face. Now *"-zashi"* (< *sashi* < *sasu* = to point at, to aim at, to pierce) means approximately "direction" or, if I may say so, "intention" (including, if you wish, intention in Husserl's phenomenological sense). Today we commonly use the expression *"mana-zashi."* *"Mana"* means the eye. Consequently, *"mana-zashi"* corresponds exactly to the gaze.

Now, it seems to me that there is a remarkable difference between *"mana-zashi"* and *"omo-zashi."* What kind of difference? I think that this difference lies precisely in the fact that *"omo-zashi"* (the features, the intention of the face) includes in itself a complex or pluridimensional intentionality, whereas in *"mana-zashi"* we have only (at least comparatively speaking) a unidimensional intentionality or, more exactly, a one-way intentionality.

To say it differently: *"Omo-zashi"* is what is seen by the other and, at the same time, what sees itself, and also, maybe, what sees itself as an other. That is to say: This word includes itself in itself, as well as the other, and, moreover, itself as an other. In other words, it already includes in itself a structure of reciprocity and reversibility.

On the other hand, as Sartre has described very clearly, *"mana-zashi"* (the gaze) only includes in itself what it sees in one direction. This is to say that, according to Sartre, it is never possible to succeed in building a true reciprocity starting exclusively from the gaze.

Personally I love the word *"omo-zashi,"* since, as you can see, it is a very elegant and delicate expression that directly indicates the way human society should be in its true meaning without egoism. In modern Japanese, unfortunately, this word is almost completely obsolete. I suppose that this is due, at least partially, to the unwelcome—in this regard—influence that Sartre had on Japanese philosophers, who have abandoned this marvelous expression, rich in connotations.

In any event, having analyzed the structure of *"omo-zashi"* (what is seen by the other, what sees itself, and what sees itself as an other), the natural conclusion follows that *"omote"* possesses exactly the same structure. Therefore *"omote,"* which is the foundation of *"omo-zashi,"* is what is seen by the other, what sees itself, and what sees itself as an other.

As you probably know, prior to entering the stage the nō actor wears the mask in a room called the "Kagami-no-Ma" (Mirror Hall), which is traditionally considered a sacred space. Here the actor transmogrifies into the ultrahuman dimension of the spirit of the ancestors. (Moreover, behind the stage there is a big plank known as the "Mirror Board" [Kagami-Ita], which has depicted on it an old pine tree that stands for the god. This is not a real mirror. We must notice, however, that on the nō stage the structure of the mirror appears almost everywhere symbolically and actually.)

In the Kagami-no-Ma, the actor puts on the mask; he sees in the mirror his own face or his own mask; at the same time, he is seen by his mask in the mirror and, finally, he sees himself transmogrified in some deity or demon. Afterward he walks onto the stage as an actor who has changed into a deity or demon or—which is to say the same thing—as a deity or demon who has taken the bodily form of this actor. To say it differently: The actor enters the stage as a self transmogrified into an other or as an other transmogrified into the self.

Here we witness the typical manifestation of the structure of *"omote"* as I described it a while ago. What is important to notice now is the fact that the structure of *"omote"* is evidently the structure of the mask, as we have seen, but at the same time it is also the structure of the face. The reason is that the face also is what is seen by the other, what sees itself, and what sees itself as an other.

It seems to me that it is precisely this common structure which grounds the fact that in Japanese we use the same word to indicate the mask and, at the same time, the face. Obviously I am reminded here of the fact that the word *"persona"* in Latin means the person as well as originally indicating the mask at the same time.

But in the cultural history of Japan we do not have the same historical development starting from *"persona"* seen as the mask during the Roman period, going through *"persona"* seen as the fundamental concept of hypostasis in Christian theology, and finally reaching the notion of individual and autonomous "person" or "personality" during the modern age. I wonder whether this was a misfortune or not for us Japanese. It is certainly a complicated problem, very difficult to solve. For the time being, however, I will content myself with noticing a big difference between Western and Japanese culture.

3

There is another extremely remarkable thing concerning the word *"omote."* As we have seen, *"omote"* means the mask, the face, but at the same time it also means the surface.

What is surprising to me is that *"omote,"* with the connotation of surface, does not mean in the Japanese language or thought "the appearance" as op-

posed to some ideal entity (as in the case of Platonism) or to some real substance (as in the case of Kant's "thing-in-itself"). It is true, however, that the
word *"omote"* is sometimes used to designate the exterior as opposed to the interior (for example, *"omote"* as the exterior of a house). But the word *"omote"* is
always originally as well as semantically opposed to the word *"urate"* (= behind, opposite, reverse; *"-te"* = hand, direction, way). *"Omo-te"* and *"ura-te"* are
therefore, at least in principle, always strictly reversible and reciprocal. Just as
in our everyday visual world, visibility and invisibility are evidently reversible
according to perspective, I would dare to say that in Japanese traditional
thought, visibility and invisibility are in principle always strictly reversible
and reciprocal.

Zeami,[31] the founder of nō with his father Kan'ami, has talked about the
"riken no ken" (the view of detached view, the view from a far away view: *"ri"*
= detached, from far away). According to him, the true actor must always see
his own image from far away, even from behind, from his back:

> As concerns the dance, it is said that "the eyes look ahead and the mind looks
> behind." This expression means that the actor looks in front of him with his
> physical eyes, but his inner concentration must be directed to the appearance of
> his movements from behind. This is a crucial element in the creation of what I
> have referred to above as the Movement Beyond Consciousness. The appearance
> of the actor, seen from the spectator in the seating area, is a detached *(riken)* view
> of the actor himself, the outer image of the actor. What an actor himself sees,
> on the other hand, forms his own internal image of himself *(gaken: ga* = I). It is
> not a detached view. In order to see himself from a detached point of view, the
> actor must put himself in the audience's place. Only then can it actually be said
> that an actor has truly grasped the nature of his appearance. For an actor to grasp
> his true appearance implies that he has under his control the space to the left
> and to the right of him, and to the front and to the rear of him. In many cases,
> however, an average actor looks only to the front and to the side, and so never
> sees what he actually looks like from behind. If the actor cannot somehow come
> to a sense of how he looks from behind, he will not be able to become conscious
> of any possible vulgarities in his performance. Therefore, thanks to the detached
> view, the actor comes to share the same view as the audience, to obtain a visual
> knowledge of his own body that the eyes cannot perceive, and so maintain a
> graceful appearance in which the five parts of the body are harmoniously coor-
> dinated. Such an action truly represents "putting the mind behind." To repeat
> again, an actor must come to have an ability to see himself as the spectators do,
> grasp the logic of the fact that the eyes cannot see themselves, and find the skill
> to grasp the whole—left and right, ahead and behind. If an actor can achieve

---

31. Zeami Motokiyo (?1364–1443), son of Kan'ami (1333–1384), is the author of most of the nō plays
that are performed today. He also wrote several theoretical treatises on the performance and appreciation
of nō.

this, his peerless appearance will be as elegant as that of a flower or a jewel and will serve as a living proof of his understanding.[32] [Zeami, *Kakyō* (A Mirror Held to the Flower)]

Let me evoke another example related to the reversibility of the seen and the unseen. In the traditional poetics and aesthetics of Japan (including the dramaturgy of nō), it is called *"yūgen,"* a kind of delicate vision that shows what is usually hidden or invisible (sometimes the world inhabited by the dead, phantoms: *"yūkai"*). (*"Yū"* = dark; *"gen"* = black, deep; *"kai"* = world, domain, space.)

In any event, in traditional Japanese thought there is neither the category of Cartesian substance nor any kind of rigid or fixed dualism between soul and body, exterior and interior, seen and unseen. It seems to me that nothing is more alien to Japanese thought than Cartesian dualism.

Perhaps in Japan, in order to remain faithful to traditional thought, there is no need either to "reverse Platonism" or to "reexamine the metaphysics of presence, the onto-theo-teleological metaphysics." In short, in Japanese traditional thought there is nothing but surfaces—or, to say it differently, there is nothing but grids of surfaces that are, at least in principle, strictly reversible, the one into the other.

As I pointed out earlier, on the nō stage (including the "Kagami no Ma"), which is surrounded several times symbolically and physically by the structure of the mirror, there is nothing but the play of various surfaces or various reflections (including, of course, the song *"utai"* and the chorus *"ji-utai"*). We can say that we find here a sort of "écriture" or "text" which contains in itself various layers and dimensions. We do not find, therefore, any trace of "phonocentrism." There is nothing but a play of identity and difference, without any strictly fixed identity. Even the "persons" (first, second, and third personal pronouns) are not strictly fixed. . . .

On the nō stage, even the world of the dead *"yūkai"* and our world, the terrestrial world, the unseen and the seen, finally put themselves in a relationship of reversibility and reciprocity.

4

Nothing exists but surfaces, grids of surfaces. Nothing but *"omote."* Nothing but reflections. Nothing but shades. Therefore, there are no substantial beings, no being that has been fixed in its sameness.

Nothing exists but a world of diverse and infinite metamorphoses.

Again, I could evoke here another remarkable peculiarity of the Japanese

---

32. Adapted from Rimer and Yamazaki, *On the Art of the Nō Drama,* p. 81. The original text appears in Tanaka, *Zeami Geijutsu Ronshū,* pp. 124–125. For a discussion of this passage see Michele Marra, "Zeami and Nō: A Path Towards Enlightenment," *Journal of Asian Culture* 12 (1988):37–65.

language: The word *"kage,"* which designates the shade, the reflection, at the same time also means the light. We say *"tsuki-kage"* (the moonlight) or *"ho-kage"* (the light of fire: *"ho" < "hi"* = fire).

This reminds us of some mystical vision of a John of the Cross,[33] which underlines the fact that shade and light are the same thing. It evokes, for example, the fact of the transparent shade of a glass bottle, which indicates symbolically or metaphorically the way of being of the entire terrestrial world.

Personally I believe there are not a few similarities between this kind of mystical vision and the Japanese traditional thought of "original enlightenment" in Tendai Buddhism.[34]

Yet we also recall another remarkable characteristic of the word *"kage"*: *"kage"* (shade, light) also means the image, the silhouette. We say *"hito-kage"* (a person's silhouette) and also *"omo-kage"* (face, features; *"omo" < "omote"*). (*"Omo-kage"* means approximately the same thing as *"omo-zashi,"* which I mentioned above.)

Once we take into account all the meanings of the word *"kage,"* we can now say that the world is made of nothing but *"kage."*

Nothing exists but shades. Nothing exists but reflections. Nothing exists but light. Nothing exists but images.

Therefore, nothing exists but *"kage."*

Indeed, in the world nothing exists but reflections.

In Japanese we use the word *"utsuru"* to say "to be reflected" and the word *"utsusu"* for "to reflect."

But what is always very striking is the fact that the word *"utsuru"* also means "to go by, to change" (as in *"toki ga utsuru"* = time goes by).

Nothing exists but reflections: consequently, this means that nothing exists but what is reflected in succession or reciprocally; nothing exists but changes; nothing exists but happenings; nothing exists but what transmogrifies infinitely.

There is the expression *"utsutsu."* This means "to be conscious of the actual presence of something, to be awake." (See *"utsutsu-gokoro"*: consciousness of reality, live contact with reality.) I am not sure that we can establish a strict lin-

---

33. Saint John of the Cross (San Juan de la Cruz, 1542–1591), is the religious name of Juan de Yepes y Alvarez, the most profoundly lyrical of Spanish poets and one of the great mystics of all time.

34. *Hongaku* (original enlightenment) is a Buddhist trend of thought which postulates that enlightenment is originally ingrained in all sentient beings and is not the result of special religious training. "The principle of hongaku was also very important in the tradition of Japanese Tendai. There it was translated into an entire panoply of philosophical moves, each of which stressed in one way or another that the world of birth and dying is also the world of true enlightenment. The emphasis throughout was on *being* enlightened rather than on *becoming* enlightened, and in Tendai there was even a refusal to make a sharp distinction in this matter between mankind and other sentient beings. It was therefore a logical consequence for Tendai thinkers such as Ryōgen (912–985) and Chūjin (1065–1138) to use the principle of hongaku as the basis for their extended arguments in favor of recognizing that even plants and trees are in possession of Buddha-nature *(sōmoku-jōbutsu)."* See William R. LaFleur, *The Karma of Words: Buddhism and the Literary Arts in Medieval Japan* (Berkeley: University of California Press, 1983), p. 22.

guistic relationship between the words *"utsutsu"* and *"utsuru."* I think, however, that between these two words exists, at least as a probability, a very close affinity. In any event, it is evident that the state of consciousness *"utsutsu"* is always considered to be something that is never distinctly separated, at least virtually, from the stage of dreaming and folly, although it is both formally and semantically opposed to dreams or folly. We often use the expression *"yume-utsutsu"* (*"yume"* = dream) to indicate a kind of ecstatic feeling or a feeling of extreme confusion that haunts us from the midst of daily life.

We can say that behind the domain of the *"utsutsu"* state we continuously find the vast domain of dreams or the oneiric world that reflects itself onto the other domain. It may be that we cannot tell exactly which of the two domains is the reflection and which is the original (as indicated by Taoist thought, which has continued to exert a great influence on the tradition of Japanese culture). . . .[35]

In any event, it is the same thing as the meditation on the shore of a deep water that reflects the world, as G. Bachelard has described so impressively in his *Water and Dreams.*[36] We cannot distinguish which one is the truest and deepest reality: the image or its reflection in the deep water.

You might wish to remember some impressive scenes from Ozu's movies that take place on the shore of the sea, of a river, or of a lake. . . .

There is also the word *"utsusemi."* It has often been used, since long ago, to evoke the ephemeral nature of human beings. It is often written with the Chinese characters indicating "empty" and "cicada." In the original Japanese language, however, it was written *"utsushi-mi": "utsushi"* = real, earthly, probably, in my opinion, < *"utsutsu," "utsuru," "mi"* = body, person, originally *"omi"* = person.

"Utsushi-mi," therefore, means the person on earth, the terrestrial human being, the real human being, the visible human being that is nothing but a reflection of something unseen and transcendental. . . .

5

Nothing exists but *"omote."* Nothing exists but surfaces. Nothing exists but *"kage."* Nothing exists but reflections that are reflected, that pass by, that transmogrify endlessly.

---

35. See, for example, Chuang Tzu's (ca. 399–295 B.C.) renowned dream of being a butterfly, as narrated in the Taoist classic, *Chuang Tzu.* "Once Chuang Chou dreamt he was a butterfly, a butterfly flitting and fluttering around, happy with himself and doing as he pleased. He didn't know he was Chuang Chou. Suddenly he woke up and there he was, solid and unmistakable Chuang Chou. But he didn't know if he was Chuang Chou who had dreamt he was a butterfly, or a butterfly dreaming he was Chuang Chou. Between Chuang Chou and a butterfly there must be *some* distinction! This is called the Transformation of Things." See Burton Watson, trans., *The Complete Works of Chuang Tzu* (New York: Columbia University Press, 1968), p. 49.

36. Gaston Bachelard (1884–1962), *L'Eau et les Rêves: Essai sur l'Imagination de la Matière* (Paris: J. Corti, 1942).

Then what does "to think" mean?

Or what do people "think"?

In Japanese, "to think" is *"omo-u"* *("omo-fu")*. *"Omo-u,"* therefore, means "to think" or "to meditate." *("Omo-i,"* *"omo-hi"* = thought, meditation, feeling.)

What, then, is *"omo-u"* or *"omo-i"?*

We can say that in *"omo-i"* various surfaces *("omote")* or various reflections *("kage")* are gathered, are concentrated, and are reflected *("utsuru")* in the soul.

When we think, even if we meditate in total solitude, we gather, we concentrate the entire *"omote,"* the entire *"kage":* everything that is seen by the other, everything that sees itself (including, perhaps, the unseen, the dead), and eventually everything that sees itself as an other.

As a result, then, *"omo-u,"* to think, to meditate, means to gather, to concentrate everything that sees and is seen, everything that is reflected and is transmogrified *("utsuru")* in the world, and finally also everything that sees itself as an other, as an *"utsushi-mi."*

But what is actually reflected, after all, in the I as *"utsushi-mi"* or, more generally, in human being as *"utsushi-mi,"* in living being as *"utsushi-mi"?* What is the ground of all beings whose being is reflected in all beings, but perhaps is itself not reflected anywhere?

Without any doubt, at least according to traditional Japanese thought, we can express it, especially in popular culture, only indirectly or metaphorically. It has been identified with various names, such as the way (in the Taoist sense),[37] emptiness,[38] nothingness.[39]

---

37. See, for example, the beginning of Lao Tzu's *Tao Te Ching* (Classic of the Way and Its Virtue: fourth century B.C.): "The way that can be spoken of / Is not the constant way; / The name that can be named / Is not the constant name. / The nameless was the beginning of heaven and earth; / The named was the mother of the myriad creatures. / Hence always rid yourself of desires in order to observe its secrets; / But always allow yourself to have desires in order to observe its manifestations. / These two are the same / But diverge in name as they issue forth. / Being the same they are called mysteries, / Mystery upon mystery— / The gateway of the manifold secrets." See D. C. Lau, trans., *Lao Tzu: Tao Te Ching* (New York: Penguin, 1963), p. 57.

38. *Kū* is the central concept of the Buddhist "Three Treatise" school *(Sanron),* which was known in India as the Mādhyamika (Middle Doctrine) school. "The central concept of the school is Emptiness *(Śūnyatā)* in the sense that the nature and characters of all dharmas, together with their causation, are devoid of reality. Thus, all differentiations, whether being or non-being, cause or effect, or coming-into-existence or going-out-of-existence, are only 'temporary names' and are empty in nature. The only reality is Emptiness itself, which is the Absolute, Ultimate Void, the Original Substance, or in Chinese terminology, the correct principle *(cheng-li).* As such it is equivalent to Nirvāna and the Dharma-body." See Wing-Tsit Chan, *A Source Book in Chinese Philosophy* (Princeton: Princeton University Press, 1969), p. 357.

39. *Wu* (Jap. *mu*), "nonbeing." "There is nothing wrong in rendering *wu* as a negative. However, in some cases it has to be interpreted. For example, *wu-hsin* is not just 'no-mind' but 'no deliberate mind of one's own,' and *wu-wei* is not simply 'inaction' but 'taking no unnatural action,' or in Buddhist usage, 'not produced from causes.' Boodberg thinks *yu* and *wu* should not be rendered as 'being' and 'non-being,' because they are essentially transitive verbs. But in *Lao Tzu,* chs. 2, 40, etc., and in many places in the *Chuang Tzu,* for example, they are not verbs and mean exactly 'being' and 'non-being.'" See Chan, *Source Book in Chinese Philosophy,* p. 791.

Yet I believe that the meaning of the famous sentence at the end of Goethe's *Faust,* "*Alles Vergängliche ist nur ein Gleichnis*" (which I would translate, or rather interpret, as "Everything that goes by in this earthly world is nothing but metaphor"), is since time immemorial a very familiar feeling for us Japanese.

Traditionally, we have tried for a long time to express in nō this deep, inexpressible feeling, the deepest "*omo-i*" in our heart, through very light gestures that are very reduced or slightly ritualized—for example, by slightly tilting the mask *("omote")* and thus expressing some sort of "*omo-zashi*" that is extremely delicate, refined, that is, "*yūgen.*"

Even today, when Ozu moves or slightly tilts the ordinary perspective, putting the camera very low, and, for example, makes two young sisters in mourning for the death of their father rise with a slightly ritualized gesture in the blue sky of autumn that occupies most of the scenes, we evidently experience this feeling that I have been talking about: We clearly experience something similar to a prayer contained in the depth of our heart.

Modoki: The Mimetic Tradition in Japan
by Sakabe Megumi

1

COMEDY AIMS at representing *(mimeisthai)* characters that are worse than actual people, while tragedy represents characters that are actually better than real persons.[40] On this, Aristotle says in his *Poetics,* is based the difference between comedy and tragedy.[41] After having presented this distinction, Aristotle relates it to the author's characters:

---

40. This essay was originally published in French as " '*Modoki*'—Sur la Tradition Mimétique au Japon," *Acta Institutionis Philosophiae et Aestheticae* 3 (1985):95–105. The author translated it into Japanese as "Modoki: Nihon ni Okeru Mōhōteki Saigen no Dentō ni Tsuite" and included it in his *Kagami no Naka no Nihongo,* pp. 83–106.

41. "Since living persons are the objects of representation, these must necessarily be either good men or inferior—thus only are characters normally distinguished, since ethical differences depend upon vice and virtue—that is to say either better than ourselves or worse or much what we are. It is the same with painters. Polygnotus depicted men as better than they are and Pauson worse, while Dionysius made likeness. Clear-

We have, then, a natural instinct for representation and for tune and rhythm—for the meters are obviously sections of rhythms—and starting with these instincts men very gradually developed them until they produced poetry out of their improvisations. Poetry then split into two kinds according to the poet's nature. For the more serious poets represented fine doings and the doings of fine men, while those of a less exalted nature represented the actions of inferior men, at first writing satire just as the others at first wrote hymns and eulogies.[42]

In this reduction of the distinction between comedy and tragedy to the distinction between characters according to the author's nature, we witness a simple presentation of a historical fact rather than the explanation of its efficient cause. Because of its own nature, this explanation does not provide us with a key to the essence of comedy and tragedy.[43] As for the essence of tragedy, Aristotle gives his famous definition that culminates in what he calls the realization of the purification *(catharsis)* of certain kinds of emotions, such as pity and fear.[44] With regard to comedy, however, he does not provide us with a detailed definition as he had done for tragedy, since, in any event, we lack the part of the *Poetics* that was supposed to deal with satire and comedy.

If we locate ourselves within the boundaries of Aristotle's theory of drama, we are naturally left with at least a big problem to rethink and to solve: What is the essence of comedy and tragedy, and what relationship exists between the two? We find, for sure, in other works by Aristotle, a few lines that deal with the essence of laughter,[45] and if we look for theories on the comic among modern authors, we will find Hegel, Baudelaire, Bergson, Plessner, and many others discussing this subject. It seems to me, however, that we lack a global view that would determine the respective place of comedy and tragedy as well as their mutual relationship in our mental life. Is it possible to arrive at such a view simply by comparing the different theories on the comic to those on tragedy that have appeared since Aristotle? Or is it not that we still lack a way

---

ly each of the above mentioned arts will admit of these distinctions, and they will differ in representing objects which differ from each other in the way here described. In painting too, and flute-playing and harp-playing, these diversities may certainly be found, and it is the same in prose and in unaccompanied verse. For instance Homer's people are 'better,' Cleophon's are 'like,' while in Hegemon of Thasos, the first writer of parodies, and in Nicochares, the author of the *Poltrooniad,* they are 'worse.' It is the same in dithyrambic and nomic poetry, for instance . . . a writer might draw characters like the Cyclops as drawn by Timotheus and Philoxenus. It is just in this respect that tragedy differs from comedy. The latter sets out to represent people as worse than they are today, the former as better." See Aristotle, *The Poetics,* trans. W. Hamilton Fyfe (Cambridge, Mass.: Harvard University Press, 1927), pp. 9–11.

42. Aristotle, *Poetics,* p. 15.

43. Original note: "Actually, Aristotle was always so free from prejudging from the standpoint of what we would call today modern subjectivity that he treated the character *(ethos)* as a more superficial component than praxis or *'ta pragmata.'*"

44. Original note: "It is not my intention here to discuss the problem of interpretation of the Aristotelian notion of *'catharsis.'* I bring myself to present it provisionally according to a very popular interpretation."

45. Original Note: "Cf. Aristotle, *Nichomachean Ethics,* 1128a–b; idem, *Parts of Animals,* 673a."

to go deeper into human nature, a way that would enable us to solve this problem? After all, should we not return to Aristotle's point of departure when we consider comedy and tragedy as a pair?

Actually, we often see in the field of theatrical performance, in a broad sense, that in the history of humanity and in most parts of the world, comic and tragic work as a pair. In ancient Greece, for example, the staging of tragedies was always accompanied by the staging of satire. In Japan, the representation of nō has for a long time been combined with that of *kyōgen* (a kind of farce). And in Korea, on the occasion of representations of masked dances, the comic element is always placed side by side and mixed with the serious.

What, then, is the common denominator we could use as a ground for our study of the comic as well as the tragic? If we could find a perspective from which to answer this question, we would understand at least a little more clearly than usual the deepest nature of man, which must be two-sided and which, because of the modern, narrow understanding of human nature, often escapes the modern man who is living in the "serious" society of our epoch.

2

It is easy to see that in order to answer the question I have posed, we must inevitably start to revise a few fundamental concepts, among which, so long as we use the conceptual framework of Western thought, is the notion of mimesis. Here I would like to make a detour, however, by examining a Japanese concept that approximately corresponds to mimesis: *modoki*.[46] After this examination, it will be relatively easy to explore a more advanced interpretation of mimesis and a few other Western philosophical concepts strictly related to it.

What, then, is the meaning of *"modoki"*? According to the current usage of the word, *"modoki"* is almost exclusively employed as a suffix indicating that something is done or is pretended to be done in imitation of its form, its appearance, or its ambience. For example:

> *"Gan-modoki"*: a kind of fried pâté of soybeans (tofu) used in vegetarian cuisine as an imitation of wild goose meat.

> *"Kare wa shibai-modoki ni shaberu"*: he speaks as if he were on stage (*shibai* = theater).

According to the most ancient usage of the word, which goes back to the Heian period (tenth century), *"modoki"* (and its verbal form *"modoku"*) meant, first, a poorly done imitation (= "magahi"); false, counterfeit. For example:

> *"Kono nana-tose ni naru ko chichi wo modokite koma-udo to fumi wo tsukuri kawashikereba"* (*Utsubo Monogatari*): Since this seven-year-old child, by imitating his father, has exchanged letters with the Koreans.

---

46. Original note: "The word that most correctly corresponds to 'mimesis' as imitation is *'mono-mane.'*"

And, second, it especially meant reproach or criticism of somebody else. For example:

> *"Yō naki furumai no tsumorite hito no modoki wo owanto suru koto to obosedo" (Genji Monogatari):* Although he feared being criticized by the world after committing so much nonsense.

To this day, a third meaning of *"modoki"* is still very much alive in the popular tradition and seems to be the original acceptation of the word—that is, the character in popular acts who essentially plays a comic and ridiculous role by imitating the main actor and making fun of him. In most sacred dances in Japanese Shintoism *(kagura)* as well as in the masked dances of Korea, we can surmise the play or interpretation of *"modoki"* to be originally a parody of a deity or a demon who appeared in human disguise. Once we have discovered this original scene, it will not be difficult to retrace from it the process through which appeared all the meanings of the word I have been enumerating. In fact, as for the derivation of the first meaning (poor imitation, counterfeit) from its original meaning, there is almost no need to fill in the intermediary steps between these two meanings. As for the second meaning (reproach or criticism of somebody else), we need only remember that parodies often assume the meaning of "reproach" or "criticism."

Actually, it is sometimes said that *"modoki"* has the same root as the word *"modoru"* (to return)[47] or that it is the transitive verbal form of *"modoru."*[48] It is also said that it might mean *"modoritoku"* (to talk or to reason in return).[49] In my opinion, it would be much more convenient to assume that *"moto"* (origin) is the root of *"modoki"* or to conjecture that *"moto-toki"* (the interpretation of origin) is the original form of this word, *"moto-doki.* This is because, as I have pointed out, the meaning of "to reproach" or "to criticize in return" is nothing but a derivative.

In any event, it is exactly in the play of *"modoki"* that the celebrated folklorist and poet Orikuchi Shinobu (1887–1953) found the prototype of traditional Japanese performing arts. I would like to present a few passages he wrote on this subject. According to Orikuchi, the word *"modoki"* was not originally limited to the meanings of "reproach" or "mockery":

> Generally speaking, we think that the word *"modoku"* is only used to indicate "to offer opposition to," "to contradict," or "to reproach." But in the ancient use of this word it seems to have had a larger meaning: At least in the history of the performing arts, it is evident that it also meant "to counterfeit," "to explain," "to reinterpret in the name of someone," and "to tone down the explanations." For example, an expression such as *"hito no modoki ofu"* (to receive reproaches)

---

47. Original note: "See the word *'modoki'* in the *Iwanami Kogo Jiten.*"
48. Original note: "See the word *'modoki'* in the *Dai-Genkai.*"
49. Original note: "Ibidem."

originally meant "to be mocked by others while representing something of which you cannot help feeling ashamed." Thus the word seems to have always meant "to counterfeit" or "to imitate."[50]

In the tradition of nō there is a major act entitled *"okina"* (the old man) that is played as an opening piece—particularly at the time of festivals at the beginning of the year, or in order to consecrate a new theater, and so forth. Since time immemorial, *okina* has normally been composed of three parts: (1) *senzai,* the opening dance played by an actor without mask; (2) *okina,* the main dance by a deity with a white mask, who comes from the other world and takes the body of an old man; and (3) *sambasō,* the third dance by another old deity who wears a black mask. Here is a paragraph by Orikuchi on the role played by the *samba-sō:*

On the opposition between *"okina"* and *"samba-sō"* I once thought as follows: In the tradition of Japanese performing arts, there is always the introduction of an accompaniment by the play of *modoki* if there is a main play. The word *"modoku,"* "to be opposed to," thus means that something like a demon or a spirit who mocks and irritates the deity puts himself next to the god, in opposition to him. From this origin the word has inherited the meaning of "to contradict." When the word is used in relation to Japanese theater, however, *"modoku"* has a broader meaning that goes from "to mock someone" to "to interpret" or "to make understandable the meaning of the main act through an explanatory representation." It is exactly this role of *modoki* that the *samba-sō* plays in relation to *okina:* The *samba-sō* is played in a very disorderly fashion in opposition to the sacred and symbolic representation of *okina.* The *samba-sō* has come to be thought the additional provider of an easy explanation of the dances and ritual chants of the *okina* by the white mask. The word *"modoku"* has thus come to indicate "to translate by an explicatory interpretation." The explicatory staging that benefited such and such a house, where the dance and ritual chants took place, was the representation of the *samba-sō.* The representation of the act of sowing or of the crow's flight, for example, although unrelated to the original thing, has broadened through interpretation the fixed meaning of an act of the past. The *samba-sō* interprets the meaning of the chant and the dance of the *okina* by explaining his religious acts and their contents that are destined to flatter the people of the house or the village in question. This kind of interpretation is precisely the raison d'être of the *samba-sō* in relation to the *okina,* and it is this role of *modoki* that is played by the *samba-sō.*[51]

Searching for the origin of *"modoki"* in some popular performances in the Japanese countryside, Orikuchi found the following:

50. Orikuchi Shinobu, *Orikuchi Shinobu Zenshū,* vol. 2: *Kodai Kenkyū (Minzoku Gakuhen,* vol. 1) (Tokyo: Chūō Kōronsha, 1975), p. 409.

51. *Orikuchi Shinobu Zenshū,* vol. 17, pp. 10–11.

It seemed to me that the original meaning of the role of *modoki* became very clear when I looked at the staging of *dengaku,* which is always performed in the mountainous northern regions of Enshū and Shinshū together with *kagura* during the Flower Festival *(hana-matsuri).*[52] The latter, which shares the same origin with *dengaku,* is made of a *nembutsu-odori* and a dance in the fashion of *shōmon-shi* (master of popular Shinto rites). *Modoki* is sometimes the role of an interpreter; at other times it is the role of the *okotsuki* (madman), or simply a secondary role. In any event, the *modoki* accompanying the *okina* possesses at the same time the characteristics of these three roles. The genuine definition of *modoki* is the role played in accompanying the *okina* and—by entering the scene a moment after him, although it is simultaneously with him in contemporary performances— in repeating in a stronger voice what the *okina* has said. He takes the disguise of an *onyō-ji* (magician) or a *shugen-ja* (monk), playing at the same time the role of interpreter and the secondary role. Sometimes he enters the scene together with the *oni* (demon) who, this time, plays the main role. In this instance, the *modoki* engages, as an auxiliary character, the *oni* in a dialogue of questions and answers.

The form of *okina* is repeated several times. The so-called *negi,* the *nakato-barai* (who seems to play the role of the ritualist from the Nakatomi family in charge of purification), or the *kaidō-kudari* (procession along the way on the seashore), are all repetitions of the role of *okina,* which add a sort of variation to the representation. They narrate the story of the actor *negi* who arrives in this village from a faraway country in order to play the role of the *okina.* In this respect the *negi* is the *modoki* of *okina.* But *okina* and *modoki* have their own *modoki,* called *okotsuki* (madman), who plays violently and in a disorderly fashion. Moreover, you can usually see another form of *modoki* accompanying the *okina: koku-jō* (the old man with a black mask). Sometimes, in some regions, this is called *samba-sō;* in others, it may be called *shōjokkiri* or also *sarugaku.* In most cases this seems to be the role of the one who interprets and develops for the nonspecialist what *okina* does and says. Therefore, this character plays a special role on the scene: to interpret metaphorically with regard to certain concrete facts what has been named by the *okina.* He speaks more quickly, more comically, and more trivially than the *okina,* showing to a greater or lesser degree an obscene nature.[53]

According to Orikuchi, through this combination of the main role *okina* and *modoki* seen as a prototype structure or unity of Japanese theater, we can also see the opposition or battle between the newly arrived deity and the autochthonous demons. Following the paragraph just mentioned, Orikuchi continues. Although many people have thought generally the same thing since

---

52. This is a festival commemorating the birth of the historical Buddha on the eighth day of the Fourth Month.

53. *Orikuchi Shinobu Zenshū,* vol. 2, pp. 411–412.

the modern age began, from the perspective of the history of Japan's religious life, this order seems reversed:

> This is what I thought about the *samba-sō*. At first it might have been a visit of demons and spirits who were not genuine deities but animistic beings inhabiting the countryside and the mountains everywhere. People in the past believed that these were always malevolent against humans for having invaded and stolen their land. At least people believed themselves to be surrounded by this kind of demon or malevolent spirit, which was always ready to revolt against humanity. People took advantage, therefore, of all occasions either to oppress or convert them, making them take a vow of loyalty and bring benefits to people. Far from cursing people, they finally came to visit them and bring them benefits during certain periods of the year. These deities of a lower degree have, therefore, risen to a higher status, abandoning their animistic nature through a kind of purification. They were finally worshiped as deities in temples. Among them are a few whose genealogy can be established, and others whose origin is not very clear and yet they are privileged by the government as gods of a high degree. It was by analogy that people came to think that even the authentic god of the highest status brings benefit to humanity. In any case, in Japan's rural villages there remains a strong belief that demons or spirits come to benefit and protect those houses and those masters who pay their respects to them.[54]

Here are a few passages in which Orikuchi clearly indicates the relationship between the authentic deity and the autochthonous demons:

> There is a character who practices the rites called *modoki-kaikō* (to open the mouth of the *modoki*). In *sarugaku* this is called *wokashi*, while in the *ennen-mai* he is the *modoki*. In *dengaku* (dance of the rice field), *modoki* was deemed to play such an important role that he also entered the dances of Buddhist temples. *Hyottoko* (a masked comic character with fat lips) is a character who has survived to our days. "*Modoki*" means "*modoku*": to oppose. In the tradition of Japanese arts we already find a form of *modoki* in duet songs. In fact, it was originally the dialogue between the deity and the spirit that later became the duet between two opposing parties (*uta-gaki*). Thus, at the beginning, there were variant forms of *modoki* everywhere. Among the nō masks, there is one called *ō-beshimi;* coming from the verb "*beshimu*," "*beshimi*" means "to twist the mouth in order to maintain silent." When the deity addresses the spirit with questions and answers, the spirit obstinately struggles to keep his mouth shut or, if later he starts opening his mouth, he always says something different from the answer or simply contradicts the deity. The mask of *ō-beshimi* expresses these two aspects. Generally speaking, there are proofs attesting the existence of masks in Japan since ancient times, although under the strong influence of masks of foreign origin that spread quickly, traces of original Japanese masks have almost dis-

---

54. *Orikuchi Shinobu Zenshū*, vol. 17, pp. 11–12.

appeared. *"Kaikō"* means "to force someone to open his mouth for an answer," and the one who is so forced plays the secondary or auxiliary role *(waki-yaku)*. *Shite* (the protagonist) is the deity; the *waki* is his partner. The role of *waki* became *kyōgen* by branching off in various characters. *Kyōgen,* therefore, is more ancient than *nō-gaku.* The mask of the *ō-beshimi,* completely guarding his silence, has two meanings: to transmit the orders of the sovereign god as well as to listen to them. Consequently, *ō-beshimi* is at the same time a demon *(oni)* and a deity.[55]

In the character of the *ō-beshimi,* which is a typical form of *modoki,* we can easily find the manifestation of an ambiguity; he presents himself at the same time as a disobedient character and as a loyal interpreter. Generally speaking, we can also find in a few words related to *modoki* the ambiguities and contradictions that sometimes correspond to those of the *ō-beshimi.* For example, *"wokashi,"* the word that indicates the *modoki* of the *sarugaku,* which ordinarily means "comic," also indicates "transgression." *Waki,* the secondary and subordinate role, means at the same time "interpretation."

It was precisely because of the dynamic and ambiguous character of the deuteragonist *(waki, okashi, modoki)* that the pair of deity and his *modoki* could become a prototype and produce almost an infinite series of variations in the tradition of Japanese performing arts. We might think of several series of pairs, for example, starting with the pair of *nin-jō* (master) and *sainō* (talented man) in traditional Shinto rites and reaching, through the intermediary of several popular performing arts, to the pair of *dai* (the big) and *shō* (the small) in kabuki. "If there were ever a history of Japanese theater that did not describe the role of *modoki,* it would be a trifle."[56]

As I will be saying, all these transformations of the deity/*modoki* pair were engendered by the dynamism of opposition between the serious and the nonserious, the operation of meaning (acceptance, transmission, interpretation) and the operation of nonmeaning (annihilation through doubling, mockery), and, finally, between obedience and disobedience. Because of this dynamism, several series of doublings and transformations of this prototype pair were able to come to life in the history of the Japanese performing arts.

According to Orikuchi, today's nō, part of which is still called *"waki-nō,"* was originally a role for the *waki.* And, contrary to the current practice, *kyōgen* originally preceded the performance of nō. Everything started with the rite of the *modoki-kaikō,* the defeat and the opening of the *waki* or *modoki*'s mouth by the deity—the submission of demon or spirit to the deity—followed by the play of the *modoki (sai-nō no waza),* which was actually the original form of *kyōgen.* On the other hand, the nō originated from the dance of an actor of *sarugaku* after the play of the *modoki*—a dance that had the char-

55. *Orikuchi Shinobu Zenshū,* vol. 3, pp. 10–11.
56. *Orikuchi Shinobu Zenshū,* vol. 1, p. 138.

acter of a *modoki* and a repetition of the victorious and inaugural dance of the main deity.[57]

Even the privileged piece of the *okina*, the most important part of the nō, which is always treated as "a piece that is nō and at the same time is not," does not escape this qualification of *waki* or *modoki*. On the original form of *okina* in the traditional popular performing art known as *hana-matsuri*, Orikuchi has this to say:

The entrance on stage of the *okina*, the *negi* (priest, grand priest), and the *miko* (priestess) is followed by the appearance of several *modoki*. In the *hana-matsuri*, *modoki* is an essential role that brings the variations of seriousness and nonseriousness, and it is the latter that accompanies the *okina*. His role in primitive performances was the magnified repetition of the *okina*'s words, but at the present time he repeats them simultaneously or by reading a text. Therefore, the word *"modoki,"* which at times also means "to be opposed to," in medieval performances in Japan means "the auxiliary role." Having also the connotation of "to interpret" or "to imitate," *"modoki"* means equally "the interpreter of the *okina*," since he gives his interpretation by performing certain modifications of words and actions.

Personally I think the *negi* was the main actor of whom the *okina* was a *modoki*. In Mikawa province there still remains the idea of treating the *okina* as *sarugaku* (an exemplary form of *modoki*). In the *dengaku* of the Hōrai-ji temple, for example, the *okina*, going by the name of *sarugaku*, performs an imitation of what is played. It is simply as a result of the belated prosperity enjoyed by the actors of *sarugaku* in the big cities that *okina* became the main actor. But Japanese performances continued to redouble repetitively the original representation for many centuries in their history. In this instance, we find the same structure: *Okina* is the *modoki* of the *negi*, who, in his turn, is accompanied by his own *modoki*, who is again a double representation of the masked character of the *hyottoko*, who behaves in a disorderly fashion. *Hyottoko*, another example of which we find in the *sato-kagura* of the Kantō region, is a kind of *modoki* taken in his nonserious meaning of "opposing himself to someone" or "going the opposite way."

To sum it up, despite the important role played in contemporary *hana-matsuri*, the *okina* must have been an auxiliary performance that was introduced quite late. The performance of the *hana-matsuri* is mainly divided into three parts: (1) the story of the *negi* who, working as a *nakatomi-barai*, has traveled through several countries in order to spread the *kagura*; (2) the play of the *oni* who, coming from the mountain, put his feet on earth in order to consecrate it; (3) the ceremony of flower cultivation *(hana-sodate)*. No matter what, the *okina* can only be a secondary role.[58]

---

57. See *Orikuchi Shinobu Zenshū*, vol. 12, p. 156; vol. 3, p. 242; vol. 2, p. 441.
58. *Orikuchi Shinobu Zenshū*, vol. 17, pp. 348–349. Original note: "In more detail Orikuchi shows how we can see in the paragraphs quoted in note 53 an example of the prototype pair of main and secondary roles which, in turn, have their own *'modoki'* (very comical)."

The Japanese performing arts indeed have "continued to redouble repetitively the original representation for many centuries in their history." This process, of course, has been invigorated by the dynamism of the prototype opposition between the main role and the *modoki,* the serious and the nonserious, meaning and nomeaning, obedience and disobedience.

3

After this detailed presentation of the factual structure by which the prototype pair of the deity and his *modoki* functions and changes in the history of the Japanese performing arts, it should not be too difficult to see the meaning behind it. I will try, therefore, to retrace here the implications that follow almost directly from such a structure.

What is the meaning of this structure or matrix of the Japanese performing arts? In other words, what does this prototype opposition mean between the main role and the *modoki,* the serious and the nonserious, meaning and nomeaning, obedience and disobedience? What strikes us first is that this opposition has such a comprehensive range that it comprises at once the total register of human existence, starting from the high and going all the way down. The dynamic structure of this prototype opposition offers us something like a mimesis that is at the same time interpretative and hermeneutical—a scheme that allows us to understand the underlying structure functioning in the depth of human existence, even prior to the formation of the so-called individual and conscious personality. The two extremities of human existence manifest each other in their strict, inseparable coordination as well as in their dynamic opposition. At the same time, this dynamism goes beyond the range of Aristotle's spirit that takes as its standard the mediocre person and then defines tragedy and comedy as the mimesis of the most noble and the must vulgar person, respectively.

Starting from the mimetic pair of the main deity and his *modoki,* could we not arrive at a larger model of mimesis, one that overcomes the strictly anthropological model devised by Aristotle, and thus integrate in it another sense of mimesis or *mimeisthai,* "to strive to be like the transcendent Being that is god"? Once we have obtained this kind of model, it would be extremely easy to enrich it—for example, by relating it to the notion of the "sacred" that, from its very origin, included both concepts of sainthood and pollution[59] or, moreover, by integrating into this model the Bergsonian idea of laughter, after making the needed modifications and reductions in order to reach a deeper and more detailed understanding of this phenomenon. It would be equally easy to adopt and integrate in our prospect the notion of Rabelaisian laughter or the idea of absolute or grotesque comicality of Baudelaire, as well as his con-

---

59. Original note: "See R. Callois, *L'Homme et le Sacré* (Paris: Gallimard, 1950), in which the notion of the 'sacred' almost corresponds to the Japanese word 'serious' *(yuyushi)*."

cept of laughter in general, as a manifestation of humanity's double nature. In fact, Baudelaire wrote as follows:

> Laughter is satanic, and therefore profoundly human. It is in man the result of the idea of his own superiority and, as a matter of fact, as laughter is essentially human, it is essentially contradictory, which is to say that laughter is at the same time a sign of infinite greatness and of infinite misery, infinite misery with respect to the absolute Being of which laughter possesses the notion, infinite greatness with regard to animals. Laughter springs from the eternal shock between these two infinities. The comic, the power of laughter is in the laughing person, and not in the object of laughter.[60]

4

I wish to recall a very interesting and remarkable fact: In Korean, the mask (which generally has a more or less sacred character) is called *"talu,"* a word that also means "pollution." In my opinion, we have here the same kind of double, opposed, or even contradictory meaning that we find in the Latin word *"sacer,"* as well as in a few Japanese and Chinese words. (In Chinese there is a general phenomenon called *"han-kun,"* according to which the same word, or more precisely the same character, can have at the same time one meaning and the opposite or contradictory one.) In any event, can we not regard this fact concerning the mask as another variation of the same essentially double structure of human beings, as in the case of the prototype of *modoki?* Do we not find the same structure at work almost everywhere in the different manifestations of human nature?

There is a Japanese word, *"huru-mai,"* or behavior (*huru-mau* = to behave oneself) that might be derived from *"huri (wo suru)"* (to imitate, to simulate, to feign) and from *"mai"* (dance). It can mean at the same time the playing of people on stage as well as people's ordinary and daily behavior. Here we have another manifestation of the same double structure—proving this time the continuity between theatrical play and daily behavior, which are both grounded in the same structure. Most human daily behavior might retain a trace, however weak, of the ancient performance of the dance and play of the main deity and his *modoki*. In fact, as the prototype of performances, the *modoki* can also be at the same time the prototype of the *huru-mai*, or human behavior in general, or, if you prefer, of human "play" in general.[61] In other words, the *modoki*, a mimesis that understands and interprets itself, is in a sense human-

---

60. Original note: "Baudelaire, *De l'Essence du Rire, Oeuvre* [*sic*] *Complètes* (Paris: Ed. de Seuil), p. 373."

61. Original note: "The dance (*'mai'*) of the deity was also called *'kamiasobi'* (the deity's play). Related to this we might remember of course a series of publications whose theme is the notion of 'play,' such as, for example, works by Huizinga, Caillois, and Fink. It would be interesting to compare their findings with the notions of 'modoki,' 'huru-mai,' 'asobi,' etc., particularly if we consider that the word 'huru-mai' could be in some way related to the expression 'hureru' (to touch, to be possessed)."

ity's *furu-mai* par excellence. From this perspective, then, the human being is nothing but a *modoki*. And this is the reason why the human being reflects and interprets himself in the mirror of *modoki*'s different aspects.[62]

5

We still have at least one problem to solve: Is this enlarged and enriched model of the structure of *modoki* that I have outlined valid for ethical considerations? And how?

I will leave the answer to my readers.

Yet one thing seems certain to me: The play of the *modoki,* who contradicts and mocks the embodied deity, reminds us that we are not gods, even if we can momentarily be possessed by them.

Are we more imbued with humanism and a sense of humor than the ancient inhabitants of the Japanese archipelago?

---

62. Original note: "Personally I see here a structural variation of the theory of St. Augustine's *imago Dei.* It is remarkable to witness a close affinity between laughter and prayer, as far as they are both expressions of cosmic sentiments."

ELEVEN

The Complicity of Aesthetics
Karatani Kōjin

KARATANI KŌJIN (b. 1941) has established himself as one of the leading literary critics of contemporary Japan and has mastered a good deal of respect in the West as well, where two of his numerous books have recently been translated.[1] A professor at Kinki University, Karatani is the chief editor of *Critical Space (Hihyō Kūkan)*—probably the first Japanese journal to seriously engage Western scholarship on issues of Japanese culture.

Karatani has written extensively on the complicity of Western hermeneutic strategies in constructing what we today call "Japan." In his opinion, aesthetics played a distinctive role in developing a major paradox in the evaluation of the Japanese arts. His argument goes as follows: The traditionalist school led by Okakura Kakuzō, which privileged native paintings and sculptures over the imported arts from the West, was actually the most modern and the most oriented to the West. After all, the originator of the movement was a scholar from Salem, Massachusetts, Ernest Fenollosa, who heavily relied on Hegelian and Spencerian philosophies.[2]

Karatani reminds us that the traditional arts of Japan were "discovered" by Westerners who were discontented with the modernity of their own culture and therefore searched in Japan for ways to overcome modernity. Japan came to be discovered by the West through its art—particularly the *ukiyo-e* of the Edo period, which exercised a considerable influence on French impressionist painters. Vincent van Gogh's oft-repeated wish of wanting "to see things like a Japanese," indicates that "Japan" came to the West as a fiction in the images that were produced within the aesthetic

---

1. See Karatani Kōjin, *Origins of Modern Japanese Literature* (Durham: Duke University Press, 1993), and Karatani Kōjin, *Architecture as Metaphor: Language, Number, Money* (Cambridge, Mass.: MIT Press, 1995).

2. "'The traditionalist faction' that propelled with passion the cause of the art school and the museum was the most vocal faction propounding modernism and westernization." See Karatani Kōjin, "Bijutsukan to Shite no Nihon: Okakura Tenshin to Fenorosa," *Hihyō Kūkan* 2(1) (1994):60. I recapitulate the remainder of the essay in the following paragraph.

realm. The Western market was ready to accept works of art that presented "Japan" in its most aestheticized manner—an argument that can easily be applied to literature as well when one considers that the most popular Japanese writers in the West (Tanizaki Jun'ichirō, Kawabata
Yasunari, and Mishima Yukio) share in the production of an aestheticized
Japan.

Art in Japan became "modern" when in the West the same genre was
held in suspicion of modernity. This happened to literature as well, a field
whose importation from the West coincided with its Western critique.[3]
Karatani argues that if Japan's nineteenth century corresponds to the Edo
period, then Japan discovered Europe's nineteenth century after its own
nineteenth century had already finished. Japan discovered the notion of interiority at a time when the West was actually looking for a world less
metaphysically conceived and less constrained by the rigidity of a strong
subject and a strong point of view. The European fascination with things
Japanese *(Japonisme)* and a world of painting that was not directly tied by
the rules of perspective is related, in Karatani's opinion, to the Japanese
text's lack of interiority or objectivity. It was exactly this lack of "spiritual
depth" that the Japanese tried to suppress by turning to the Western nineteenth century.

Westerners, however, started highlighting whatever of Japan could be
conceived of as an absence of form, content, or structure organized around
a precise and definite center. Martin Heidegger's interest in Japan, for example, followed from the fact that he saw in Kuki Shūzō's notion of *iki,* or
tension of possibilities, a description of what he named *Abgrund,* or "abyssal
depth," which is a jump beyond the structured depth of metaphysical
thought. The numerous Western studies on the Japanese concepts of impermanence *(mujō)* and formlessness were also results of reading Japan as a
text along the lines of an exteriorized presence that refuses to be caught in
the stability of a secret and hidden interiority. This condition, in Karatani's
judgment, might have slowed down the process of Japanese "modernization" but is turning out to be a major condition for the acceleration of
Japan's postmodernism—thus explaining Japan's preeminence in the postmodern world.[4]

---

3. "Today's 'modern literature' emerged only during the last decade of the nineteenth century. Whereas in Europe at this time literature and philosophy were seeking to deny the very idea of a nineteenth century—and looking to other alternatives—Japanese literature was barely beginning to conceive of its own
nineteenth century." See Karatani Kōjin, "One Spirit, Two Nineteenth Centuries," in Masao Miyoshi and
H. D. Harootunian, eds., *Postmodernism and Japan* (Durham: Duke University Press, 1989), p. 259.

4. Karatani, "One Spirit, Two Nineteenth Centuries," pp. 265–267.

In *Origins of Modern Japanese Literature* Karatani traces the process of Japan's discovery of Western perspectivism, which objectifies what is portrayed in visual and literary texts by reducing the focus of vision to the fixed position of the viewer. Such a mode of representation collided with medieval models of pictorial representation which posited a transcendental space that allowed the representation of reality in terms of the depiction of concepts. By importing the Western nineteenth century—Karatani argues—Japan discovered in the 1890s the notion of landscape. "Landscape" implies that the subject is alienated from the external world—as the viewer of Leonardo da Vinci's *Mona Lisa* immediately realizes by noticing the split between the woman's face in the foreground and the portrait of nature in the background. Such a discovery produced what Karatani calls "inversion," which is the erroneous perception that a newly devised construct existed from time immemorial and is thus felt as natural.[5]

Prior to the "discovery" of Western modernity, reality had been perceived as the reproduction of Chinese texts *(kanbun)* into images of nature *(kachō fūgetsu),* which were far from being natural. Strict rules codified which birds were singing in which season on which flowers. The structure of perception was crystallized to the point that reality could never be seen as it showed itself to the viewer—or it strongly conditioned the viewer as to what he was allowed to see. The Japanese discovery of "landscape" entailed a series of epistemological inversions. New conceptions of writing were sought that would match the orality of speech without the cumbersome intrusion of Chinese characters *(genbun itchi).* More attention was paid to the actual workings of nature in the composition of poetry (the "sketches" of Masaoka Shiki). The naked face finally appeared on stage, unprotected by the layers of powder traditionally applied to the face of the kabuki actor in an attempt to imitate the movement of dolls (Ichikawa Danjūrō of the Shintōza kabuki troupe). In a word, the discovery of "landscape" by Japanese artists corresponds to the Japanese discovery of "meaning," "reality," and "interiority."

Karatani describes "interiority" as immediacy to the self brought about by the correspondence of voice and reality. In his opinion, the discovery of interiority was a result, and not the cause, of the *genbun itchi* movement, which aimed at erasing the presence of Chinese characters that stood in the way of the immediacy of expression. Interiority was grounded in the alleged "transparency" of expression, thus forcing authors to reduce the ex-

---

5. Karatani Kōjin, "The Discovery of Landscape," in *Origins of Modern Japanese Literature,* pp. 11–44.

teriority of writer and language and repress the figurative *(kanji)* in favor of hearing the inner voice.[6] In a hermeneutical move analogous to the presentation of the Japanese birth of interiority as the textual result of the debate on issues related to the *genbun itchi,* Karatani argues that it was the literary form of the confession which brought to life the author's "true self," thus making interiority the product of a compulsion to confess on the part of an author, who found himself part of what Karatani calls "confession as system." Karatani describes the popularity that confession achieved in the literature of the Meiji period in terms of the ideological implications of the notion of confession. He points out that the strength of confession lies in its power to disguise itself as an oppositional force to external authority—while, in fact, it is an expression of will-to-power on the part of the defeated. A facade of weakness hides the power of a subject who becomes master of himself by asserting himself in an act of authority. Such an act contributed to the establishment of a new form of subjectivity in modern Japan.

According to Karatani, the notion of a strong self that came to Japan with the concept of interiority was a manifestation of absolute authority that, rooted in the monotheistic structure of Christianity, informed the new definition of imperial power given in the Meiji period. Whereas prior to the opening of Japan to the West, the distinction, in terms of authority, between emperor, shogun, and daimyo was left ambiguous, with the Meiji Restoration the government proclaimed the supreme authority of the emperor. The complicity of the Western model of modernity in setting up the newly conceived notions of "authority" and "interiority" was also at work in the development of the government's homogenization and centralization policies during the third decade of the Meiji period—exactly the time when writers were faced with problems of interiority and confession.[7]

Since confession is part and parcel of humanity's dialogue with God in the Christian faith—Karatani continues—the exposure of Japan to this literary genre also meant a confrontation with issues related to Christianity. The redemptive structure of God's love of the repentant sinner implies the presence of sickness, without which no healing can take place. This, according to Karatani, explains the "sudden appearance of illness" in Japan as a literary topos after 1890. Pain is a necessary condition for redemption since, without illness and suffering, there would not be anything from

6. Karatani Kōjin, "The Discovery of Interiority," in *Origins of Modern Japanese Literature,* pp. 44–75.
7. Karatani Kōjin, "Confession as a System," in *Origins of Modern Japanese Literature,* pp. 76–96.

which people need to be liberated. In Christianity, Karatani argues, illness is a sin because it attacks the mortal part of the body. It is a curse to be ashamed of. Christianity justifies it through redemption whereas its secularized form, the novel, displaces it through metaphors. The aestheticization and mythologization of illness in modern literature make good health appear a sign of vulgarity. This notion of illness as metaphor was particularly "contagious" in the formation of modern Japanese subjectivity and, according to Karatani, it was another example of Catholic hermeneutics at work in Japan at the end of the nineteenth century. A stark opposition between illness and health was promoted by a medical community whose authority was grounded on an "imaginary subject"—a construct that empowered the "scientific" method with absolute control over the health of modern man. The Japanese subject was increasingly becoming the product of Western modernity.[8]

Karatani reminds his readers that the formation of a Japanese subjectivity at the end of the nineteenth century was a complex process involving an entire series of "inversions" whose historicity is often lost in discussions of literature. He argues that the sudden interest of Japanese writers in children's literature, for example, was based on the birth of a landscape known as "the child," which required a modern definition of childhood. Unlike premodern societies, in which the boundary between childhood and adulthood was much less evident, the contemporary role assigned to the child must be seen from the perspective of the modern notion of division of labor. The alleged recovery of innocence on the part of a Japanese writer who wants to see the world from the eyes of a child must be historicized—Karatani reminds us—in order to be understood. Once we realize that such a writer cannot operate from outside the modern landscape of childhood, we are faced with the true paradox of inversion: a series of manipulations of and by Western hermeneutics that easily goes undetected.

In the case of poetics related to "children's innocence," for example, the excessive self-consciousness that has made the romantic subject so complicated in the West becomes the object of an inversion when it tries to relieve the subject of the burden of fear and anxiety by becoming once more "like newborn babes" (1 Peter 2:2) in the Christian spirit of Peter's words. This "inversion" is accompanied by an entire series of concepts developed by the German romantics, such as "self-expression," "originality," and "ge-

---

8. Karatani Kōjin, "Sickness as Meaning," in *Origins of Modern Japanese Literature,* pp. 97–113.

nius," which erase the presence of an earlier landscape made of "collabora-
tive authorship, citation, allusion, and imitation." All these hermeneutical
moves become an object of an even deeper amnesia when the package of
modernity reaches Japan, and writers are under the illusion of escaping
modernity by looking at the world with the innocence of the child. Moreover, these writers believe that by digging into their childhood they have
finally found a way to uncover their deeper "self" whereas, in fact, they at
best uncover the system that makes them feel they are actually able to do
so. Forgetting the historicity of such a process is tantamount to forgetting
one's complicity with the system that one mistakenly believes one is challenging and criticizing.[9]

Karatani describes the Western hermeneutics of modernity as a kind of
perspectival configuration, based on the linear perspective system, that
aims at making the viewer feel the "depth" of things. "Depth" in the
West, then, is the result of a technique of drafting by vanishing point that
also informed much of modern Japanese literature. It is premised on the
existence of the transcendental, from which the notions of "verticality,"
"strata," and "substrata" also came. This vanishing point made possible
the transparency of words and things. Karatani argues that Japanese writers of the beginning of the century were certainly aware of the complicity of Western hermeneutics in the writing of literature. What was lacking, according to him, was an awareness of the historicity of the
phenomenon known as "perspectival configuration," which made Japanese writers and scholars side with the spokesmen of modernity, giving the
impression that those who resisted and questioned modernity were necessarily at fault.

In the 1891–1892 debate on "submerged ideals" between Tsubouchi
Shōyō and Mori Ōgai, for example, the latter was shown by critics to have
emerged the winner because he expounded the idealist theory of the one-
point perspective system. The paradox resulting from the debate was that
Ōgai later joined his rival in understanding that perspectival configuration was nothing but a specific hermeneutical strategy—the result of a series of inversions grounded in Western metaphysics. Ōgai's attempt to de-
center such a perspective was a questioning of the transcendental meaning
of the vanishing point, which was, after all, what Shōyō had argued about
in the debate. Karatani's reevaluation of the role played by Shōyō in the
debate is not meant, however, to search for truth behind specific

---

9. Karatani Kōjin, "The Discovery of the Child," in *Origins of Modern Japanese Literature*, pp. 114–135.

hermeneutical strategies but to bring back to memory the working of hermeneutics in the formation of discourses. Unless the interpreter interrogates the self-evidence of epistemological apparatuses—such as "author," "self," "expression," and "depth"—modernity cannot be subjected to a true critique and debates such as this one cannot be seen in a truly historical light.[10]

After all, Karatani himself confesses to have been informed, in the writing of *Origins of Modern Japanese Literature,* by the genealogical method of Friedrich Nietzsche and Michel Foucault, which is an attempt at uncovering the historical nature of all constructs, including the process that compels people to internalize them as natural. To put it in Karatani's words: "This genealogical method attempts to expose the way in which we take what has been historically produced as natural, the contingent as the necessary."[11] This explains Karatani's questioning of the notion of a "theory" that has lost its exteriority—its ability to doubt—contenting itself with being reduced to a mere language game. To this kind of theory he opposes "criticism" *(hihyō),* which he describes as "a ceaseless movement" that does not hesitate to question itself as a method by inquiring into the historicity of the hermeneutical act. Instead of the expression "hermeneutical act," however, Karatani uses the words "critical space" *(hihyō kūkan),* which he also applied to the title of his influential journal.

The same methodology informs the essay "Edo Exegesis and the Present," which is translated here. In this essay Karatani analyzes the Japanese discourse on reason and the heart (aesthetics), as it developed in the eighteenth century, by presenting the configurations that led to the reinterpretation of Chinese concepts in light of the political situation of Edo Japan. Through this search, Karatani reminds his readers of what preceded the "perspectival configuration" leading to the discovery of interiority. At the same time, the essay explores analogies in the relationship between language, aesthetics, and the market that can be found in what scholars usually define as premodern (Edo) and postmodern (contemporary) Japan. Issues related to modernity again become central to understanding such relationships—confirming once more the crucial role played by the Japanese late nineteenth century (Meiji) in the formation of the Japanese notion of "modern" subjectivity, the fundamental target of Karatani's critique.

---

10. Karatani Kōjin, "On the Power to Construct," in *Origins of Modern Japanese Literature,* pp. 136–154.

11. Karatani Kōjin, "Afterword to the Japanese Paperback Edition," in *Origins of Modern Japanese Literature,* p. 186.

Edo Exegesis and the Present
by Karatani Kōjin

1

Recently everybody has been speaking of a revival of Edo culture.[12] Actually, I myself have written about thinkers of the Edo period,[13] although this activity of mine was unrelated to such a revival. Yet I can understand the reasons behind this boom, and I think I can almost foresee where such a boom is taking us. Before the war, around the late 1930s, a kind of Edo revival occurred— and by this I do not simply mean that people read Motoori Norinaga and the works of nativist scholars. "Historical novels" were widely popular, for example, and "movies with a historical content" were equally popular. "Historical" clearly referred to the Edo period. They all reflected the present age onto the Edo period, so that they were not particularly motivated by any interest in history—far from it. It was a lack of interest in "history" and this feeling of occlusion that created the "historical novel."

This genre is not unrelated to the intellectual tendency that is best represented by the slogan "overcoming the modern."[14] Kuki Shūzō's *Structure of Iki,*[15] for example, is perhaps the first attempt to give a philosophical mean-

---

12. This is the text of a lecture that Karatani delivered at Waseda University on 1 November 1985. The text, "Edo no Chūshakugaku to Genzai," appears in Karatani Kōjin, *Kotoba to Higeki* (Tokyo: Daisanbunmeisha, 1989), pp. 90–127.

13. The Edo period, also known as the Tokugawa period from the name of the shogunal house in charge of the government at the time, goes from 1600 to 1868.

14. *"Kindai no chōkoku"* ("overcoming the modern") was the topic discussed in a famous roundtable of 1942 that was organized by Kawakami Tetsutarō (1902–1980), chief editor of the journal *Bungakkai.* Thirteen participants gathered to discuss the meaning of Western modernity and Japanese ways of overcoming it. Among the discussants were the critics Kobayashi Hideo (1902–1983), Kamei Katsuichirō (1907–1966), and Nakamura Mitsuo (b. 1911), the poet Miyoshi Tatsuji (1900–1964), the novelist Hayashi Fusao (1903–1975), the philosophers Nishitani Keiji (1900–1990) and Shimomura Toratarō (b. 1902), the historian Suzuki Shigetaka (1907–1988), the theologian Yoshimitsu Yoshihiko (1904–1945), the medical doctor Kikuchi Seishi (1902–1974), the composer Moroi Saburō (1903–1977), and the journalist Tsumura Hideo (b. 1907). For a brief discussion of this roundtable see Masayuki Ninomiya, *La Pensée de Kobayashi Hideo: Un Intellectuel Japonais au Tournant de l'Histoire* (Geneva: Librairie Droz, 1995), pp. 33–41.

15. Kuki Shūzō (1888–1941) provided an aesthetic representation of the Edo period in his work *Iki no Kōzō* (The Structure of Iki, 1926, published in 1930), seeing it as an age dominated by the notion of "erotic allure" *(bitai).* According to Kuki, this seduction was the result of the cultural synthesis of two cultural moments of the Japanese tradition: the moment of Buddhist renunciation *(akirame)* and the Confucian moment of honor or pride *(ikiji)* derived from the ethics of the military class *(bushidō).* These two moments maintained in a state of tension a relationship between man and woman that could never be fulfilled or realized—what Kuki called *iki,* or chic refinement. A condition of *iki* was freedom from all kinds of necessity and the opening of possibility. While love was a simple necessity, *iki* was a transcendental possibility—

ing to the sensibility and lifestyle of the Japanese living during the late Edo period. Yet this was again an "Edo" found within the topic of the so-called overcoming of Western modernity. If I am allowed a simplification, the Edo revival had the following characteristics. First of all, it is closed to historical consciousness. We could call this the consciousness of "the end of history." Nothing is left for us to achieve further. In the case of the years before the war, this was the result of the suppression and breakdown of Marxism. Secondly, and related to the first characteristic, is the tendency of trying to be self-sufficient within a closed space. Rather than an exclusionist nationalism, this sense of self-sufficiency was like a feeling that there was nothing left to be learned from the West.

Today's Edo revival is basically similar to the situation I just described. That is to say, it is linked to the trend called postmodernism. Although there is no specific suppression, people are no longer moved by the concept that history reaches a specific goal or that it should achieve something. In this sense, I feel that the notion of the "end of history" is infiltrating everywhere. Furthermore, this is related to a "consumer society." Here I feel that people do not produce anything material but simply create difference = information. And the Japanese start feeling that at this point they have nothing to learn from the West and are rather at the vanguard.

By the time I decided to study thinkers of the Edo period, this trend had become conspicuous. As I thought about "the overcoming of modernity" of the late 1920s and early 1930s, I felt that I should go back to the Edo period. Since people such as Kobayashi Hideo,[16] Yasuda Yojūrō,[17] Nishida Kitarō,[18]

---

the erotic allure that knows renunciation and is built on a spiritual energy or tension. Too much showiness (*hade*) is contrary to the notion of renunciation and is therefore considered vulgar (*gebin*). Iki finds its objectivation in bodily expressions, such as the way of speaking and walking. Kuki gives the example of Edo paintings of women after a bath (*yuagari sugata*), in which a recent state of nudity is merely suggested but never clearly presented. In order for *iki* to exist, the lingering fragrance of the woman's body must suggest eroticism through an imagined memory. Kuki also applied the category of *iki* to specific lines in design, such as parallel lines that express the duality between ideal tension and reality. Kuki also saw this duality in the tension between wood and bamboo in Japanese architecture. Ultimately Kuki reduces the phenomenon of *iki* to an exercise in nationalistic hermeneutics, specifying *iki* as the memory of an image that allows the Japanese people to recognize this aesthetic experience as something peculiarly Japanese in its ability to manifest the essence or being of the nation. See Kuki Shūzō, *Iki no Kōzō* (Tokyo: Iwanami Shoten, 1979). For an ideological critique, though somehow reductionist, of Kuki's aesthetic project, see Leslie Pincus, *Authenticating Culture in Imperial Japan: Kuki Shūzō and the Rise of National Aesthetics* (Berkeley: University of California Press, 1996).

16. Kobayashi Hideo (1902–1983), literary critic, took a strong position against Marxist and post–World War I avant-garde literature. He interrupted his activity as a social commentator during World War II, concentrating instead on classical Japanese literature and the aestheticization of Japan.

17. Yasuda Yojūrō (1910–1981), literary critic, founded the Japanese Romantic school (Nihon Rōman-ha) in 1935 advocating the reawakening of the Japanese national spirit and the traditional appreciation of beauty. He contributed directly to the rise of ultranationalism in the late 1930s and 1940s.

18. Nishida Kitarō (1870–1945) is the most important philosopher of modern Japan. Author of *The Study of Good* (*Zen no Kenkyū*, 1911), he formulated the concept of "pure experience" in which all dualisms—

and Kuki Shūzō[19] depended, after all, on the thought of the Edo period, I felt that we had no other way but to follow the same wheel tracks. That is to say, I wanted to know how, in Edo thought, a mode—a mode to which we always return despite our efforts to hunt for novelties—is produced in its thorough form and how such a form comes into being.

Earlier I wrote a book titled *Origins of Modern Japanese Literature*[20] in which I said that "modern literature" appeared within an inversion that occurred in the third decade of the Meiji period.[21] But the third decade of the Meiji period corresponds in the Christian era to the end of the nineteenth century. That is to say, what we call modern Japanese literature is basically the literature of the twentieth century. To say it differently, we are in a modern literature that is not yet one hundred years of age. If we put aside the political order and all economic relationships, in sensibility and lifestyle the nineteenth century for Japan was virtually the Edo period. It was not a situation of underdeveloped belatedness in need of modernization, however, but, in a sense, a perfectly refined formation that could hardly be further perfected. I think it is important to remember that the foundation upon which modern Japanese literature, or modern consciousness, came into existence was not something like a feudal society or a cultural stage of belatedness. Strangely enough, it was something concluded—taken to the point that it could not go any further.

What I did in *Origins of Modern Japanese Literature* was to show that the notions of "literature" and "interiority," which we take as self-evident, are at most nothing but a product of the late nineteenth century. This was not necessarily meant to deny "modern literature" and the "modern," however. I simply stated that we are in that space and these are not simply concepts. Coming into the 1980s, I began to feel that what I had until then fought against had finally turned inside out. This is because all those notions that "modern literature" had actually considered values—such as, for example, "interiority" and "depth"—began to be simply jeered at by people. I do not feel the presence of any thought

---

subject and object, mind and body, spirit and matter—are allegedly erased. He further refined the concepts of "pure experience" and "absolute will" in his main work on aesthetics, *Art and Morality* (*Geijutsu to Dōtoku*, 1923). In *Hataraku Mono kara Miru Mono e* (From the Acting to the Seeing, 1927), Nishida articulated his notion of *basho:* the "place," or topos, of "absolute nothingness" wherein the "true self" is revealed. He was the founder of the Kyoto school of philosophy, named for the university where he taught from 1910 until his retirement in 1928.

19. Kuki Shūzō (1888–1941), philosopher, studied in Europe with Heinrich Rickert, Henri Bergson, and Martin Heidegger. He taught the history of philosophy at Kyoto University after his return to Japan in 1929. Besides engaging in the phenomenological study of *iki* in the Edo period, Kuki also tackled the notion of the "accidental" as related to the human emotion of wonder in *The Problem of the Accidental* (*Gūzensei no Mondai,* 1935).

20. Karatani Kōjin, *Nihon Kindai Bungaku no Kigen* (Tokyo: Kōdansha, 1980). For an English translation see Karatani, *Origins of Modern Japanese Literature.*

21. That is, the years 1887–1896.

in that jeering. What we have today is precisely the nineteenth-century Edo from which modern Japanese literature indisputably came. This is not a return to the Japanese tradition, but I believe that the present situation has disclosed those elements which are at the foundation of, at best, a little more than eighty years of modern consciousness and modern systems.

I used the phrase "nineteenth century," but usually we employ the expressions Edo period or Genroku,[22] Bunka,[23] and Bunsei[24] periods. However, I venture to follow the Western calendar. There are several reasons for my doing so, but by using the Western calendar we avoid the separation that we feel when we employ expressions such as the Meiji[25] or the Taishō[26] periods, which tend to enclose us. By the way, when I think of Western philosophy, people today usually speak of thinkers from Descartes,[27] Spinoza,[28] and Leibniz[29] to Kant[30] and Hegel,[31] as of philosophers of the seventeenth and eighteenth centuries. They read Leibniz or Spinoza, not as objects of historical studies, but as contemporaries. Being Westerners, they feel that these philosophers are not that far away from them. But when we say Edo period, the Japanese thinkers of the eighteenth century look like people of a previous age that is unrelated to us. Thinkers such as Itō Jinsai,[32] Ogyū Sorai,[33] and Motoori Norinaga[34] end up looking antiquated. Is this not strange and unfair? Accordingly, shouldn't we put into brackets at once the subdivisions of the Edo period, thus relinquishing the practice of using the terms, for example, Bunka and Bunsei, and just call it "the nineteenth century"?

In Japan, modernization has advanced since the Meiji Restoration, but in literature this occurred thirty years later. This is why in Japan the nineteenth century is basically the Edo period. To summarize the nineteenth century in one word, I would refer to the *Structure of Iki* by Kuki Shūzō cited earlier. According to him, *iki* is "the absolutization of possibility as possibility"—which is to say, stopping one step prior to reaching a place or prior to transcending

---

22. Genroku period (1688–1703).

23. Bunka period (1804–1817).

24. Bunsei period (1818–1829).

25. Meiji period (1868–1911).

26. Taishō period (1912–1925).

27. René Descartes (1596–1650).

28. Baruch Spinoza (1632–1677).

29. Gottfried Wilhelm Leibniz (1646–1716).

30. Immanuel Kant (1724–1804).

31. Georg Wilhelm Friedrich Hegel (1770–1831).

32. Itō Jinsai (1627–1705), Confucian scholar, produced several commentaries on the Chinese classics, such as *Old Interpretations of the Analects* (*Rongo Kogi,* 1712) and *Old Interpretations of Mencius* (*Mōshi Kogi,* 1720).

33. Ogyū Sorai (1666–1728), Confucian scholar, was one of the major proponents of *kogaku* or ancient (Chinese) learning. Among his major works are *Explanation of the Way* (*Bendō,* 1717) and *Explanation of Terms* (*Benmei,* 1717).

34. Motoori Norinaga (1730–1801), the leading *kokugaku* or nativist scholar.

it. Hasumi Shigehiko[35] uses the expression "to stop in the shallow while being tempted by depth," and I think that this in a sense expresses the structure of the phenomenon known as *iki*.

I think that in modern literature the first person to critique the notion of *iki*—although he used the word *"sui"*[36]—was Kitamura Tōkoku.[37] We have his essays "A Consideration of *Sui* Extended to *The Aloes-Wood Pillow*"[38] and "The Pessimist Poet and Women"[39] in which he opposed to *iki* "romantic love" *(ren'ai)*, the passionate love depicted by Stendhal.[40] Tōkoku was a Christian, and the notion of "romantic love" spread during the Meiji period from within the churches. The Christian church, especially the Protestant church, was a place where men and women were equal. Therefore, churches were special places separated from Meiji society. From there romantic love spread and reached many people, among whom was Tōkoku. "Romantic love" was a new concept.[41]

I said that it spread from Christian churches, but "romantic love" also rebelled against Christianity. Accordingly, de Rougemont found the origin of "romantic love" in a heretic school of Christianity (the Cathars).[42] After a

---

35. Hasumi Shigehiko (b. 1936), president of the University of Tokyo, is the author of the influential *Introduction to the Critique of Fiction (Monogatari Hihan Josetsu)* and *Essays on Natsume Sōseki (Natsume Sōseki Ron).*

36. While *iki* implies the chic lifestyle and up-to-dateness of the inhabitants of downtown Edo, *sui* is usually related to the traditional "refinement" of merchants in the Kansai area and has stronger ethical connotations. The character *"sui"* came to be read *"iki"* in Edo, maintaining the implication that the man of *iki* must be conversant with the world of the pleasure quarters. The most celebrated man of *iki* in Edo was Kinokuniya Monzaemon, who had the entire Yoshiwara red-light district booked for a whole night—thus employing all the courtesans there and shutting the main entrance gate. See Nakao Tatsurō, *Sui, Tsū, Iki: Edo no Bi Ishiki Kō* (Tokyo: Miai Shoten, 1984).

37. Kitamura Tōkoku (1868–1894), poet and essayist, was a major theorist of the Meiji romantic movement. Prior to his suicide at age twenty-six, he published several articles in the journal *Bungakkai* on the modern notions of romantic love and interiority.

38. "Sui wo Ronjite Kyara-makura ni Oyobu," in *Tōkoku Zenshū*, vol. 1 (Complete Works of Kitamura Tōkoku) (Tokyo: Iwanami Shoten, 1950), pp. 265–271.

39. "Ensei Shika to Josei," in *Tōkoku Zenshū*, vol. 1, pp. 254–264.

40. Henri Beyle Stendhal (1783–1842), French writer.

41. Commenting on a passage from Karatani's *Origins of Modern Japanese Literature,* Brett de Bary, the editor of the English translation, makes the following point: "Karatani refers to the distinction between two words for 'love' in contemporary Japanese: *koi* and *ren'ai.* Building on Kitamura's observation, Karatani claims that 'love' in Edo literature was exclusively referred to by the term *koi,* which always connotes sexual love. The term *ren'ai* came into use only during the Meiji period, when Kitamura Tōkoku's writings on the subject were particularly influential. *Ren'ai* may refer to platonic, idealized love, as well as to sexual love, but, because of its early association with Japanese Christianity and literary romanticism, is often translated into English as 'romantic love.' In contemporary speech it is used to describe a 'love' marriage *(ren'ai kekkon)* as opposed to an arranged marriage *(miai kekkon).* See Karatani, *Origins of Modern Japanese Literature,* p. 201, n. 6.

42. The Cathars are medieval heretics, active from the eleventh century on, whose name comes from the Greek word *"katharos,"* or pure. Here Karatani refers to Denis de Rougemont, *Love in the Western World* (Princeton: Princeton University Press, 1956).

while, Tōkoku ended up by rejecting the Christian faith. He relied on the transcendentalism of the American Emerson.[43] Emerson thought of God, not as a personal other, but as a transcendental being immanent in everyone. Since it is inherent to everyone, it is possible to reach him. Tōkoku considered "romantic love" a union of love with the other sex. Seen from the perspective of *iki,* this is absolutely vulgar *(yabo),* since in *iki* allure stops at the level of allure and should not reach the level of materialization. Moreover, you should not be lost in confusion as a result of this lack of materialization. You should not fall into despair. Such an attitude would be "vulgar." If *iki* is to stand within a transcendentalism that cannot reach the other, then vulgarity and barbarism clearly stem from Tōkoku's transcendentalism.

Modern literature starts like this, that is, together with "romantic love." In Natsume Sōseki,[44] for example, whether he deals with triangles or other relationships, literature reaches the height of vulgarity. Able to go against this flow, perhaps, are works such as Nagai Kafū's *Strange Tale East of the River*[45] and Kawabata Yasunari's *Snow Country.*[46] These works appeared around 1935 at the time of "art's renaissance." In short, they are linked to the "Edo revival" of the Shōwa period that I mentioned earlier. In sum, we can think that in the ultimate analysis the point reached by Edo literature and the nineteenth century was absolutely not the arrival at the transcendent world, but a stopping just in front of it. If this is the renunciation accompanying *iki,* then, contrary to this, what we call modern literature is undoubtedly vulgar and barbarous, since it tries to reach somewhere. It has a "purpose." It has an "end." It must always proceed in that direction . . . or so they say.

But the "Edo period" from the seventeenth to the eighteenth century is different from that of the nineteenth century. That was rather "vulgar," and this applies to thinkers as well. But when people speak of "Edo," they usually mean the nineteenth century. What is perceived in Europe, and especially in France, as "peculiarly Japanese" is all "nineteenth-century Edo."

Impressionist paintings are a typical example. Van Gogh[47] repeatedly wrote in his letters that he wanted to see things like a Japanese. Although he says "Japanese," he actually knew only Japanese paintings. These were clearly paintings at the level of *iki,* not the paintings of the Genroku period. That is to say, he meant nineteenth-century paintings. The "Japanese" of whom van

---

43. Ralph Waldo Emerson (1803–1882), American philosopher and poet, developed a movement of thought known as transcendentalism in the essay "Nature" (1836). This was a form of mystic idealism and Wordsworthian reverence for nature.

44. Natsume Sōseki (1867–1916) is still considered the greatest novelist of the Meiji period. Translations of his main works are available in all the major European languages.

45. Nagai Kafū (1879–1959) published *Bokutō Kidan* in serialized form in the newspaper *Asahi Shinbun* from April to June 1937.

46. Kawabata Yasunari (1899–1972) wrote *Yukiguni* mostly before and during the war (1935–1947).

47. Vincent van Gogh (1853–1890) is generally considered the greatest Dutch painter after Rembrandt. He was a powerful influence on the current of expressionism in modern art.

Gogh speaks, when he says that he wants to see like them, are located at the limit of a process of refinement prior to our entering "the modern period." Westerners discovered the Japanese "nineteenth century" during the latter half of the nineteenth century—exactly when Westerners were trying to exit that century.

The impressionists and van Gogh thought that this was "Japan" without even considering that it was actually the Edo period. Their excitement was enormous. For them, Japan was a big occasion to deny Western "modernity." It should come as no surprise, therefore, if, after a century, we link our rediscovery of Edo and the "nineteenth century" to the achievement of the present postmodern condition. The "Edo taste" of the Japanese, whether it was Nagai Kafū's or Kuki Shūzō's, was mediated by the "Japanese taste" of the West.

As you know, Roland Barthes wrote a book on Japan called *Empire of Signs*.[48] Here he takes all his examples of what is "typically Japanese" from the Japanese nineteenth century. Therefore, for Barthes as well, Japan basically becomes a nineteenth-century Japan. Westerners seem to be interested in the later Edo and tend to call it "Japan." It is the same thing with Kojeve.[49] We can criticize this attitude as a kind of "orientalism"—the projection of a Western problem onto the mirror known as Japan. But when we look at contemporary Japan, we cannot settle the problem so easily.

Until now, the matter ended by saying that this was an arbitrary, Western way of seeing things. Yet we cannot be content with it. The reason is that contemporary Japanese literature and thought in general—I think we could call it postmodernism—appear to be influenced by the West and appear to stand at the level of advanced capitalism and yet, at the same time, are nothing but the disclosure of an Edo literature that was found, at the most, only eighty years ago—after peeling off the outer layer, that is, the ground of Edo literature was exposed.

In the literature of the Bunka and Bunsei periods, linguistic games and wordplay—that is to say, parodies and puns—were dominant. "Shallowness" rather than "depth," frivolous and minor works, prevailed. For example: in *Ten Thousand Streams* the copywriter Itoi Shigesato[50] turned a *senryū*[51] into a parody, and again *senryū* were products of the nineteenth century [*sic*]. We can almost say that in the nineteenth century authors only wrote this kind of light work, the same kind of works that Tanaka Yasuo[52] is producing to-

---

48. Roland Barthes, *Empire of Signs* (New York: Noonday Press, 1989).

49. Alexandre Kojève (1902–1968), a major French scholar of Hegel.

50. Itoi Shigesato, *Itoi Shigesato no Manryū Kopī Hito Juku* (Tokyo: Bungei Shunjū, 1988). Itoi (b. 1947) has written extensively on the media and popular culture.

51. *Senryū* are pungent and satiric verses, conceived as 5–7–5-syllable stanzas, which were practiced and collected by an Edo writer whose pen name was Kari Senryū (1718–1790).

52. Tanaka Yasuo (b. 1956) won the 1980 Bungei Prize for his novel *Somehow Crystal (Nantonaku Kurisutaru)*.

day. There was a great abundance of books like catalogs of the red-light districts, books on everything related to so-and-so, on how to behave in such-and-such a place, which brands are the good ones and so forth. At one time Masamune Hakuchō[53] called this age "the heaven of idiocy." In any event, in the nineteenth century the Japanese reached the peak of superficiality and frivolity. Until a century ago there were plenty of things that we find fashionable today.

If we want to use the word "light," we can say that words in contemporary literature are light. This lightness has freed itself from the yoke of "meaning." You will not find a writer today, for example, who talks about "self-expression." Until twenty years ago, I think there were people talking about self-expression in literature. Since Kitamura Tōkoku, I believe there were people who hallucinated with self-expression. But this is not a problem with contemporary writers, and no reader would be interested in this topic.

And while I am on the topic of "lightness," let me say that lightness also refers to "the present reality." The word "realism," as the representation of reality, does not exist. I believe that contemporary literature is headed toward a complete denial and contempt for any word that carries the burden of meaning and reality, toward the unmaking of these words, one after another. In the end, they make words extremely light. They make them shallow. They avoid the heavy load of meaning. There are books on the situation of mass-produced images that argue from the perspective of the contemporary consumer society, but there is no other area that has progressed to such an extremity as contemporary Japan with regard to consumerism and information. The West will never become like that.

That is to say, it has been no more than eighty years that words in Japan have been loaded with the heaviness of meaning, truth, and objects. Tōkoku, mentioned earlier, is just an example, but for the first time with modern literature words have been made to carry heavy weights. In the Japanese literature of the nineteenth century words did not carry such a heavy burden. They were empty. In the latter half of the eighteenth century, the literature known as *gesaku*[54] followed this procedure quite self-consciously. Most of the authors of *gesaku* belonged to the school of Ogyū Sorai and, on the one hand, brought with them the consciousness of the intelligentsia. On the other hand, I think they also had an ironically critical consciousness that made them part of a movement which denied that knowledge as parody.

But with the arrival of the Bunka and Bunsei periods, that is, the nineteenth century, this critical consciousness disappeared and simply became light. It simply became *gesaku*. Moreover, the real literature that was not *gesaku*, and was actually against it, also disappeared. I do not know whether the present situation in Japan has reached a similar point. But I do feel that the tension

---

53. Masamune Hakuchō (1879–1962), writer and critic.
54. Popular fiction of the Edo period dealing with worldly matters, humor, and parodies.

we find in modern literature has already gone. Until about 1970, the light consciousness of *gesaku* was pretty much undermined, but with the arrival of the 1980s it has increasingly become of the *gesaku* type.

2

In contemporary Japan, poststructuralism and deconstruction have now become intellectual fads. Of course, I myself have been thinking along similar lines but, in the boom of the recent years, it was inevitable for me to come to think in a different manner. To a certain degree, I have written about this in my *Criticism and the Postmodern.*[55] In that book I problematized the fact that the up-to-date problem of contemporary thought showed itself in the form of poststructuralism as a critique of, to use Derrida's word, "logocentrism." The critique of such Western thought was already present in Japan in a different form and was received, therefore, as an old acquaintance. The most advanced thought in the Western world, on further reflection, was only natural for us Japanese and did not look like anything new. It had already made its appearance in the intellectual genres mentioned earlier.

Even among the various ideologues who were called "the overcomers of modernity" before the war, a good deal of anti-Western thought from the West was absorbed and assimilated. This is a topic that is usually handled with too much ease. Even in today's postmodernism there is a similar tendency. Moreover, seen against the contemporary trend of a world divided into blocs, sooner or later Japanese postmodernism could be considered a reprint of all the opinions expressed in the debate on "overcoming modernity." Yet the people who took part in that debate actually relied on thinkers of the Edo period. For example, as you well know, what we should consider the lifework of Kobayashi Hideo was his *Motoori Norinaga.*[56]

Moreover, some people say that Nishida Kitarō is the only original and systematic philosopher in Japan who has attempted to discuss Zen from the perspective of Western logic. In this sense, however, the Chu Hsi school[57] is more original and systematic. Actually, Nishida's philosophy is similar to the thought of the Chu Hsi school. Both have their point of departure from Zen, and both try to cover all matters. The philosophers of the Edo period tried to criticize the Chu Hsi school, and this took the form of exegesis. Although this critique was not systematic, we cannot say that such attempts were not philosophy or thought. When we think about it, even in the West people do not

---

55. Karatani Kōjin, *Hihyō to Posuto-Modan* (Tokyo: Fukutake Shoten, 1985).

56. Kobayashi Hideo, *Motoori Norinaga* (Tokyo: Shinchōsha, 1982).

57. Shushigaku, or the study of Chu Hsi (1130–1200), was one of the main schools of Neo-Confucianism supported by the shogun during the Edo period. Established by Hayashi Razan (1583–1657), the school included the names of Fujiwara Seika (1561–1619), Kaibara Ekiken (1630–1714), Muro Kyūsō (1658–1734), and Yamazaki Ansai (1618–1682).

think of the works of Vico,[58] Nietzsche,[59] Rousseau,[60] and Kierkegaard[61] as philosophy. Even Marx did not leave a system and, therefore, cannot be classified as a philosopher. And yet no one will think of Thomas Aquinas[62] and Hegel as the only philosophers on earth! People say that the Chu Hsi school is not Japanese, and yet it would have been impossible without the Buddhist philosophy from India and, to say it in different words, without communications in Asia. It was the same with the system of Thomas Aquinas, whose development would have been impossible without Jewish, Greek, and Arabian thought. The notion of originality, in the sense of beginning, is not such a valuable idea. There is no "original" philosophy. They all come from the outside. The same thing applies to the origin of Greek philosophy, which was born out of foreigners and communications in the Mediterranean. The person who actually suppressed this and fixed the origin as fundamental truth was Plato and his metaphysics. This was not only the case with Greece, since it also happened in India and China. There were mutual influences, however, so that Aristotle's thought entered the Buddhist logic of India (causality).

Itō Jinsai says that the "way" *(michi)* is the place where people come and go. This sounds quite banal, and yet it shows exceptional understanding. That is: he brought the notion of "communication" to the explanation of truth and origin (ground). However, he acquired this knowledge from the *Analects.*[63] Therefore, we should avoid thinking in terms of a philosophy that is peculiarly Japanese. This is not the way Edo thinkers thought at the time. Chu Hsi learning was a "worldly" thought, and they wrestled with it head-on. This is the only way in which "originality" is born.

In a sense, the history of Edo thought is nothing but a critique of the rational system known as the Chu Hsi school. Whether "reason" *(ri)* is the equivalent of *logos* remains doubtful and problematic, but the critique of "reason" is thoroughly performed, reaching its final phase in Motoori Norinaga. When

---

58. Giambattista Vico (1668–1744), Italian thinker, is the author of the *New Science* (*La Scienza Nuova,* 1725).

59. Friedrich Wilhelm Nietzsche (1844–1900), German philosopher and poet, is the author, among other works, of *The Birth of Tragedy* (*Die Geburt der Tragödie,* 1872), *Thus Spake Zarathustra* (*Also Spracht Zarathustra,* 1883–1892), *Beyond Good and Evil* (*Jenseits von Gut und Böse,* 1886), and *The Will to Power* (*Der Wille zur Macht,* posthumous).

60. Jean-Jacques Rousseau (1712–1778), French thinker, is the author, among other works, of *Speeches on the Sciences and the Arts* (*Discours sur les Sciences et les Arts,* 1750), *Speeches on the Origin of Inequality* (*Discours sur l'Origine de l'Inégalité,* 1755), *The Social Contract* (*Du Contract Social,* 1762), and *The Confessions* (*Les Confessions,* 1781–1788).

61. Sören Kierkegaard (1813–1855), Danish thinker, is the author, among other works, of *The Concept of Anxiety, Fear and Trembling and The Sickness unto Death,* and *The Concept of Irony.*

62. St. Thomas Aquinas (1224/1225–1274), Christian philosopher from Italy, systematized Latin theology in his *Summa Theologiae* and *Summa Contra Gentiles.*

63. *Lun Yü (Rongo)* or *The Analects of Confucius.* For an English translation see Arthur Waley, trans., *The Analects of Confucius* (New York: Vintage, 1938).

we mention the nativist school, the name of Hirata Atsutane[64] comes up. He moved backward from Norinaga's position in the direction of "reason" once again. This is why I think Norinaga reached the final stop in the critique of Chu Hsi's thought.

Of course, Norinaga's criticism did not come out of the blue. Prior to him, a critique of the Chu Hsi school had already begun with Itō Jinsai and Ogyū Sorai and involved such people as Keichū[65] and Kamo no Mabuchi.[66] Norinaga himself emphasized that he came, not from the Confucian lineage, but from the nativist tradition following Keichū and Mabuchi. But rather than from Mabuchi, he was influenced by Jinsai and Sorai, and so we cannot think of him as belonging only to the nativist genealogy. No matter what, Norinaga also belongs to the group of scholars who critiqued the Chu Hsi school.

The reason behind my long-lasting fascination with the Edo period was the fact that I saw it as a kind of landscape—a landscape where there is no need to think too much of its exterior and whose set linguistic system, which transforms the terminology of its own account, comes easily into view. On the other hand, when attempts were made after Meiji to overturn the previously accepted intellectual tradition, new concepts were promptly borrowed not from the inside but from outside the system. Of course there were circumstances forcing this process. As a result, the epistemological problems that were addressed in the previous tradition were not completely exhausted but suddenly jumped into the new language.

When you read the philosophy of Nishida today, you might feel how different his language is from ours and how hard it is to approach. In fact, Nishida's philosophy continues to live in a much more familiar shape in Marxists such as Kakehashi Akihide[67] and Umemoto Katsumi,[68] as well as in psychopathologists such as Kimura Bin.[69] It is unlikely that today's young peo-

---

64. Hirata Atsutane (1776–1843) studied under the son of Motoori Norinaga, Haruniwa. He argued for the existence of a Japanese written language allegedly predating the introduction of Chinese characters—a proposition that he developed in his *Japanese Writing in the Divine Script* (*Shinji Hifumi Den,* 1819).

65. Keichū (1640–1701) worked extensively on the Japanese classics from a philological point of view. Among other works, he is the author of the *Man'yō Daishōki,* a monumental commentary on the *Ten Thousand Leaves.*

66. Kamo no Mabuchi (1697–1769) is the author of the *Study of the Man'yōshū* (*Man'yō Kō,* 1760–1768), a massive study on the *Ten Thousand Leaves.* He strongly advocated the native cultural heritage, as one can see from his *Study of Our National Temper* (*Kokui Kō,* 1765). For an English translation of the latter by Harry Harootunian, see *Readings in Tokugawa Thought* (Chicago: Center for East Asian Studies, University of Chicago, 1994), pp. 129–148.

67. Kakehashi Akihide (b. 1902), philosopher, is the author of *The Philosophical Category of Matter* (*Busshitsu no Tetsugaku Gainen,* 1959).

68. Umemoto Katsumi (1912–1974) is the author of *Materialism and Man* (*Yuibutsuron to Ningen,* 1947) and *Materialistic Views of History and Morality* (*Yuibutsu Shikan to Dōtoku,* 1949). His *Materialistic Views of History and the Present* (*Yuibutsuron to Gendai,* 1967) became a best-seller and had a profound impact on Japanese Marxist thought in the postwar era.

69. Kimura Bin (b. 1931) is a professor at Kyoto University.

ple will notice the continuity, however. This being the case, the thought of the hundred years following Meiji looks very indistinct. Instead, in the history of Edo thought there is a kind of purity in which you clearly see the shape of thorough battles and the signs of inversions with regard to a single word. This does not mean, however, that at that time Japanese thinkers thought in some sort of isolation. Actually—and in a sense different from today's—Edo thinkers were truly international. They all read Chinese writings on their own, and they all wrote in Chinese. In fact, when the books by Sorai later crossed over to China they were rated as true novelties.

In the world of East Asia, Chinese was the common language, in the same fashion that Latin was for Europe. Therefore, we cannot absolutely speak of isolationism with regard to the intelligentsia of the Edo period. Moreover, in the second half of the eighteenth century, Dutch studies entered Japan with vigor. Even if people could not read the Western books directly, they could rely on Chinese translations. And they thought that the notion of "reason" as it developed in the Chu Hsi school had a global, universal value whether it applied to Japan, China, or India. I think it is important to realize that they premised their discourse on this universality. Norinaga's critique was not locked in some sort of nationalism, but took account of this "globalism."

When we think of the Edo period, we already have some social and economic notions in mind, so that we end up by moving to easy criticisms of the history of Edo thought from our modern perspective. Whenever we exercise our thinking faculties, we necessarily move within a linguistic system and temporarily stand in the "present reality," which is premised on a theoretical system. Therefore, despite our attempts at "looking at reality," if we cannot critique this theoretical system we will never be able to achieve anything. I think we are correct to simplify the matter by saying that knowledge in the Edo period started from the Chu Hsi school. But if we bring in our contemporary perspectives on society and the economy in order to critique the linguistic system of the Chu Hsi school, then we have a problem. And yet it is inevitable for a process of inversion and criticism to start from within some kind of theoretical and linguistic system. Actually, it would not be an exaggeration to say that this is all there is to the matter. Of course, although every single process signifies a real event, there is no immediacy to it.[70]

---

70. This confirms Brett de Bary's critique of Karatani's notion of history: "The notion that modernity cannot be transcended is one rigorously adhered to in this text, in a way that both powerfully informs Karatani's argument and leads it in paradoxical twists. These are paradoxes such as that pointed out to me by an American student reader of Karatani who once asked, gingerly but with unassailable logic, 'If Karatani wishes to reject a linear concept of history, how can he say that there was no concept of interiority in Japanese literature before the third decade of the Meiji period?' This apparent contradiction is inseparable from Karatani's epistemological stance vis-à-vis modernity, which may be best characterized as historicist. In each essay of his book, Karatani seeks to analyze the ideological nature of what have been seen as the simply existing objects (objects which are taken as 'objectively' existing, as Karatani repeatedly asserts, as if they were

Although it looks as if in China Confucianism continued all along, in fact Buddhism and Taoism were dominant until about the tenth century. Against these religions, the Chu Hsi school came out as the peak of the movement that tried to revive the most Confucian elements of Confucianism. A characteristic of the Chu Hsi school, or rather of Confucianism, is the thought that we are in this world. While Buddhism and Taoism are ultraworldly and involve the problems of seclusion and tonsure, Confucianism does not acknowledge the existence of anything outside this world. Accordingly, politics and human relationships become central issues in Confucianism. I believe that Confucianism is this kind of thought. But the Chu Hsi school shows, rather than this Confucian flavor, a strong Buddhist influence, and it became a truly theoretical science.

In Chu Hsi learning, there is a distinction between reason (*li*) and matter (*ch'i*). To make it easy, if we take *li* to mean original principle and *ch'i* to indicate substance, then the material world and the natural world exist and so does a natural law. In that case, for example, although we might call it Newton's law or the law of gravity, where on earth do we find it? Is it located in the natural world or outside? Such a problem commonly surfaces, but it is one difficult to solve. When we think of such a law as reason, then we are faced with the question of whether this reason comes prior to the natural world or after. The Chu Hsi school says "first reason then matter," arguing that reason precedes matter. However—they continue—it does not precede as a result of a split. Reason is a kind of transcendental being, something like an idea that does not reside in the natural world. Rather, they follow a path of integration in which reason, in a sense, is nothing but matter and is comprised of it.

'out there') of modern Japanese literary representation—be it landscape, the inner self, the child, illness—by asking readers to be mindful that what appears to them to be timeless nature in fact has a point of origin, a historicity which has been repressed. Karatani reminds us that young Japanese studying Western oil painting in the early Meiji period, for example, could not in fact 'see' the scenes their Italian teacher, Antonio Fontanesi, sent them out to sketch. . . . Yet Karatani's call for a historicizing awareness must be self-contradictory, for in relativizing modern perspectives or common sense it raises the question of the historical epoch as a 'limit,' a boundary of understanding, beyond which understanding itself cannot penetrate. As a historicist, then, Karatani faces a problem similar to that confronted by Georg Lukacs in his consideration of the relationship between history and consciousness. 'The most basic question to which Lukacs' theory of class consciousness is addressed,' writes Andrew Feenberg, 'concerns whether any vantage point exists *inside* a given culture from which that culture appears, not as a transhistorical limit on consciousness, but as a merely historical stage in the development of consciousness.' . . . Thus, while on the one hand he [Karatani] uses the concept of history and origins to defamiliarize the natural and commonsensical in Japanese modernity, Karatani on the other must insist on the radical unknowability of the other-than-modern. . . . William Haver has lucidly analyzed the reasons for this paradoxical quality of Karatani's historicism by elaborating on Karatani's notion of an inversion, or *tentō,* as the origin of Japanese modernity. Karatani's inversion, Haver notes, presents us with a model of knowing, or 'discovery,' which is doubled, constituted in equal parts of 'blindness and insight.' As Haver writes, 'origin or *kigen* in Karatani's deployments refers both to the originary 'event' of a dialectical *tentō,* and at the same time to the *forgetting* and repression of that event . . . origin as the originary forgetting of one's historicity.'" See Karatani, *Origins of Modern Japanese Literature,* pp. 6–7.

The Chu Hsi school is characterized by the equation of interiority and transcendence—meaning that although heaven and earth are transcendent, at the same time they exist inside humankind. This way of thinking also applies to yoga and Buddhism, and in the West, as well, a mystic such as Eckard[71] argued along the same lines. It is the same with Jung's[72] school of psychology, which argues that beneath the I there is a bigger I. Therefore, by concentrating upon oneself, we tune into the bigger self. To say it differently: self-cognition is the realization of this bigger self within oneself. If we reach toward the world, in other words, we will see that it is grounded in the fact that we are God. Just at that very moment when the Chu Hsi school shows its theoretical strength, it appears to be a method for a training very similar to Zen.

The Chu Hsi school argues that existence is what ought to be. To say that one's actual existence is what ought to be means that one has reached this ideal existence. To put it in a simple form: anyone can become a sage through training. With regard to the sage, they say, "training of the self, order in the country," which is to say that leading a virtuous life corresponds to the management of the state. Such a way of thinking was vehemently attacked by Sorai, who actually ridiculed it. Even today's politicians say they start by first mending their conduct. The same thing happened in the Edo period: when the economy begins to falter, people start taking to frugality. Taking the lead, the lords embarked on policies of thrift. But Sorai understood that such actions do not lead anywhere. In fact, the notion of trying to solve financial hardships by forcing people to feel that, since the lord was exercising frugality, they too should avoid an extravagant lifestyle only results in oppressing the lower classes.

With regard to the physical laws and principles, the physical laws are the principles of things, while principles are the moral law. The "way" is divided into the way of heaven, the way of earth, and the way of man, which are all related to each other like concentric circles. This system is similar to the medieval "chain of being" in the West. The microcosm and the macrocosm become concentric circles, so that the cleansing of the self becomes the cleansing of the world. On the other hand, when the world is in disarray, people too are confused. To rectify the situation, people must cultivate themselves. This is a kind of cosmology, and the Edo period was basically sustained by the cosmology of the Chu Hsi school. This was fitting precisely the class society of Edo, so that lower classes and higher classes, the world and the cosmos, run along parallel lines in concentric circles.

Now, just as a precautionary measure, let me add that we cannot put together the Chinese and Japanese versions of the Chu Hsi school. In the case of China, for example, Chu Hsi and the literati came out of the public examina-

---

71. Johannes Eckard (?1260–1327), also known as "Meister Eckard," was a German Dominican who is regarded as the founder of German mysticism.

72. Carl Gustav Jung (1875–1961), Swiss psychiatrist, is the founder of analytical psychology.

tion system. This system was based on tests leading to the higher civil service—basically continuing from the Tang period until the twentieth century.
Thanks to this system, so long as you were capable you could become a high-
ranking official no matter which social class you came from. This group of government officials were readers of books—literati who formed a new class of
politicians. It was only natural for a group of people who had essentially gone
beyond the class system to think that in man dwelled God.

Their thought was a perfect example of Confucian rationalism. Therefore,
they were extremely critical of folk-religious beliefs in demons and the other-
world. Since "they do not speak of superhuman mental derangements," it was
a rational and progressive group. Even with regard to the physical laws, they
believed in the existence of a "reason" in this natural world and tried to investigate it. A while ago I mentioned only the inner training. But in the Chu
Hsi school there is also much concern with the exploration of the "reasons" behind the natural world.

Today, when we think of Japanese words that include the character for "reason" *(ri)*, we can list the expressions logic *(ronri)*, theory *(genri)*, truth *(shinri)*,
reason *(risei)*, and also argument *(rikutsu)* and principle *(dōri)*. We use the word
"reason" *(ri)* in several different ways. But when we translate these expressions
into English or some other European language, they assume a completely different meaning. On the other hand, when we think of how often we use the
character "reason" *(ri)* in our translations, we understand the tremendous impact that the Chu Hsi school had on Japan and how much of our thinking is
based on the theoretical system of the Chu Hsi school. Therefore, critiques
against the notion of reason as well must be conducted on the whole with regard to different situations.

3

Before presenting a critique of the notion of reason, I want to explain the differences between the Chinese and the Japanese Chu Hsi schools of thought.

In the case of Japan, research within the Chu Hsi school was not carried out
by a class of readers who were chosen according to an examination system that
was open to everyone, as in the case with China. The research of the Chu Hsi
school in Japan was premised on the need to establish a theory that would
strengthen the legitimacy and structure of personal political power within the
Tokugawa shogunate, which had come to power through military might.
Moreover, the Chu Hsi school had entered Japan prior to the Edo period. In
the background of the Kenmu Restoration of Emperor Go-Daigo there was the
influence of the Chu Hsi school,[73] which also informed the *Chronicle of Direct*

---

73. With the short-lived Kenmu Restoration (1334–1336), Go-Daigo (1288–1339) attempted to recover political power from the Kamakura *bakufu* run by the Hōjō regents.

Descent of Gods and Sovereigns (Jinnō Shōtōki), written by Kitabatake Chikafusa at that time.[74] These were people, excited by the Chu Hsi school, who started promoting direct imperial rule. These people—Kitabatake Chikafusa above all—struggled to interpret the continuity of Japanese history with the concept of legitimacy, and as a result they came up with the idea of the emperor's direct involvement in the affairs of state.

This thought did not come out of Japan, however. Go-Daigo's personal rule of the Kenmu years came out suddenly—as in the case of the abrupt excitement following the reading of Marxist works. It is difficult to explain the eighty years of the Northern and Southern courts from the perspective of those times. Perhaps everyone read works of the Chu Hsi school and lost their mind. Of course—just as in the beginning of the Shōwa period, when everybody in the intelligentsia converted to Marxism, there were actually contradictions in the labor movement and in capitalism—there was also a base sustaining the Kenmu Restoration. I believe that the leading role, however, was played by ideas. For people at the center of power, the establishment of a rational ground upon which to legitimize changes of political power was a major problem. In Japan, in order to explain this well, the emperor is constantly invoked. A theoretical formulation of the problem occurred at the time of the Kenmu Restoration, and it was grounded in the Chu Hsi school of thought.

Usually people say that the cult of the emperor is an outcome of the nativist school, but this is a mistake. Although the slogan "revere the emperor and expel the barbarians" originally came from the Mito school,[75] for example, the Mito school was part of the Chu Hsi school. The Chu Hsi school used the image of the emperor in order to theorize the legitimacy of the *bakufu* by showing that the shogun was "the emperor's shogun." For them, reverence for the emperor was merely a formal issue. The anti-*bakufu* clique simply reversed the trick. Without the Chu Hsi school, there would not have been the cult of a "single, eternal imperial line." Sorai and Norinaga were critical of this kind of Chu Hsi school and, therefore, even in Norinaga's case, they have no relationship with the notions of imperial reverence and the expulsion of foreign ideas from Japan. "To revere the emperor and expel the barbarians" is, rather, the thought behind the orthodox Chu Hsi school.

Even if we consider Chu Hsi learning a philosophy imported in order to sustain the Tokugawa system, since Japan at the time was a feudal society, the the-

---

74. Kitabatake Chikafusa (1293–1354), historian of Emperor Go-Daigo's Southern Court, explained in the *Jinnō Shōtōki* (1339) the legitimacy of the Southern Court in order to challenge the legitimacy of the Northern Court set up by the new shogun, Ashikaga Takauji. For an English translation see H. Paul Varley, trans., *A Chronicle of Gods and Sovereigns: Jinnō Shōtōki by Kitabatake Chikafusa* (New York: Columbia University Press, 1980).

75. *Mitogaku* was an Edo school of thought that originated in the Mito domain with Tokugawa Mitsukuni. A combination of nativist, Shinto, and Neo-Confucian thought, the school was very influential on the protagonists of the Meiji Restoration.

oretical discourse and the people who actually lived in that reality hardly matched. The notions that humankind was originally related to the universe, and that transcendence dwelled within people, were acceptable to people who, like the Chinese, were selected equally according to their intellectual skills. They were inadequate to a society, like Tokugawa society, that was based on social status. To people like Jinsai and Sorai, the details of Chu Hsi thought must have smelled of deception. Since the soldier achieves his power by military might, Chu Hsi thought and the military class do not match. Especially for someone like Jinsai, who started his life as a merchant, it was only natural that Chu Hsi thought would look alien. I believe that people like him were quite aware of the gap between words and their life. Because of this gap, it would be impossible to expect them to explain this thought from a point of view grounded in reality.

The greatness of Itō Jinsai lies in the facts that his philosophy is not based on his life and that his critique of the Chu Hsi system of learning was carried on from within that system. From the very beginning, the Chu Hsi system was limited by the fact that although some of its elements did indeed work in Japan, others could not absolutely match the reality of those times. A critique of the school's notion of reason had to be conducted from within the system, and we can say that Jinsai started this debate.

So far as I can judge from my readings, there have been two tendencies in the study of the history of Edo thought. The most representative work is Maruyama Masao's *Studies in the History of Japan's Political Thought*.[76] In this book Maruyama attaches great importance to Sorai and proceeds from the viewpoint that Sorai's antirational attitude paved the way to Japanese modernity—thus arguing that modernity appeared in Japan as a critique of the rationalism of the Chu Hsi school. A diametrically opposite view has strongly made its way, however, and has actually become the general trend. Representative of this latter view is Minamoto Ryōen,[77] who advocates the birth of Japanese modernity using precisely the rationalism of the Chu Hsi school. Maruyama Masao followed the Hegelian method of dialectics by first positing the presence of the Chu Hsi school from which later came an oppositional movement. But as Maruyama himself stated later, the Chu Hsi school actually began to spread from Jinsai. That is to say, rather than positing a Chu Hsi school at the beginning, against which an oppositional movement followed later, we should say that Chu Hsi scholars absorbed Jinsai and Sorai in some form. To a certain degree, the Chu Hsi school was flexible to change. In the same way, people involved in Dutch studies were mostly members of the Chu Hsi school—for example, Arai Hakuseki,[78] whose rationalism is breathtaking

---

76. Maruyama Masao, *Nihon Seiji Shisōshi Kenkyū* (Tokyo: Tokyo Daigaku Shuppankai, 1952).

77. See, for example, Minamoto Ryōen, *Tokugawa Gōri Shisō no Keifu* (Tokyo: Chūō Kōronsha, 1972).

78. Arai Hakuseki (1657–1725), scholar, poet in Chinese, historian, autobiographer, and political figure, is the author of *Seiyō Kibun* (Hearing about the West, 1715) and a famous autobiography, *Oritaku Shiba no Ki* (Told Round a Brushwood Fire, ca. 1716–1717).

even from today's point of view. Arai Hakuseki was a contemporary of Sorai but also, politically speaking, a rival.

At the end of the shogunate, after Arai Hakuseki, figures such as Sakuma Shōzan[79] appear, who tried to understand Western science within the framework of the Chu Hsi school. For example, he used Neo-Confucian terminology to express the notion of physics. As we can see from his Japanese translations of Western terms, he assimilated Western science by starting from the premise, shared by Chu Hsi scholars, that this world is rational. From this comes Sakuma Shōzan's famous slogan: "Japanese spirit and Western technology." I think that this dichotomy between "the Yamato spirit" and "Western skills" is still alive in contemporary Japan. This explains the boldness shown by the Japanese with regard to science and technology, as well as their readiness to develop these sciences with no hesitation. For example, Japanese scholars are the most radical when it comes to biology and the study of life. Essentially the Japanese feel well at ease in situations in which a mixture of "skills" and "spirit" usually causes great anxiety. Probably this is another extension of the Japanese version of Chu Hsi learning.

Of course, the fact that rationalism enabled the development of the natural sciences applies to the West as well. We can say it with regard to both Descartes and Bacon.[80] Bacon is generally known for his inductionism and empiricism but, strictly speaking, he also tacitly started from the premise that truth exists in this natural world, manifesting itself. At the base of Western rationalism is the belief that truth exists in this world, as well as the fact that our inability to see the truth, which should be essentially visible, depends on our ignorance. This belief has sustained the development of Western science, and it is also related to the theories on revolution. The main thrust of vulgar Marxism is that deception on the part of a selfish agent must be removed in order to restore the truth. I think we should use the word "faith" to describe the notion that truth is at the root of this world and that this truth has the potential of being thought and realized.

According to the medieval thinker Thomas Aquinas, faith is reason. Rationality and belief are united in one body. Contrary to this thought is the transcendentalization of God on the part of the Protestants, following their claim that faith cannot be attained by reason. In the same fashion, even in the critiques of the Japanese Chu Hsi school, people like Jinsai cut the link between interiority and transcendence. To the claim made by the Chu Hsi school that anyone can become a sage, Jinsai opposed the view that the sage is more than man. That is, he emphasized the need to transcend the equation of interiority and transcendence. This move was common to both East and

79. Sakuma Shōzan (1811–1864) advocated the experimental methodology of the West and the adoption in Japan of Western technological skills.

80. Francis Bacon (1561–1626) presented his theory of scientific method in the *Novum Organum* (1620).

West, and, in this sense, we should compare the work of Jinsai with the work of Luther.[81]

I shall return to this point later, but I think we can say that the critique of the Chu Hsi school was a critique of the belief that reason—that is, truth, theory, and human reason—dwell within humankind. However, the critique of the Chu Hsi school did not start from "speculation." Both Maruyama Masao and Minamoto Ryōen address the problem only from a philosophical standpoint. When this approach does not work, they try to explain the issues by grafting their explanations onto "reality."

4

Well, the three scholars Jinsai, Sorai, and Norinaga began their criticism of the Chi Hsi school from the perspective of "textuality." For Jinsai, the theory of the Chu Hsi school was not of great concern. The only important thing was *The Analects.* Earlier I said that Jinsai can be compared to Luther, and actually Luther as well was not concerned with Catholic doctrine. He emphasized, rather, "a return to the Bible."

There is a sentence that is always quoted when explaining Jinsai. It comes from one of the Five Classics and Four Books,[82] *The Great Learning:* "The feeling of sympathy is the edge of humaneness."[83] "The feeling of sympathy" means to feel pity for others, to sympathize with them, to feel somebody else's pain. "Humaneness" corresponds to love, but "the edge of humaneness" in the Chu Hsi school indicates "the appearance of humaneness." Namely, there is an essence known as "humaneness" and a manifestation known as "edge." Against this interpretation of the Chu Hsi school, Jinsai argued that humaneness cannot be located somewhere from the beginning and, moreover, that "the edge of humaneness" is "the beginning of humaneness." In real life, for example, when someone is on verge of dying, the action of offering help without even thinking about it is the beginning of humaneness—"the edge of humaneness"—and this humaneness does not exist as reason.

Against the thought that the essence comes first and then emerges as appearance, Jinsai presented the view that first you have action, and, as a result, this becomes reason. He realized that no matter how much you turn upside down the notion of "first reason then matter," arguing instead for "first mat-

---

81. Martin Luther (1483–1546) led the Reformation in Germany.

82. The Five Classics: *Book of History, Book of Odes, Book of Rites, Book of Changes,* and *Spring and Autumn Annals.* The Four Books: *Analects of Confucius, Book of Mencius, Great Learning,* and *Doctrine of the Mean.*

83. In fact this quotation comes from the *Book of Mencius.* "This feeling of distress (at the suffering of others) is the first sign of Humanity. This feeling of shame and disgrace is the first sign of Justice. This feeling of deference to others is the first sign of propriety. This sense of right and wrong is the first sign of wisdom. Men have these four innate feelings just as they have four limbs." See W. A. C. H. Dobson, trans., *Mencius* (Toronto: University of Toronto Press, 1963), p. 132.

ter then reason," you are still simply transforming idealism into materialism. This was not a true reversal. Kaibara Ekiken[84] carried out the proposition "first matter then reason," but he could not change the dichotomous and oppositional structure of reason and matter. On the other hand, Jinsai realized that no matter whether you opt for "first reason then matter" or for "first matter then reason," this is still a purely theoretical issue after all. To the field of theory and the field of philosophical research, he opposed the field of "practice." Moreover, Jinsai bracketed both the way of heaven and the way of earth, subsuming them under "the way of man." In other words: He focused on the relationships between people. His method is similar to Kant's dialectics, but with Jinsai you can equally say that the world has a beginning and that it does not. Or, realizing that humanity cannot answer such problems, Jinsai rejected the idea of pursuing the "reason" of heaven and earth.

The Chu Hsi school acknowledges the existence of an original principle and investigates "physical laws." But Jinsai thought it was a mistake to hypothesize arbitrarily such a "reason," and thus he preferred to focus on the study of "the human way." Rather than addressing original principle and theory with another theory, he privileged practice. He did not simply deny "reason." Nor did he argue about which came first, the idea or matter, since these were nothing but theoretical speculations. What is truly important for Jinsai is practice: action. For Jinsai, Confucianism is "virtuous behavior," certain action for sure. Moreover, the "way" does not exist as a "principle" but is a "coming and going," that is, "communication."

In the Chu Hsi school, as I mentioned earlier, "reason" dwells in every single human being, and so too does transcendence. To say it differently: Every single human being is originally endowed, to use a Buddhist expression, with Buddha nature—everybody is a buddha. In a humanistic form of Christianity, as in the case of Hegel, every single human being is a god. To say it in Chinese fashion, every single human being is originally a sage. Accordingly, anyone with the proper training can reach the stage of sagehood. As a result, in the case of Buddhism, there is no longer need for the historical Buddha, since everybody is a buddha. Personally, however, I do not really believe this. An other known as the Buddha, or Jesus, must actually exist; but if we take every human being to be originally a buddha or a god, the historical Jesus and Buddha become unnecessary.

It is the same thing with the Chu Hsi school, which was originally Zen. When we speak of Buddhism with regard to China, we speak of Zen, which included the Pure Land school. The Chu Hsi school was a critique of Zen seen from the viewpoint of Confucianism. Nevertheless, the system of the Chu Hsi

---

84. Kaibara Ekiken (1630–1714) wrote works on botany, history, natural history, philology, and education. He expressed doubts about the Chu Hsi school in his *Taigiroku* (Record of Major Doubts, 1714). For an English translation see Martin Pierce Griggs, trans., "*Taigiroku* by Kaibara Ekiken," in *Readings in Tokugawa Thought* (Chicago: Center for East Asian Studies, University of Chicago, 1994), pp. 69–97.

school shares basically the same structure with Zen. Therefore, we do not need a person such as Confucius. The Chu Hsi school has no need for the historical Confucius. Accordingly, *The Analects* simply belong to the intellectual system known as the Chu Hsi school, and they are simply commented upon. Confucius is merely the person who pronounced them, and nothing more.

If I had to sum up Jinsai's critique of the Chu Hsi school, I would say that it is the discovery of transcendence, or exteriority. By this I do not mean that he transcended God or heaven, since this had already been done by the Chu Hsi school. To explain the notion of transcendence as truly seen by Jinsai, I would simply call it the "other." He read the "real nature" of the Chu Hsi school as "what is given by birth." Now, "what is given by birth" differs in each person. Although Mencius said that "human nature is good," Confucius simply called it "affinity." Wittgenstein[85] used the words "family resemblance," meaning that the similarities are of the degree found in the likeness among family members. Although one looks like the other, there is nothing in common—which is to say that human nature involves the presence of many and different elements given by birth. We cannot say that in each human being we find the same "reason," or "nature," or "good."

After all, what Jinsai saw as transcendence or exteriority was the realization that the "other" was simply different from himself. It was an "other" that could absolutely not be identified with the self. For the Chu Hsi school, "human nature" is the essence and "human passions" are phenomena. Therefore "humaneness" was "human nature," while "love" was "a human passion." To love a person as an expression of passion was still considered an immature stage, since people were required to love in a deeper sense as an expression of "humaneness." Jinsai thought there was no such essence called love, however, nor the "idea" of love. Neither was there something called "humaneness." The only thing that actually existed was love. In fact, he argued that the actual love which was so deeply despised by the Chu Hsi school, the real, concrete, love, was actually the beginning and the end. There was no "humaneness" beyond that love, which was belittled as a simple start. I think that Jinsai took as his central problem this relationship with the "other."

Jinsai—and the same thing can be said with regard to Chu Hsi—was originally a practitioner of Zen and, like the Chu Hsi school, started from the outset with the "heart." That is, his inquiry began from a person's internal state. From there he proceeded to think about the difficulties of enlightenment, as well as the procedure of how to reach it. This is nothing but Zen. However, he realized that this internal state did not exist. Jinsai realized that we are posited in a relationship with the other, and this other is never the same as us. In other words: Between us and the other there is not the same *logos*.

---

85. Ludwig Josef Johann Wittgenstein (1889–1951) is the author of the *Tractatus Logico-Philosophicus* (1922).

Jinsai located language exactly in this place of heterogeneous communication. If there were a "reason" in man from the beginning, he could do without education since he could realize everything by himself. This is why, in the Chu Hsi school, the "*teachings* of Confucius" are needless. Instead, Jinsai emphasized the importance of precisely "Confucius' teachings." When we communicate in this world of heterogeneous relationships, "the teachings of Confucius" are what provide us with sameness. For Jinsai, therefore, Confucius is a sage but not in the sense that everybody can become a sage—rather, a sage as "an absolute other." It would be something like Jesus in Christianity. For Jinsai, people prior to Confucius were not sages.

The situation is different with Sorai, who placed Confucius at the end of the line of sages (ancient kings). For Jinsai, Confucius was the only sage. In Confucianism, even people who lived prior to Confucius are called sages. Jinsai emphasized the meaning of the appearance of the sage known as Confucius, however, arguing that we should pay attention to what unfolded with his appearance or, to use his words, "love." If the Chu Hsi school or any other theoretical system posits the uselessness of the sage, then there is no way to understand the meaning of what comes with the appearance of the sage. This is the critique that Jinsai brought to the Chu Hsi school.

To go back to my original point, it is important to remember that the occasion for Jinsai—as it was for Sorai and Norinaga—to think along these lines actually came from his reading *The Analects.* This might sound a little bit too concrete, but when one learns to read writings in Chinese *(kanbun),* he depends on the return marks that allow him to read the text in the correct order—just as is done today. However, it was essential for both Jinsai and Sorai to stop that practice. By transliterating Chinese into Japanese, one has the feeling of actually reading the Chinese text, but that is not really Chinese or Japanese. The transliteration of the Chinese text is a midway solution upon which we tend somehow to agree. Sorai read directly, using Chinese pronunciations, and even studied with Chinese teachers. In any event, such a sensibility toward language was actually the starting point for Jinsai.

The linguistic theory of Jinsai is generally neglected, however, since it is not clearly expressed. Maruyama Masao stresses the interiority and subjectivity of Jinsai, arguing that Sorai came out with a system and a language of externality that go well beyond Jinsai's. There is no doubt that Maruyama is correct with regard to Sorai, who provided a clear methodology for language. Whenever Sorai taught *kanbun* to a student, for example, he never explained the meaning of the text from the beginning. First of all, he had the student read the text in Chinese until the student could not take it any longer. In the meantime, the student learned the Chinese pronunciations and started understanding the text's meaning.

Even when Sorai read *The Analects,* he did not begin by clearly defining the meaning of each word as the Chu Hsi scholars did. He felt it was not enough to read only *The Analects.* He thought people should also examine the literature and other documents of the same age, as well as those of previous and later ages. By getting used to those expressions, one finally had the feeling of what was written in *The Analects*. Rather than trying to define the meaning of words, one was asked to first of all erase "meaning." To use the words of Wittgenstein, one experiences the use of language. Although he did not clearly state it methodologically, Jinsai was already proceeding along these lines. Jinsai differed from Sorai in that he dealt with *The Analects* as if they were completely dissimilar from earlier and later texts. He thought that the words of *The Analects* were the peak of expression, unmatched in ancient and modern times. What did he mean by this?

As you can easily notice when reading *The Analects,* you find many inconsistencies in terms of the content. The reason is that *The Analects* take the form of answers by Confucius to statements by different people, so that the content is determined by the context established at the time of the discussion. A sentence such as "A friend coming from afar, isn't that delightful?," for example, does not make any sense unless we understand the context. I think the meaning lies in the joy of discovering that someone aspires to the same things we do and thinks the same way we do. And yet, no matter how hard you concentrate on the words, you cannot come up with a correct interpretation. It is as if at a certain time, all of a sudden, Confucius' words come clear for an instant. It is the same with the Bible, where Jesus' words are always addressed to an other within a specific context. If you take them as fragments and decontextualize them, then the statements become mutually contradictory and cannot be collected into the doctrine known as Christianity. They would be extremely heterogeneous with regard to the theology of Thomas Aquinas.

What Jinsai noticed in the words of *The Analects* was their "dialogic character." This, of course, is different from Plato's "dialogue." If we take dialogue in its Platonic sense, then we mean a dialogue between like-minded persons, who share something in common, since it would be a dialogue with an other who possesses the same *logos* that I possess. As we can see from the expression "common search" that Plato put in Socrates' mouth, Plato's dialogue with the other, after all, is nothing but a dialogue with himself. Hence rather than a dialogue, we should talk of a "monologue," since "dialogue" implies a meeting with an other, that is, someone who is different from us. More than anything else, *The Analects* are this kind of "dialogue." On the other hand, *Mencius* is a monologue in the form of a dialogue, easy for scholars to understand.

It is important to remember that Jinsai's school was this kind of "dialogue"—a school in the form of a seminar that rejected the stiff relationship of teacher and student. This is something that did not exist in the Edo period, of course, and perhaps does not exist even today. Since Sorai simply lectured in a one-sided way, he was like the other Chu Hsi scholars. We can say that the linguistic theory of Jinsai shows in his way of approaching *The Analects,* as well as in his teaching methodology. Scholars of political science such as Maruyama Masao simply do not understand this.

Therefore, we can say that with Jinsai the act of "reading" finally began. Jinsai understood that the meaning of words is not established by definitions but surfaces gradually from the practical use of words. Jinsai wrote a book in the format of an elucidation of words, but this came after thirty or forty years of dialogues with his students (although I should not use this word). Actually, Jinsai's understanding of Confucius was based on extreme contextualization, always inquiring as to whom Confucius was addressing when saying something, or when being unwilling to say it, or unwilling to answer.

5

So far I have been talking mainly about Jinsai. Next I would like to turn to Sorai and to Norinaga.

As I mentioned earlier, Jinsai is a very interesting figure when seen in his individuality. But when we line up Jinsai, Sorai, and Norinaga, all of a sudden our interest for Jinsai disappears. The same thing happens when we rank Kant, Hegel, Marx, and Kierkegaard; in this case Kant is simply reduced to the person who came first, and Hegel becomes the one before Marx. When we take them as individuals, however, reading the actual texts written by Kant and Hegel, we realize how tremendously fascinating they are. Planning to work on Norinaga, I started with Jinsai and felt that he was becoming increasingly interesting. Then I also felt that Sorai was interesting, but not in the sense meant by Maruyama Masao. I think it is a mistake when intellectual historians line up people in a historical sequence and then argue about them. To speak in such historical terms, it becomes a kind of intellectual history deprived of content. By following Jinsai in his methodology of reading texts, however, we find in Jinsai's writings a completely different kind of fascination.

Jinsai's denial of "reason" is, in this case, a denial of the meaning that conceals the Text. I think that contemporary criticism actually comes from this kind of literature and exegetical works. Even in the case of Derrida,[86] when he deals with the problem of *écriture,* "Text" should essentially be written in capital letters. For by Text Derrida means the Bible, particularly the New Testament. You often hear the slogan "Free the text," but this is not what a Text is.

So long as we do not realize that everything is in the Text, it is impossible to free the Text from meaning. In order to do so, you need a belief. You cannot critique the theoretical system of the Chu Hsi school that encloses *The Analects* unless you think that *The Analects* are authentic and that everything has been written in *The Analects.* Therefore, the Text is not an option, but it must be a Text in capital letters. After concealing the Text in capital letters,

---

86. Jacques Derrida (b. 1930), French philosopher, is a major representative of the deconstructionist school. He is the author of, among other works, *L'Écriture et la Différence* (Writing and Difference, 1967), *De la Grammatologie* (Of Grammatology, 1967), *Marges de la Philosophie* (Margins of Philosophy, 1972), *La Dissémination* (Dissemination, 1972), and *La Vérité en Peinture* (Truth in Painting, 1978).

Derrida tacitly includes this meaning in the notion of *écriture*. In this sense, it was very important for Jinsai to proceed in his critique of "reason" by making *The Analects* into a Text and by thinking that everything was included in it. I think I can go so far as to say that the most valuable thing in the thought of the Edo period was Jinsai's discovery of the Text in this sense.

Jinsai did not care about the "matter" of "the way of heaven" and "the way of earth." To repeat: He only problematized "the human way," or "the way of man." He discovered the "way" in the relationship with the other, or in the love for the other. This is not a subjective move. Sorai, however, found the "way" in the social system or in politics. Sorai saw in the outside system the "way" as it was built by the ancient sage-kings of China, and he criticized Jinsai for leaning too much toward interiority in a Buddhist fashion. This, however, was clearly not the case. Conversely, the morality that we find in Jinsai disappears from Sorai's discourse on politics. To say it differently: He deprived *The Analects* of their only chance of ever becoming a world religion.

Sorai argued that humaneness and love are not ethical problems at all or problems related to interiority. He said that humaneness is a way of governing the country and pacifying its people. Maruyama Masao evaluated Sorai in terms of his bringing about a feeling of political responsibility and political ethics. Macchiavelli[87] said it is not important for a ruler to be a moral person so long as he looks moral, and for Sorai as well this kind of political ethics was important. He said that it does not matter whether a ruler is an ethically good or bad person as an individual. No matter how deeply he studies Confucianism, what makes a politician is his ability to actually run the country and provide the people with peace.

At the time of Sorai, the shogun was the infamous Tokugawa Tsunayoshi, also known as "The Dog Shogun,"[88] a strange fellow who personally lectured on Confucianism. Since it was the lord who lectured, all the retainers were forced to listen. The shogun must have thought himself to be a good lecturer, but for the retainers it was certainly an inconvenience. It was the same with his ordinances on the protection of animals (the Edicts on Compassion for Living Things), which must have made Tsunayoshi proud of his morality. The actual effects that these ordinances had on his people were disastrous, however, and contrary to the image of the moral ruler. Therefore, a criticism of such behavior on Tsunayoshi's part was certainly included in Sorai's thought. Nothing is more distressful than a moral leader. In this sense, according to Maruya-

---

87. Niccolò Macchiavelli (1469–1527), political theorist, is the author of *Il Principe* (The Prince, 1513), a treatise on statecraft.

88. Tokugawa Tsunayoshi (1646–1709), the fifth Tokugawa shogun, ruled from 1680 to 1709. He drew criticism by promulgating from 1685 onward the highly unpopular "Edicts on Compassion for Living Things," which ordained the death sentence for killing a dog. This earned him the sobriquet "The Dog Shogun."

ma Masao's evaluation of Sorai, Sorai's concern for a political system that was free of moral considerations, focused on interiority, marked the beginning of modern thought.

Sorai's thought is different from Macchiavelli's, however, as well as from Han Fei Tzu's.[89] We must not forget that he was a Confucian and, therefore, politics was rigidly grounded in rites. To forget this—and to consider Sorai the patriarch of modern political science—is a double mistake because it tends to forget, as Maruyama did, that the Confucian political system includes insights related to humans and human desire.

The Chu Hsi school often used the expression "leave human desire and follow the rules of heaven." When he uses the word "desire," I think that Sorai really means "passions." In the Chu Hsi school, human desires are urges kept inside an isolated human being. Consequently—they think—it is possible to reach "the brightness of the mirror and the stillness of water" by rejecting those urges through knowledge and training. But as Hegel pointed out, passions are desires for an other and always require the mediation of an other. In this sense, if we mean urges within an isolated person, we might possibly overcome them. On the other hand, since passions always imply a relationship with the other, they cannot be overcome by training. Moreover, to be passionate is not a problem of personal freedom and responsibility.

To be more precise, Sorai wrote about these views in his *Political Discourses.* At that time, during the Genroku period, in Edo, whether you were a soldier or a farmer, everybody imitated the merchants. Everyone left for Edo, so that the city population expanded enormously. Not only did the status of each individual become obscure, but everybody followed the current fashions, increasingly indulging in lavish lifestyles. The passions and desires of that age took on a shape that could not be grasped by the Chu Hsi school. This trend further developed in the Bunka and Bunsei periods, but the "passions" of a consumer society clearly started to appear in the Genroku era. The status society did not show any resistance to these developments. This might be related to the permeation of a monetary economy, in which there was no room for the oppositional dualism of human desire and the rules of heaven as postulated by the Chu Hsi school. The conflictual phenomenon of someone else's desire, or desire mediated by others, spread well beyond the status society. As a result, it invited economical difficulties to Edo. Which position did Sorai take on this issue?

The heterogeneity between Sorai's political thought and the legalist followers of Han Fei Tzu stemmed mainly from Sorai's belief that politics is related to rites—that is, to etiquette and music. For Sorai "humaneness" was not a problem of "love," as Jinsai had put it, but had everything to do with polit-

---

89. Han Fei Tzu (d. 233 B.C.), Chinese philosopher of the legalist school, according to whom a state must be governed by the union of authority, methods, and laws.

ical skills. Sorai argued that the ancient sages had created these skills through the ages. What kinds of skills did he mean exactly? He meant the "rites," not the laws or punishments. To say it even more concretely: Since rites take the form of etiquette, I could further simplify the matter by saying that they defined difference by form. For Sorai the Genroku period witnessed the disappearance of human difference. While speaking about status, people were actually moved by someone else's desire, and in practice everyone was doing the same thing. This created a tremendous conflictual phenomenon whose power could not be stopped even though it was bringing the feudal system to bankruptcy. This might have been good for merchants, but it inevitably forced the Tokugawa system to face the crisis of collapse.

How could this crisis be controlled? By restoring "etiquette." In order to check this process of equalization, which came to be incessantly encouraged by a reciprocally conflictual difference, there was no other way than to establish an "etiquette" suitable to a status society. Sorai thought that with the establishment of this "etiquette" it was possible to curb the progress of a consumer society. That did not work out well, of course, and it could not work out.

I believe that Sorai thought there is nothing inside us which allows us to regulate ourselves and that the only constraints could come from the system of rites. To urge someone, commanding him to curb his desires, is futile. This simply creates the difference that puts desire in motion, putting an end to equalization, and thus eliciting the opposite effect. Consequently, politics should not appeal to the interiority and the morality of the single individual, but should be carried out as a technique, a system from the outside. I think that this looks deceptively similar to modern political science.

6

Since I am bringing my talk to a conclusion, I might sound biased in what I am going to say. But looking at the issue from the perspective of the critique of "reason," I believe that Norinaga brought a sense of closure to the positions of Jinsai and Sorai. The works of Jinsai and Sorai centered on the Four Books and the Five Classics, starting with *The Analects*. On the other hand, Norinaga's Text was mainly literature: the *Kojiki,* the *Genji Monogatari,* or, basically, Japanese poetry *(waka)*.

To use the traditional classification of reason, feelings, and will, Jinsai did not problematize the realm of reason, that is, theory and truth or falsehood, privileging instead the realm of the will. (Of course, we should say that Jinsai worked from within a different realm of knowledge from the realm that was made of knowledge, feelings, and will.) In any event, I think that Jinsai tried to think from within the realm of the will—or, to use the classification of truth, good, and beauty, the realm of good. He was quite indifferent to the realms of feelings and beauty, however. Although he dealt with literature, when it came to the evaluation of beauty he often followed a logic that adhered strictly to "reason." It was the same with Mabuchi.[90]

Now, the reason behind the importance attributed to poetry ever since the ancient past was that poetry sang the "true heart" of people. And since it gave voice to the true heart, poetry was thought to move the heart of the gods. This had already been mentioned by Ki no Tsurayuki in his preface to the *Kokinshū*.[91] During the Edo period, seventeenth-century scholars such as Kagawa Kageki[92] and Kamo no Mabuchi explained the fascination of poetry in terms of its ability to express the sincerity of our true feelings. Jinsai did not think there was a "true heart," of course, yet he defended literature inasmuch as it expressed people's sincere feelings.

This is something that you hear repeated even today, for example, in the method of understanding the literary text in terms of circumstances—as when you hear that a text "grasps the situation well." In this case, the situation is the truth. It follows, then, that the excellence of the fiction known as literature depends on its ability to show the truth. Here, after all, literature is in the service of sincerity and truth. People defending literature and poetry also support the idea that literature actualizes the truth, although in a different way from philosophy, or that it actualizes the truth exactly because it is literature.

With Norinaga, however, things are completely different. What was the true heart for Norinaga? It was not an adulterous heart, of course, or a vicious heart. He never defined the true heart by indicating something specific. Rather, he wanted to smash the very differentiation between "what is true and what is false," which was housed in the true heart. It was the same with Jinsai and Sorai. They too criticized the thought that words are in the service of truth and reason. But with Norinaga, the critique took a different direction.

Earlier I mentioned the categories of reason, feelings, and will. Norinaga privileged the realm of feelings. He used the words "to know the pathos of things," and this was the realm of the emotions. Whether they are passions or emotions, in philosophy these things must usually be controlled. Namely, moralists problematize the method of controlling their passions. On the other hand, Norinaga criticized the thought that feelings are located outside the sphere of reason and must always be restrained by reason. Hence the famous expression "to know the pathos of things." This does not mean "to know things" or "there is pathos"—although, of course, "to know the pathos of things" is itself a form of knowledge. It is not a knowledge of the kind that comes from recognizing an object or differentiating between truth and falsehood, however, or good and evil. It is basically aesthetic.

---

90. Kamo no Mabuchi (1697–1769).

91. Ki no Tsurayuki (ca. 872–945), poet, critic, and diarist, is the main compiler of the *Collection of the Poems of Yesterday and Today* (*Kokinshū*, 905).

92. Kagawa Kageki (1768–1843) was actually an eighteenth- and nineteenth-century *waka* poet and critic who composed the collection *Keien Isshi* (A Shoot from the Judas-Tree Garden, 1830).

Norinaga acknowledged the presence of reason in the realm of feelings, which he thought to be even more primeval than truth and good. In Norinaga's "knowing the pathos of things," the pathos *(aware)* does not simply refer to sadness. It also indicates a kind of emotion, an experience of something that goes deeper than the usual realm of epistemology. Norinaga reduced "the pure experience" that precedes cognitive judgment to the expression "to know the *pathos* of things."

In a sense, by using the expressions "the world of the gods" and "the ancient way" Norinaga transposed into a Japanese context the teachings of Sorai. Yet in these expressions there is a realization that goes beyond not only truth and falsehood but also good and evil. He said that when someone dies, for example, he goes to the land of the Yellow Springs whether he was a virtuous or a wicked person. Here we have a contradiction that cannot be helped. What he meant, however, was that it is wrong to think of death only in terms of sadness, to justify it arbitrarily according to the notions of good and evil, and thus waiting for mercy in the other world. Norinaga disavowed this attitude, calling it "Buddhist-like" and "Chinese-like."

Originally we live thinking that death is simply sad, and all the rest is only theory. And yet when something does not match the theory, we feel a sense of absurdity and come out with ideas such as "the last judgment" in order to dispose of the difficulty. Actually, Hirata Atsutane, who came after Norinaga, imported Christianity into Shintoism, so that people went to paradise or hell according to their goodness or wickedness. Again, there was a fall into dualisms.

The sense in which Norinaga uses the verb "to know" in "to know the pathos of things" is different from what is generally meant and goes into a much deeper level of human consciousness. This level is "the other shore of good and evil," that is, the way of the gods, which we must know. Of course, Norinaga does not talk about it theoretically. Rather, he uses a close exegetical reading and explanation of the Text. He carries out his criticism by avoiding the question, "what is reason?," thus bringing to the limits the line of questioning initiated by Jinsai.

Maruyama Masao provided the analogies of Jinsai being like Kant, and Sorai like Hegel, but I would say that Jinsai was like Kierkegaard, Sorai like Marx, and Norinaga like Nietzsche. Nietzsche studied Greek philology and tried to uncover an "ancient way" with it, a way that was prior to Christianity and to Platonism. He took a critical stance against Platonic reason (philosophy) by locating cognition in the depth of "tragedy" in *The Birth of Tragedy*. In this sense, we can say that Norinaga is similar to Nietzsche.

Although it goes without saying that I am critical of Norinaga, I have talked repeatedly about this matter on other occasions. What I want to say today is a warning against simply disavowing or mocking him. Today we can count on the knowledge of new ideas, but this does not mean that people in the Edo period did not think. In a sense, their intellectual development and search took the form of an unparalleled thoroughness and ineluctability. Shouldn't this be an encouragement for us?

Although in the West the critique of philosophy comes from within the field of philosophy itself, such a critique is usually conducted from the outside fields of religion and the arts. This is done by bringing in the notion of the other as transcendence, which philosophy discards. This was Kierkegaard's criticism of Hegel. But this was also the case with atheism. Marx, for example, in *Capital,* brought the asymmetric relationship of money (god) and commodity (man) into the world of "sameness" of classical economy. As for the critique from the realm of the arts (beauty), probably Nietzsche is the most representative example. From this point of view, we can also easily see it in the deconstruction of philosophy (the Chu Hsi school) on the part of Jinsai, Sorai, and Motoori.

In today's lecture I wanted everybody to be aware of these problems. I am delighted if some interest was raised that might lead to further research on your part. Here I shall end my talk.

GLOSSARY

ametsuchi no shirabe 天地の調べ

araware 現象

ashi 惡シ

Ashihara no Nakatsukuni 葦原の中国

awaremu 愛 (to love)

awaremu 憐 (to feel for someone)

aya 文

basho 場所

bi 美

Bi to wa Nani zo ya 美とは何ぞや (What Is Beauty?)

bigaku 美学

bijutsu 美術

Bijutsu Shinsetsu 美術説 (True Conception of the Fine Arts)

Bikan ni Tsuite no Kansatsu 美感に就いての観察 (Observations on Aesthetic Pleasure)

bimyōgaku 美妙学

Bimyōgaku Setsu 美妙学説 (Theory of Aesthetics)

biteki bunka 美的文化

biteki hanchū 美的範疇

biteki seikatsu 美的生活

Biteki Seikatsu wo Ronzu 美的生活を論ず (Debate on the Aesthetic Life)

bun 文

bunpō 文法

busshitsu 物質

butsuri 物理

chi 知

chiteki bunka 知的文化

dai 大

dōtoku no sei 道徳の性

Edo no Chūshakugaku to Genzai 江戸の注釈学と現在 (Edo Exegesis and the Present)

egoteki 回互的

eitan 詠歎

enbi 婉美

fūdo 風土

Fūga Ron: Sabi no Kenkyū 風雅論——さびの研究 (On *Refinement:* A Study on *Sabi*)

Fujitani Mitsue 富士谷御杖

Fukada Yasukazu 深田康算

ga 雅

geijutsu 芸術

Geijutsu Keishiki to Shite no Mikanseiteki na Mono 芸術形式としての未完成的なもの (Incompleteness as Artistic Form)

genjitsu 現実

gen-ninshō 原人称

genshō 現象

genso 元素

genzen 現前

gijutsu 技術

Haga Yaichi 芳賀矢一

hana 花

Hihyō Kūkan 批評空間 (Critical Space)

hirenzoku 非連続

Hisamatsu Sen'ichi 久松潜一

hito 他者

hō 法

hōben 方便

hōgen 法眼

hokkai 法界

hōsoku 法則

hōunji 法雲地

Hyakugaku Renkan 百学連環 (Encyclopedia)

Hyakuichi Shinron 百一新論 (New Theory of the One Hundred and One)

i 意
ichidai genso 一大元素
idō seibun 異同成文
Iki no Kōzō いきの構造 (The Structure of *Iki*)
ikō 移行
Imamichi Tomonobu 今道友信
inshō 印象
in'yu 因由
Ishi Bigaku 維氏美学 (The Aesthetics of Mr. V.)
ishiki 意識
itami 痛み
ji 辞
jikaku 自覚
jinbun 人文
jinen no shirabe 自然の調
jinen no sugata 自然の姿
jitsuzai 実在
Jōdōe 成道会
jodōshi 助動詞
joshi 助詞
jūji 十地
jutsugo 述語
kagaku 化学
Kagaku Teiyō 歌学提要 (Summary of Poetics)
Kagami no Naka no Nihongo 鏡の中の日本語 (Japanese Inside the Mirror)
Kagawa Kageki 香川景樹
kage 影
kage 陰/蔭
kagyakusei 可逆性
Kamen no Kaishakugaku 仮面の解釈学 (The Hermeneutics of Masks)
kan 感
Kanbishin to Nikukan 観美心と肉感 (The Heart of External Beauty and Physical Sensation)
kandō 感動
Kanga-kai 鑑画会
kanjō 感情
kanju 感受

kannen 観念
Kanō Naganobu 狩野栄信
Kanō Osanobu 狩野養信
kanzen chōaku 観善懲悪
Karatani Kōjin 柄谷行人
kashuron 佳趣論
kata 方 (direction)
kata 型 (pattern)
katachinaki sugata かたちなき姿
katachinaki tokoro かたちなき所
Katō Chikage 加藤千蔭
Kawase Hideharu 河瀬秀治
kawayushi 怜ユシ
Keichū 契沖
Keijijōgakuteki Tachiba kara Mita Tōzai Kodai no Bunka Keitai 形而上学的立場から見た東西古代の文化形熊 (The Forms of Culture of the Classical Periods of East and West Seen from a Metaphysical Perspective)
Kejō 化成
ki-itsu 帰一
Kikuchi Dairoku 菊地大麗
kimi/hito 君/臣
Kinsei Bigaku 近世美学 (Modern Aesthetics)
Kinsei Bigaku Shisō Ippan 近世美学思想一斑 (Outline of Modern Aesthetic Thought)
kireji 切れ字
ko 虚
kō 好
kobetsuka 個別化
Kōbu Bijutsu Gakkō 工部美術学校
kokoro 意
kokū 虚空
koto 言
koto 事
kotoba 神語
kotonari 事成り
kotonari/sa-i 差異
kū 空
Kū to Soku 空と即 (Emptiness and Sameness)

Kuki Shūzō　九鬼周造
Kusanagi Masao　草薙正夫
kyakkan　客観
magokoro　誠実
makoto no omote　真の面
Man'yōshū no Shizen Kanjō　万葉集の
　自然感情 (Feelings Toward Nature
　in the *Man'yōshū*)
mono　物
Mori Ōgai　森鷗外
mu　無
muichimotsu　無一物
mujō　無常
mumei no shūgōteki na tōitsu no kinō
　無名の集合的な統一の機能
mushō　無生
myōsō　妙想
myōtai　妙体
Nakae Chōmin　中江兆民
Nenokuni　根の国
Nihon Bijutsu Kyōkai　日本美術協会
Nihon Geijutsu no Rinen　日本芸術の
　理念 (The Concept of Japanese Art)
Nihon Kaiga no Mirai　日本繪画の未
　來 (The Future of Japanese Painting)
Nihon Kodai Bungaku ni Okeru Bi no Ruikei
　日本古代文学における美の類
　型 (Patterns of Beauty in Ancient
　Japanese Literature)
Niimanabi Iken　新学異見 (A Different
　Opinion on New Learning)
nikushi　憎シ
ningen　人間
nin-jō　人長
ninjō　人情
Nishi Amane　西周
Nishida Kitarō　西田幾多郎
Nishitani Keiji　西谷啓治
nō　能
nori　法
noru　宣る
Okakura Kakuzō (Tenshin)　岡倉覚
　三 (天信)

okashi　可笑シ
omo　重
omofu　思ふ
Ōmori Ichū　大森惟中
omoshiroshi　面白シ
omote　表
omotsuhe　面つ方
omoya　母屋
Ōnishi Hajime (Sōzan)　大西祝 (操山)
Ōnishi Yoshinori　大西克禮
onozukara　おのづから
oshie　教
Ōtsuka Yasuji　大塚保治
rekishi　歴史
ri　理
riken no ken　離見の見
ryōshin　良心
Ryūchikai　龍池会
saigenzenka　再現前化
sainō　才の男
Sakabe Megumi　坂部恵
sakai　境界
Sangai　三界
Sano Tsunetami　佐野常民
san'ya kaihin ni toji　山野海浜に投じ
sei　正
seigi no kankaku　正義の感覚
seimei ishiki　生命意識
seiryakujō kansetsu no mokuteki　政略上
　間接ノ目的
shan mei liang ueng　善美能良
shigaku　詩学
shiki soku zekū, kū soku zeshiki　色即是
　空, 空即是色
Shimamura Hōgetsu　島村抱月
shime　標
shimenawa　標縄
Shinbi Kōryō　審美綱領 (Outline of
　Aesthetics)
Shinbi Ron　審美論 (Theory of Aes-
　thetics)
Shinbiteki Kankan wo Ronzu　審美的感
　官を論ず (On Aesthetic Senses)
shinjin　身心

shinjin ichinyo   心身一如
shinri   心理
shirabe   調
shiru   知る
shiru   領る
shirushi   徴/標
shirushi   著し
shirushi   標
shisō   思想
shō   小
Shōbōgenzō   正法眼蔵
shōji   初地
Shōsetsu Shinzui   小説神髄 (Essence of the Novel)
shoyūken   所有権
shugo   主語
shukan   主観
shutai   主体
sōgosei   相互性
soko   底
soku   即
sōzōryoku   想像力
sugao   素顔
sujime   痕跡
sumu   住 (to live)
sumu   澄 (to become clear)
Ta Hsüe   大学 (The Great Learning)
taiken   体験
Takamanohara   高天原
Takayama Chogyū   高山樗牛
takumeru ga gotoku, kazareru ga gotoku   巧めるが如く飾れるが如く
tanoshi   楽シ
ten'i   転移
teniwoha   てにをは
tetsugaku   哲学
Toyama Masakazu   外山正一
Tōyōteki Geijutsu Seishin   東洋的芸術精神 (Artistic Spirit of the East)
Tsubouchi Shōyō   坪内逍遥
tsumi no naki sayō   罪ノ無キ作用

Tsunashima Ryōsen   綱島梁川
Uji   有時
ura   裏
ureshi   嬉シ
ushinron   有心論
utsuri   映り
utsuri   移り
utsushi   現し/顕し
utsushimi   うつし身
utsutsu   現
Waka ni Shūkyō Nashi   和歌に宗教なし (There Is No Religion in *Waka*)
waki   脇 (deuteragonist)
waki   分き (interpretation)
Watsuji Tetsurō   和辻哲郎
wokashi   可笑し (comic)
wokashi   犯し (transgression)
wu hu   嗚呼
yojō   余情
yojōbi   余情美
Yōjō no Ronri   余情の論理 (The Logic of Passional Surplus)
yojō yōen   余情妖艶
yorokobashi   悦シ
yoshi   善シ
yū   有
yūen   優婉
yūgenbi   幽玄美
Yūgen to Aware   幽玄とあはれ (*Yūgen* and *Aware*)
yume   夢
yumegokochi   夢心地
yū soku mu, mu soku yū   有即無, 無即有
Zeami   世阿弥
zen   善
zenbigaku   善美学
zenbi nōkō   善美能好
Zen no Kenkyū   善の研究 (The Study of Good)
zoku   俗

CHRONOLOGY

1818 Birth of Antonio Fontanesi.
1825 Birth of Eugène Véron.
1828 Birth of Hippolyte Taine.
1829 Birth of Nishi Amane.
1834 Birth of Fukuzawa Yukichi.
      Birth of Theodor Fechner.
1841 Birth of Antonio Ragusa.
1842 Birth of Karl Robert Eduard von Hartmann.
1843 Death of Hirata Atsutane.
1844 Birth of Friedrich Wilhelm Nietzsche.
1847 Birth of Nakae Chōmin.
1848 Birth of Toyama Masakazu.
      Birth of Johannes Volkelt.
1851 Birth of Theodor Lipps.
1853 Birth of Vincent van Gogh.
      Birth of Ernest Fenollosa.
1854 Birth of Jean-Marie Guyau.
1855 Birth of Kikuchi Dairoku.
1858 Birth of Tsubouchi Shōyō.
1859 Birth of Henry-Louis Bergson.
1862 Birth of Mori Ōgai.
      Birth of Okakura Tenshin.
1863 Birth of George Santayana.
1864 Birth of Ōnishi Hajime.
      Birth of Futabatei Shimei.
1865 *Philosophy of Art* by Hippolyte Taine.
1867 Birth of Haga Yaichi.
      Birth of Natsume Sōseki.
1868 Birth of Ōtsuka Yasuji.
      Birth of Kitamura Tōkoku.
      Geschichte der Ästhetik in Deutschland (History of Aesthetics in Germany) by R. H.
        Lotze.
1869 *Philosophy of the Unconscious* by Eduard von Hartmann.

1870 Nishi Amane translates Joseph Haven's *Mental Philosophy: Including the Intellect,
     Sensibilities, and Will* (1857). The translation, *Shinrigaku* (Psychology), is completed
     in 1871.

1871 Birth of Nishida Kitarō.
     Birth of Shimamura Hōgetsu.
     Birth of Takayama Chogyū.

1872 The word *"bijutsu"* is used to translate "art" in the Japanese catalog for the exhibit of
     the 1873 Vienna Exposition.
     Die Geburt der Tragödie (The Birth of Tragedy) by Friedrich Wilhelm Nietzsche.
     Kritische Geschichte der Ästhetik (Critical History of Aesthetics) by M. Schasler.

1873 Birth of Tsunashima Ryōsen.

1874 *Outlines of the World's History, Ancient, Medieval, and Modern, with Special Relation to the
     History of Civilization and the Progress of Mankind* by William Swinton.

1875 Birth of Carl Gustav Jung.

1876 *Vorschule der Ästhetik* (Elementary Course in Aesthetics) by Theodor Fechner.
     Foundation of the Kōbu Bijutsu Gakkō (Technological Art School) in Tokyo.

1877 *Bimyōgaku Setsu* (Theory of Aesthetics) by Nishi Amane (published in 1907).
     Physiological Aesthetics by Grant Allen (1848–1899).

1878 *L'Esthétique* by Eugène Véron.
     Ernest Fenollosa reaches Japan.

1879 Birth of Nagai Kafū.
     Formation of the Ryūchikai (Dragon Pond Society).
     Shūji Oyobi Kabun (Rhetoric and Belles Lettres) by Kikuchi Dairoku—translation of an
     anonymous article from Chambers' *Encyclopedia*, edited by Robert and William
     Chambers between 1859 and 1868.

1882 Death of Antonio Fontanesi.
     Death of Ralph Waldo Emerson.
     Bijutsu Shinsetsu (True Conception of the Fine Arts) by Ōmori Ichū from a lecture of
     Ernest Fenollosa.

1883 Birth of Karl Jaspers.
     Nakae Chōmin translates as *Ishi Bigaku* (The Aesthetics of Mr. V.) Eugène Véron's
     L'Esthétique (first volume).
     Also Spracht Zarathustra (Thus Spake Zarathustra) by Friedrich Wilhelm Nietzsche
     (completed in 1892).

1884 Nakae Chōmin translates as *Ishi Bigaku* (The Aesthetics of Mr. V.) Eugène Véron's
     L'Esthétique (second volume).
     Foundation of the Kanga-kai (Painting Appreciation Society).
     L'Esthétique Contemporaine (Contemporary Aesthetics) by Jean-Marie Guyau.

1885 *Shōsetsu Shinzui* (Essence of the Novel) by Tsubouchi Shōyō.

1886 *Bi to wa Nani zo ya* (What Is Beauty?) by Tsubouchi Shōyō.
     Jenseits von Gut und Böse (Beyond Good and Evil) by Friedrich Wilhelm Nietzsche.
     Ästhetik (Aesthetics) by Eduard von Hartmann (completed in 1887).
     Grundzüge der Wissenschaft des Schönen und der Kunst (Basic Elements of the Science of
     the Beautiful and of Art) by Max Schasler.
     George William Knox (1853–1912) teaches aesthetics at Tokyo Imperial University.

1887 Death of Theodor Fechner.
     The Ryūchikai is renamed Nihon Bijutsu Kyōkai (Japanese Art Society).
     Waka ni Shūkyō Nashi (There Is No Religion in *Waka*) by Ōnishi Hajime.

Ludwig Busse (1862–1907) teaches aesthetics at Tokyo Imperial University until 1892.

L'Art au Point de Vue Sociologique (Art from the Sociological Point of View) by Jean-Marie Guyau.

Philosophie des Schönen (Philosophy of Beauty) by Eduard von Hartmann.

1888 Death of Jean-Marie Guyau.

Bijutsu to Shūkyō (Art and Religion), by Ōnishi Hajime.

Birth of Ōnishi Yoshinori.

Birth of Kuki Shūzō.

1889 Death of Eugène Véron.

Birth of Martin Heidegger.

Birth of Watsuji Tetsurō.

The Kōbu Bijutsu Gakkō is renamed the Tokyo Bijutsu Gakkō (Tokyo Art School).

1890 Death of Vincent van Gogh.

Nihon Kaiga no Mirai (The Future of Japanese Painting) by Toyama Masakazu.

1891 Dispute between Mori Ōgai and Tsubouchi Shōyō about "submerged ideas" (*botsurisō*)—continues until 1892.

1892 *Einleitung in die Ästhetik* (Introduction to Aesthetics) by Karl Groos (1861–1946).

Shinbi Ron (Theory of Aesthectics) by Mori Ōgai—a partial translation of Eduard von Hartmann's *Philosophie des Schönen* (Philosophy of the Beautiful), which Mori continued until 1895.

1893 Death of Hippolyte Taine.

Raphael von Koeber (1848–1923) teaches aesthetics at Tokyo Imperial University until 1914.

1894 Death of Kitamura Tōkoku.

Birth of Hisamatsu Sen'ichi.

1895 *Kanbishin to Nikukan* (The Heart of External Beauty and Physical Sensation) by Ōnishi Hajime.

Shinbiteki Kankan wo Ronzu (On Aesthetic Senses) by Ōnishi Hajime.

Aesthetic Principles by Henry R. Marshall (1852–1927).

Ästhetische Zeitfragen (Aesthetic Questions) by Johannes Volkelt.

1896 *The Sense of Beauty* by George Santayana.

1897 Death of Nishi Amane.

Kinsei Bigaku Shisō Ippan (Outline of Modern Aesthetic Thought) by Ōnishi Hajime.

1898 Takayama Chogyū replaces Ōnishi Hajime as lecturer of aesthetics at Waseda University.

1899 Birth of Kawabata Yasunari.

Shinbi Kōryō (Outline of Aesthetics) by Mori Ōgai together with Ōmura Seigai (1868–1927).

Kinsei Bigaku (Modern Aesthetics) by Takayama Chogyū—based on Max Schasler's (1819–1879) *Kritische Geschichte der Ästhetik* (Critical History of Aesthetics) and Robert Zimmermann's (1824–1898) *Geschichte der Ästhetik als Philosophischer Wissenschaft* (History of Aesthetics as Philosophical Science).

1900 Death of Toyama Masakazu.

Death of Ōnishi Hajime.

Death of Friedrich Wilhelm Nietzsche.

Birth of Nishitani Keiji.

Birth of Kusanagi Masao.

Appointment of Ōtsuka Yasuji to the first Chair of Aesthetics at Tokyo Imperial
University. He will keep the chair until his retirement in 1929.

Bikan ni Tsuite no Kansatsu (Observations on Aesthetic Pleasure) by Takayama Chogyū.

Shinbi Kyokuchi Ron (Treatise on What Is Highest in Aesthetics) by Mori Ōgai—
translation of Otto Liebman's *Zur Analyse der Wirklichkeit: Eine Erörterung der
Grundproblem der Philosophie* (On the Analysis of Reality: Articulation of the Basic
Problems of Philosophy, 1876).

1901   Death of Nakae Chōmin.

Death of Fukuzawa Yukichi.

Biteki Seikatsu wo Ronzu (Debate on the Aesthetic Life) by Takayama Chogyū.

1902   Death of Takayama Chogyū.

Birth of Kobayashi Hideo.

Shinbi Kashō Ron (Treatise on Aesthetic Appearance) by Mori Ōgai—partial translation
of Karl Groos' *Einleitung in der Aesthetik* (Introduction to Aesthetics).

1903   *The Ideals of the East* by Okakura Tenshin.

Leitfaden der Psychologie (Guide to Psychology) by Theodor Lipps.

Ästhetik (Aesthetics) by Theodor Lipps—completed in 1906.

1905   Birth of Jean-Paul Sartre.

System der Ästhetik (System of the Aesthetic) by Johannes Volkelt—completed in 1914.

1906   Death of Karl Robert Eduard von Hartmann.

Ästhetik und Allgemeine Kunstwissenschaft (Aesthetics and General Art-Science) by
M. Dessoir.

1907   Death of Tsunashima Ryōsen.

Birth of Kamei Katsuichirō.

1908   Death of Ernest F. Fenollosa.

Birth of Maurice Merleau-Ponty.

1909   Death of Futabatei Shimei.

1910   Birth of Yasuda Yojūrō.

Appointment of Fukada Yasukazu to the first Chair of Aesthetics at Kyoto Imperial
University.

1911   *Zen no Kenkyū* (The Study of Good) by Nishida Kitarō.

1912   *Epochs of Chinese and Japanese Art* by Ernest Fenollosa.

1913   Death of Okakura Tenshin.

1914   Death of Theodor Lipps.

1916   Death of Natsume Sōseki.

1917   Death of Kikuchi Dairoku.

1918   Death of Shimamura Hōgestu.

1922   Death of Mori Ōgai.

Birth of Imamichi Tomonobu.

Beiträge zur Phänomenologie des Äesthetischen Genusses (Phenomenology of Aesthetic
Appreciation) by Moritz Geiger (1880–1937).

1923   *Geijutsu to Dōtoku (Art and Morality)* by Nishida Kitarō.

1926   *Iki no Kōzō* (The Structure of *Iki*) by Kuki Shūzō (published in 1930).

1927   Death of Haga Yaichi.

Hataraku Mono kara Miru Mono e (From Acting to Seeing) by Nishida Kitarō.

1928   Death of Antonio Ragusa.

Die Psychische Bedeutung der Kunst (The Psychic Meaning of the Arts) by Moritz Geiger.

1930   Death of Johannes Volkelt.

1931 Death of Ōtsuka Yasuji.
1935 Death of Tsubouchi Shōyō.
      Gūzensei no Mondai (The Problem of the Accidental) by Kuki Shūzō.
1936 Birth of Sakabe Megumi.
      Birth of Gianni Vattimo.
1939 *Yūgen to Aware (Yūgen* and *Aware)* by Ōnishi Yoshinori.
1940 *Fūga Ron: Sabi no Kenkyū* (On Refinement: A Study on *Sabi*) by Ōnishi Yoshinori.
1941 Death of Kuki Shūzō.
      Death of Henry-Louis Bergson.
      Birth of Karatani Kōjin.
1943 *Man'yōshū no Shizen Kanjō* (Feelings Toward Nature in the *Man'yōshū*) by Ōnishi
      Yoshinori.
1945 Death of Nishida Kitarō.
1952 Death of George Santayana.
1953 *Nihon Kodai Bungaku ni Okeru Bi no Ruikei* (Paterns of Beauty in Ancient Japanese
      Literature) by Hisamatsu Sen'ichi.
1959 Death of Ōnishi Yoshinori.
      Death of Nagai Kafū.
      Bigaku (Aesthetics) by Ōnishi Yoshinori (first volume).
1960 Death of Watsuji Tetsurō.
      Bigaku (Aesthetics) by Ōnishi Yoshinori (second volume).
1961 Death of Maurice Merleau-Ponty.
      Death of Carl Gustav Jung.
1966 Death of Kamei Katsuichirō.
1967 *Nihon Geijutsu no Rinen* (The Concept of Japanese Art) by Kusanagi Masao.
1968 Imamichi Tomonobu is appointed professor of aesthetics at the University of Tokyo.
      He retires in 1983.
1969 Death of Karl Jaspers.
1972 Death of Kawabata Yasunari.
      Yojō no Ronri (The Logic of Passional Surplus) by Kusanagi Masao.
1973 *Yūgenbi no Bigaku* (The Aesthetics of the Beauty of *Yūgen*) by Kusanagi Masao.
      Bi ni Tsuite (On Beauty) by Imamichi Tomonobu.
1976 Death of Hisamatsu Sen'ichi.
      Death of Martin Heidegger.
      Kamen no Kaishakugaku (The Hermeneutics of Masks) by Sakabe Megumi.
1980 Death of Jean-Paul Sartre.
      Nihon Kindai Bungaku no Kigen (Origins of Modern Japanese Literature) by Karatani
      Kōjin.
1981 Death of Yasuda Yojūrō.
1983 Death of Kobayashi Hideo.
1988 *Tōyōteki Geijutsu Seishin* (The Artistic Spirit of the East) by Ōnishi Yoshinori.
1989 *Kagami no Naka no Nihongo* (Japanese Inside the Mirror) by Sakabe Megumi.
1990 Death of Nishitani Keiji.

BIBLIOGRAPHY

LIST OF ABBREVIATIONS

BMS	*Bijutsu Meicho Sensho*
CR	*Chikuma Raiburarī*
GBS	*Gendai Bigaku Sōsho*
GNBZ	*Gendai Nihon Bungaku Zenshū*
KGB	*Kōdansha Gakujutsu Bunko*
KGS	*Kōdansha Gendai Shinsho*
KT	*Kanshi Taikei*
MBZ	*Meiji Bungaku Zenshū*
NKBT	*Nihon Koten Bungaku Taikei*
NKBZ	*Nihon Koten Bungaku Zenshū*
NKST	*Nihon Kindai Shisō Taikei*
NST	*Nihon Shisō Taikei*
SKT	*Shinshaku Kanbun Taikei*
SNKBT	*Shin Nihon Koten Bungaku Taikei*
SNKS	*Shinchō Nihon Koten Shūsei*

WORKS IN JAPANESE

Amagasaki Akira. *Kachō no Tsukai: Uta no Michi no Shigaku. GBS* 7. Tokyo: Keisō Shobō, 1983.

Aoki Shigeru and Sakai Tadayasu, eds. *Bijutsu. NKST* 17. Tokyo: Iwanami Shoten, 1989.

Hanawa Hokinoichi, ed. *Zoku Gunsho Ruijū,* vol. 19. Tokyo: Zoku Gunsho Ruijū Kanseikai, 1912.

Higuchi Yoshimaro et al., eds. *Chūsei Waka Shū: Kamakura Hen. SNKBT* 46. Tokyo: Iwanami Shoten, 1991.

Hijikata Teiichi. *Kindai Nihon Bungaku Hyōron Shi.* Tokyo: Hōsei Daigaku Shuppankyoku, 1973.

———, ed. *Meiji Geijutsu, Bungaku Ronshū. MBZ* 79. Tokyo: Chikuma Shobō, 1975.

Hino Tatsuo. *Motoori Norinaga Shū. SNKS* 60. Tokyo: Shinchōsha, 1983.

Hirata Toshihiro. "Yawarakai Sakabe Tetsugaku." *Risō* 646 (1990): 67–75.

Hisamatsu Sen'ichi. *Nihon Bungaku Hyōron Shi: Kinsei Kindai Hen.* Tokyo: Shibundō, 1952.

Hisamatsu Sen'ichi and Nishio Minoru, eds. *Karonshū, Nōgakuronshū. NKBT* 65. Tokyo: Iwanami Shoten, 1961.

Hoshikawa Kyotaka, ed. *Koshigen, Ge. KT* 5. Tokyo: Shūeisha, 1965.

Ijichi Tetsuo, Omote Akira, and Kuriyama Riichi, eds. *Rengaronshū, Nōgakuronshū, Haironshū. NKBZ* 51. Tokyo: Shōgakukan, 1973.

Imamichi Tomonobu. *Bi ni Tsuite.* Tokyo: Kōdansha, 1973.

———. *Eco-Ethica: Seiken Rinrigaku Nyūmon.* Tokyo: Kōdansha, 1990.

———, ed. *Kōza Bigaku.* 5 vols. Tokyo: Tokyo Daigaku Shuppan Kai, 1984–1985.

Imazeki Tenpō and Karashima Takeshi, eds. *Sōshi Sen. KT* 16. Tokyo: Shūeisha, 1966.

Ishikawa Jun, ed. *Motoori Norinaga.* Nihon no Meicho 21. Tokyo: Chūō Kōron Sha, 1984.

Isoda Kōichi. "Okakura Tenshin: Sono Rekishiteki Ichi wo Megutte." *Nihon no Bigaku* 1(4) (Spring 1985).

Kambayashi Tsunemichi, ed. *Nihon no Bi no Katachi.* Kyoto: Sekai Shisō Sha, 1991.

Kaneda Tamio. *Nihon Kindai Bigaku Josetsu.* Kyoto: Hōritsu Bunka Sha, 1990.

Karatani Kōjin. "Bigaku no Kōyō: *Orientarizumu* Igo." *Hihyō Kūkan* 2(14) (1997).

———. "Bijutsukan to Shite no Nihon: Okakura Tenshin to Fenorosa." *Hihyō Kūkan* 2(1) (1994).

———. *Hihyō to Posuto-Modan.* Tokyo: Fukutake Shoten, 1985.

———. *Kotoba to Higeki.* Tokyo: Daisanbunmeisha, 1989.

Kidō Saizō, ed. *Tsurezuregusa. SNKS* 10. Tokyo: Shinchōsha, 1977.

Kitamura Tōkoku. *Tōkoku Zenshū,* vol. 1. Tokyo: Iwanami Shoten, 1950.

Kobayashi Hideo. *Motoori Norinaga.* Tokyo: Shinchōsha, 1982.

Kon Eizō, ed. *Bashō Kushū. SNKS* 51. Tokyo: Shinchōsha, 1982.

Kubota Jun, ed. *Senzai Waka Shū.* Tokyo: Iwanami Shoten, 1986.

———. *Shinkokin Waka Shū, Ge. SNKS* 30. Tokyo: Shinchōsha, 1979.

Kubota Jun and Kawamura Teruo, eds. *Gappon Hachidaishū.* Tokyo: Miyai Shoten, 1986.

Kuki Shūzō. *Iki no Kōzō.* Tokyo: Iwanami Shoten, 1979.

Kusanagi Masao. *Yūgenbi no Bigaku.* Tokyo: Hanawa Shobō, 1973.

Marra, Michele. "Yowaki Shii: Kaishakugaku no Mirai wo Minagara (Weak Thought: A Look at the Future of Hermeneutics)." *Nichibunken Forum* 95 (1997).

Maruyama Masao. *Nihon Seiji Shisōshi Kenkyū.* Tokyo: Tokyo Daigaku Shuppan Kai, 1952.

Mekada Makoto. *Tōshisen. SKT* 19. Tokyo: Meiji Shoin, 1988.

Minami Hiroshi. *Nihonjin Ron: Meiji kara Kyō made.* Tokyo: Iwanami Shoten, 1994.

Minamoto Ryōen. *Tokugawa Gōri Shisō no Keifu.* Tokyo: Chūō Kōronsha, 1972.

Mori Rintarō. *Ōgai Zenshū,* vol. 23. Tokyo: Iwanami Shoten, 1973.

Morioka Kenji, ed. *Kindaigo no Seiritsu: Goi Hen.* Tokyo: Meiji Shoin, 1990.

Nakamura Toshisada, ed. *Kōhon Bashō Zenshū,* vol. 5: *Renku Hen, Ge.* Tokyo: Kadokawa Shoten, 1968.

Nakamura Yukihiko, ed. *Kinsei Bungaku Ronshū. NKBT* 94. Tokyo: Iwanami Shoten, 1966.

Nakao Tatsurō. *Sui, Tsū, Iki: Edo no Bi Ishiki Kō.* Tokyo: Miyai Shoten, 1984.

Nishida Kitarō. *Ippansha no Jikakuteki Taikei.* Tokyo: Iwanami Shoten, 1929.

———. *Nishida Kitarō Zenshū,* vol. 7. Tokyo: Iwanami Shoten, 1965.

Nishitani Keiji. *Nishitani Keiji Chosaku Shū,* vol. 13. Tokyo: Sōbunsha, 1987.

Okazaki Yoshie. *Geijutsu Ron no Tankyū.* Tokyo: Kōbundō, 1941.

Ōkubo Tadashi, ed. *Motoori Norinaga Zenshū,* vol. 8. Tokyo: Chikuma Shobō, 1972.

Ōkubo Toshiaki, ed. *Nishi Amane Zenshū,* 2. Tokyo: Munetaka Shobō, 1960.

Okumura Tsuneya, ed. *Kokin Waka Shū. SNKS* 19. Tokyo: Shinchōsha, 1978.

Ōnishi Hajime. *Ōnishi Hakase Zenshū.* 7 vols. Tokyo: Nihon Kokusho Sentā, 1982.

Ōnishi Yoshinori. *Bigaku,* vol. 2: *Biteki Hanchū Ron.* Tokyo: Kōbundō, 1960.

———. *Yūgen to Aware.* Tokyo: Iwanami Shoten, 1939.

Ono Susumu, Satake Akihiro, and Maeda Kingorō, eds. *Iwanami Kogo Jiten.* Tokyo: Iwanami Shoten, 1974.

Orikuchi Shinobu. *Orikuchi Shinobu Zenshū,* vol. 2: *Kodai Kenkyū (Minzoku Gakuhen,* vol. 1). Tokyo: Chūō Kōronsha, 1975.

Oyama Tokujirō, ed. *Saigyō Zenshū.* Tokyo: Gogatsu Shobō, 1978.

Saigō Nobutsuna, ed. *Nihon Bungaku Kōza,* vol. 1: *Hōhō to Shiten.* Tokyo: Nihon Bungaku Kyōkai, 1987.

Sakabe Megumi. *Kagami no Naka no Nihongo: Sono Shikō no Shujusō. CR* 22. Tokyo: Chikuma Shobō, 1989.

———. *Kamen no Kaishakugaku.* Tokyo: Tokyo Daigaku Shuppan Kai, 1976.

Sakazaki Shizuka, ed. *Nihon Garon Taikan,* vol. 1. Tokyo: Arusu, 1927.

———. *Nihonga no Seishin.* Tokyo: Tōkyōdō, 1942.

Sasaki Ken'ichi. *Bigaku Jiten.* Tokyo: Tokyo Daigaku Shuppan Kai, 1995.

Satō Dōshin. *Nihon Bijutsu Tanjō: Kindai Nihon no "Kotoba" to Senryaku.* Tokyo: Kōdansha, 1996.

Shida Nobuyoshi. "Hisamatsu Sen'ichi: Bungaku Shi to Bungaku Hyōron Shi." *Kokubungaku: Kaishaku to Kanshō* 57(8) (1992).

Shimamoto Haruo. "Ishi Bigaku to Nakae Atsusuke." In *Meiji Bunka Zenshū,* add. 1. Tokyo: Nihon Hyōronsha, 1970.

Shumoru, J. A., ed. *Geijutsu ni Okeru Mikansei. BMS* 17. Tokyo: Iwazaki Bijutsu Sha, 1971.

Takayama Chogyū Shū, Anezaki Chōfū Shū, Sasakawa Rinpū Shū. GNBZ 13. Tokyo: Kaizōsha, 1956.

Takayama Rinjirō. *Chogyū Zenshū,* vol. 1: *Bigaku Oyobi Bijutsu Shi.* Tokyo: Hakubunkan, 1914.

Takeuchi Toshio, ed. *Bigaku Jiten.* Tokyo: Kōbundō, 1974.

Tanaka Yutaka, ed. *Zeami Geijutsu Ronshū. SNKS* 4. Tokyo: Shinchōsha, 1976.

Tokieda Motoki. *Kokugogaku Genron: Gengo Kateisetsu no Seiritsu to Sono Tenkai.* Tokyo: Iwanami Shoten, 1941.

Watanabe Kazuyasu. *Meiji Shisō Shi: Jukyōteki Dentō to Kindai Ninshiki Ron.* Tokyo: Perikansha, 1978.

———. "Ōnishi Hajime: Hihyōshugi to Bigaku." *Nihon no Bigaku* 2(7) (1986).

Watsuji Tetsurō. *Nihon Seishin Shi Kenkyū.* Tokyo: Iwanami Shoten, 1940.

Yamamoto Masao. *Tōzai Geijutsu Seishin no Dentō to Kōryū.* Tokyo: Risōsha, 1965.

Yamaori Tetsuo. *Sei to Shi no Kosumogurafī.* Kyoto: Hōzōkan, 1993.

Yoshikawa Kōjirō, Satake Akihiro, and Hino Tatsuo, eds. *Motoori Norinaga. NST* 40. Tokyo: Iwanami Shoten, 1978.

WORKS IN WESTERN LANGUAGES

Addiss, Stephen. *Zenga and Nanga: Paintings by Japanese Monks and Scholars.* New Orleans: Museum of Art, 1976.

Aristotle. *The Poetics.* Translated by W. Hamilton Fyfe. Cambridge, Mass.: Harvard University Press, 1927.

Baumgarten, Alexander Gottlieb. *Aesthetica.* Frankfurt: Johann Christian Kleyb, 1750.

Beardsley, Monroe C. *Aesthetics from Classical Greece to the Present: A Short History.* University: University of Alabama Press, 1982. Originally published in 1966.

Bowring, Richard John. *Mori Ōgai and the Modernization of Japanese Culture.* Cambridge: Cambridge University Press, 1979.

Brower, Robert H., trans. *Conversations with Shōtetsu (Shōtetsu Monogatari).* Ann Arbor: Center for Japanese Studies, University of Michigan, 1992.

Brower, Robert H., and Earl Miner. *Japanese Court Poetry.* Stanford: Stanford University Press, 1961.

Chan, Wing-Tsit. *A Source Book in Chinese Philosophy.* Princeton: Princeton University Press, 1969.

Cleary, Thomas, trans. *Shōbōgenzō: Zen Essays by Dōgen.* Honolulu: University of Hawai'i Press, 1986.

Couvreur, Séraphin. *Mémoires sur les Bienséances et les Cérémonies,* vol. 1. Paris: Cathasia, 1950.

De Man, Paul. "Sign and Symbol in Hegel's *Aesthetics.*" *Critical Inquiry* 8(4) (Summer 1982):761–775.

De Rougemont, Denis. *Love in the Western World.* Princeton: Princeton University Press, 1956.

Dilworth, David A., trans. *Nishida Kitarō's Fundamental Problems of Philosophy: The World of Action and the Dialectical World.* Tokyo: Sophia University, 1970.

Dobson, W. A. C. H., trans. *Mencius.* Toronto: University of Toronto Press, 1963.

Drabble, Margaret, and Jenny Stringer. *The Concise Oxford Companion to English Literature.* Oxford: Oxford University Press, 1987.

Eagleton, Terry. *The Ideology of the Aesthetic.* Oxford: Blackwell, 1990.

Editorial Committee of Festschrift for Tomonobu Imamichi, ed. *Aesthetica and Calonologia*. Tokyo: Bunkensha, 1988.

Einem, Herbert von. *Michelangelo*. London: Methuen, 1973.

Eisenwerth, J. A. Schmoll, ed. *Das Unvollendete als Künstlerische Form*. Bern and Munich: Francke AG Verlag, 1959.

Fechner, Gustav Theodor. *Vorschule der Ästhetik*. Leipzig: Breitkopf & Härtel, 1925.

Ferry, Luc. *Homo Aestheticus: The Invention of Taste in the Democratic Age*. Chicago: University of Chicago Press, 1993.

Frey, Dagobert. *Architecture of the Renaissance from Brunelleschi to Michael Angelo*. The Hague: G. Naeff, 1925.

Gilbert, Katharine Everett, and Helmut Kuhn. *A History of Esthetics*. Bloomington: Indiana University Press, 1954. Originally published in 1939.

Gover, Charles E. *The Folk-Songs of Southern India*. Madras: South India Saiva Siddhanta, 1959. Originally published in 1871.

Guyau, M. *L'Art au Point de Vue Sociologique*. Paris: Félix Alcan, 1914.

———. *Les Problèmes de l'Esthétique Contemporaine*. Paris: Félix Alcan, 1884.

Hartmann, Eduard von. *Philosophy of the Unconscious: Speculative Results According to the Inductive Method of Physical Science*. New York: Harcourt, Brace, 1931.

Haven, Joseph. *Mental Philosophy: Including the Intellect, Sensibilities, and Will*. Boston: Gould & Lincoln, 1857.

Havens, Thomas R. H. *Nishi Amane and Modern Japanese Thought*. Princeton: Princeton University Press, 1970.

Hegel, G. W. F. *Introductory Lectures on Aesthetics*. Translated by Bernard Bosanquet. London: Penguin, 1993.

Heidegger, Martin. *Basic Writings from Being and Time (1927) to The Task of Thinking (1964)*. New York: HarperCollins, 1993.

———. *On the Way to Language*. New York: Harper & Row, 1971. Originally published in 1959.

Hirota, Dennis. *Wind in the Pines: Classic Writings of the Way of Tea as a Buddhist Path*. Fremont, Calif.: Asian Humanities Press, 1995.

Hisamatsu, Sen'ichi. *The Vocabulary of Japanese Literary Aesthetics*. Tokyo: Centre for East Asian Cultural Studies, 1963.

Howland, Douglas. "Nishi Amane's Efforts to Translate Western Knowledge: Sound, Written Character, and Meaning." *Semiotica* 83(3/4) (1991).

Hume, Nancy G., ed. *Japanese Aesthetics and Culture*. Albany: SUNY Press, 1995.

Hurvitz, Leon, trans. *Scripture of the Lotus Blossom of the Fine Dharma*. New York: Columbia University Press, 1976.

Inagaki, Hisao. *A Dictionary of Japanese Buddhist Terms*. Union City, Calif.: Heian International, 1989.

Jaspers, Karl. *Philosophy*, vol. 1. Translated by E. B. Ashton. Chicago: University of Chicago Press, 1969.

Johnson, Galen A., ed. *The Merleau-Ponty Aesthetics Reader: Philosophy and Painting*. Evanston, Ill.: Northwestern University Press, 1993.

Jusdanis, Gregory. *Belated Modernity and Aesthetic Culture: Inventing National Literature.* Minneapolis: University of Minnesota Press, 1991.

Kant, Immanuel. *Critique of Judgment.* New York: Hafner, 1951.

Karatani, Kōjin. *Architecture as Metaphor: Language, Number, Money.* Cambridge, Mass.: MIT Press, 1995.

———. "One Spirit, Two Nineteenth Centuries." In Masao Miyoshi and H. D. Harootunian, eds., *Postmodernism and Japan.* Durham: Duke University Press, 1989.

———. *Origins of Modern Japanese Literature.* Durham: Duke University Press, 1993.

Katō, Hilda. "The *Mumyōshō* of Kamo no Chōmei and Its Significance in Japanese Literature." *Monumenta Nipponica* 23(3–4) (1968).

Kaufman, Walter. *The Portable Nietzsche.* New York: Viking, 1954.

Keene, Donald, trans. *Essays in Idleness: The Tsurezuregusa of Kenkō.* New York: Columbia University Press, 1967.

Kuo, Hsi. *An Essay on Landscape Painting.* Translated by Shio Nakanishi. London: John Murray, 1935.

LaFleur, William R. *The Karma of Words: Buddhism and the Literary Arts in Medieval Japan.* Berkeley: University of California Press, 1983.

Lau, D. C., trans. *Lao Tzu: Tao Te Ching.* New York: Penguin, 1963.

Legge, James. *The Chinese Classics,* vol. 1: *Confucian Analects, The Great Learning, The Doctrine of the Mean.* Hong Kong: Hong Kong University Press, 1970.

———. *The Chinese Classics.* Vol. 3, pt. 1. London: Oxford University Press, 1939.

Marra, Michele. "Japanese Aesthetics: The Construction of Meaning." *Philosophy East and West* 45(3) (1995).

———. "Zeami and *Nō*: A Path Towards Enlightenment." *Journal of Asian Culture* 12 (1988).

Miner, Earl, Hiroko Odagiri, and Robert E. Morrell. *The Princeton Companion to Classical Japanese Literature.* Princeton: Princeton University Press, 1985.

Miyoshi, Masao, and H. D. Harootunian, eds. *Postmodernism and Japan.* Durham: Duke University Press, 1989.

Momokawa, Takahito. "'Mono no Aware'—The Identity of the Japanese." *Kokubungaku Kenkyū Shiryōkan Kiyō* 13 (1987).

Murakata, Akiko, ed. *The Ernest F. Fenollosa Papers: The Houghton Library, Harvard University.* Tokyo: Museum Press, 1987.

Nakamura, Hajime. *Ways of Thinking of Eastern Peoples: India, China, Tibet, Japan.* Honolulu: University of Hawai'i Press, 1964.

Nietzsche, Friedrich. *The Birth of Tragedy and The Genealogy of Morals.* New York: Doubleday, 1956.

Ninomiya, Masayuki. *La Pensée de Kobayashi Hideo: Un Intellectuel Japonais au Tournant de l'Histoire.* Geneva and Paris: Librairie Droz, 1995.

Nishida, Kitarō. *An Inquiry into the Good.* Translated by Masao Abe and Christopher Ives. New Haven: Yale University Press, 1990.

Nishitani, Keiji. *Religion and Nothingness.* Berkeley: University of California Press, 1982.

————. *The Self-Overcoming of Nihilism.* Translated by Graham Parkes with Setsuko Aihara. Albany: SUNY Press, 1990.

Notehelfer, F. G. "On Idealism and Realism in the Thought of Okakura Tenshin." *Journal of Japanese Studies* 16(2) (1990).

Okakura, Kakuzō. *Collected English Writings.* 3 vols. Tokyo: Heibonsha, 1984.

————. *The Ideals of the East with Special Reference to the Art of Japan.* London: John Murray, 1903.

Okazaki, Yoshie. *Japanese Literature in the Meiji Era.* Tokyo: Ōbunsha, 1955.

Philippi, Donald L., trans. *Kojiki.* Tokyo: University of Tokyo Press, 1968.

Pincus, Leslie. *Authenticating Culture in Imperial Japan: Kuki Shūzō and the Rise of National Aesthetics.* Berkeley: University of California Press, 1996.

Rimer, J. Thomas, and Yamazaki Masakazu, trans. *On the Art of the Nō Drama: The Major Treatises of Zeami.* Princeton: Princeton University Press, 1984.

Rosaldo, Renato. *Culture and Truth: The Remaking of Social Analysis.* Boston: Beacon Press, 1989.

Ross, Stephen David, ed. *Art and Its Significance: An Anthology of Aesthetic Theory.* Albany: SUNY Press, 1994.

Sakabe, Megumi. "Dignité du Mot et Valeur de la Personne." *Acta Institutionis Philosophiae et Aestheticae* 1 (1983).

————. "La Métaphore et le Problème du Sujet." *Journal of the Faculty of Letters, University of Tokyo (Aesthetics)* 5 (1980).

————. "Le Masque, le Comportement et le Jeu." *Revue d'Esthétique* 21 (1992).

————. "Le Masque et l'Ombre dans la Culture Japonaise." *Revue de Métaphysique et de Morale* 87(3) (July–September 1982).

————. "'Modoki'—Sur la Tradition Mimétique au Japon." *Acta Institutionis Philosophiae et Aestheticae* 3 (1985).

————. "Notes sur le Mot Japonais *hureru.*" *Revue d'Esthetique,* nouvelle série 11 (1986).

————. "Sur le Fondement Affectif de l'Éthique et de l'Esthétique dans la Tradition de la Pensée Japonaise." *Acta Insititutionis Philosophiae et Aestheticae* 5 (1987).

Santayana, George. *The Sense of Beauty: Being the Outlines of Aesthetic Theory.* Cambridge, Mass.: MIT Press, 1988.

Sartre, Jean-Paul. *What Is Literature?* Translated by Bernard Frechtman. New York: Harper & Row, 1965.

Schiller, Friedrich. *Essays.* New York: Continuum, 1993.

Schumann, Hans Wolfgang. *Buddhism: An Outline of Its Teachings and Schools.* Wheaton, Ill.: Theosophical Publishing House, 1974.

Seidensticker, Edward G., trans. *The Tale of Genji.* New York: Knopf, 1976.

Sheats, Paul D., ed. *The Poetical Works of Wordsworth.* Boston: Houghton Mifflin, 1982.

Sydow, Eckard von. *Die Kultur der Dekadenz.* Dresden: Sibyllen-verlag, 1921.

Taine, Hippolyte. *Philosophie de l'Art.* Paris: Fayard, 1985.

Tanaka, Stefan. "Imaging History: Inscribing Belief in the Nation." *Journal of Asian Studies* 53(1) (February 1994):24–44.

Thomas, Roger K. "'High' Versus 'Low': The *Fude no Saga* Controversy and Bakumatsu Poetics." *Monumenta Nipponica* 49(4) (Winter 1994):455–469.

Tsuchida, Kyoson. *Contemporary Thought of Japan and China.* New York: Knopf, 1927.

Ueda, Makoto. "*Yūgen* and *Erhabene:* Ōnishi Yoshinori's Attempt to Synthesize Japanese and Western Aesthetics." In J. Thomas Rimer, ed., *Culture and Identity: Japanese Intellectuals During the Interwar Years.* Princeton: Princeton University Press, 1990.

Uyeno, Naoteru, ed. *Japanese Arts and Crafts in the Meiji Era.* Tokyo: Pan-Pacific Press, 1958.

Vattimo, Gianni. *The Adventure of Difference: Philosophy After Nietzsche and Heidegger.* Cambridge: Polity Press, 1993.

———. *The End of Modernity: Nihilism and Hermeneutics in Post-Modern Culture.* Cambridge: Polity Press, 1988.

———, ed. *Estetica Moderna.* Bologna: Il Mulino, 1977.

Vattimo, Gianni, and Pier Aldo Rovatti, eds. *Il Pensiero Debole.* Milan: Feltrinelli, 1983.

Véron, Eugène. *Aesthetics.* Translated by W. H. Armstrong. London: Chapman & Hall, 1879.

———. *L'Esthétique.* Paris: C. Reinwald, 1878.

Verri, Antonio. *Origine delle Lingue e Civiltà in Rousseau.* Ravenna: Edizioni A. Longo, 1970.

Waley, Arthur, trans. *The Analects of Confucius.* New York: Vintage, 1938.

Watson, Burton, trans. *The Complete Works of Chuang Tzu.* New York: Columbia University Press, 1968.

Watsuji, Tetsurō. *Climate and Culture: A Philosophical Study.* New York: Greenwood Press, 1961.

Weisberg, Gabriel P., and Yvonne M. L. Weisberg. *Japonisme: An Annotated Bibliography.* New York: Garland, 1990.

Yuasa, Yasuo. *The Body: Toward an Eastern Mind-Body Theory.* Albany: SUNY Press, 1987.

INDEX

ABOUT THE AUTHOR

Michele Marra is professor of Japanese literature at the University of California, Los Angeles. He has served on the faculties of the Osaka University of Foreign Studies, the University of Tokyo, and the University of Southern California. Among his numerous publications are *The Aesthetics of Discontent: Politics and Reclusion in Medieval Japanese Literature* (1991), which was named a finalist for the 1992 Hiromi Arisawa Memorial Award, and *Representations of Power: The Literary Politics of Medieval Japan* (1993).